# TRUEBLOOD™

## THE FRENCH QUARTER

TRUE BLOOD created by
**Alan Ball**

written by
**Mariah Huehner and David Tischman**

layouts by
**David Messina**

pencils by
**Claudia Balboni and Bruno Letizia**

inks by
**Elena Casagrande and Emanuel Simeoni**

colors by
**Ilaria Traversi and ScarletGothica**

letters by
**Neil Uyetake and Robbie Robbins**

series edits by
**Scott Dunbier**

story editor for HBO
**Gianna Sobol**

cover by
**David Messina**

cover colors by
**Giovanna Niro**

collection design by
**Neil Uyetake**

collection edits by
**Justin Eisinger and Alonzo Simon**

Special thanks to everyone at HBO for their invaluable assistance.

IDW founded by Ted Adams, Alex Garner, Kris Oprisko, and Robbie Robbins | International Rights Representative, Christine Meyer: christine@gfloystudio.com

ISBN: 978-1-61377-165-5

15 14 13 12 1 2 3 4

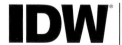

Ted Adams, CEO & Publisher
Greg Goldstein, President & COO
Robbie Robbins, EVP/Sr. Graphic Artist
Chris Ryall, Chief Creative Officer/Editor-in-Chief
Matthew Ruzicka, CPA, Chief Financial Officer
Alan Payne, VP of Sales

Become our fan on Facebook **facebook.com/idwpublishing**
Follow us on Twitter **@idwpublishing**
Check us out on YouTube **youtube.com/idwpublishing**
**www.IDWPUBLISHING.com**



Originally published as TRUE BLOOD: FRENCH QUARTER Issues #1–6.

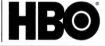

# TRUEBLOOD™

## THE FRENCH QUARTER

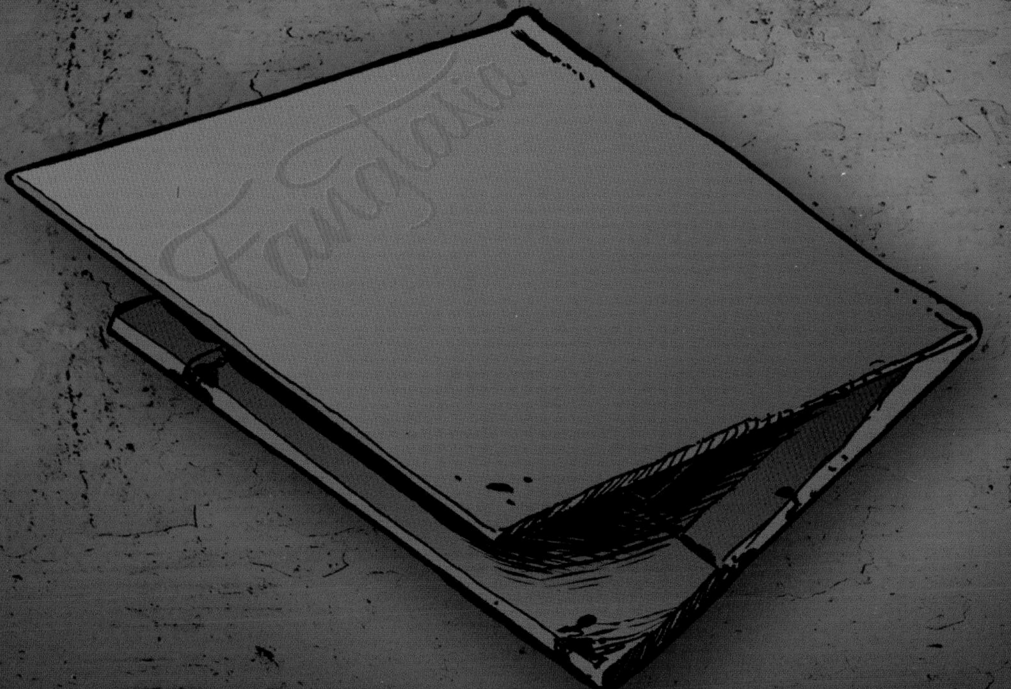
Fangtasia

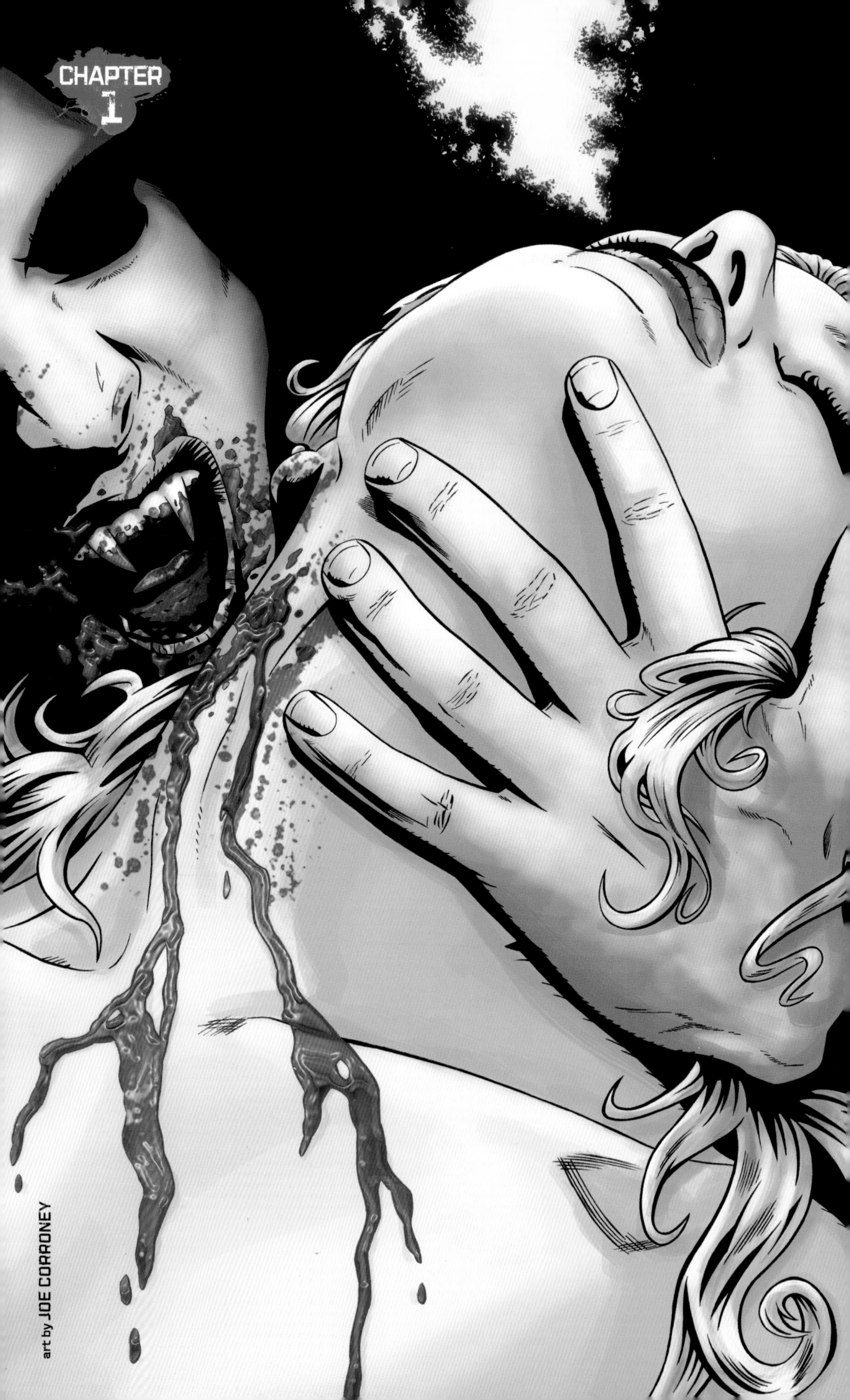
CHAPTER
1
art by JOE CORRONEY

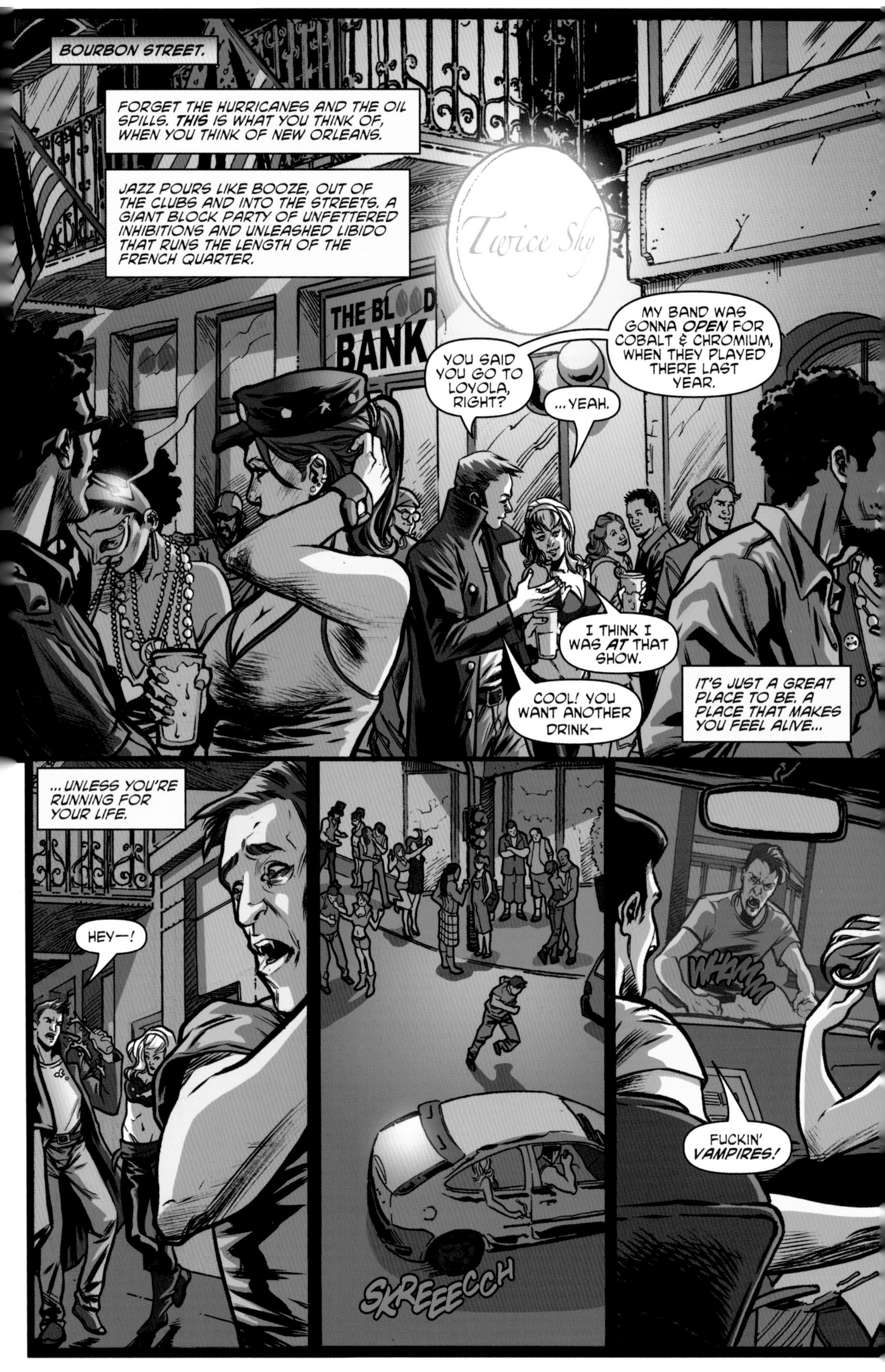
BOURBON STREET.
FORGET THE HURRICANES AND THE OIL SPILLS. THIS IS WHAT YOU THINK OF, WHEN YOU THINK OF NEW ORLEANS.
JAZZ POURS LIKE BOOZE, OUT OF THE CLUBS AND INTO THE STREETS. A GIANT BLOCK PARTY OF UNFETTERED INHIBITIONS AND UNLEASHED LIBIDO THAT RUNS THE LENGTH OF THE FRENCH QUARTER.
Twice Shy
THE BLOOD BANK
YOU SAID YOU GO TO LOYOLA, RIGHT?
...YEAH.
MY BAND WAS GONNA OPEN FOR COBALT & CHROMIUM, WHEN THEY PLAYED THERE LAST YEAR.
I THINK I WAS AT THAT SHOW.
COOL! YOU WANT ANOTHER DRINK—
IT'S JUST A GREAT PLACE TO BE. A PLACE THAT MAKES YOU FEEL ALIVE...
...UNLESS YOU'RE RUNNING FOR YOUR LIFE.
HEY—!
SKREEECCH
WHAMM
FUCKIN' VAMPIRES!

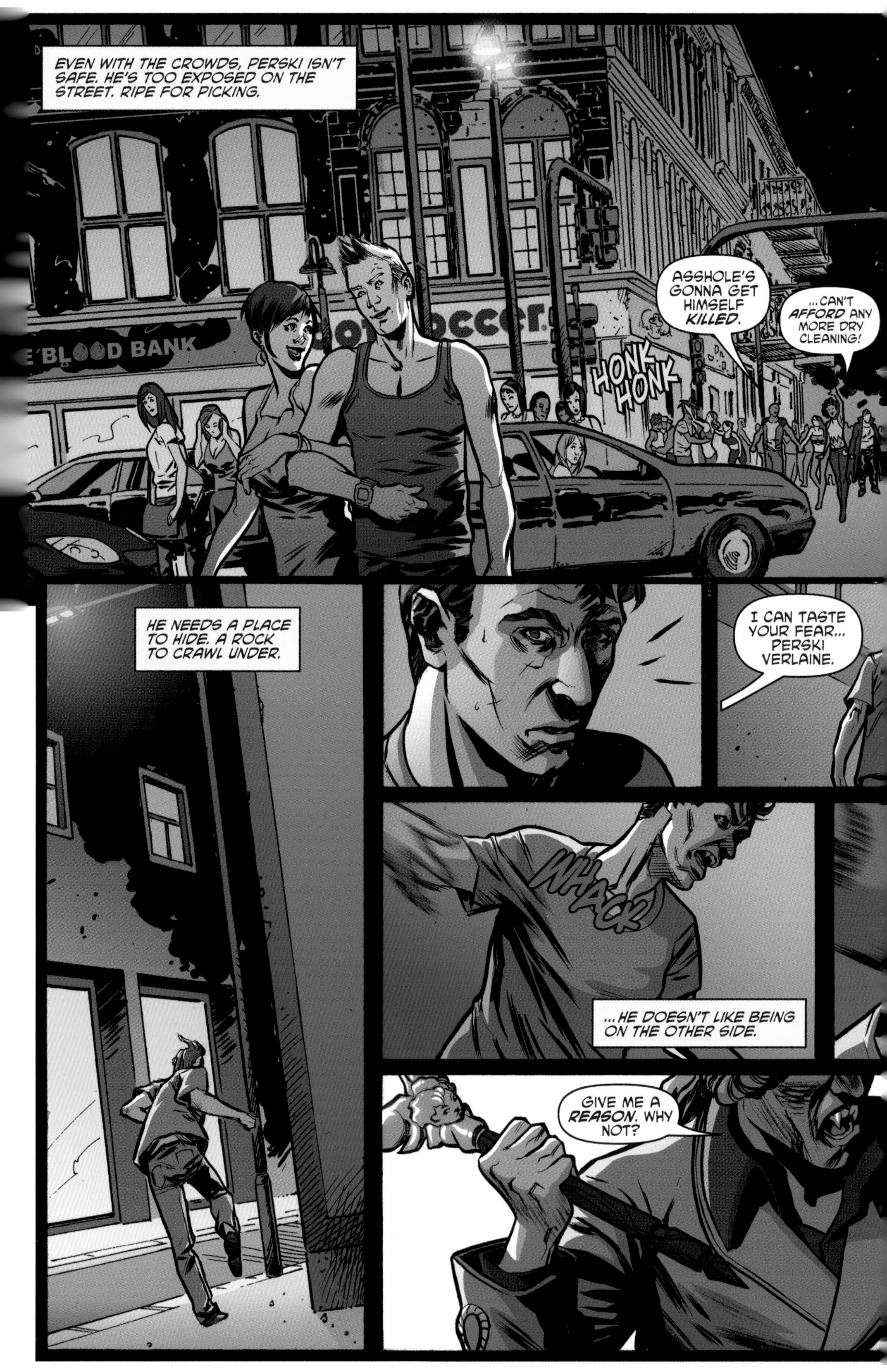
EVEN WITH THE CROWDS, PERSKI ISN'T SAFE. HE'S TOO EXPOSED ON THE STREET. RIPE FOR PICKING.
BLOOD BANK
ASSHOLE'S GONNA GET HIMSELF KILLED.
HONK HONK
...CAN'T AFFORD ANY MORE DRY CLEANING!
HE NEEDS A PLACE TO HIDE. A ROCK TO CRAWL UNDER.
I CAN TASTE YOUR FEAR... PERSKI VERLAINE.
WHACK
...HE DOESN'T LIKE BEING ON THE OTHER SIDE.
GIVE ME A REASON. WHY NOT?

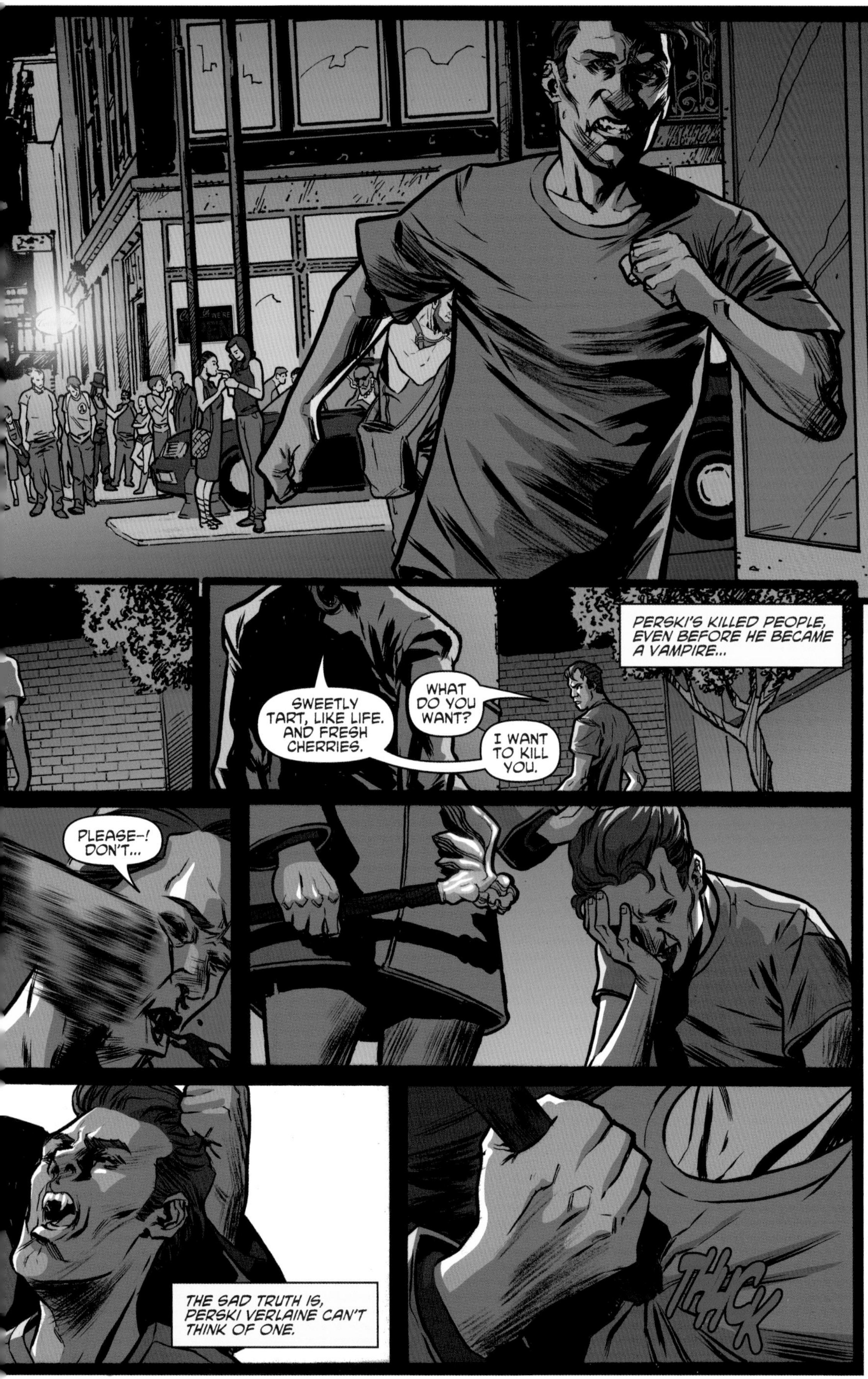
PERSKI'S KILLED PEOPLE, EVEN BEFORE HE BECAME A VAMPIRE...
SWEETLY TART, LIKE LIFE. AND FRESH CHERRIES.
WHAT DO YOU WANT?
I WANT TO KILL YOU.
PLEASE-! DON'T...
THE SAD TRUTH IS, PERSKI VERLAINE CAN'T THINK OF ONE.
THCK

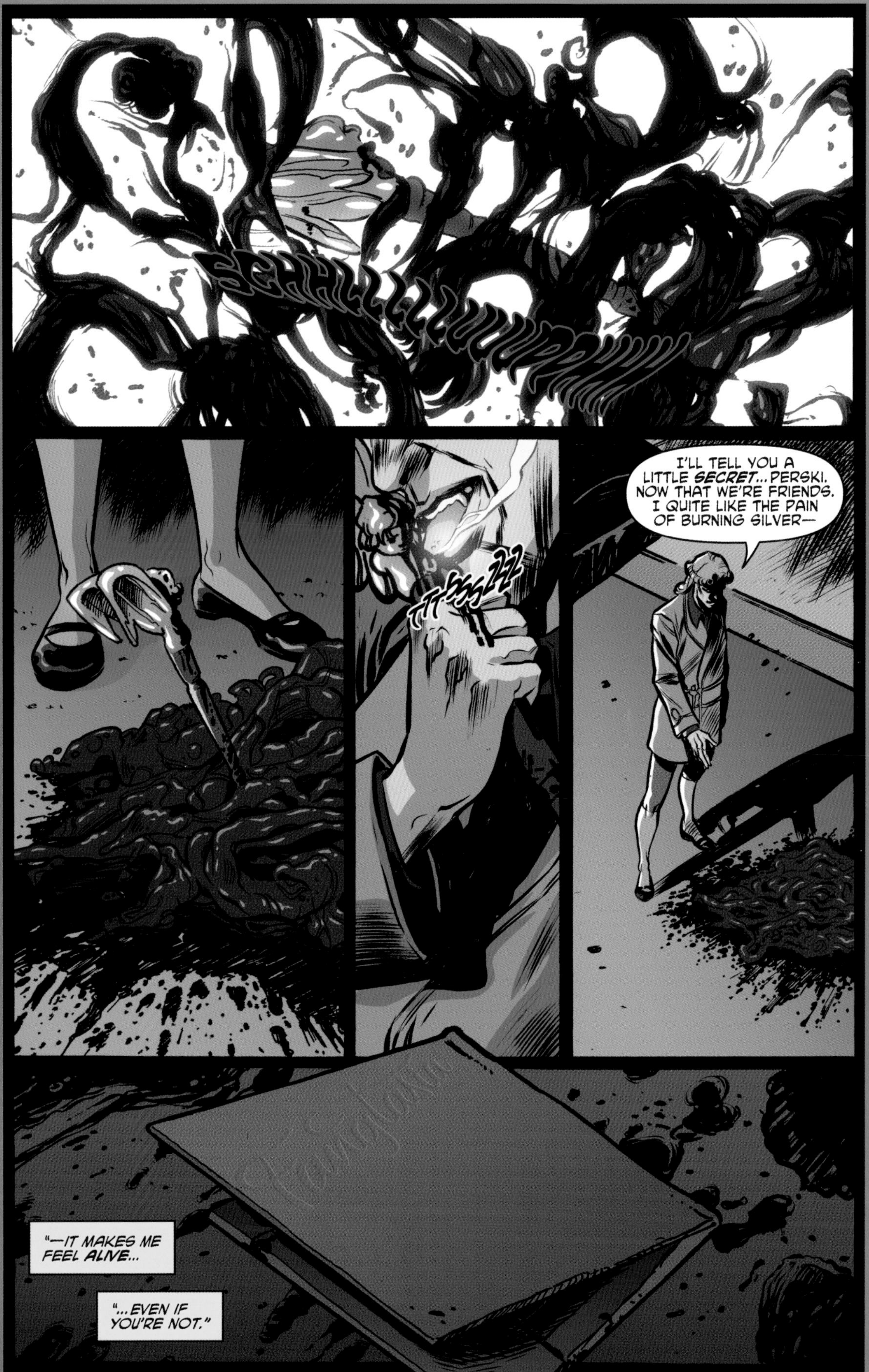

I'LL TELL YOU A LITTLE SECRET... PERSKI. NOW THAT WE'RE FRIENDS. I QUITE LIKE THE PAIN OF BURNING SILVER—
"—IT MAKES ME FEEL ALIVE...
"...EVEN IF YOU'RE NOT."

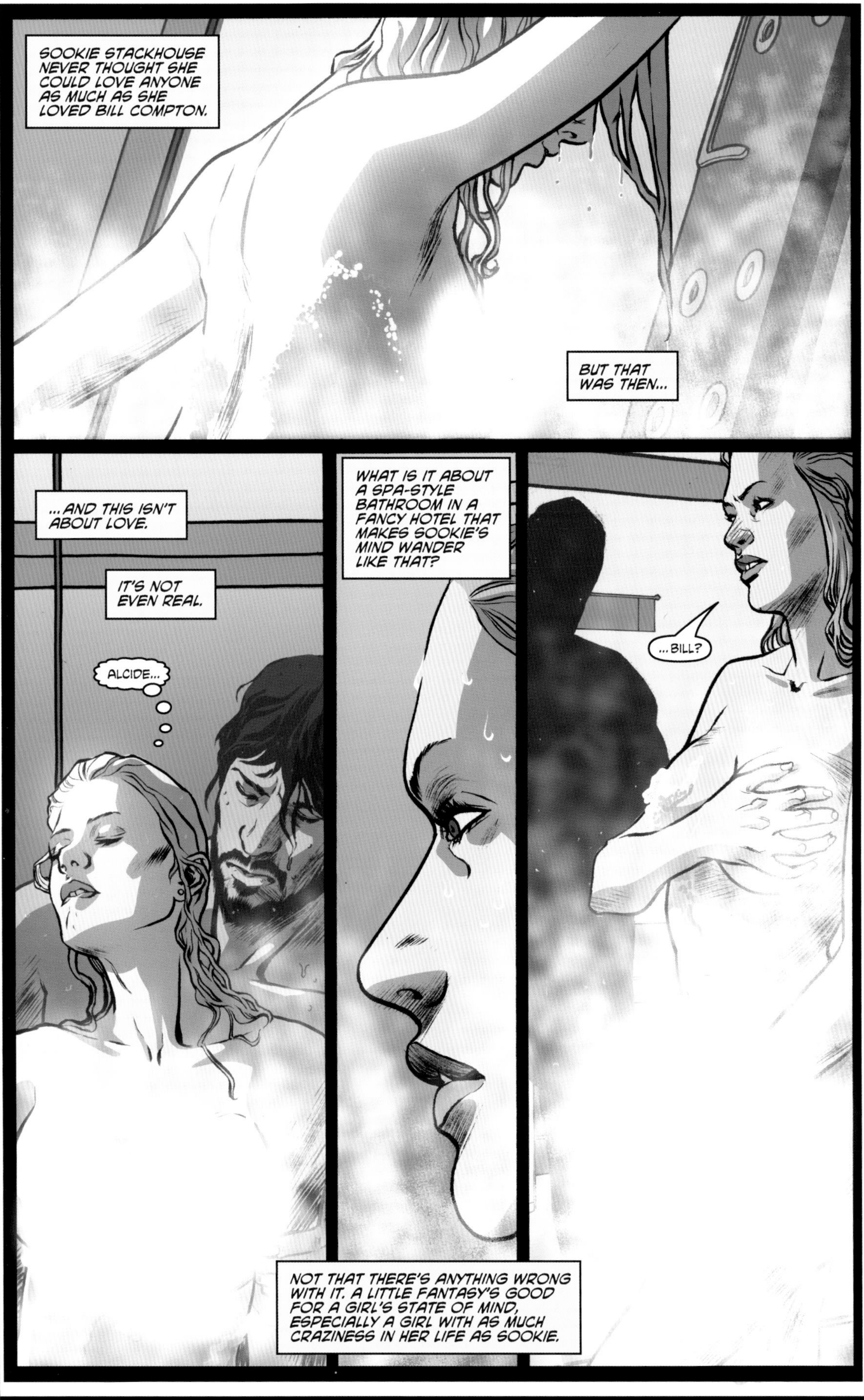
SOOKIE STACKHOUSE NEVER THOUGHT SHE COULD LOVE ANYONE AS MUCH AS SHE LOVED BILL COMPTON.
BUT THAT WAS THEN...
...AND THIS ISN'T ABOUT LOVE.
IT'S NOT EVEN REAL.
ALCIDE...
WHAT IS IT ABOUT A SPA-STYLE BATHROOM IN A FANCY HOTEL THAT MAKES SOOKIE'S MIND WANDER LIKE THAT?
...BILL?
NOT THAT THERE'S ANYTHING WRONG WITH IT. A LITTLE FANTASY'S GOOD FOR A GIRL'S STATE OF MIND, ESPECIALLY A GIRL WITH AS MUCH CRAZINESS IN HER LIFE AS SOOKIE.

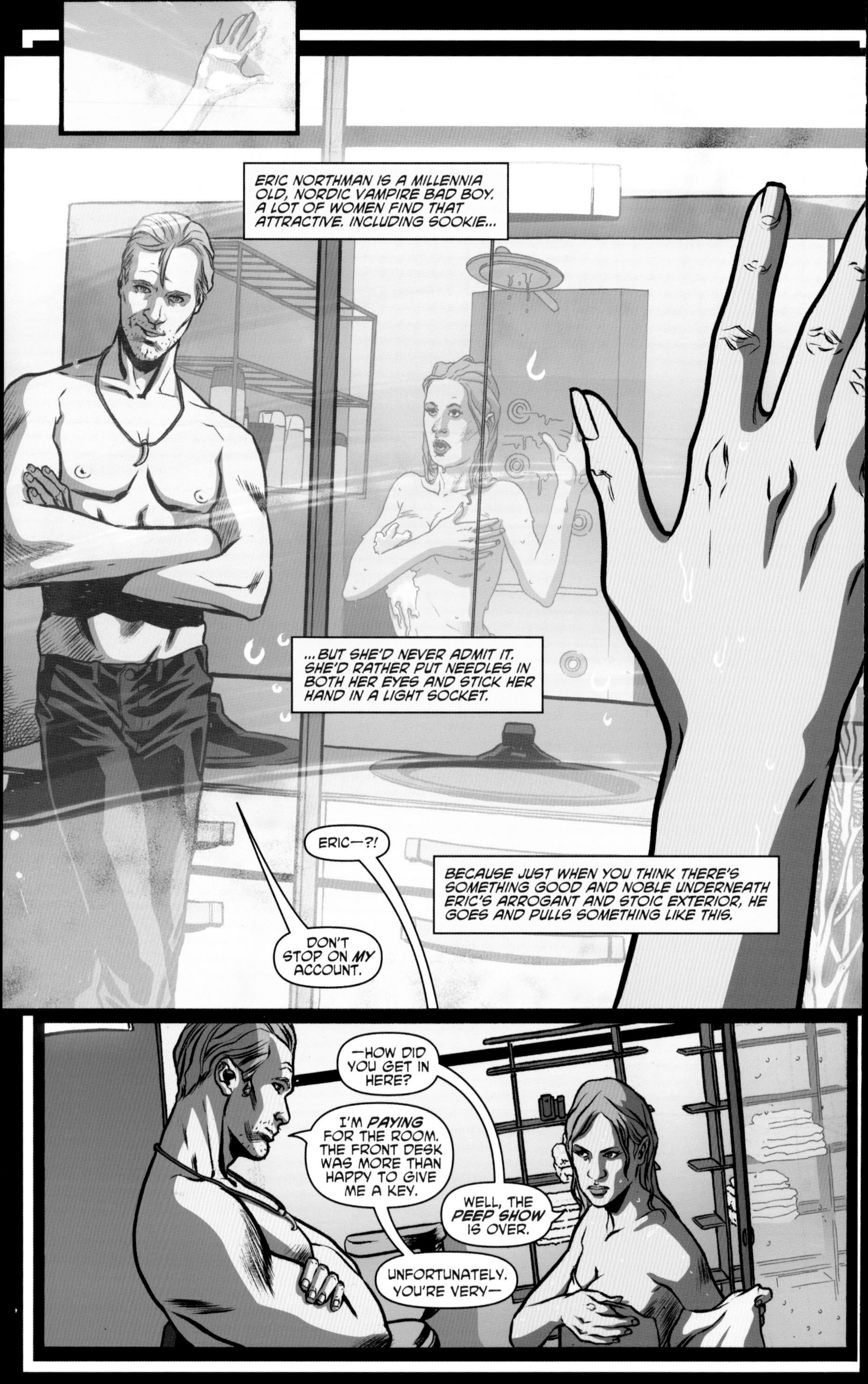
ERIC NORTHMAN IS A MILLENNIA OLD, NORDIC VAMPIRE BAD BOY. A LOT OF WOMEN FIND THAT ATTRACTIVE. INCLUDING SOOKIE...
...BUT SHE'D NEVER ADMIT IT. SHE'D RATHER PUT NEEDLES IN BOTH HER EYES AND STICK HER HAND IN A LIGHT SOCKET.
ERIC—?!
BECAUSE JUST WHEN YOU THINK THERE'S SOMETHING GOOD AND NOBLE UNDERNEATH ERIC'S ARROGANT AND STOIC EXTERIOR, HE GOES AND PULLS SOMETHING LIKE THIS.
DON'T STOP ON *MY* ACCOUNT.
—HOW DID YOU GET IN HERE?
I'M *PAYING* FOR THE ROOM. THE FRONT DESK WAS MORE THAN HAPPY TO GIVE ME A KEY.
WELL, THE *PEEP SHOW* IS OVER.
UNFORTUNATELY. YOU'RE VERY—

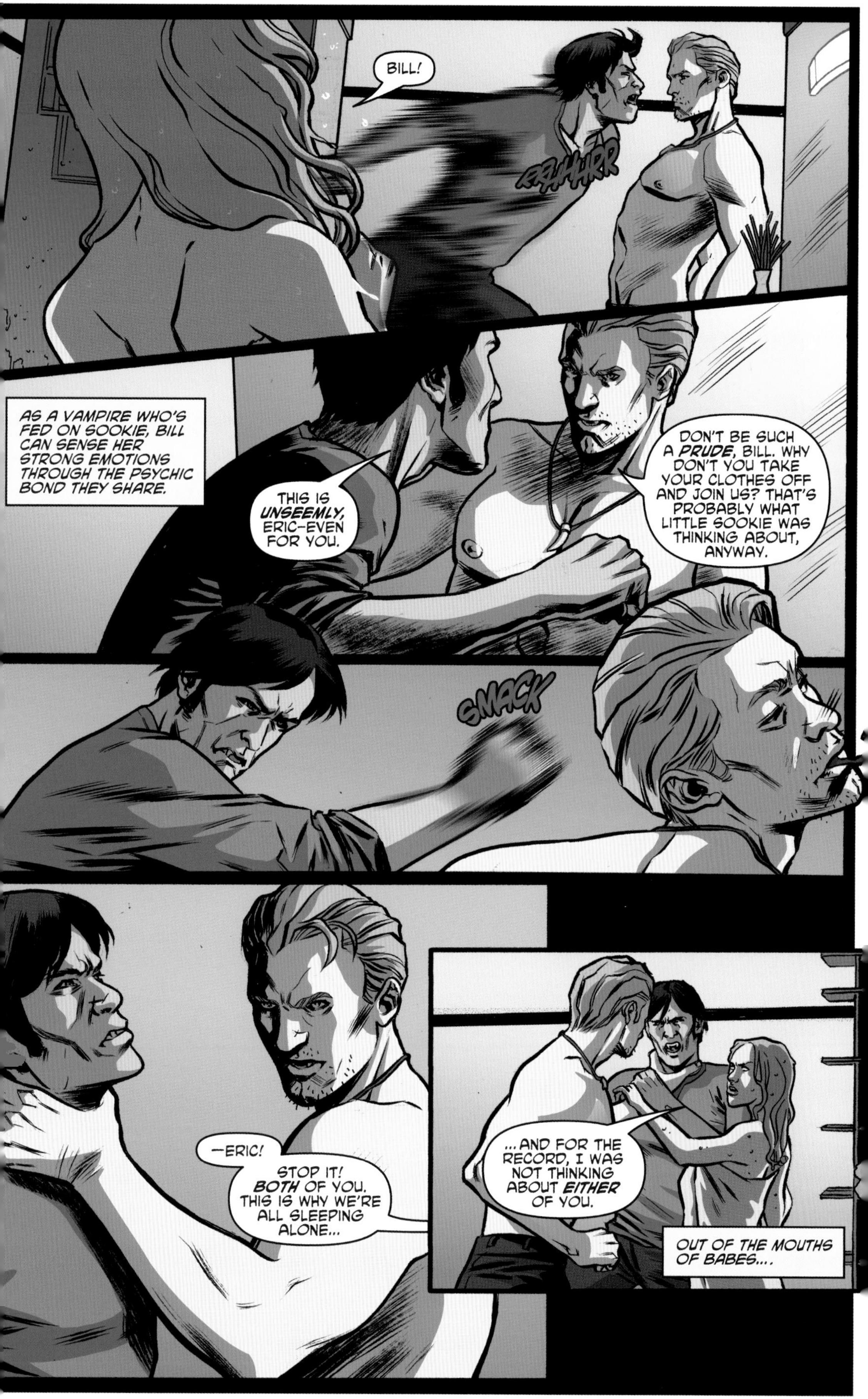
BILL!
RRAHHRR
AS A VAMPIRE WHO'S FED ON SOOKIE, BILL CAN SENSE HER STRONG EMOTIONS THROUGH THE PSYCHIC BOND THEY SHARE.
THIS IS UNSEEMLY, ERIC--EVEN FOR YOU.
DON'T BE SUCH A PRUDE, BILL. WHY DON'T YOU TAKE YOUR CLOTHES OFF AND JOIN US? THAT'S PROBABLY WHAT LITTLE SOOKIE WAS THINKING ABOUT, ANYWAY.
SMACK
--ERIC!
STOP IT! BOTH OF YOU. THIS IS WHY WE'RE ALL SLEEPING ALONE...
...AND FOR THE RECORD, I WAS NOT THINKING ABOUT EITHER OF YOU.
OUT OF THE MOUTHS OF BABES....

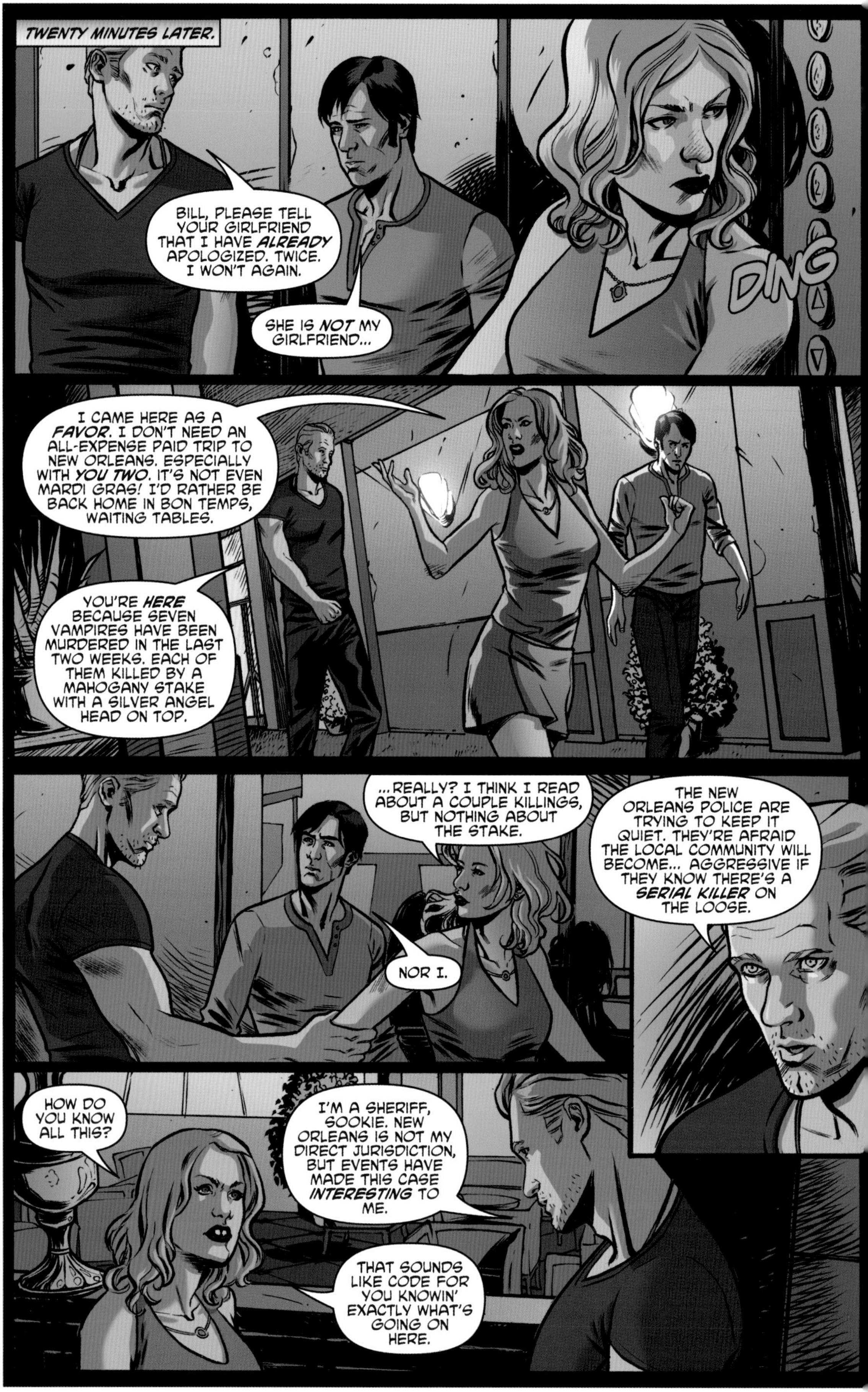
TWENTY MINUTES LATER.
BILL, PLEASE TELL YOUR GIRLFRIEND THAT I HAVE ALREADY APOLOGIZED. TWICE. I WON'T AGAIN.
SHE IS NOT MY GIRLFRIEND...
DING
I CAME HERE AS A FAVOR. I DON'T NEED AN ALL-EXPENSE PAID TRIP TO NEW ORLEANS. ESPECIALLY WITH YOU TWO. IT'S NOT EVEN MARDI GRAS! I'D RATHER BE BACK HOME IN BON TEMPS, WAITING TABLES.
YOU'RE HERE BECAUSE SEVEN VAMPIRES HAVE BEEN MURDERED IN THE LAST TWO WEEKS. EACH OF THEM KILLED BY A MAHOGANY STAKE WITH A SILVER ANGEL HEAD ON TOP.
...REALLY? I THINK I READ ABOUT A COUPLE KILLINGS, BUT NOTHING ABOUT THE STAKE.
NOR I.
THE NEW ORLEANS POLICE ARE TRYING TO KEEP IT QUIET. THEY'RE AFRAID THE LOCAL COMMUNITY WILL BECOME... AGGRESSIVE IF THEY KNOW THERE'S A SERIAL KILLER ON THE LOOSE.
HOW DO YOU KNOW ALL THIS?
I'M A SHERIFF, SOOKIE. NEW ORLEANS IS NOT MY DIRECT JURISDICTION, BUT EVENTS HAVE MADE THIS CASE INTERESTING TO ME.
THAT SOUNDS LIKE CODE FOR YOU KNOWIN' EXACTLY WHAT'S GOING ON HERE.

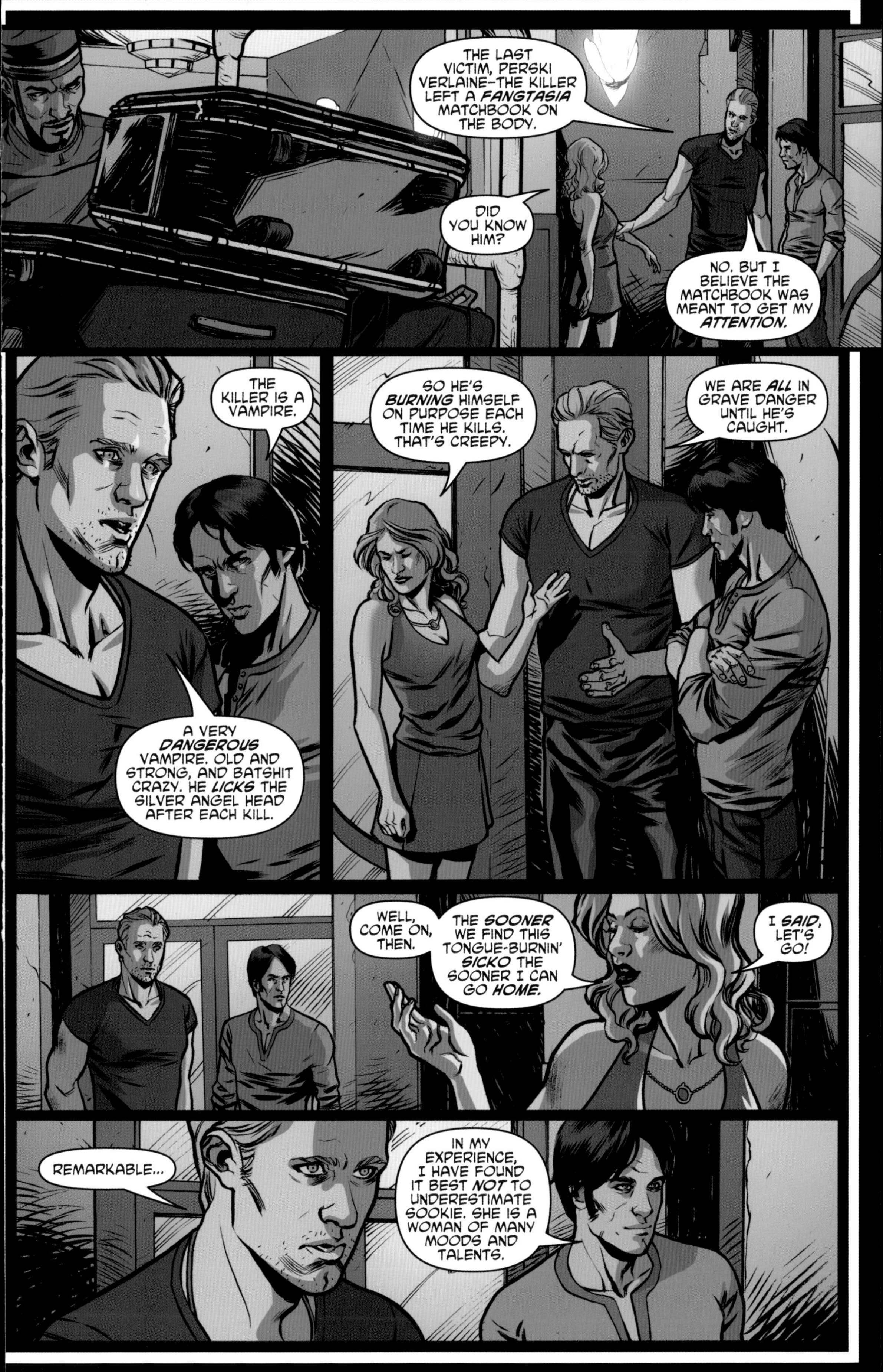
THE LAST VICTIM, PERSKI VERLAINE—THE KILLER LEFT A FANGTASIA MATCHBOOK ON THE BODY.
DID YOU KNOW HIM?
NO. BUT I BELIEVE THE MATCHBOOK WAS MEANT TO GET MY ATTENTION.
THE KILLER IS A VAMPIRE.
A VERY DANGEROUS VAMPIRE. OLD AND STRONG, AND BATSHIT CRAZY. HE LICKS THE SILVER ANGEL HEAD AFTER EACH KILL.
SO HE'S BURNING HIMSELF ON PURPOSE EACH TIME HE KILLS. THAT'S CREEPY.
WE ARE ALL IN GRAVE DANGER UNTIL HE'S CAUGHT.
WELL, COME ON, THEN.
THE SOONER WE FIND THIS TONGUE-BURNIN' SICKO THE SOONER I CAN GO HOME.
I SAID, LET'S GO!
REMARKABLE...
IN MY EXPERIENCE, I HAVE FOUND IT BEST NOT TO UNDERESTIMATE SOOKIE. SHE IS A WOMAN OF MANY MOODS AND TALENTS.

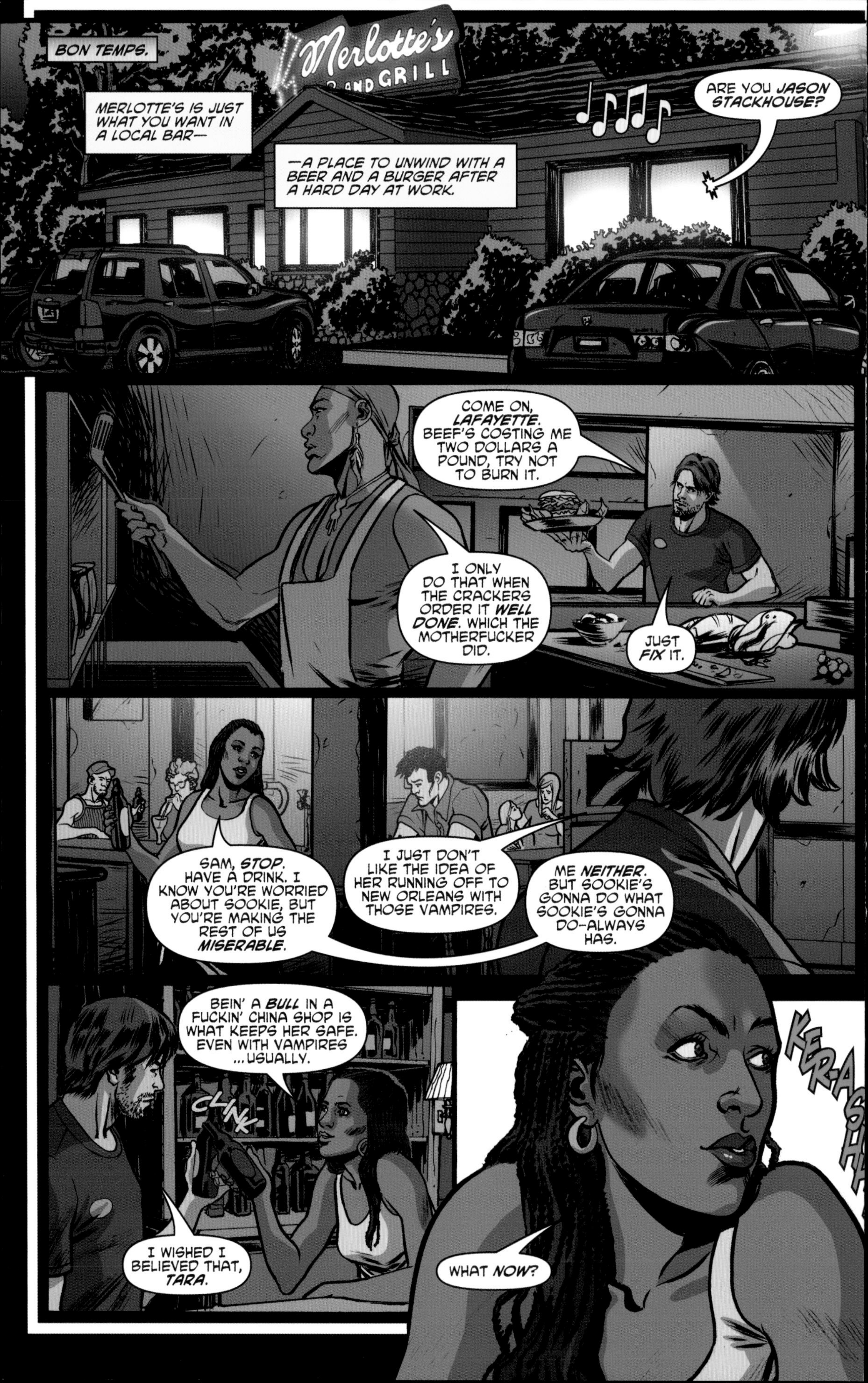
BON TEMPS.
Merlotte's AND GRILL
MERLOTTE'S IS JUST WHAT YOU WANT IN A LOCAL BAR—
—A PLACE TO UNWIND WITH A BEER AND A BURGER AFTER A HARD DAY AT WORK.
ARE YOU JASON STACKHOUSE?
COME ON, LAFAYETTE. BEEF'S COSTING ME TWO DOLLARS A POUND, TRY NOT TO BURN IT.
I ONLY DO THAT WHEN THE CRACKERS ORDER IT WELL DONE. WHICH THE MOTHERFUCKER DID.
JUST FIX IT.
SAM, STOP. HAVE A DRINK. I KNOW YOU'RE WORRIED ABOUT SOOKIE, BUT YOU'RE MAKING THE REST OF US MISERABLE.
I JUST DON'T LIKE THE IDEA OF HER RUNNING OFF TO NEW ORLEANS WITH THOSE VAMPIRES.
ME NEITHER. BUT SOOKIE'S GONNA DO WHAT SOOKIE'S GONNA DO-ALWAYS HAS.
BEIN' A BULL IN A FUCKIN' CHINA SHOP IS WHAT KEEPS HER SAFE. EVEN WITH VAMPIRES ...USUALLY.
CLINK
I WISHED I BELIEVED THAT, TARA.
KER-ASH
WHAT NOW?

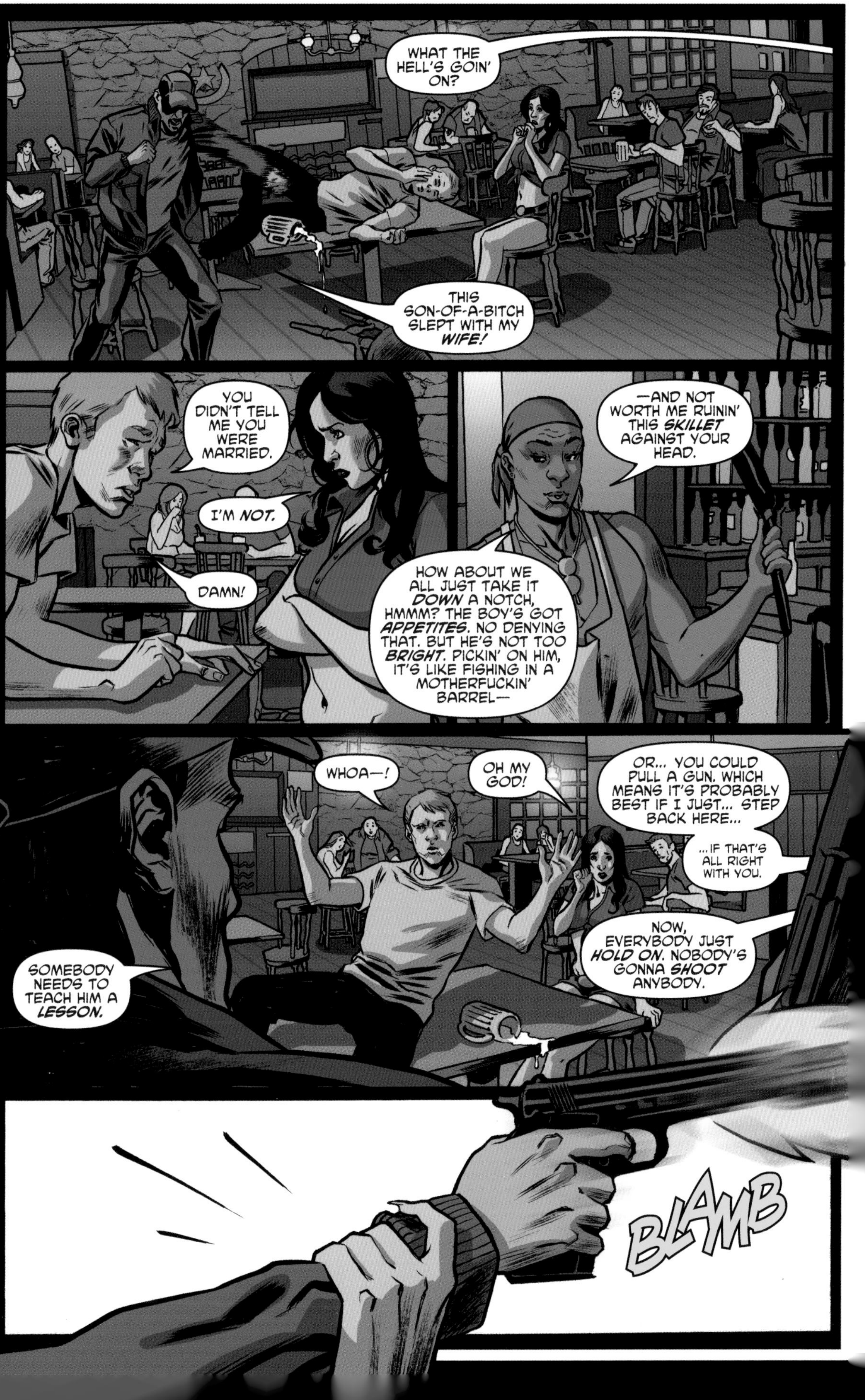
WHAT THE HELL'S GOIN' ON?
THIS SON-OF-A-BITCH SLEPT WITH MY WIFE!
YOU DIDN'T TELL ME YOU WERE MARRIED.
I'M NOT.
DAMN!
—AND NOT WORTH ME RUININ' THIS SKILLET AGAINST YOUR HEAD.
HOW ABOUT WE ALL JUST TAKE IT DOWN A NOTCH, HMMM? THE BOY'S GOT APPETITES. NO DENYING THAT. BUT HE'S NOT TOO BRIGHT. PICKIN' ON HIM, IT'S LIKE FISHING IN A MOTHERFUCKIN' BARREL—
WHOA—!
OH MY GOD!
OR... YOU COULD PULL A GUN. WHICH MEANS IT'S PROBABLY BEST IF I JUST... STEP BACK HERE...
...IF THAT'S ALL RIGHT WITH YOU.
SOMEBODY NEEDS TO TEACH HIM A LESSON.
NOW, EVERYBODY JUST HOLD ON. NOBODY'S GONNA SHOOT ANYBODY.
BLAMB

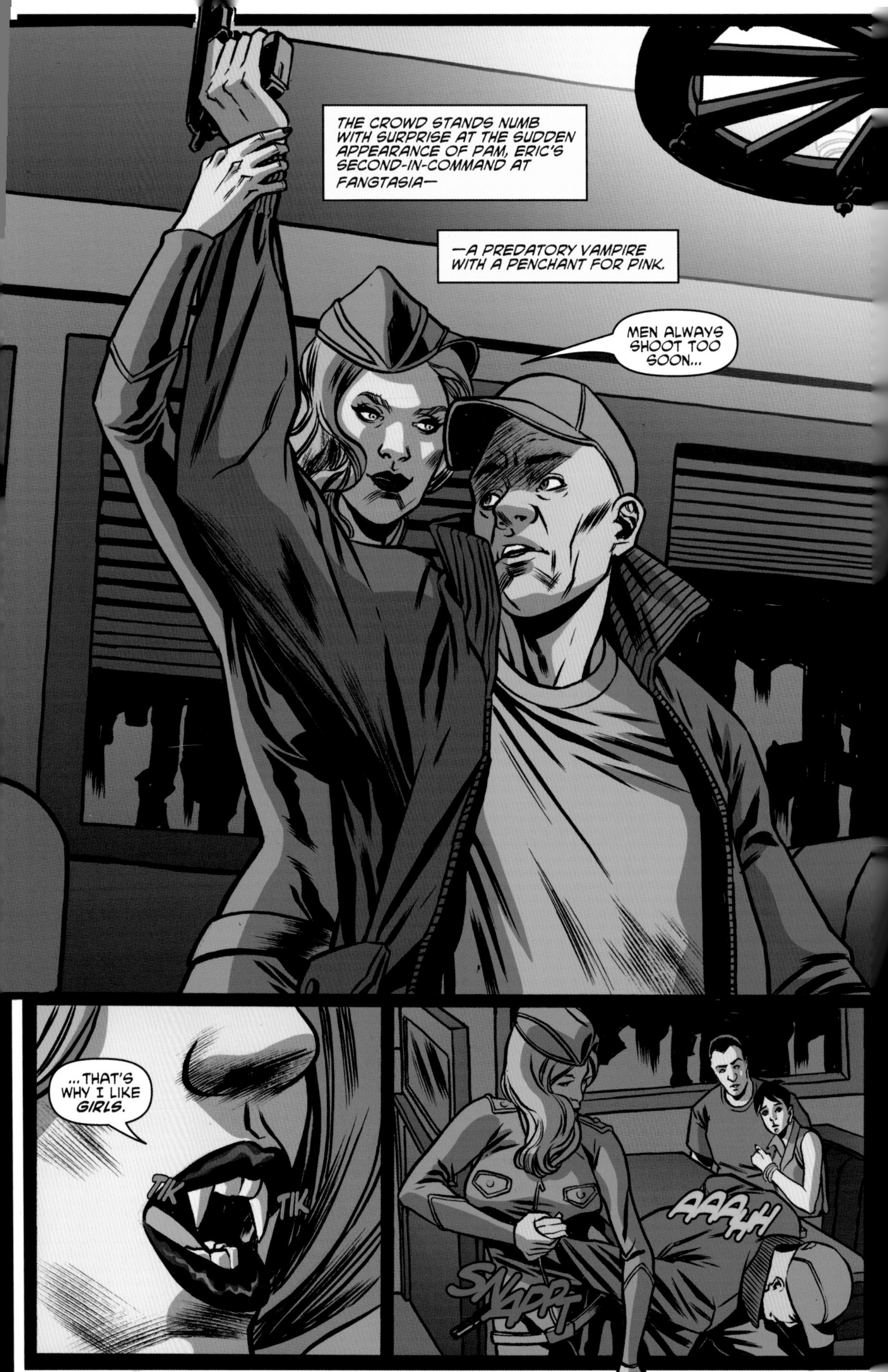
THE CROWD STANDS NUMB WITH SURPRISE AT THE SUDDEN APPEARANCE OF PAM, ERIC'S SECOND-IN-COMMAND AT FANGTASIA—
—A PREDATORY VAMPIRE WITH A PENCHANT FOR PINK.
MEN ALWAYS SHOOT TOO SOON...
...THAT'S WHY I LIKE *GIRLS.*
TIK
TIK
SNAPP
AAAAHH

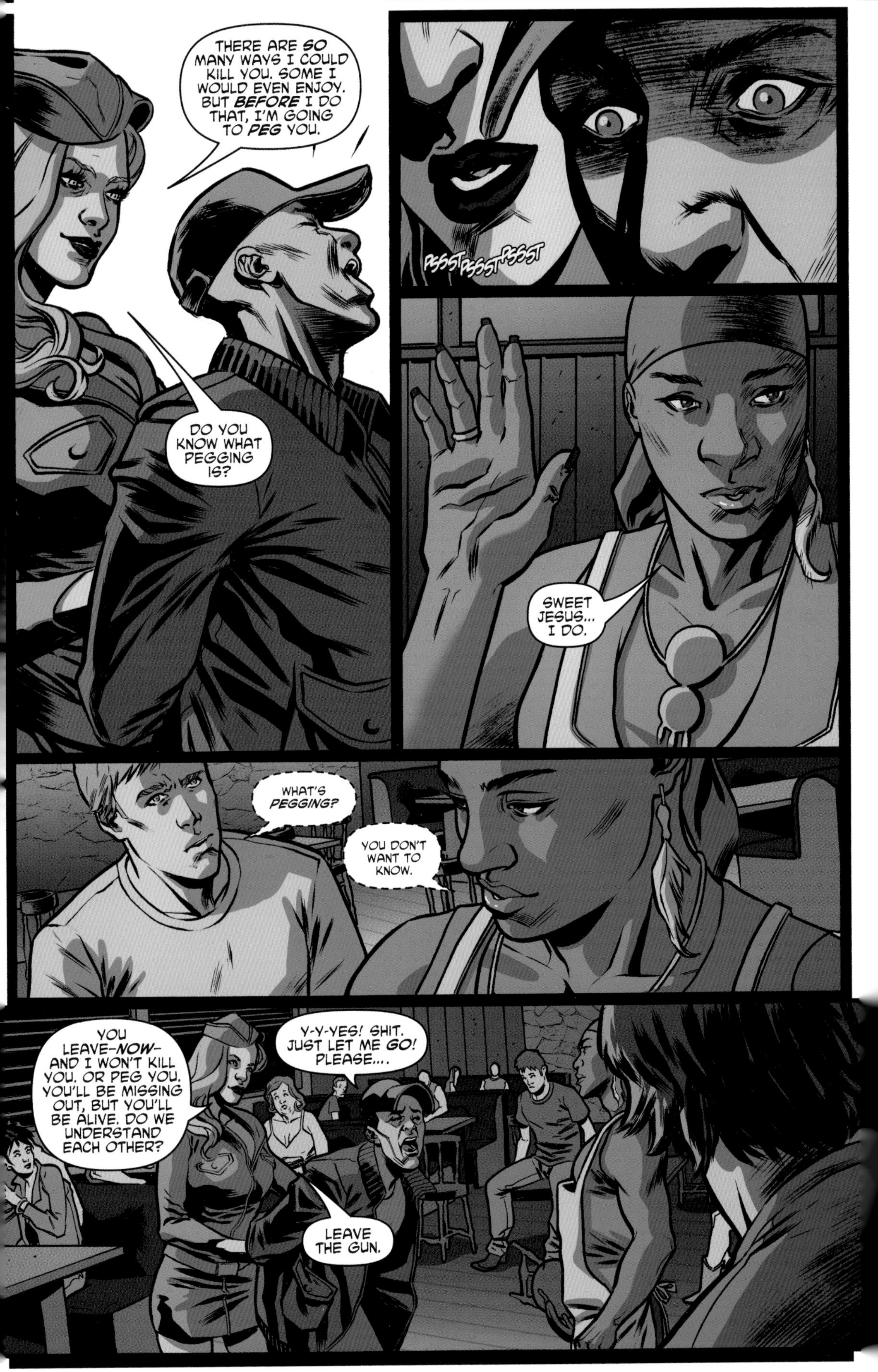
THERE ARE SO MANY WAYS I COULD KILL YOU. SOME I WOULD EVEN ENJOY. BUT BEFORE I DO THAT, I'M GOING TO PEG YOU.
DO YOU KNOW WHAT PEGGING IS?
PSSST PSSST PSSST
SWEET JESUS... I DO.
WHAT'S PEGGING?
YOU DON'T WANT TO KNOW.
YOU LEAVE--NOW--AND I WON'T KILL YOU. OR PEG YOU. YOU'LL BE MISSING OUT, BUT YOU'LL BE ALIVE. DO WE UNDERSTAND EACH OTHER?
Y-Y-YES! SHIT. JUST LET ME GO! PLEASE....
LEAVE THE GUN.

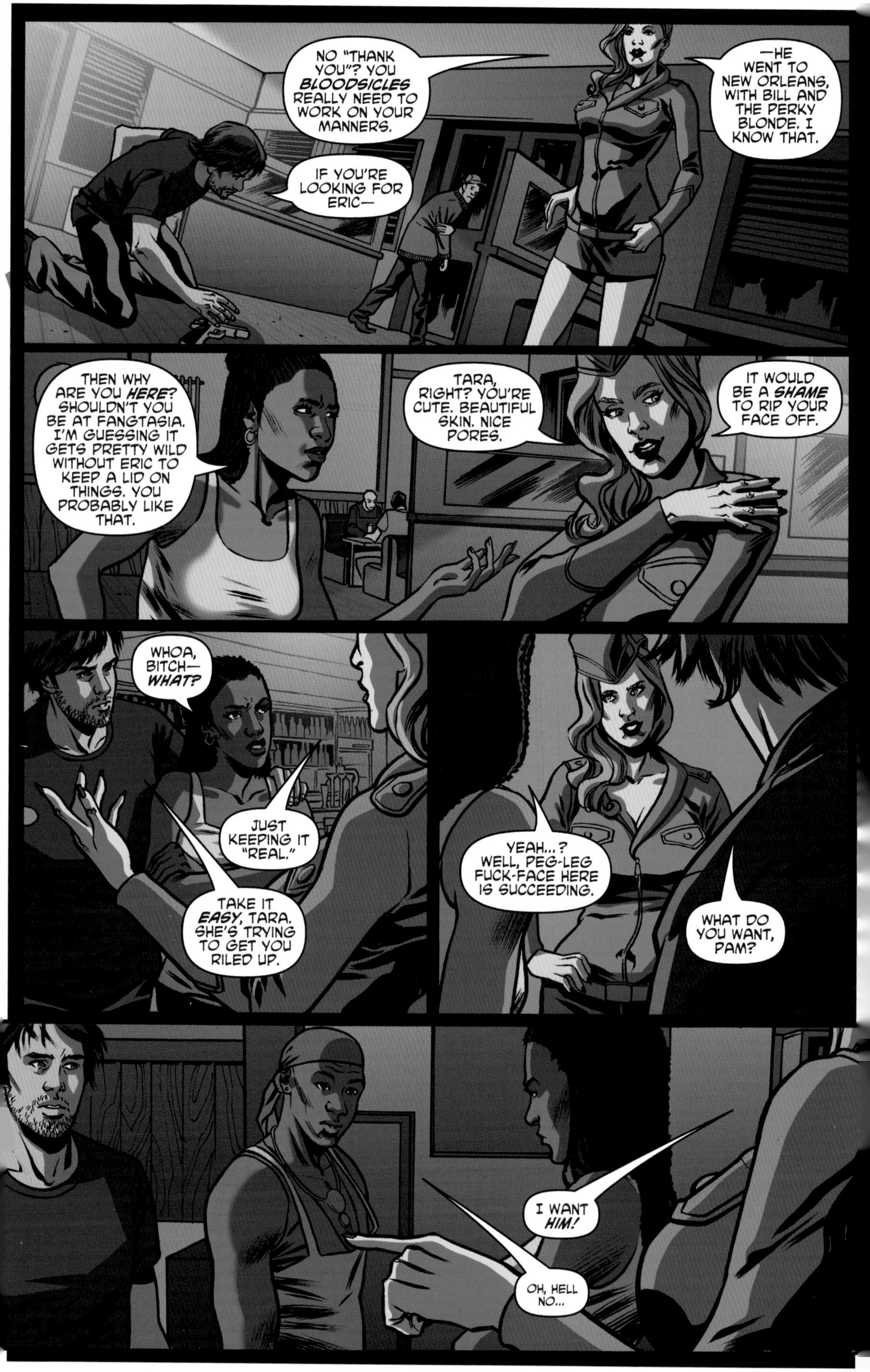
NO "THANK YOU"? YOU BLOODSICLES REALLY NEED TO WORK ON YOUR MANNERS.
IF YOU'RE LOOKING FOR ERIC—
—HE WENT TO NEW ORLEANS, WITH BILL AND THE PERKY BLONDE. I KNOW THAT.
THEN WHY ARE YOU HERE? SHOULDN'T YOU BE AT FANGTASIA. I'M GUESSING IT GETS PRETTY WILD WITHOUT ERIC TO KEEP A LID ON THINGS. YOU PROBABLY LIKE THAT.
TARA, RIGHT? YOU'RE CUTE. BEAUTIFUL SKIN. NICE PORES.
IT WOULD BE A SHAME TO RIP YOUR FACE OFF.
WHOA, BITCH— WHAT?
JUST KEEPING IT "REAL."
TAKE IT EASY, TARA. SHE'S TRYING TO GET YOU RILED UP.
YEAH...? WELL, PEG-LEG FUCK-FACE HERE IS SUCCEEDING.
WHAT DO YOU WANT, PAM?
I WANT HIM!
OH, HELL NO...

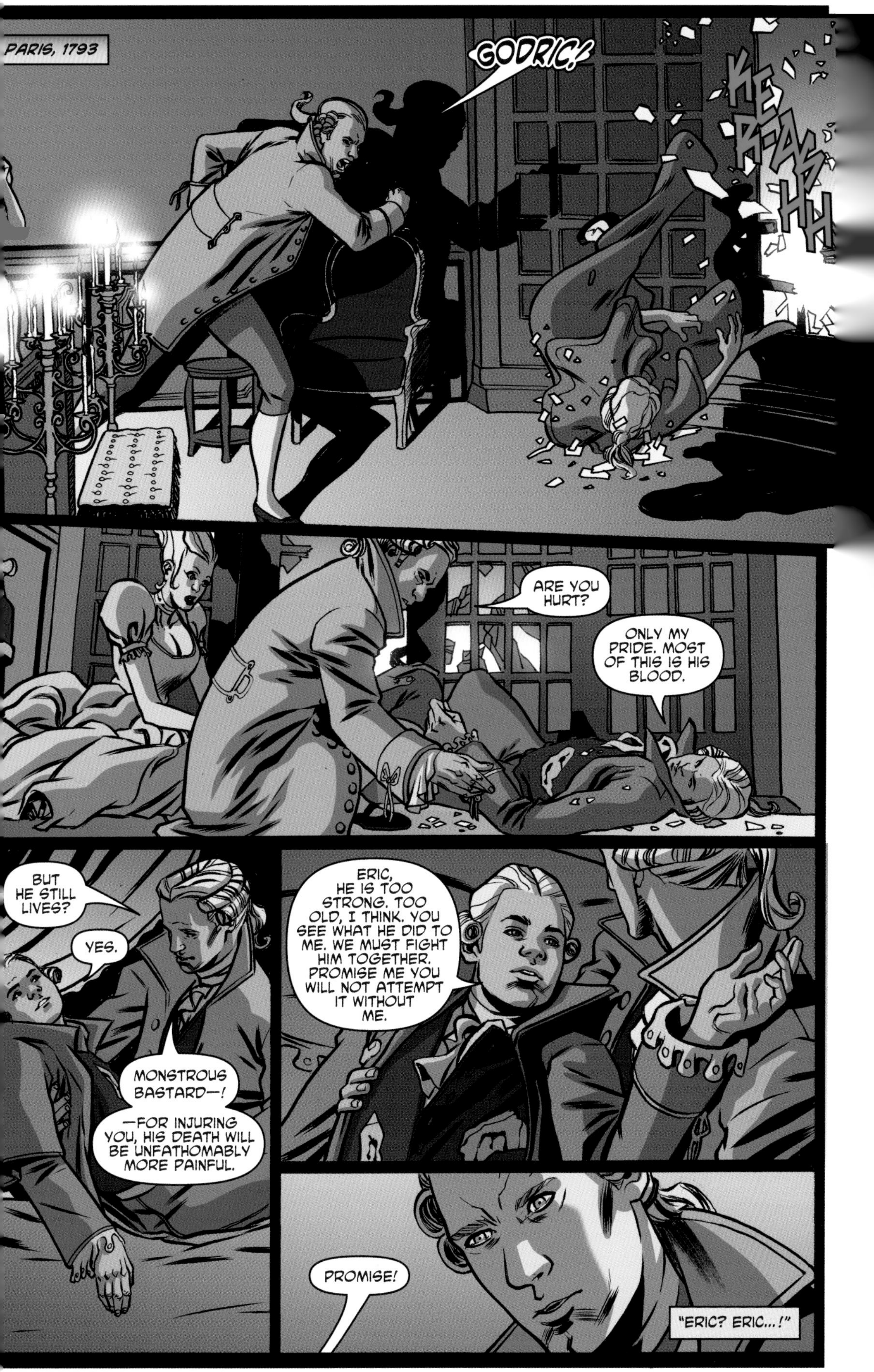
PARIS, 1793
GODRIC!
KE-R-ASHH
ARE YOU HURT?
ONLY MY PRIDE. MOST OF THIS IS HIS BLOOD.
BUT HE STILL LIVES?
YES.
MONSTROUS BASTARD—!
—FOR INJURING YOU, HIS DEATH WILL BE UNFATHOMABLY MORE PAINFUL.
ERIC, HE IS TOO STRONG. TOO OLD, I THINK. YOU SEE WHAT HE DID TO ME. WE MUST FIGHT HIM TOGETHER. PROMISE ME YOU WILL NOT ATTEMPT IT WITHOUT ME.
PROMISE!
"ERIC? ERIC...!"

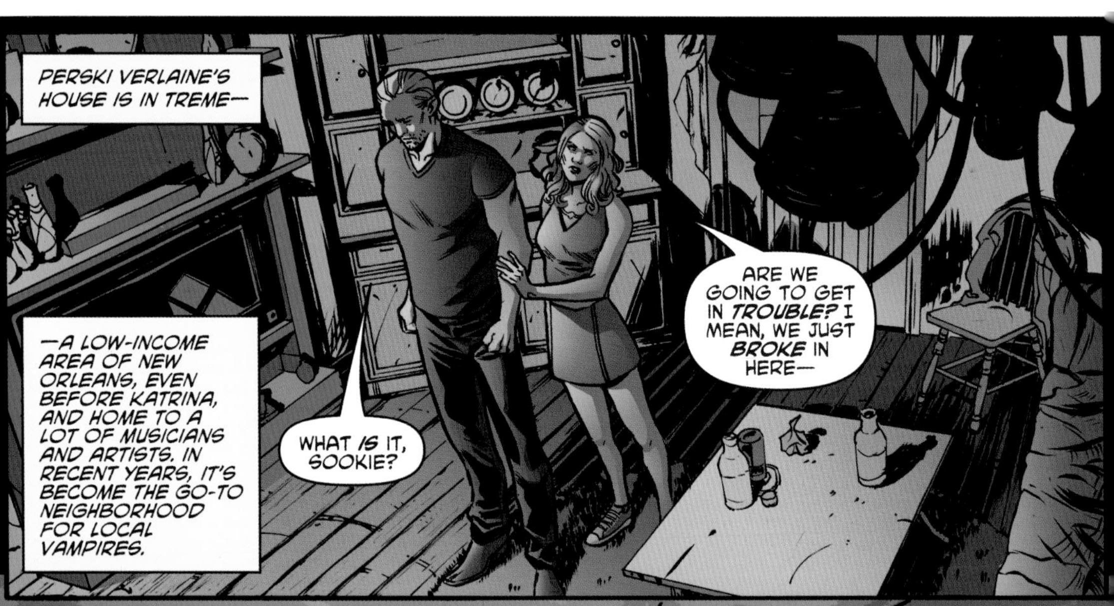
PERSKI VERLAINE'S HOUSE IS IN TREME—
—A LOW-INCOME AREA OF NEW ORLEANS, EVEN BEFORE KATRINA, AND HOME TO A LOT OF MUSICIANS AND ARTISTS. IN RECENT YEARS, IT'S BECOME THE GO-TO NEIGHBORHOOD FOR LOCAL VAMPIRES.
WHAT *IS* IT, SOOKIE?
ARE WE GOING TO GET IN *TROUBLE?* I MEAN, WE JUST *BROKE* IN HERE—

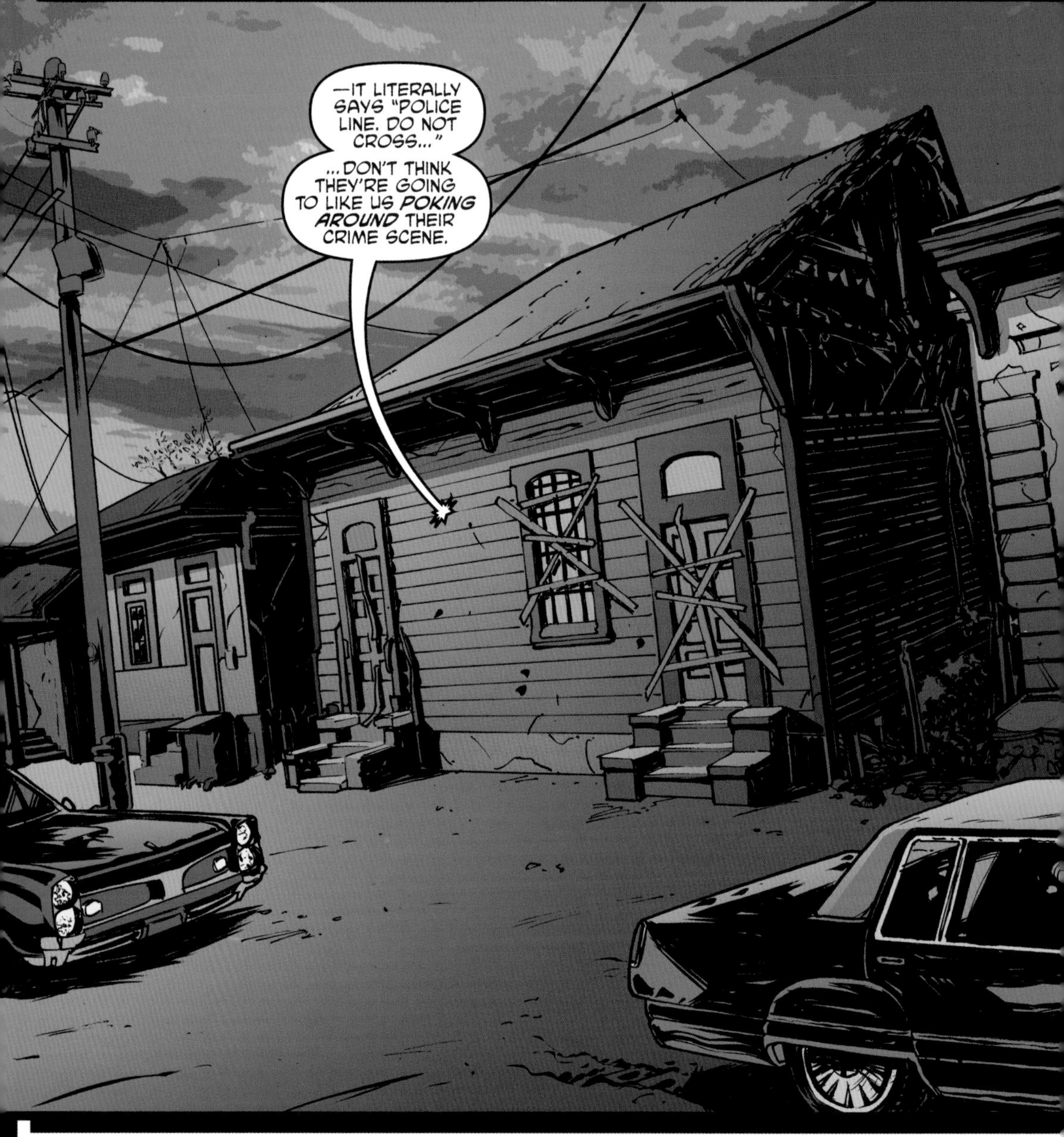
—IT LITERALLY SAYS "POLICE LINE. DO NOT CROSS..."
...DON'T THINK THEY'RE GOING TO LIKE US *POKING AROUND* THEIR CRIME SCENE.

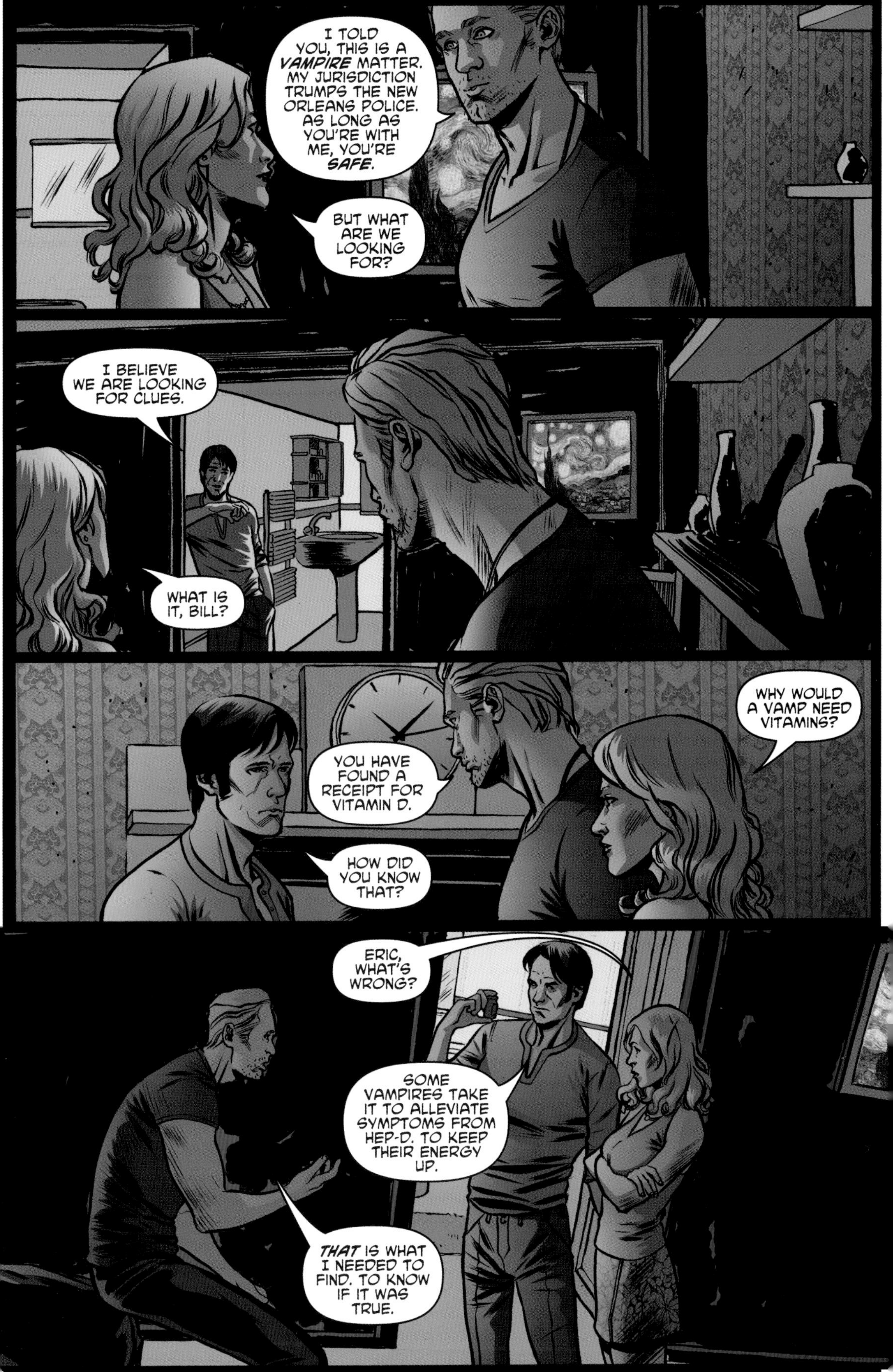
I TOLD YOU, THIS IS A *VAMPIRE* MATTER. MY JURISDICTION TRUMPS THE NEW ORLEANS POLICE. AS LONG AS YOU'RE WITH ME, YOU'RE *SAFE*.
BUT WHAT ARE WE LOOKING FOR?
I BELIEVE WE ARE LOOKING FOR CLUES.
WHAT IS IT, BILL?
WHY WOULD A VAMP NEED VITAMINS?
YOU HAVE FOUND A RECEIPT FOR VITAMIN D.
HOW DID YOU KNOW THAT?
ERIC, WHAT'S WRONG?
SOME VAMPIRES TAKE IT TO ALLEVIATE SYMPTOMS FROM HEP-D. TO KEEP THEIR ENERGY UP.
*THAT* IS WHAT I NEEDED TO FIND. TO KNOW IF IT WAS TRUE.

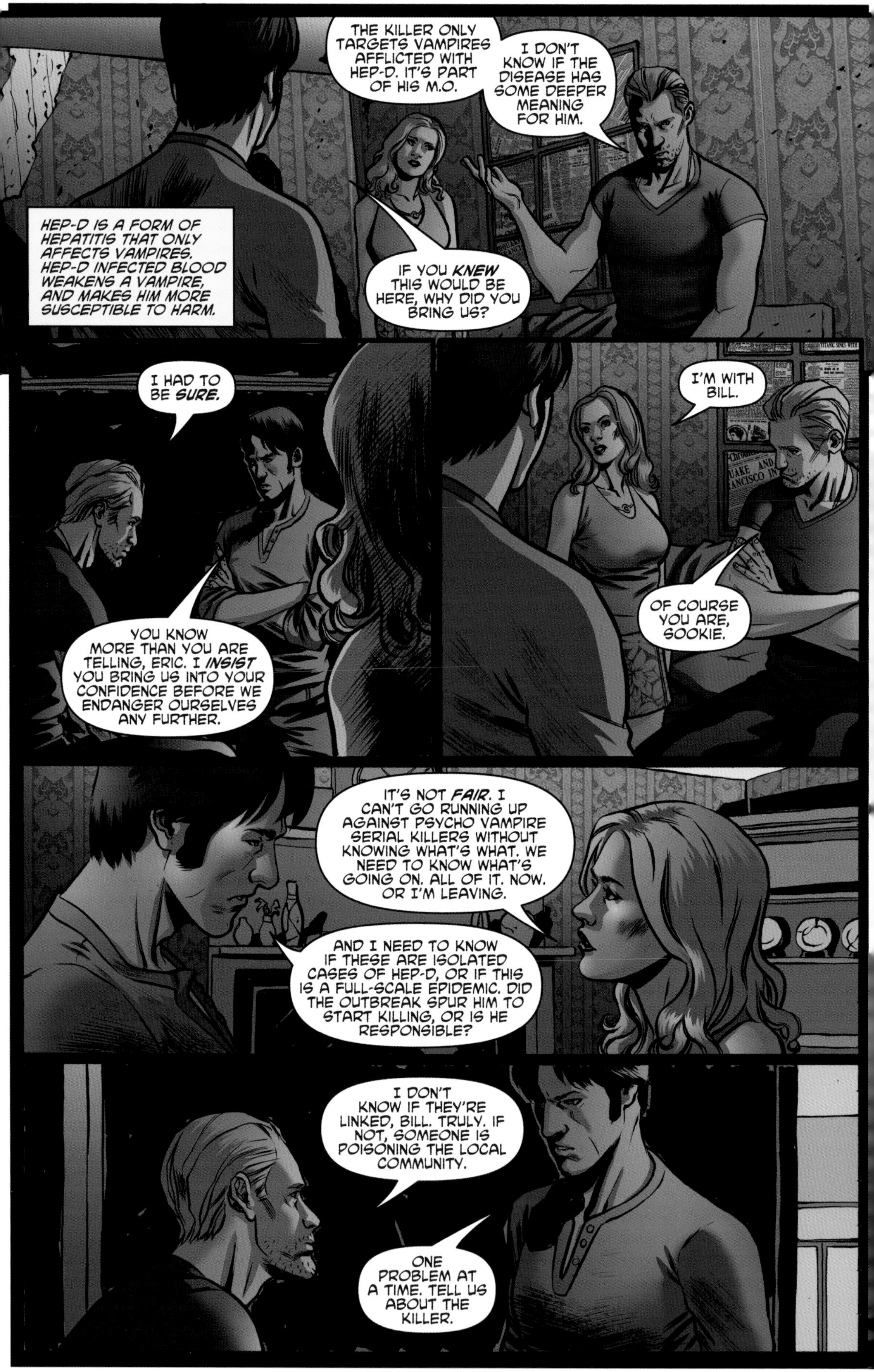
THE KILLER ONLY TARGETS VAMPIRES AFFLICTED WITH HEP-D. IT'S PART OF HIS M.O.
I DON'T KNOW IF THE DISEASE HAS SOME DEEPER MEANING FOR HIM.
HEP-D IS A FORM OF HEPATITIS THAT ONLY AFFECTS VAMPIRES. HEP-D INFECTED BLOOD WEAKENS A VAMPIRE, AND MAKES HIM MORE SUSCEPTIBLE TO HARM.
IF YOU KNEW THIS WOULD BE HERE, WHY DID YOU BRING US?
I HAD TO BE SURE.
YOU KNOW MORE THAN YOU ARE TELLING, ERIC. I INSIST YOU BRING US INTO YOUR CONFIDENCE BEFORE WE ENDANGER OURSELVES ANY FURTHER.
I'M WITH BILL.
OF COURSE YOU ARE, SOOKIE.
IT'S NOT FAIR. I CAN'T GO RUNNING UP AGAINST PSYCHO VAMPIRE SERIAL KILLERS WITHOUT KNOWING WHAT'S WHAT. WE NEED TO KNOW WHAT'S GOING ON. ALL OF IT. NOW. OR I'M LEAVING.
AND I NEED TO KNOW IF THESE ARE ISOLATED CASES OF HEP-D, OR IF THIS IS A FULL-SCALE EPIDEMIC. DID THE OUTBREAK SPUR HIM TO START KILLING, OR IS HE RESPONSIBLE?
I DON'T KNOW IF THEY'RE LINKED, BILL. TRULY. IF NOT, SOMEONE IS POISONING THE LOCAL COMMUNITY.
ONE PROBLEM AT A TIME. TELL US ABOUT THE KILLER.

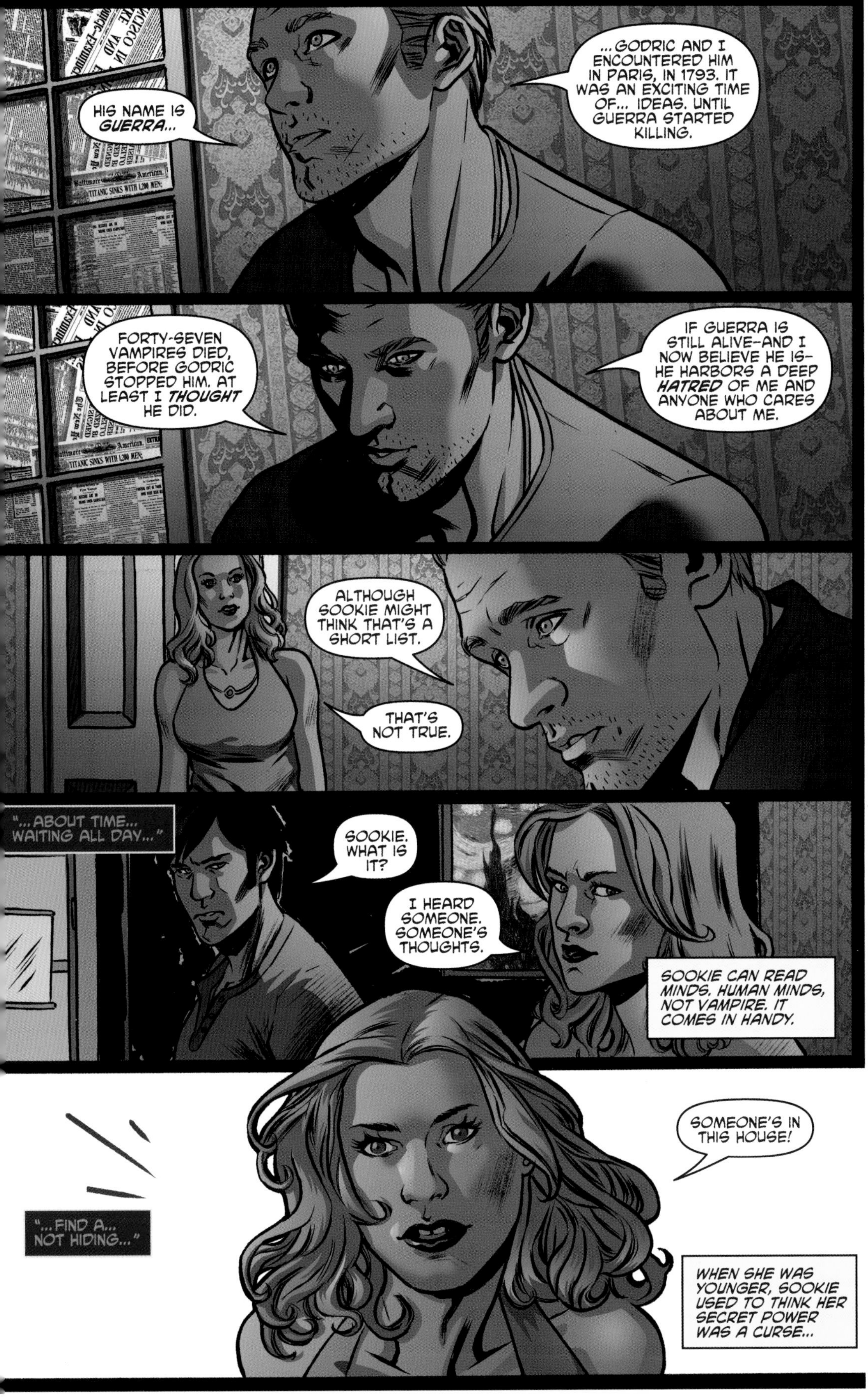
HIS NAME IS *GUERRA*...
...GODRIC AND I ENCOUNTERED HIM IN PARIS, IN 1793. IT WAS AN EXCITING TIME OF... IDEAS. UNTIL GUERRA STARTED KILLING.
FORTY-SEVEN VAMPIRES DIED, BEFORE GODRIC STOPPED HIM. AT LEAST I *THOUGHT* HE DID.
IF GUERRA IS STILL ALIVE--AND I NOW BELIEVE HE IS--HE HARBORS A DEEP *HATRED* OF ME AND ANYONE WHO CARES ABOUT ME.
ALTHOUGH SOOKIE MIGHT THINK THAT'S A SHORT LIST.
THAT'S NOT TRUE.
"...ABOUT TIME... WAITING ALL DAY..."
SOOKIE. WHAT IS IT?
I HEARD SOMEONE. SOMEONE'S THOUGHTS.
SOOKIE CAN READ MINDS. HUMAN MINDS, NOT VAMPIRE. IT COMES IN HANDY.
"...FIND A... NOT HIDING..."
SOMEONE'S IN THIS HOUSE!
WHEN SHE WAS YOUNGER, SOOKIE USED TO THINK HER SECRET POWER WAS A CURSE...

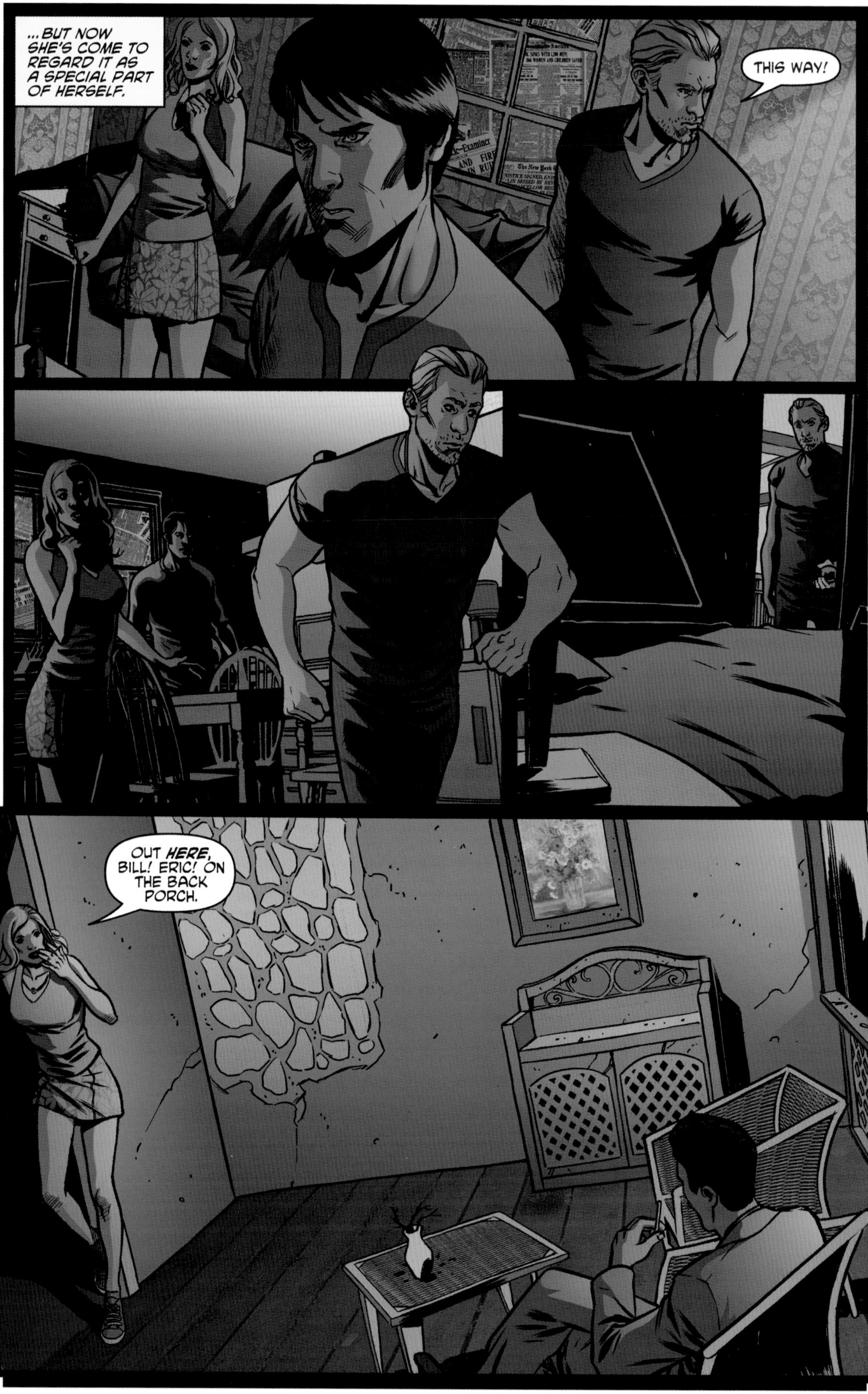
...BUT NOW SHE'S COME TO REGARD IT AS A SPECIAL PART OF HERSELF.
THIS WAY!
OUT HERE, BILL! ERIC! ON THE BACK PORCH.

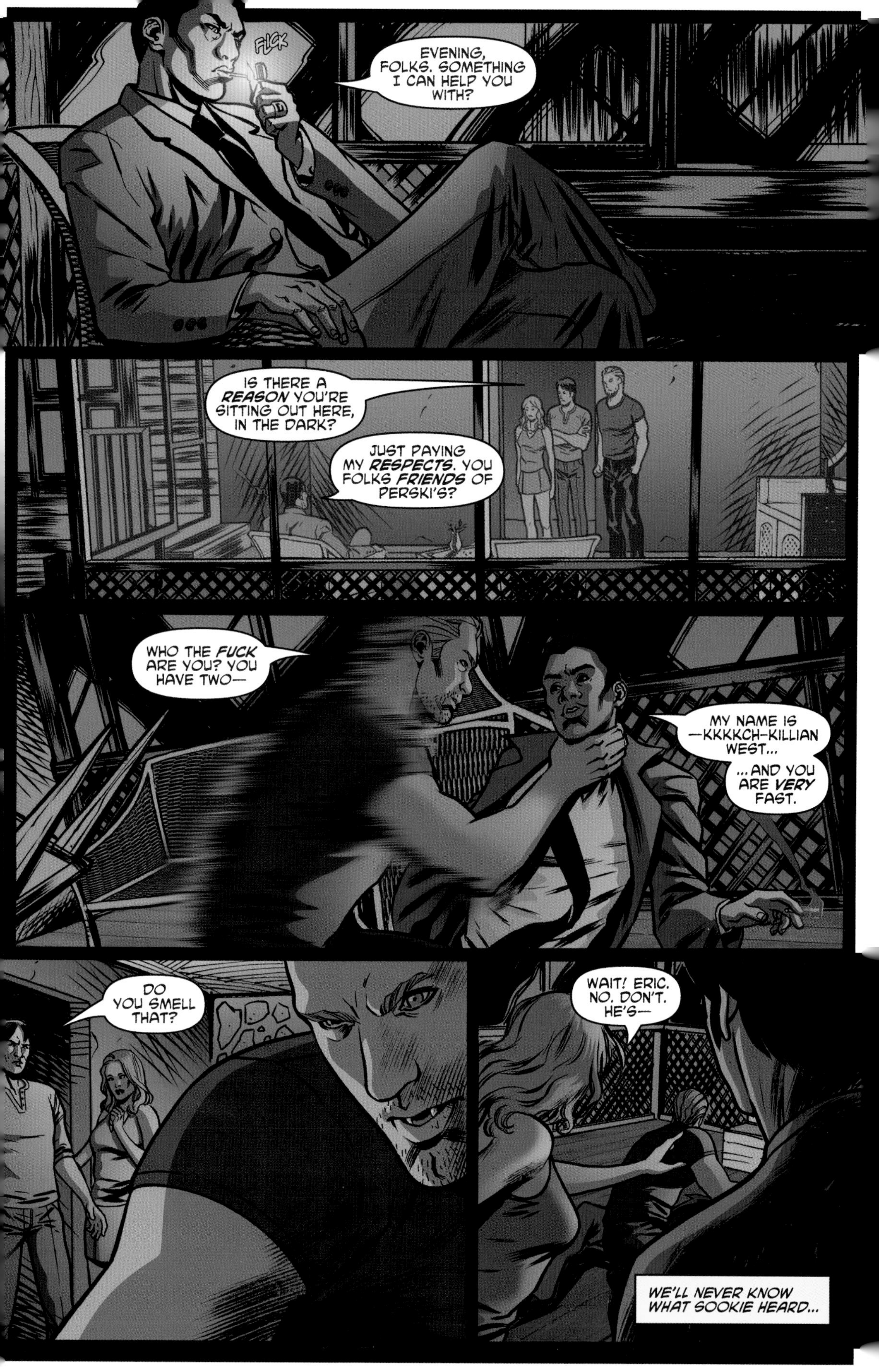
FLICK
EVENING, FOLKS. SOMETHING I CAN HELP YOU WITH?
IS THERE A REASON YOU'RE SITTING OUT HERE, IN THE DARK?
JUST PAYING MY RESPECTS. YOU FOLKS FRIENDS OF PERSKI'S?
WHO THE FUCK ARE YOU? YOU HAVE TWO—
MY NAME IS —KKKKCH—KILLIAN WEST...
...AND YOU ARE VERY FAST.
DO YOU SMELL THAT?
WAIT! ERIC. NO. DON'T. HE'S—
WE'LL NEVER KNOW WHAT SOOKIE HEARD...

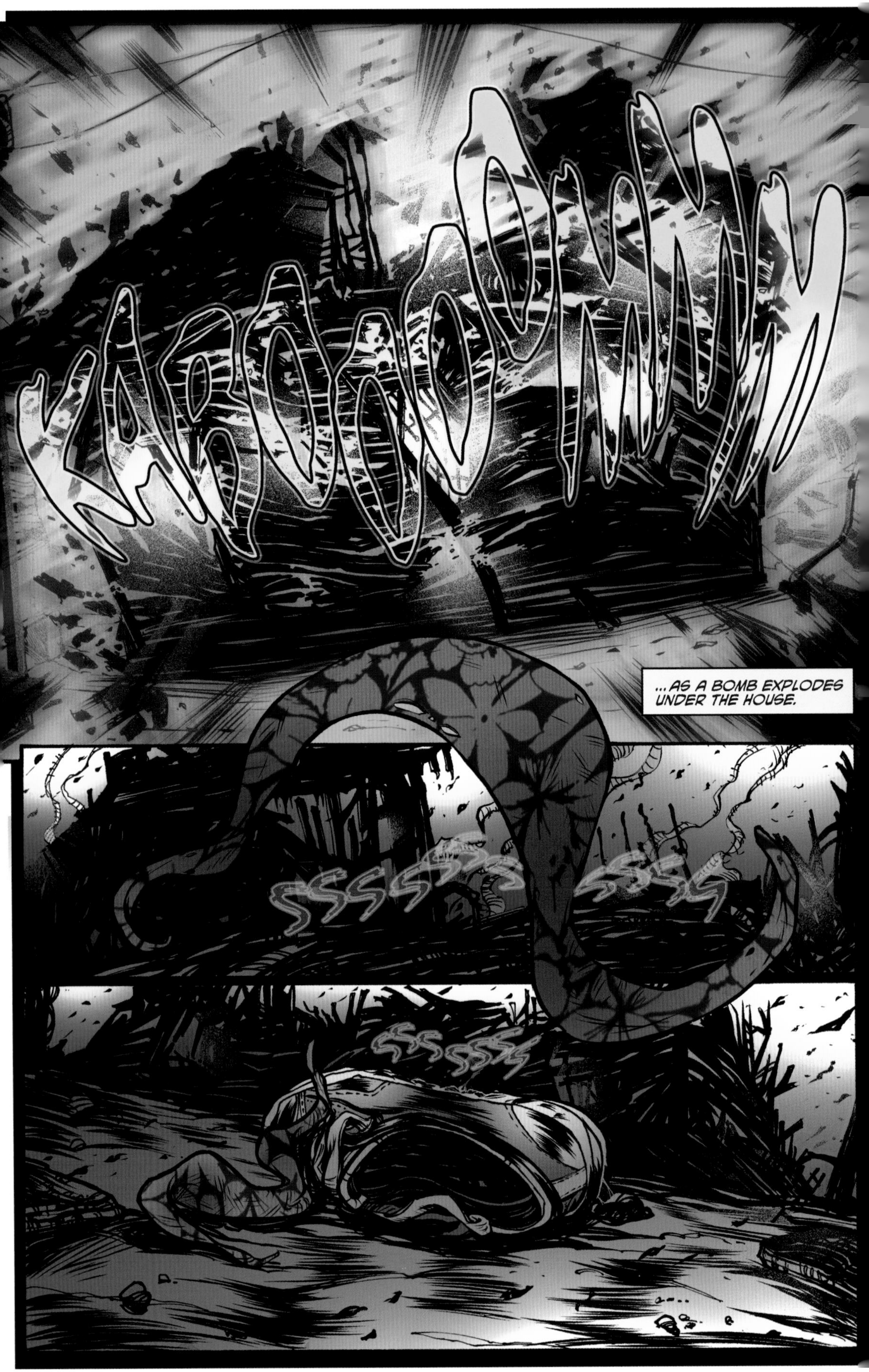
...AS A BOMB EXPLODES UNDER THE HOUSE.

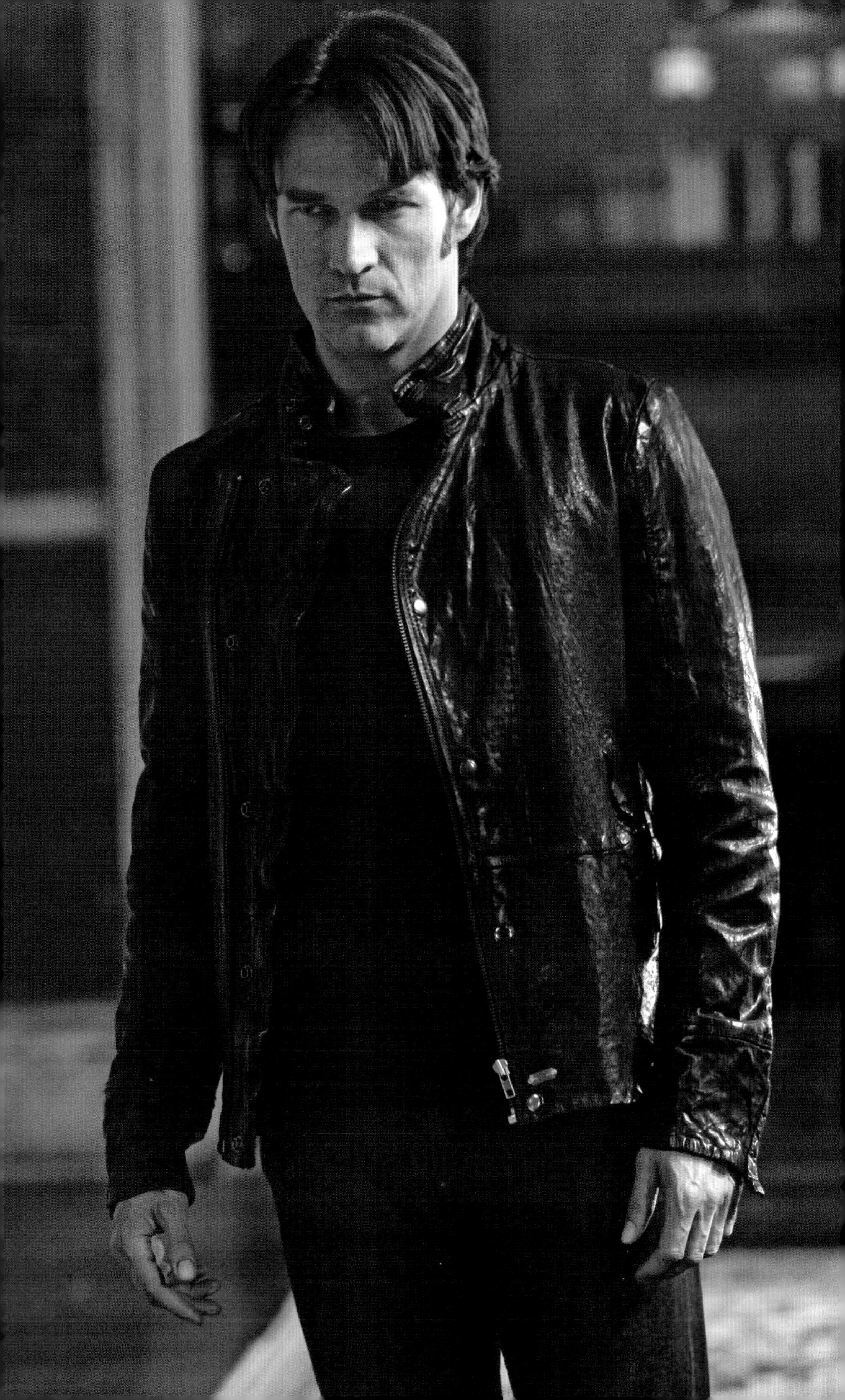

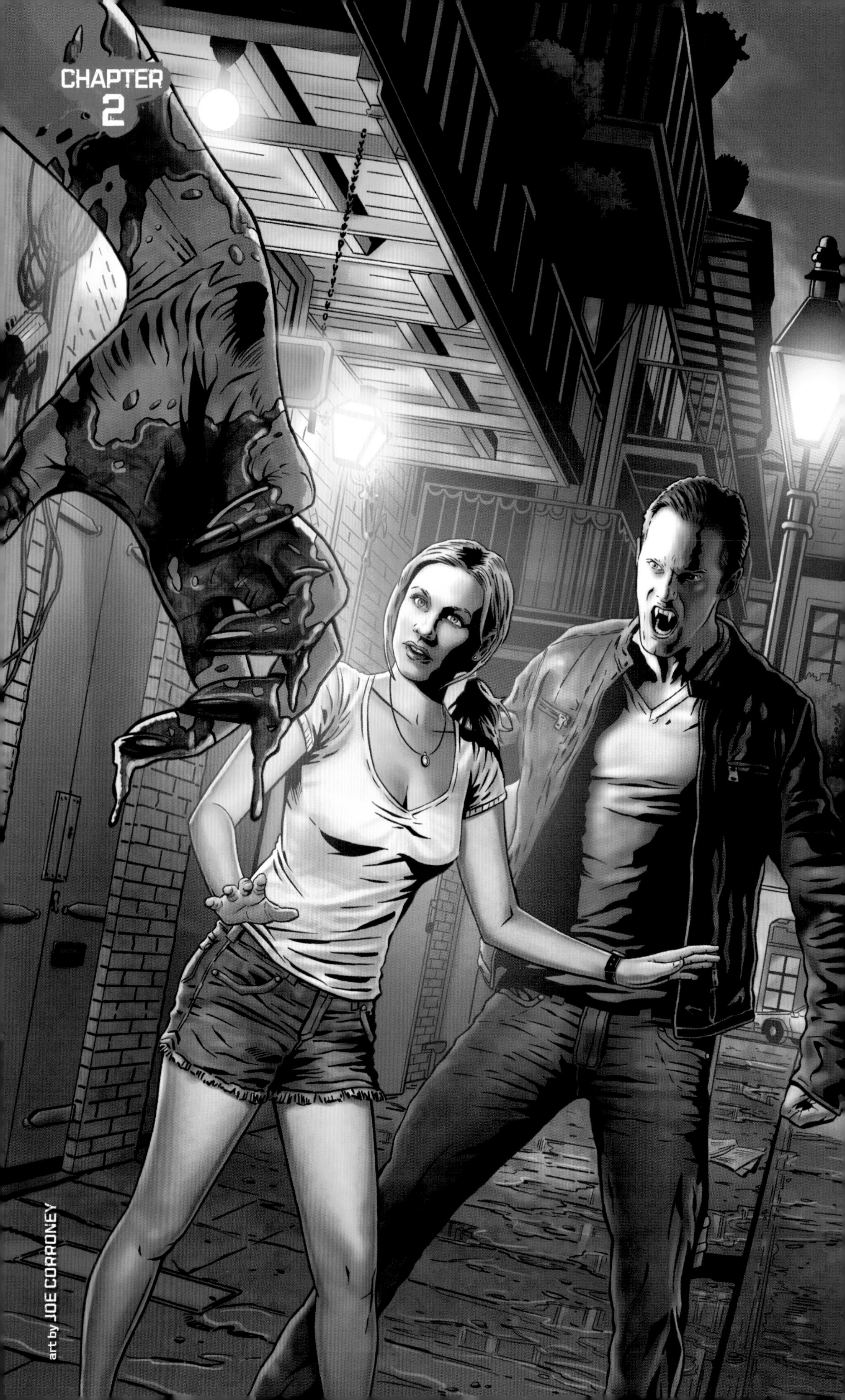
CHAPTER
2
art by JOE CORRONEY

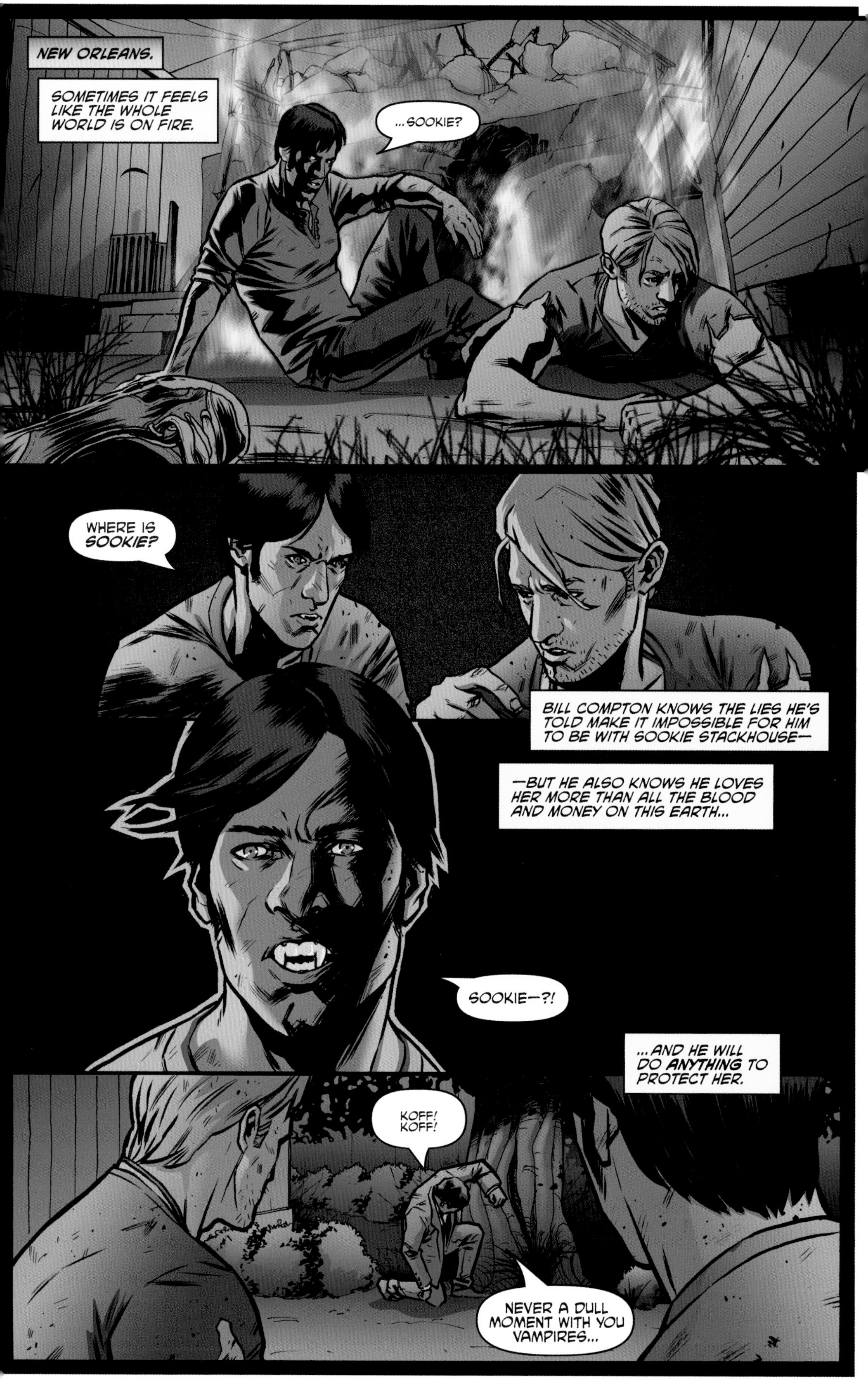
NEW ORLEANS.
SOMETIMES IT FEELS LIKE THE WHOLE WORLD IS ON FIRE.
...SOOKIE?
WHERE IS SOOKIE?
BILL COMPTON KNOWS THE LIES HE'S TOLD MAKE IT IMPOSSIBLE FOR HIM TO BE WITH SOOKIE STACKHOUSE—
—BUT HE ALSO KNOWS HE LOVES HER MORE THAN ALL THE BLOOD AND MONEY ON THIS EARTH...
SOOKIE—?!
...AND HE WILL DO ANYTHING TO PROTECT HER.
KOFF! KOFF!
NEVER A DULL MOMENT WITH YOU VAMPIRES...

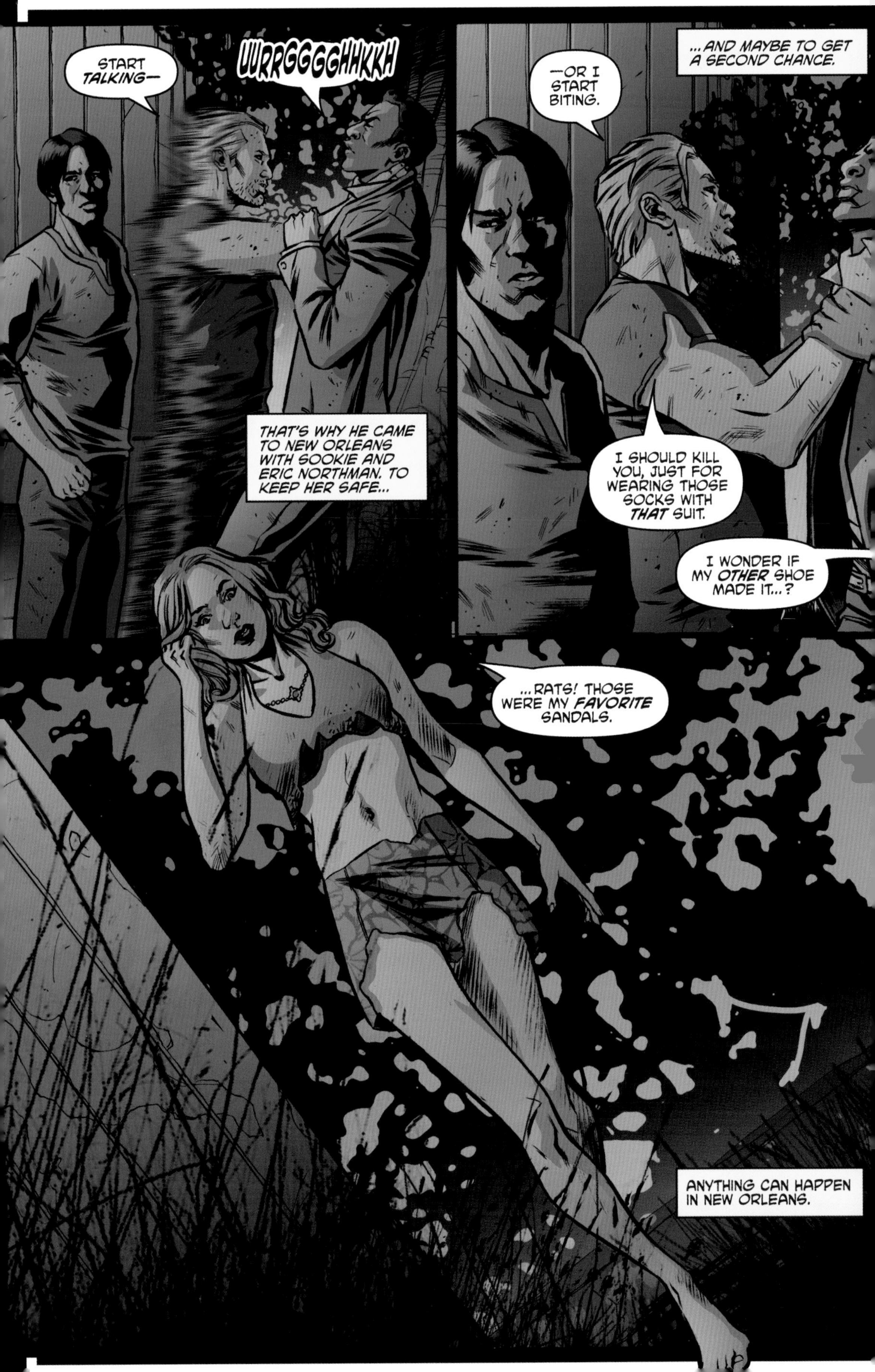
START TALKING—
UURRGGGGHHKKH
THAT'S WHY HE CAME TO NEW ORLEANS WITH SOOKIE AND ERIC NORTHMAN. TO KEEP HER SAFE...
—OR I START BITING.
...AND MAYBE TO GET A SECOND CHANCE.
I SHOULD KILL YOU, JUST FOR WEARING THOSE SOCKS WITH THAT SUIT.
I WONDER IF MY OTHER SHOE MADE IT...?
...RATS! THOSE WERE MY FAVORITE SANDALS.
ANYTHING CAN HAPPEN IN NEW ORLEANS.

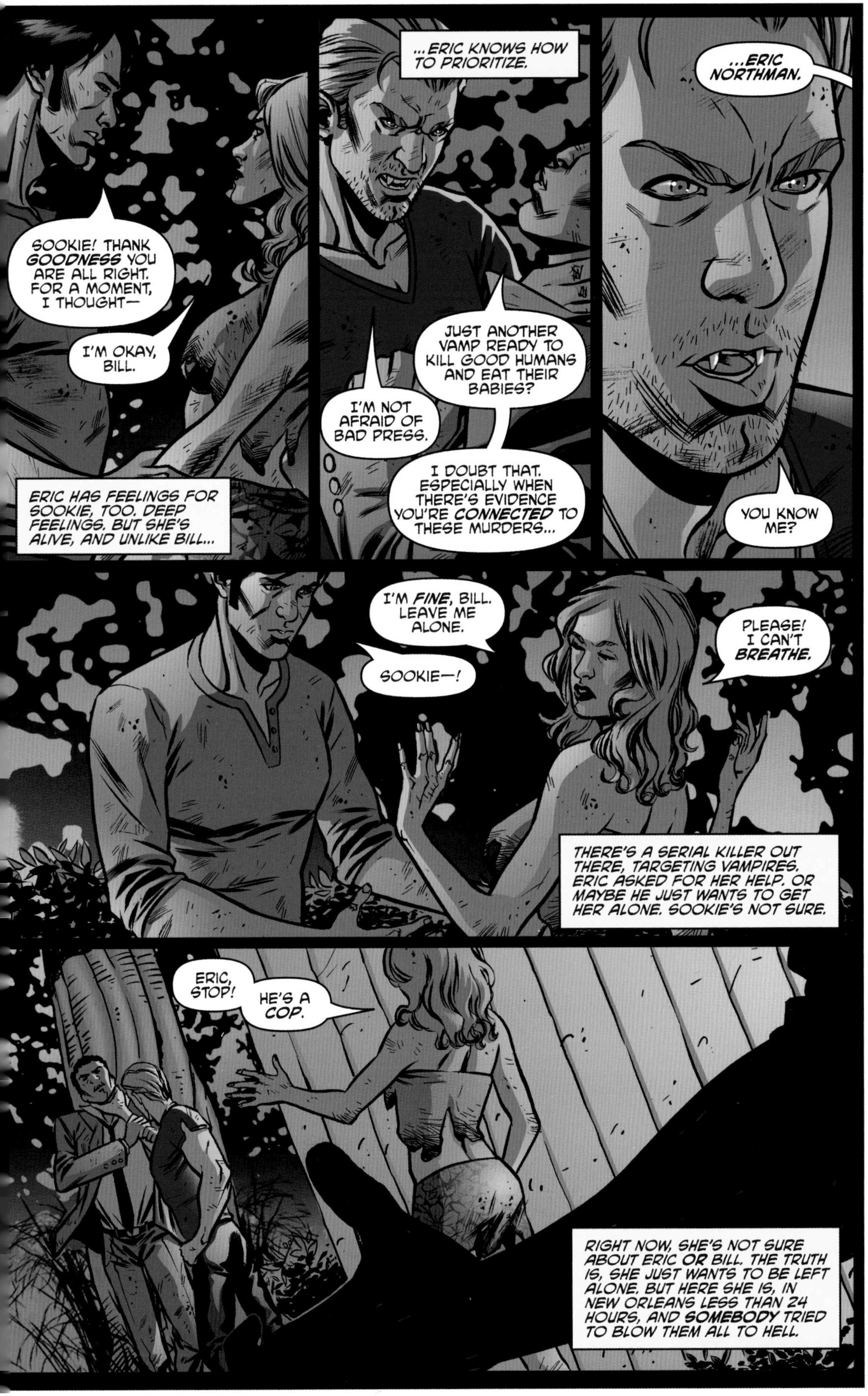
SOOKIE! THANK GOODNESS YOU ARE ALL RIGHT. FOR A MOMENT, I THOUGHT—
I'M OKAY, BILL.
ERIC HAS FEELINGS FOR SOOKIE, TOO. DEEP FEELINGS. BUT SHE'S ALIVE, AND UNLIKE BILL...
...ERIC KNOWS HOW TO PRIORITIZE.
JUST ANOTHER VAMP READY TO KILL GOOD HUMANS AND EAT THEIR BABIES?
I'M NOT AFRAID OF BAD PRESS.
I DOUBT THAT. ESPECIALLY WHEN THERE'S EVIDENCE YOU'RE CONNECTED TO THESE MURDERS...
...ERIC NORTHMAN.
YOU KNOW ME?
I'M FINE, BILL. LEAVE ME ALONE.
SOOKIE—!
PLEASE! I CAN'T BREATHE.
THERE'S A SERIAL KILLER OUT THERE, TARGETING VAMPIRES. ERIC ASKED FOR HER HELP. OR MAYBE HE JUST WANTS TO GET HER ALONE. SOOKIE'S NOT SURE.
ERIC, STOP!
HE'S A COP.
RIGHT NOW, SHE'S NOT SURE ABOUT ERIC OR BILL. THE TRUTH IS, SHE JUST WANTS TO BE LEFT ALONE. BUT HERE SHE IS, IN NEW ORLEANS LESS THAN 24 HOURS, AND SOMEBODY TRIED TO BLOW THEM ALL TO HELL.

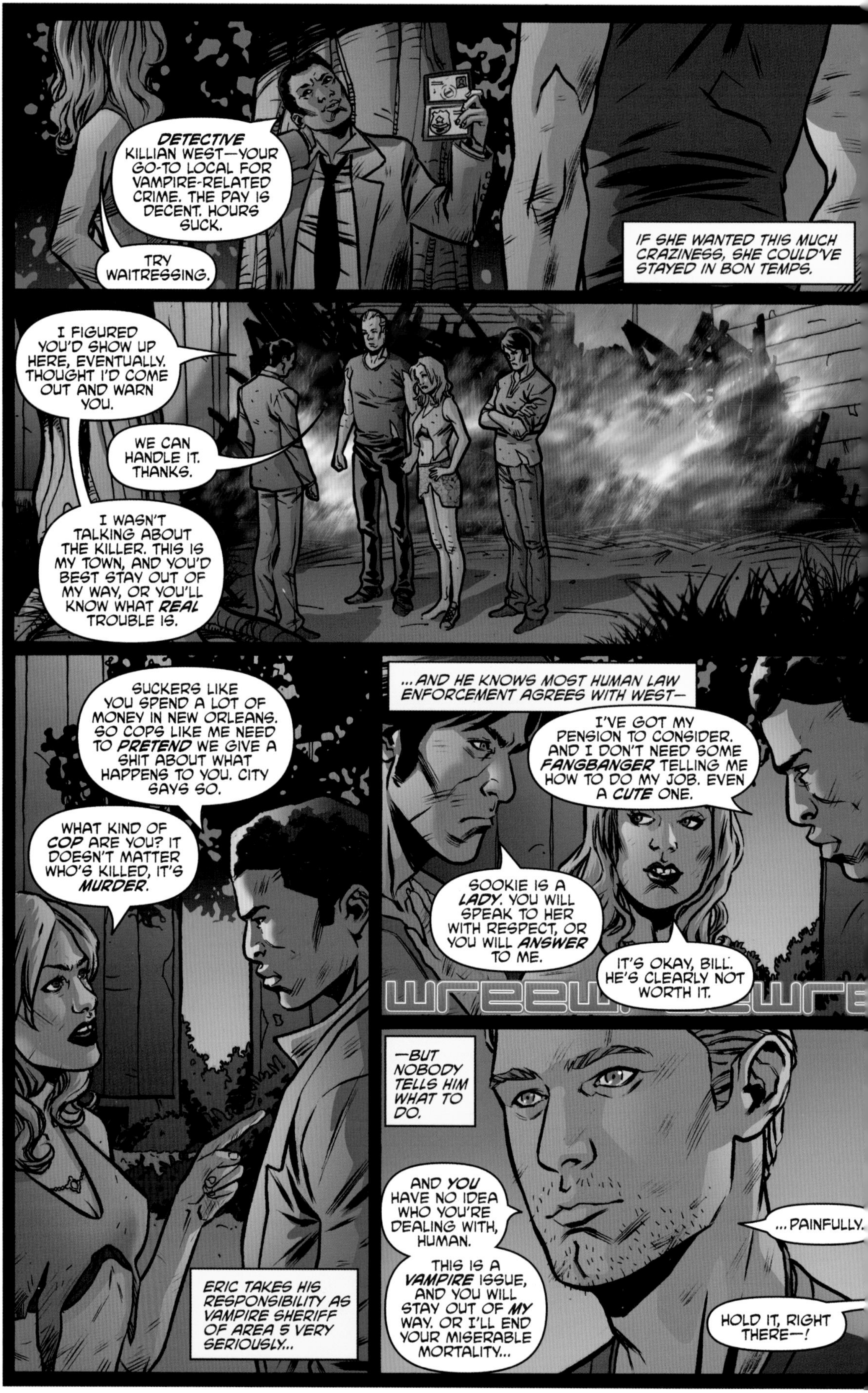

DETECTIVE KILLIAN WEST—YOUR GO-TO LOCAL FOR VAMPIRE-RELATED CRIME. THE PAY IS DECENT. HOURS SUCK.
TRY WAITRESSING.
IF SHE WANTED THIS MUCH CRAZINESS, SHE COULD'VE STAYED IN BON TEMPS.
I FIGURED YOU'D SHOW UP HERE, EVENTUALLY. THOUGHT I'D COME OUT AND WARN YOU.
WE CAN HANDLE IT. THANKS.
I WASN'T TALKING ABOUT THE KILLER. THIS IS MY TOWN, AND YOU'D BEST STAY OUT OF MY WAY, OR YOU'LL KNOW WHAT REAL TROUBLE IS.
SUCKERS LIKE YOU SPEND A LOT OF MONEY IN NEW ORLEANS. SO COPS LIKE ME NEED TO PRETEND WE GIVE A SHIT ABOUT WHAT HAPPENS TO YOU. CITY SAYS SO.
WHAT KIND OF COP ARE YOU? IT DOESN'T MATTER WHO'S KILLED, IT'S MURDER.
ERIC TAKES HIS RESPONSIBILITY AS VAMPIRE SHERIFF OF AREA 5 VERY SERIOUSLY...
...AND HE KNOWS MOST HUMAN LAW ENFORCEMENT AGREES WITH WEST—
I'VE GOT MY PENSION TO CONSIDER. AND I DON'T NEED SOME FANGBANGER TELLING ME HOW TO DO MY JOB. EVEN A CUTE ONE.
SOOKIE IS A LADY. YOU WILL SPEAK TO HER WITH RESPECT, OR YOU WILL ANSWER TO ME.
IT'S OKAY, BILL. HE'S CLEARLY NOT WORTH IT.
—BUT NOBODY TELLS HIM WHAT TO DO.
AND YOU HAVE NO IDEA WHO YOU'RE DEALING WITH, HUMAN.
THIS IS A VAMPIRE ISSUE, AND YOU WILL STAY OUT OF MY WAY. OR I'LL END YOUR MISERABLE MORTALITY...
...PAINFULLY.
HOLD IT, RIGHT THERE—!

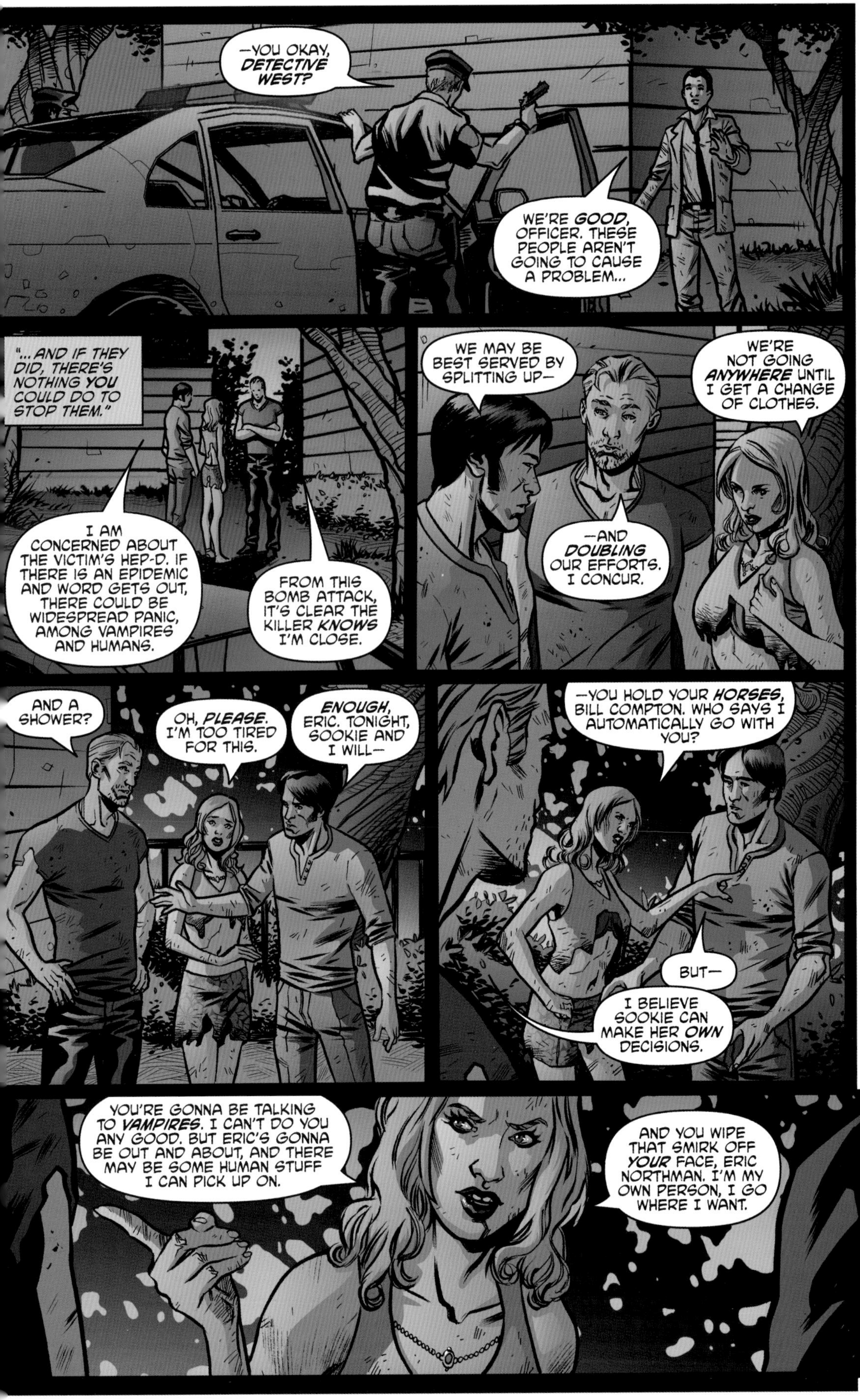
—YOU OKAY, DETECTIVE WEST?
WE'RE GOOD, OFFICER. THESE PEOPLE AREN'T GOING TO CAUSE A PROBLEM...
"...AND IF THEY DID, THERE'S NOTHING YOU COULD DO TO STOP THEM."
I AM CONCERNED ABOUT THE VICTIM'S HEP-D. IF THERE IS AN EPIDEMIC AND WORD GETS OUT, THERE COULD BE WIDESPREAD PANIC, AMONG VAMPIRES AND HUMANS.
FROM THIS BOMB ATTACK, IT'S CLEAR THE KILLER KNOWS I'M CLOSE.
WE MAY BE BEST SERVED BY SPLITTING UP—
—AND DOUBLING OUR EFFORTS. I CONCUR.
WE'RE NOT GOING ANYWHERE UNTIL I GET A CHANGE OF CLOTHES.
AND A SHOWER?
OH, PLEASE. I'M TOO TIRED FOR THIS.
ENOUGH, ERIC. TONIGHT, SOOKIE AND I WILL—
—YOU HOLD YOUR HORSES, BILL COMPTON. WHO SAYS I AUTOMATICALLY GO WITH YOU?
BUT—
I BELIEVE SOOKIE CAN MAKE HER OWN DECISIONS.
YOU'RE GONNA BE TALKING TO VAMPIRES. I CAN'T DO YOU ANY GOOD. BUT ERIC'S GONNA BE OUT AND ABOUT, AND THERE MAY BE SOME HUMAN STUFF I CAN PICK UP ON.
AND YOU WIPE THAT SMIRK OFF YOUR FACE, ERIC NORTHMAN. I'M MY OWN PERSON, I GO WHERE I WANT.

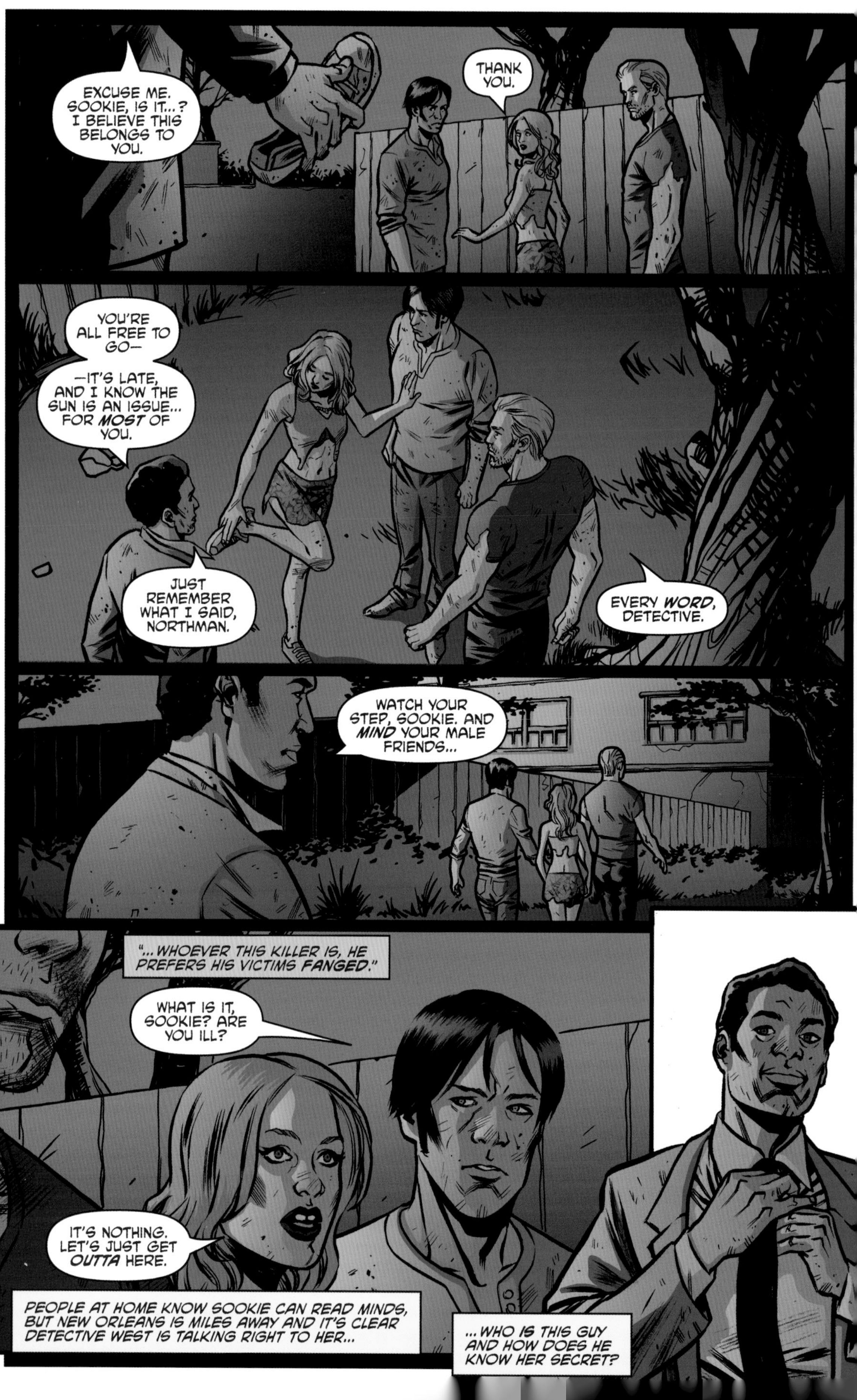
EXCUSE ME. SOOKIE, IS IT...? I BELIEVE THIS BELONGS TO YOU.
THANK YOU.
YOU'RE ALL FREE TO GO—
—IT'S LATE, AND I KNOW THE SUN IS AN ISSUE... FOR MOST OF YOU.
JUST REMEMBER WHAT I SAID, NORTHMAN.
EVERY WORD, DETECTIVE.
WATCH YOUR STEP, SOOKIE. AND MIND YOUR MALE FRIENDS...
"...WHOEVER THIS KILLER IS, HE PREFERS HIS VICTIMS FANGED."
WHAT IS IT, SOOKIE? ARE YOU ILL?
IT'S NOTHING. LET'S JUST GET OUTTA HERE.
PEOPLE AT HOME KNOW SOOKIE CAN READ MINDS, BUT NEW ORLEANS IS MILES AWAY AND IT'S CLEAR DETECTIVE WEST IS TALKING RIGHT TO HER...
...WHO IS THIS GUY AND HOW DOES HE KNOW HER SECRET?

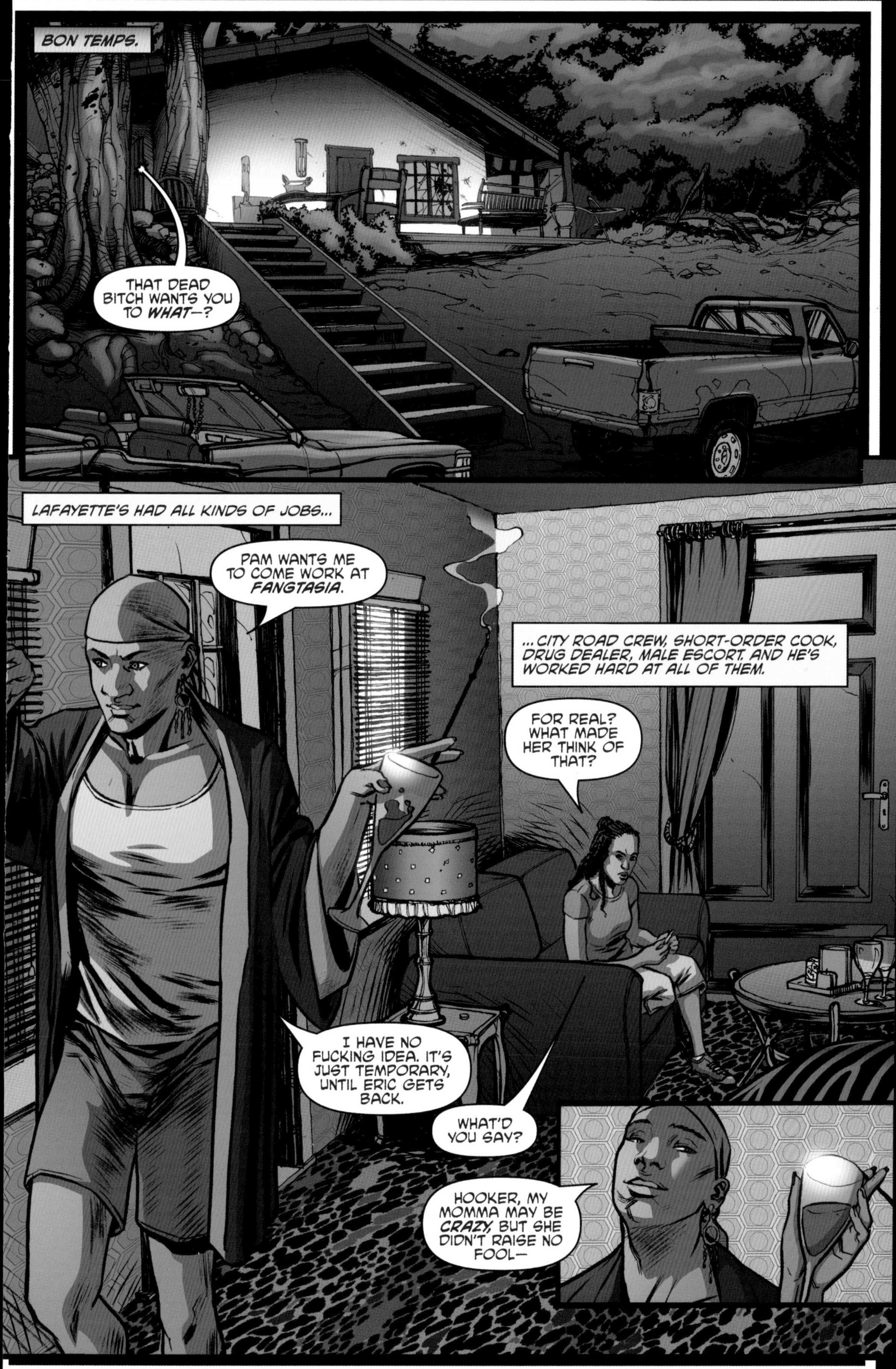
BON TEMPS.
THAT DEAD BITCH WANTS YOU TO WHAT—?
LAFAYETTE'S HAD ALL KINDS OF JOBS...
PAM WANTS ME TO COME WORK AT FANGTASIA.
...CITY ROAD CREW, SHORT-ORDER COOK, DRUG DEALER, MALE ESCORT. AND HE'S WORKED HARD AT ALL OF THEM.
FOR REAL? WHAT MADE HER THINK OF THAT?
I HAVE NO FUCKING IDEA. IT'S JUST TEMPORARY, UNTIL ERIC GETS BACK.
WHAT'D YOU SAY?
HOOKER, MY MOMMA MAY BE CRAZY, BUT SHE DIDN'T RAISE NO FOOL—

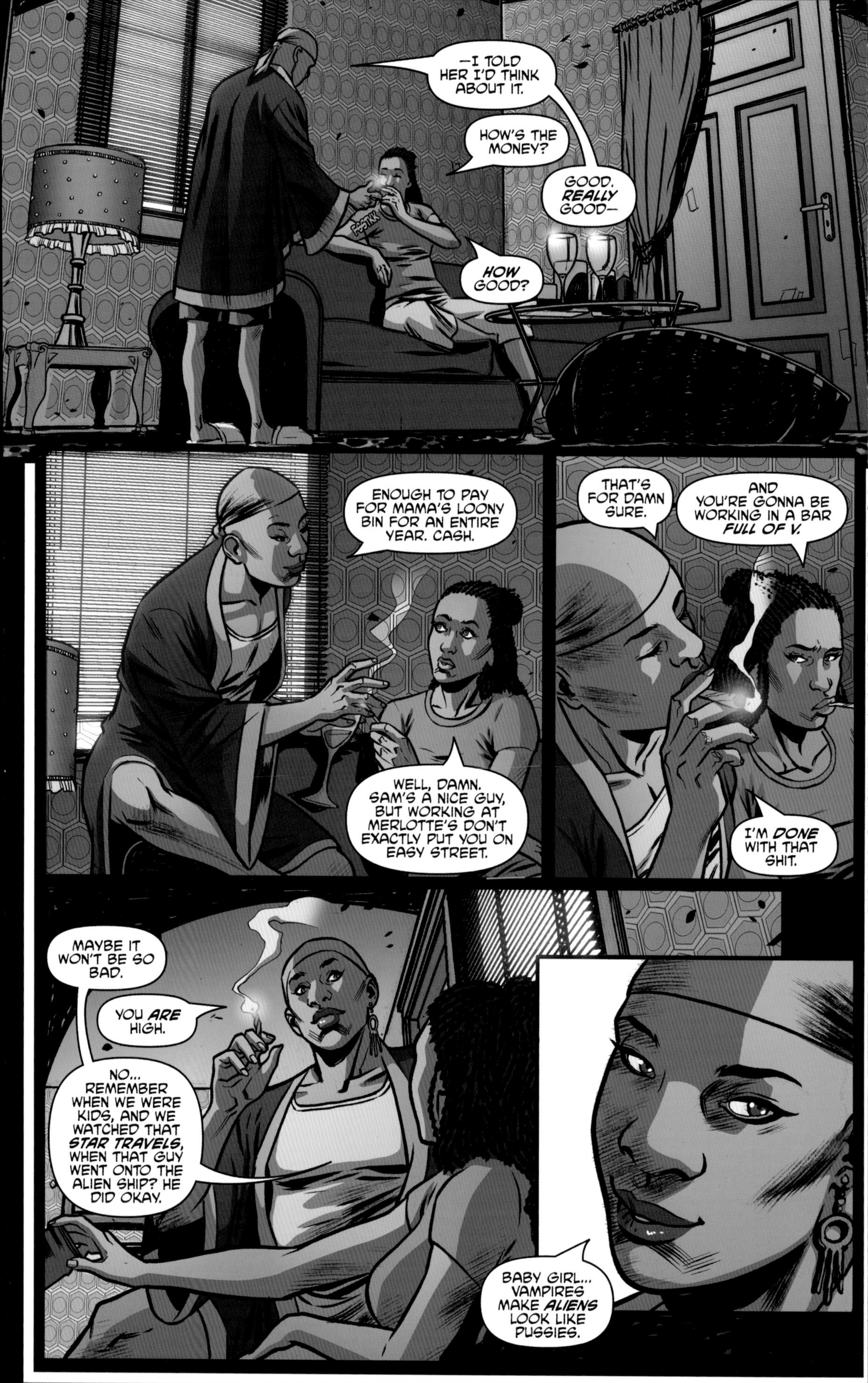
—I TOLD HER I'D THINK ABOUT IT.
HOW'S THE MONEY?
GOOD. **REALLY** GOOD—
**HOW** GOOD?
FSSTKK
ENOUGH TO PAY FOR MAMA'S LOONY BIN FOR AN ENTIRE YEAR. CASH.
WELL, DAMN. SAM'S A NICE GUY, BUT WORKING AT MERLOTTE'S DON'T EXACTLY PUT YOU ON EASY STREET.
THAT'S FOR DAMN SURE.
AND YOU'RE GONNA BE WORKING IN A BAR **FULL OF V.**
I'M **DONE** WITH THAT SHIT.
MAYBE IT WON'T BE SO BAD.
YOU **ARE** HIGH.
NO... REMEMBER WHEN WE WERE KIDS, AND WE WATCHED THAT ***STAR TRAVELS,*** WHEN THAT GUY WENT ONTO THE ALIEN SHIP? HE DID OKAY.
BABY GIRL... VAMPIRES MAKE **ALIENS** LOOK LIKE PUSSIES.

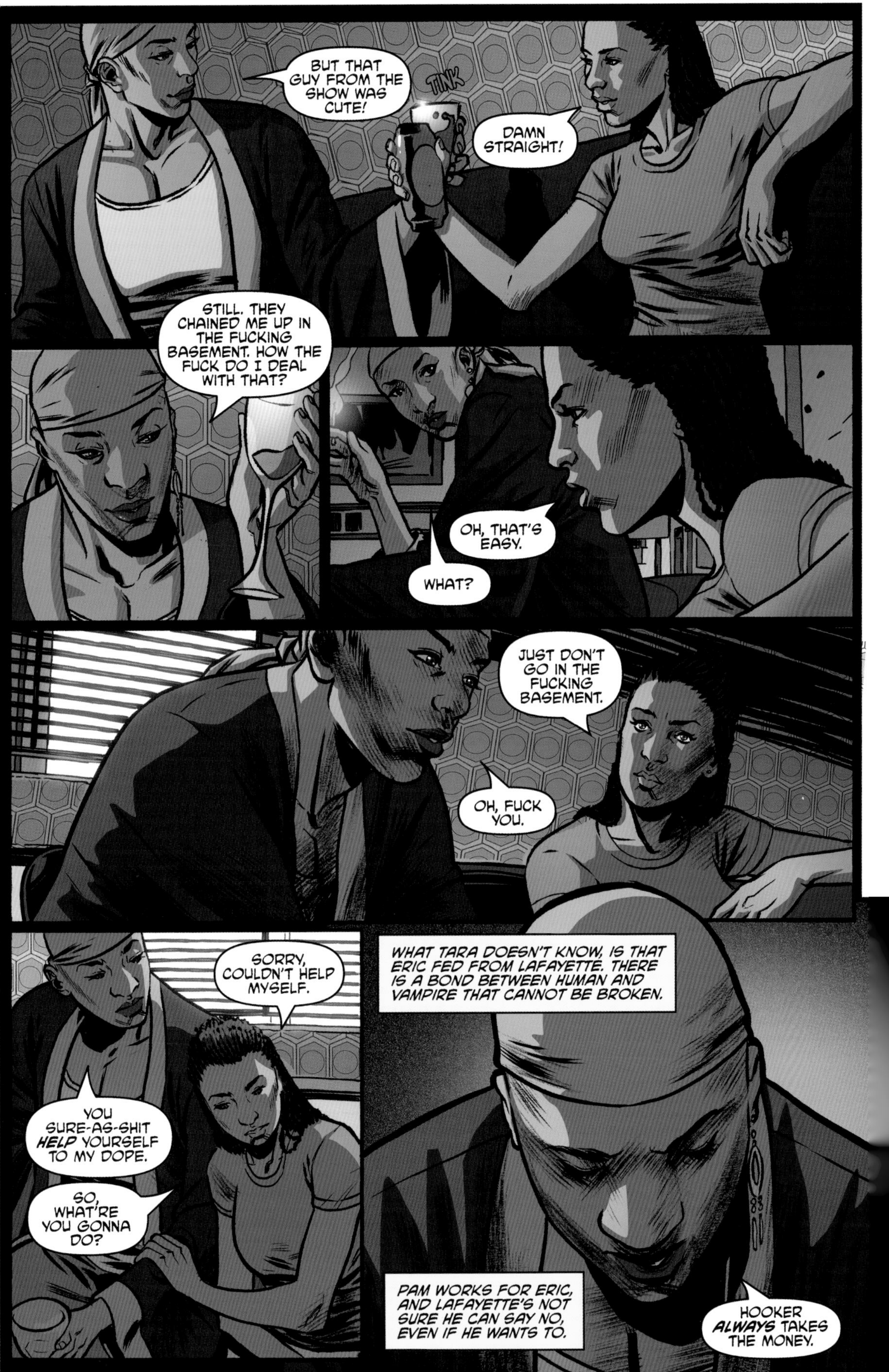
BUT THAT GUY FROM THE SHOW WAS CUTE!
TINK
DAMN STRAIGHT!
STILL. THEY CHAINED ME UP IN THE FUCKING BASEMENT. HOW THE FUCK DO I DEAL WITH THAT?
OH, THAT'S EASY.
WHAT?
JUST DON'T GO IN THE FUCKING BASEMENT.
OH, FUCK YOU.
SORRY, COULDN'T HELP MYSELF.
YOU SURE-AS-SHIT *HELP* YOURSELF TO MY DOPE.
SO, WHAT'RE YOU GONNA DO?
*WHAT TARA DOESN'T KNOW, IS THAT ERIC FED FROM LAFAYETTE. THERE IS A BOND BETWEEN HUMAN AND VAMPIRE THAT CANNOT BE BROKEN.*
*PAM WORKS FOR ERIC, AND LAFAYETTE'S NOT SURE HE CAN SAY NO, EVEN IF HE WANTS TO.*
HOOKER *ALWAYS* TAKES THE MONEY.

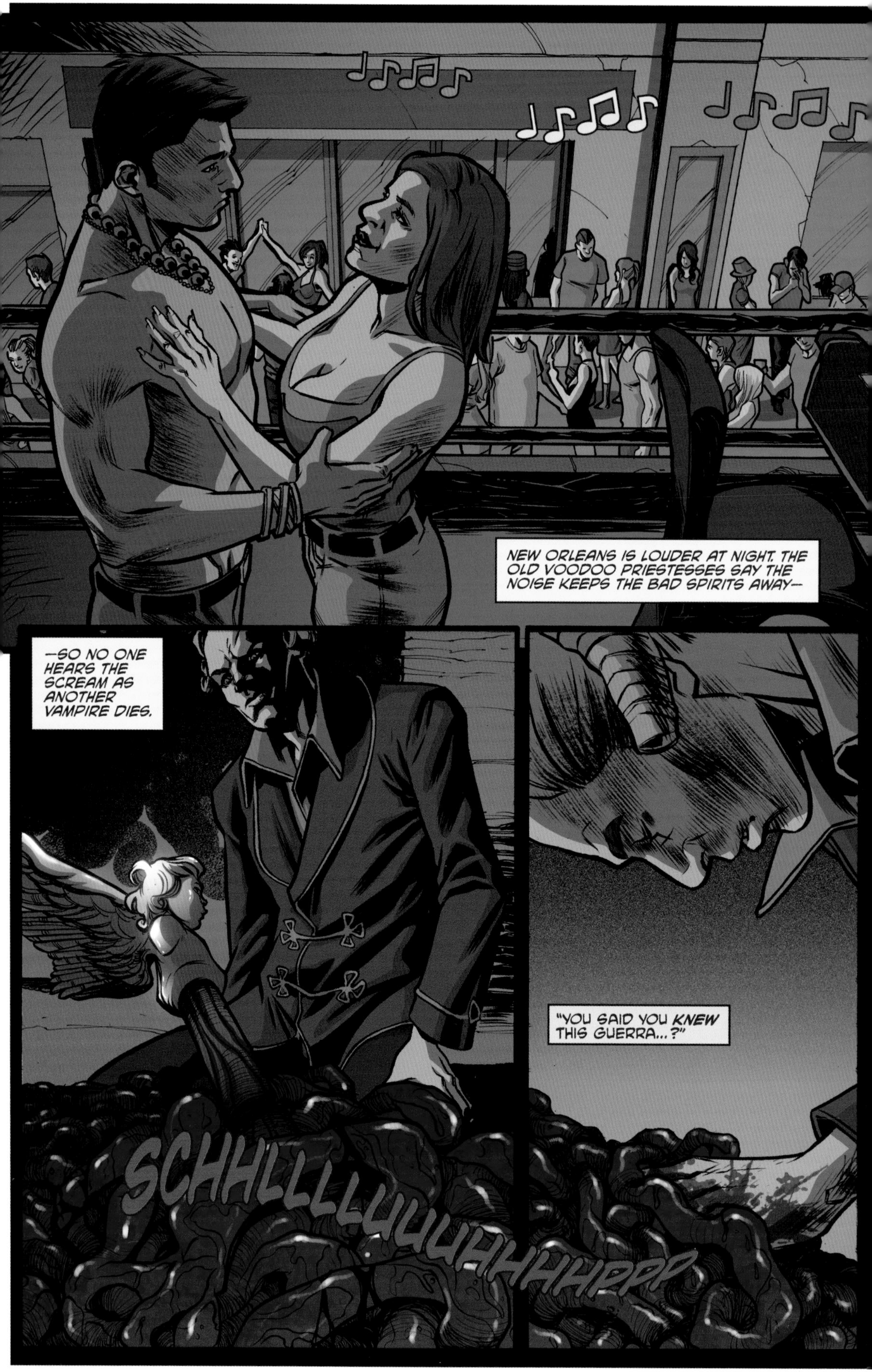
NEW ORLEANS IS LOUDER AT NIGHT. THE OLD VOODOO PRIESTESSES SAY THE NOISE KEEPS THE BAD SPIRITS AWAY--
--SO NO ONE HEARS THE SCREAM AS ANOTHER VAMPIRE DIES.
"YOU SAID YOU *KNEW* THIS GUERRA...?"
SCHHLLLLLUUUHHHHHPPP

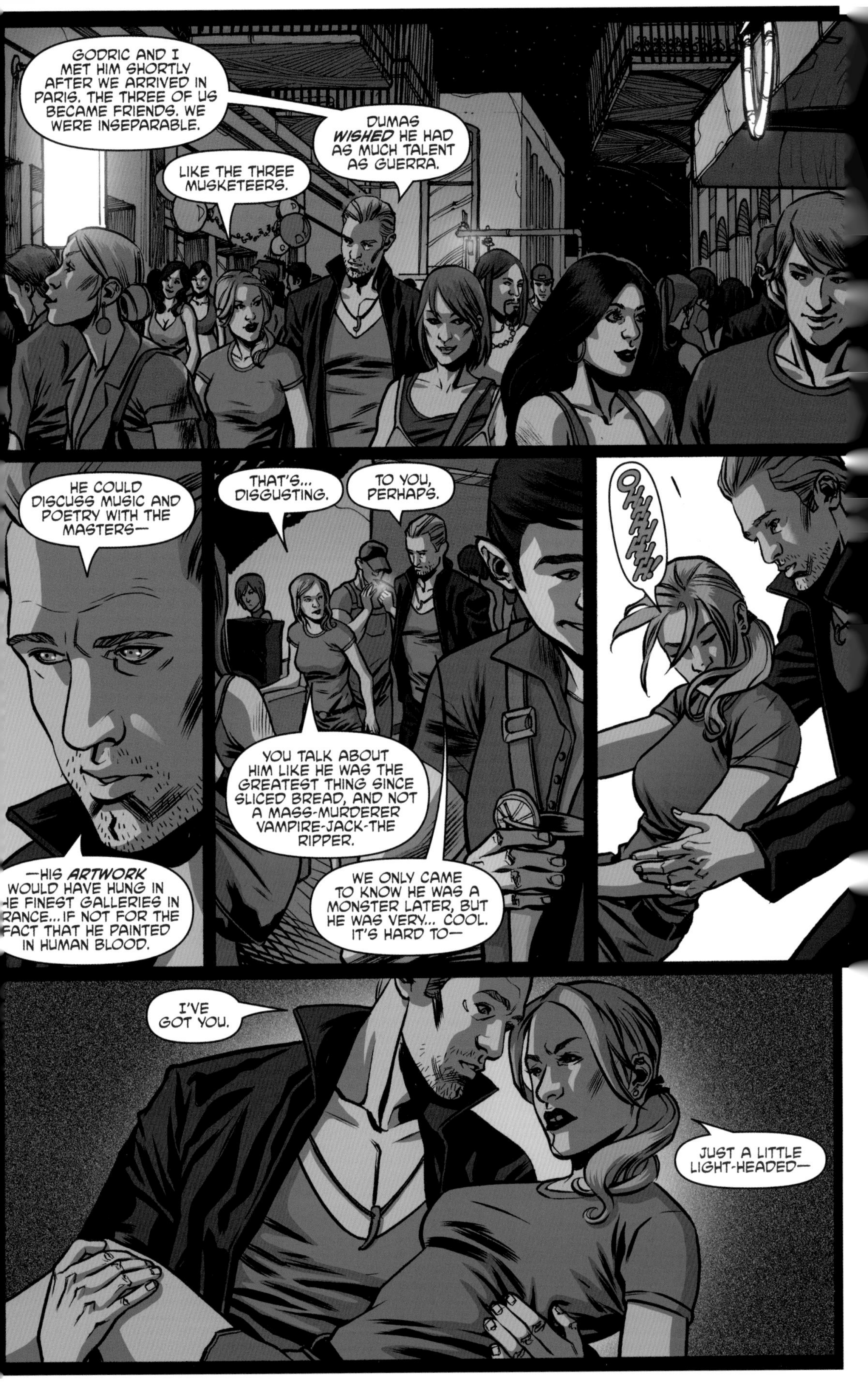
GODRIC AND I MET HIM SHORTLY AFTER WE ARRIVED IN PARIS. THE THREE OF US BECAME FRIENDS. WE WERE INSEPARABLE.
LIKE THE THREE MUSKETEERS.
DUMAS *WISHED* HE HAD AS MUCH TALENT AS GUERRA.
HE COULD DISCUSS MUSIC AND POETRY WITH THE MASTERS—
—HIS *ARTWORK* WOULD HAVE HUNG IN HE FINEST GALLERIES IN RANCE... IF NOT FOR THE FACT THAT HE PAINTED IN HUMAN BLOOD.
THAT'S... DISGUSTING.
TO YOU, PERHAPS.
YOU TALK ABOUT HIM LIKE HE WAS THE GREATEST THING SINCE SLICED BREAD, AND NOT A MASS-MURDERER VAMPIRE-JACK-THE RIPPER.
WE ONLY CAME TO KNOW HE WAS A MONSTER LATER, BUT HE WAS VERY... COOL. IT'S HARD TO—
OHHHHHH!
I'VE GOT YOU.
JUST A LITTLE LIGHT-HEADED—

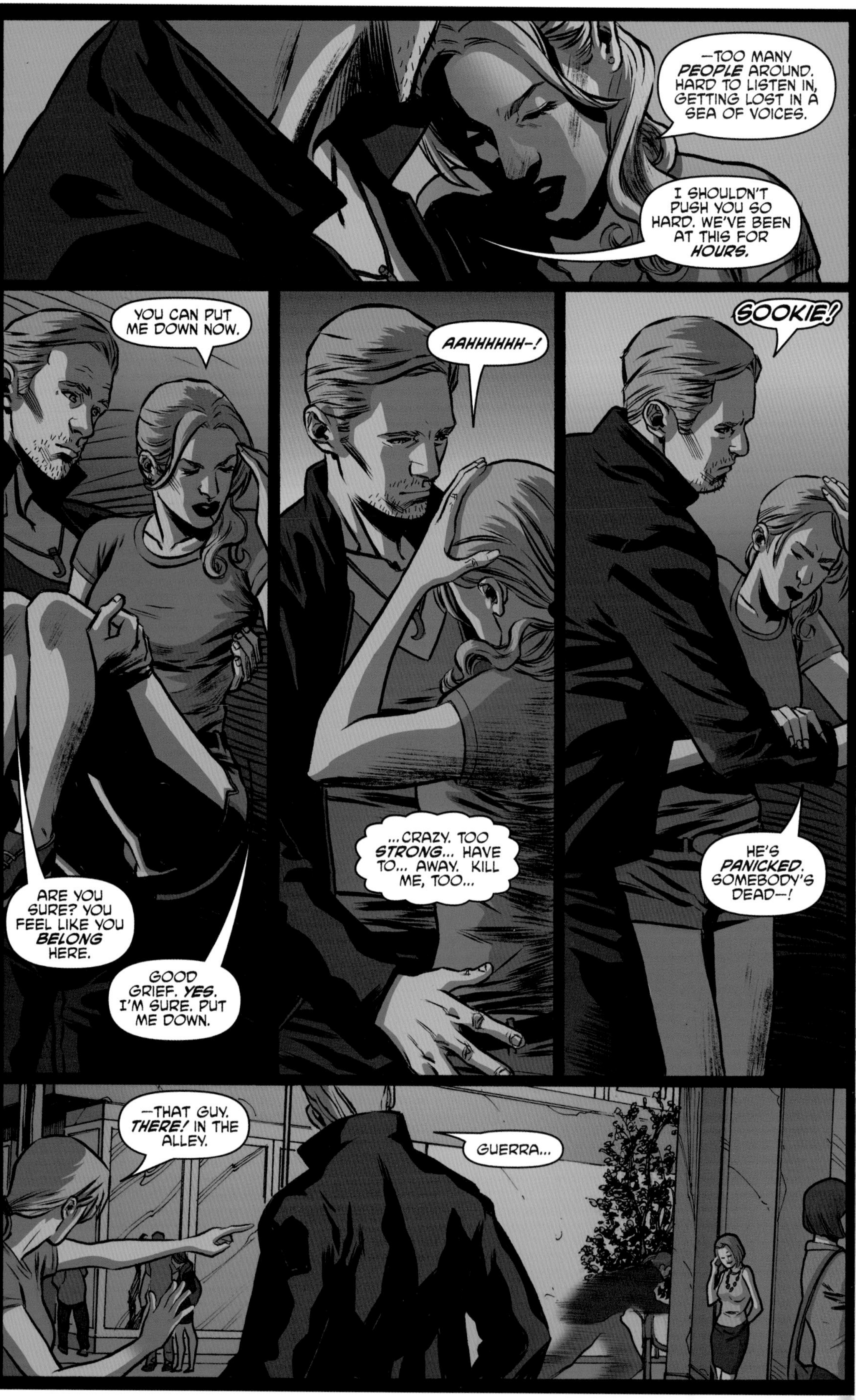
—TOO MANY PEOPLE AROUND. HARD TO LISTEN IN, GETTING LOST IN A SEA OF VOICES.
I SHOULDN'T PUSH YOU SO HARD. WE'VE BEEN AT THIS FOR HOURS.
YOU CAN PUT ME DOWN NOW.
ARE YOU SURE? YOU FEEL LIKE YOU BELONG HERE.
GOOD GRIEF. YES. I'M SURE. PUT ME DOWN.
AAHHHHHH—!
...CRAZY. TOO STRONG... HAVE TO... AWAY. KILL ME, TOO...
SOOKIE!
HE'S PANICKED. SOMEBODY'S DEAD—!
—THAT GUY. THERE! IN THE ALLEY.
GUERRA...

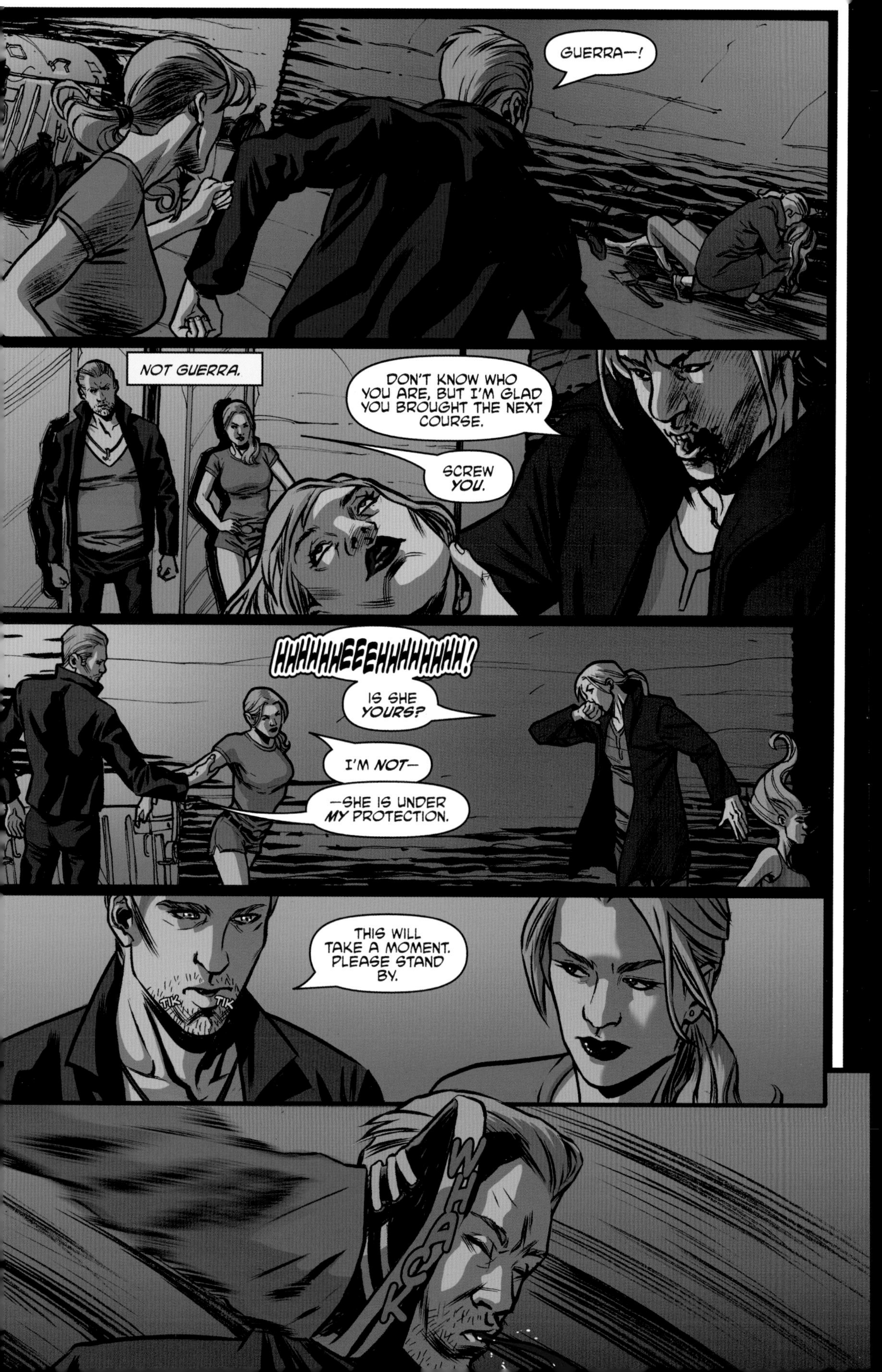
GUERRA—!
NOT GUERRA.
DON'T KNOW WHO YOU ARE, BUT I'M GLAD YOU BROUGHT THE NEXT COURSE.
SCREW *YOU*.
HHHHHHEEEHHHHHHHH!
IS SHE *YOURS?*
I'M *NOT*—
—SHE IS UNDER *MY* PROTECTION.
THIS WILL TAKE A MOMENT. PLEASE STAND BY.
TIK TIK
WHACK

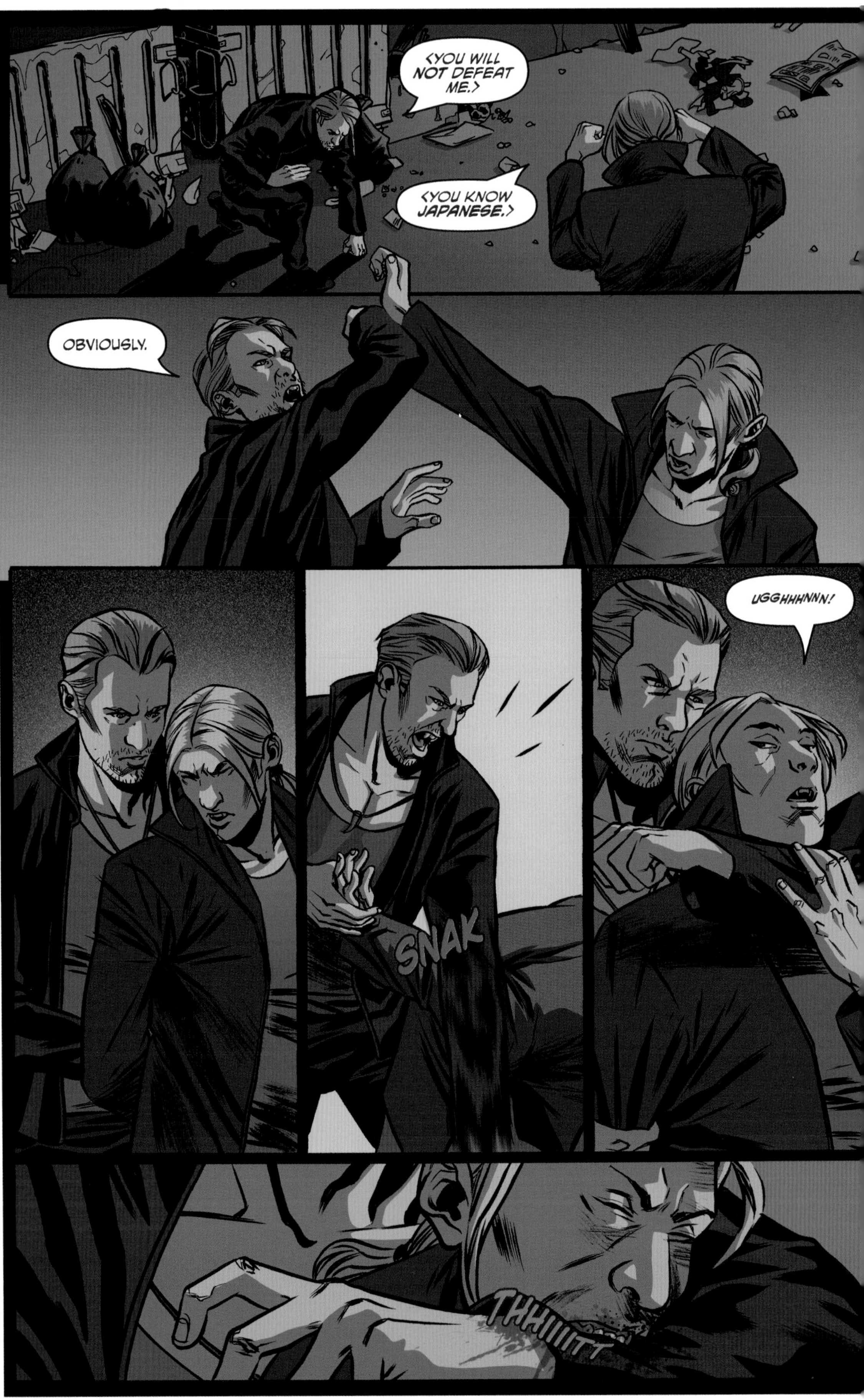

<YOU WILL NOT DEFEAT ME.>
<YOU KNOW JAPANESE.>
OBVIOUSLY.
SNAK
UGGHHHNNN!
THHIIIITT

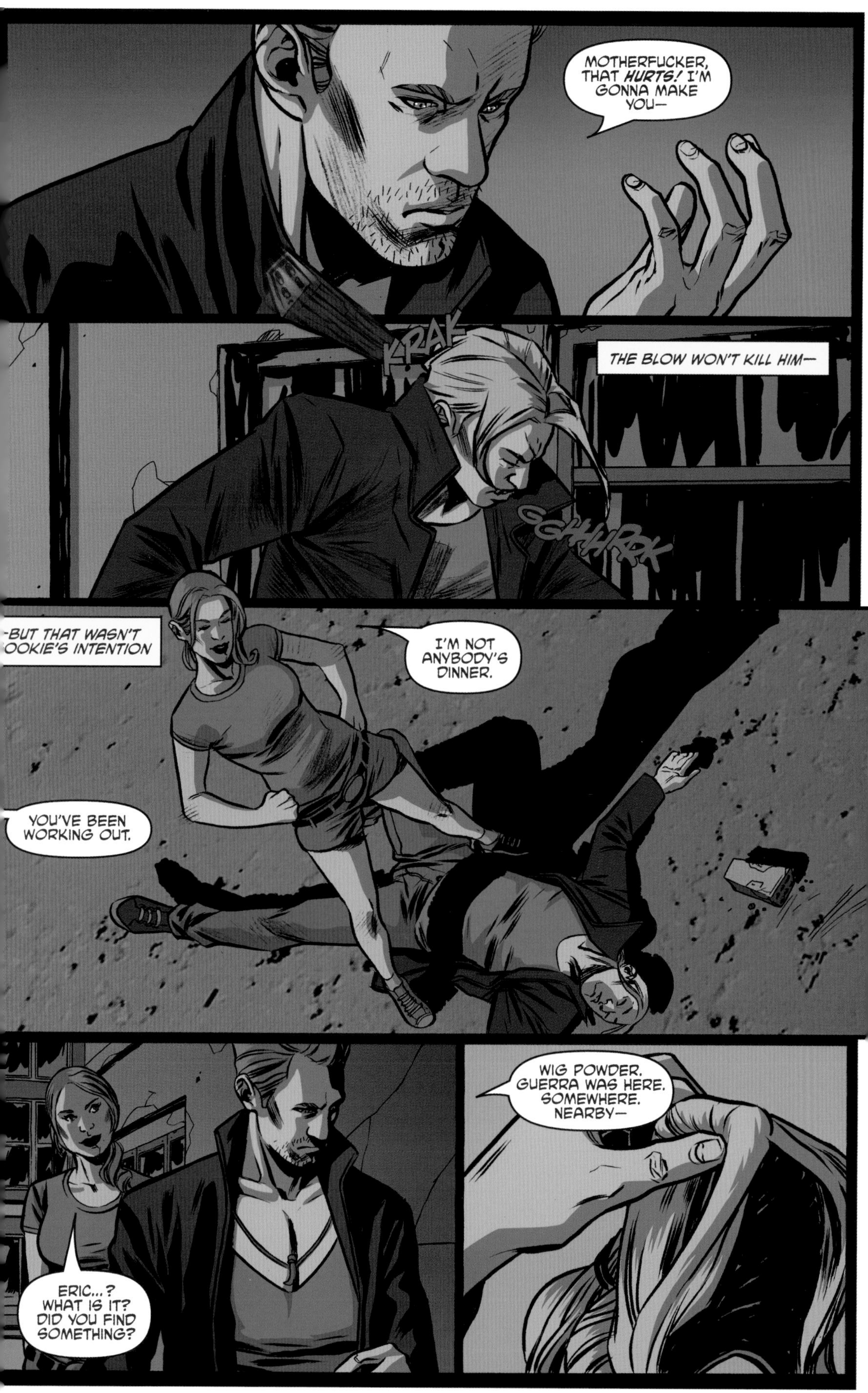
MOTHERFUCKER, THAT *HURTS!* I'M GONNA MAKE YOU—
KRAK
THE BLOW WON'T KILL HIM—
GGHHHRRK
-BUT THAT WASN'T OOKIE'S INTENTION
I'M NOT ANYBODY'S DINNER.
YOU'VE BEEN WORKING OUT.
ERIC...? WHAT IS IT? DID YOU FIND SOMETHING?
WIG POWDER. GUERRA WAS HERE. SOMEWHERE. NEARBY—

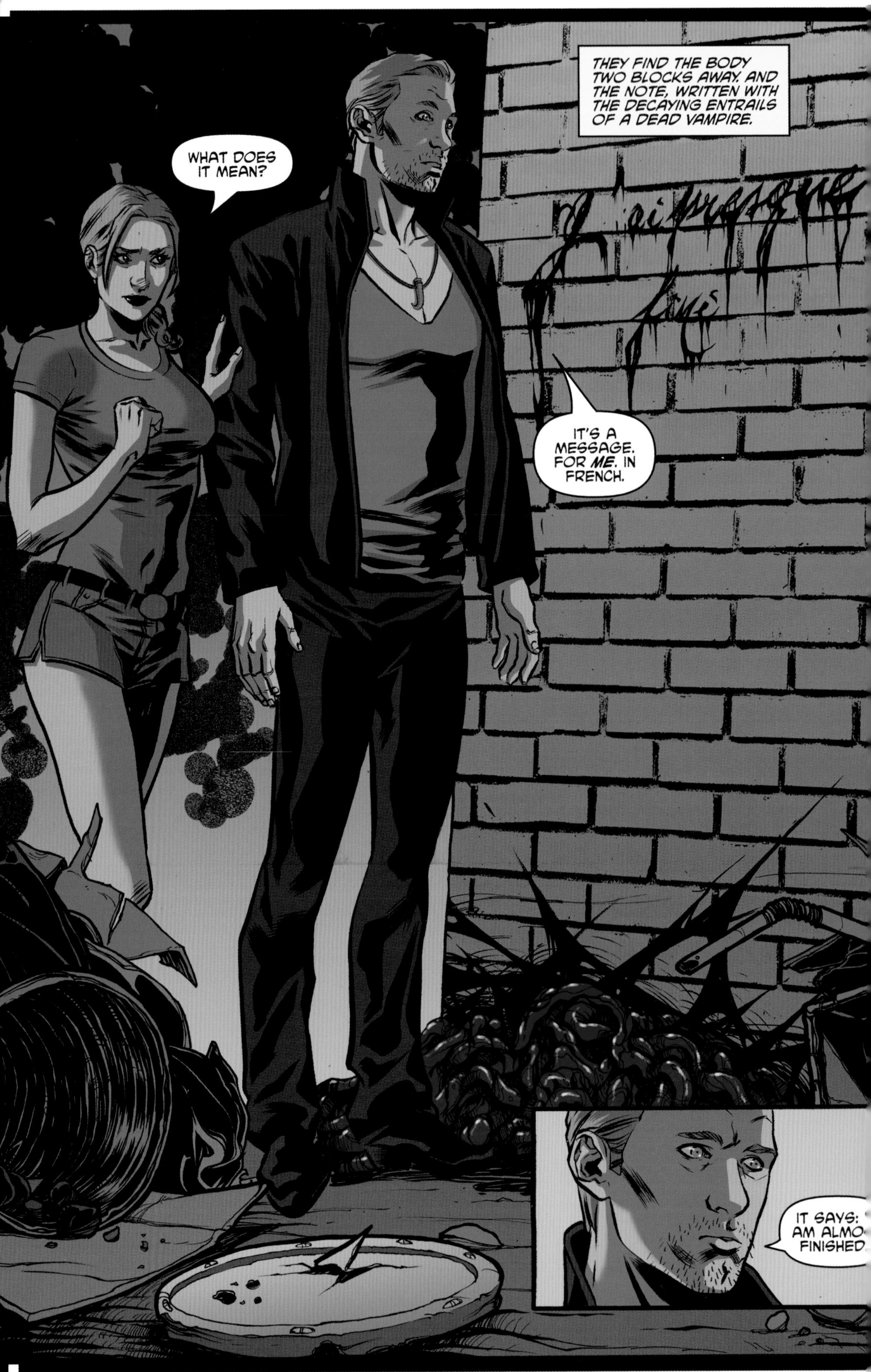
THEY FIND THE BODY TWO BLOCKS AWAY. AND THE NOTE, WRITTEN WITH THE DECAYING ENTRAILS OF A DEAD VAMPIRE.
WHAT DOES IT MEAN?
IT'S A MESSAGE. FOR *ME*. IN FRENCH.
IT SAYS: AM ALMO FINISHED

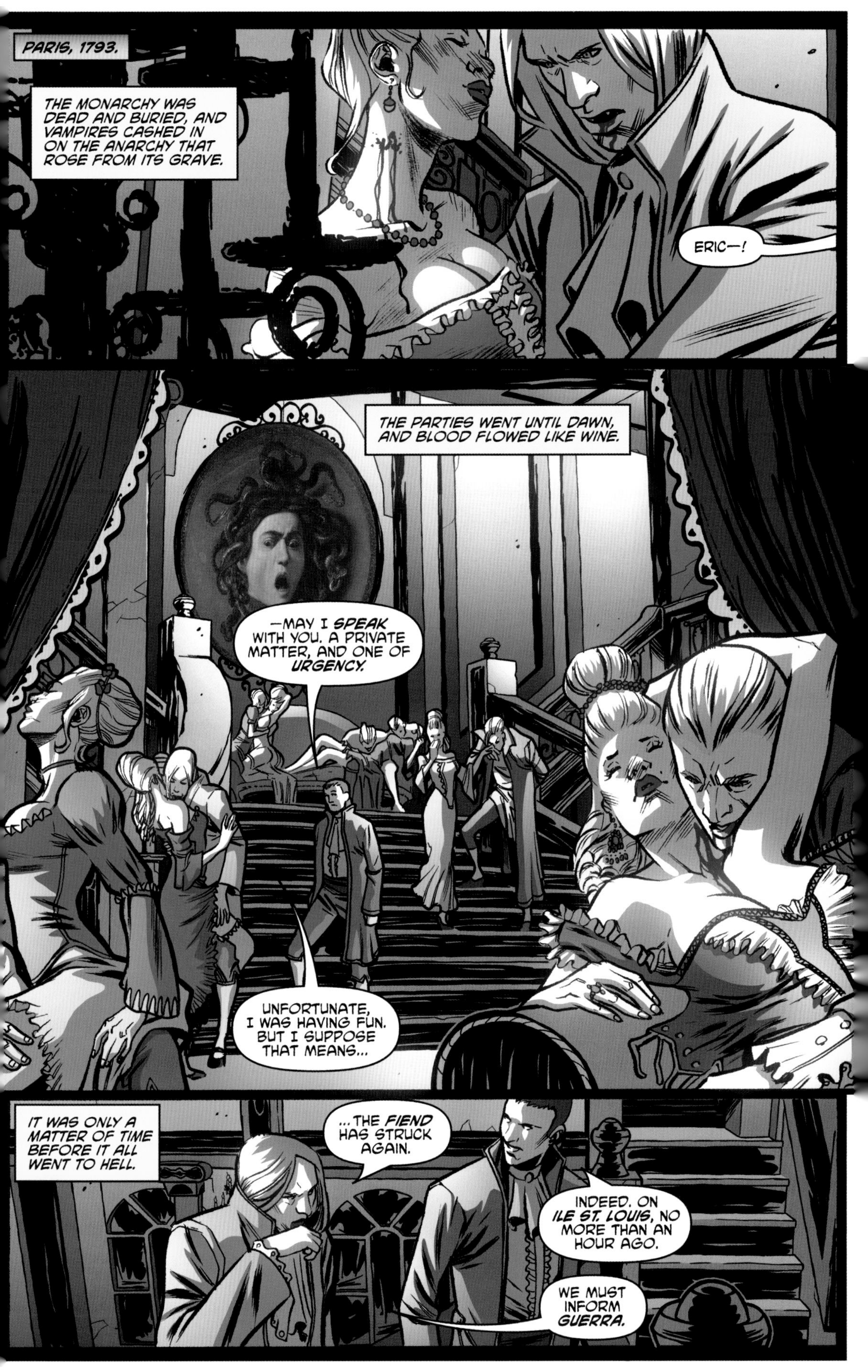
PARIS, 1793.
THE MONARCHY WAS DEAD AND BURIED, AND VAMPIRES CASHED IN ON THE ANARCHY THAT ROSE FROM ITS GRAVE.
ERIC—!
THE PARTIES WENT UNTIL DAWN, AND BLOOD FLOWED LIKE WINE.
—MAY I SPEAK WITH YOU. A PRIVATE MATTER, AND ONE OF URGENCY.
UNFORTUNATE, I WAS HAVING FUN. BUT I SUPPOSE THAT MEANS...
IT WAS ONLY A MATTER OF TIME BEFORE IT ALL WENT TO HELL.
...THE FIEND HAS STRUCK AGAIN.
INDEED. ON ILE ST. LOUIS, NO MORE THAN AN HOUR AGO.
WE MUST INFORM GUERRA.

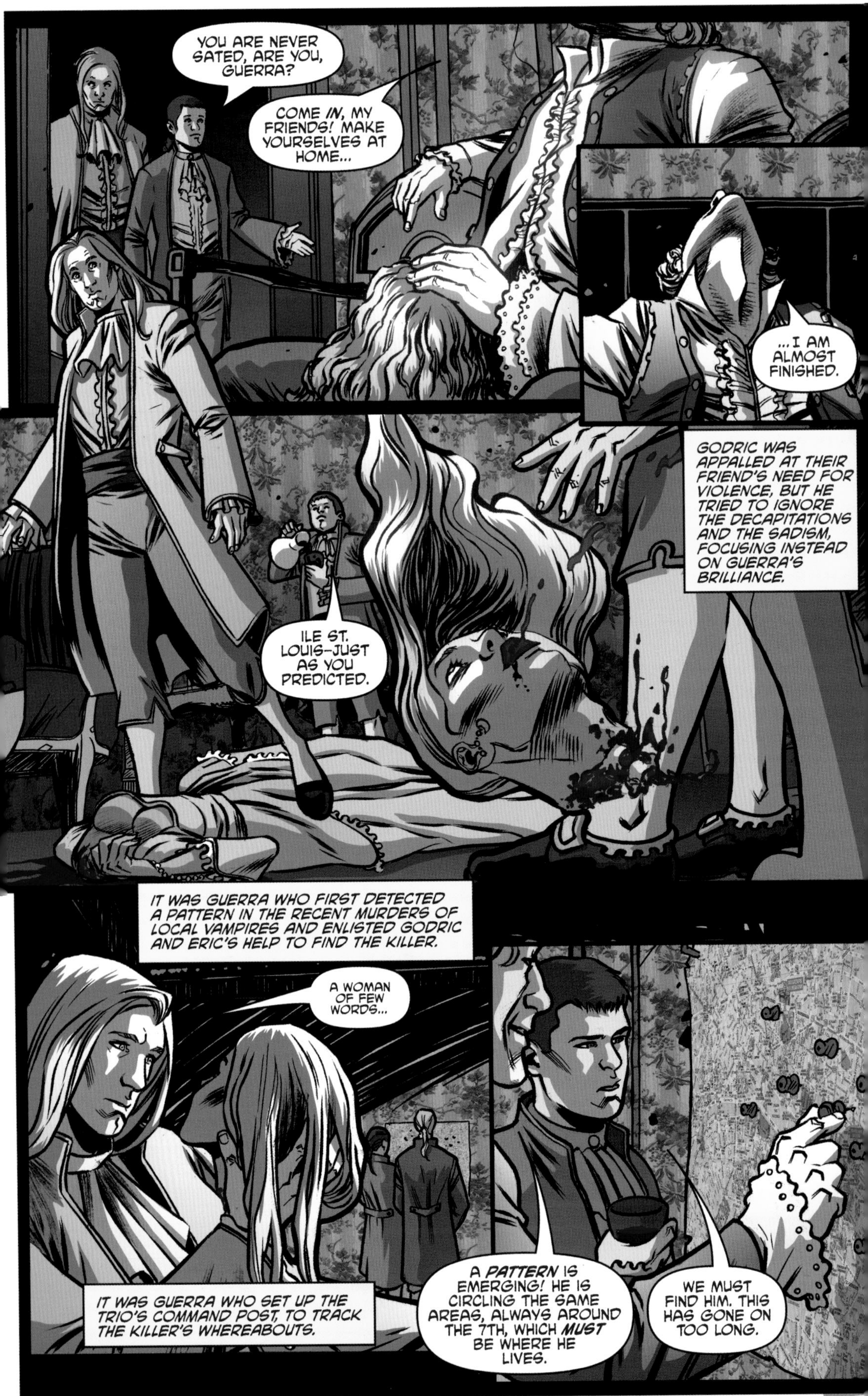
YOU ARE NEVER SATED, ARE YOU, GUERRA?
COME *IN*, MY FRIENDS! MAKE YOURSELVES AT HOME...
...I AM ALMOST FINISHED.
GODRIC WAS APPALLED AT THEIR FRIEND'S NEED FOR VIOLENCE, BUT HE TRIED TO IGNORE THE DECAPITATIONS AND THE SADISM, FOCUSING INSTEAD ON GUERRA'S BRILLIANCE.
ILE ST. LOUIS–JUST AS YOU PREDICTED.
IT WAS GUERRA WHO FIRST DETECTED A PATTERN IN THE RECENT MURDERS OF LOCAL VAMPIRES AND ENLISTED GODRIC AND ERIC'S HELP TO FIND THE KILLER.
A WOMAN OF FEW WORDS...
IT WAS GUERRA WHO SET UP THE TRIO'S COMMAND POST, TO TRACK THE KILLER'S WHEREABOUTS.
A *PATTERN* IS EMERGING! HE IS CIRCLING THE SAME AREAS, ALWAYS AROUND THE 7TH, WHICH *MUST* BE WHERE HE LIVES.
WE MUST FIND HIM. THIS HAS GONE ON TOO LONG.

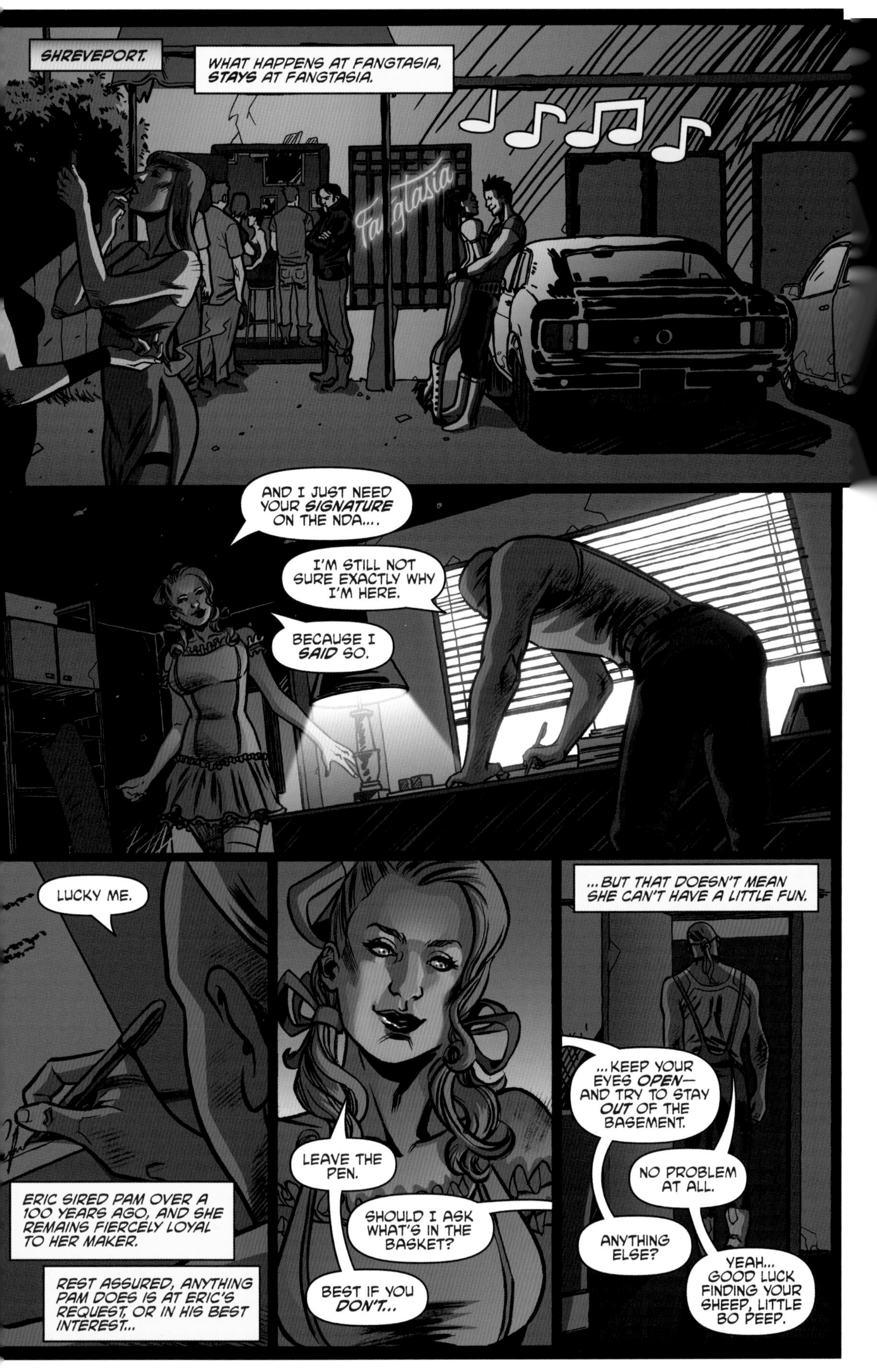
SHREVEPORT.
WHAT HAPPENS AT FANGTASIA, STAYS AT FANGTASIA.
Fangtasia
AND I JUST NEED YOUR SIGNATURE ON THE NDA....
I'M STILL NOT SURE EXACTLY WHY I'M HERE.
BECAUSE I SAID SO.
LUCKY ME.
ERIC SIRED PAM OVER A 100 YEARS AGO, AND SHE REMAINS FIERCELY LOYAL TO HER MAKER.
REST ASSURED, ANYTHING PAM DOES IS AT ERIC'S REQUEST, OR IN HIS BEST INTEREST...
LEAVE THE PEN.
SHOULD I ASK WHAT'S IN THE BASKET?
BEST IF YOU DON'T...
...BUT THAT DOESN'T MEAN SHE CAN'T HAVE A LITTLE FUN.
...KEEP YOUR EYES OPEN— AND TRY TO STAY OUT OF THE BASEMENT.
NO PROBLEM AT ALL.
ANYTHING ELSE?
YEAH... GOOD LUCK FINDING YOUR SHEEP, LITTLE BO PEEP.

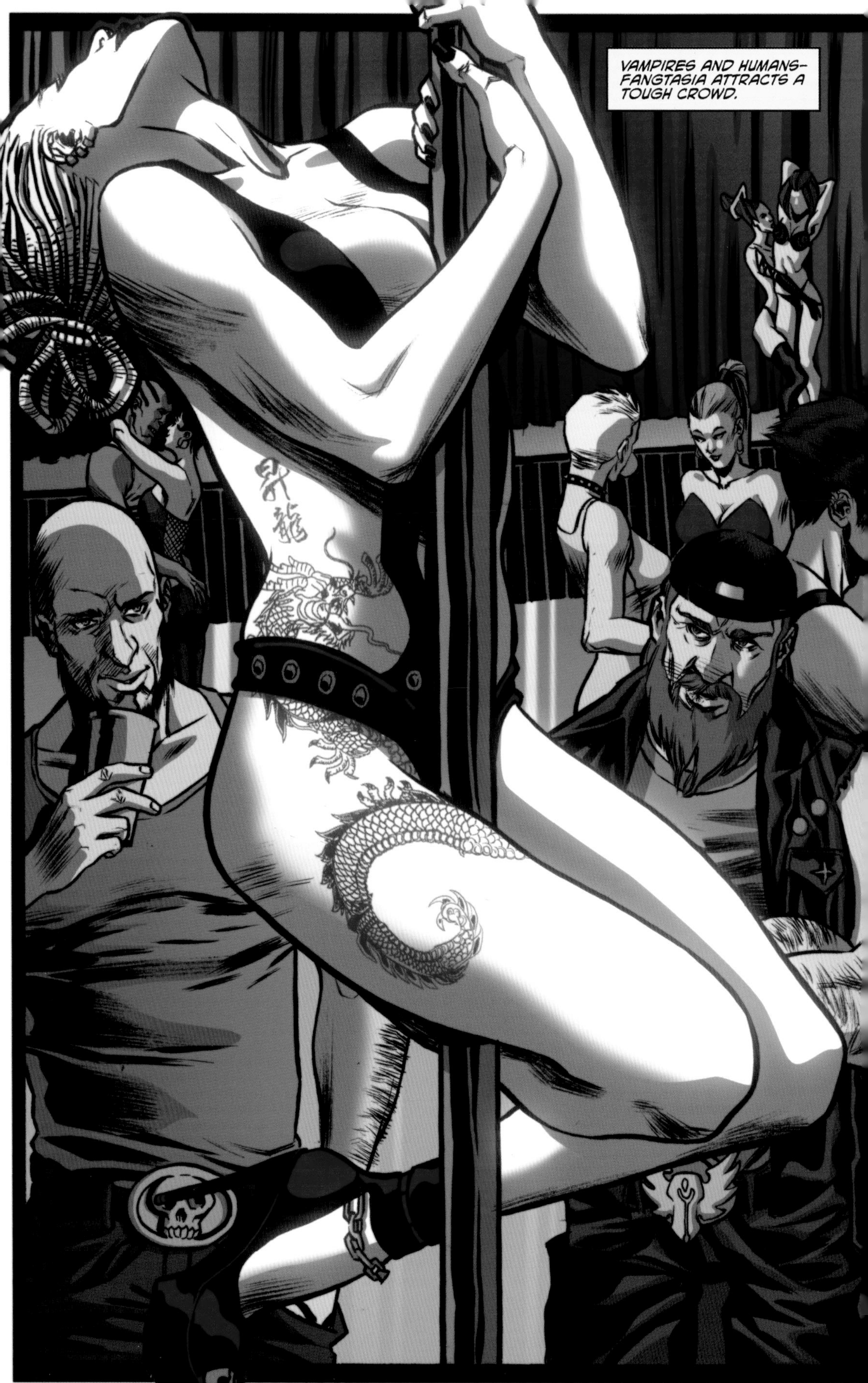
VAMPIRES AND HUMANS–FANGTASIA ATTRACTS A TOUGH CROWD.

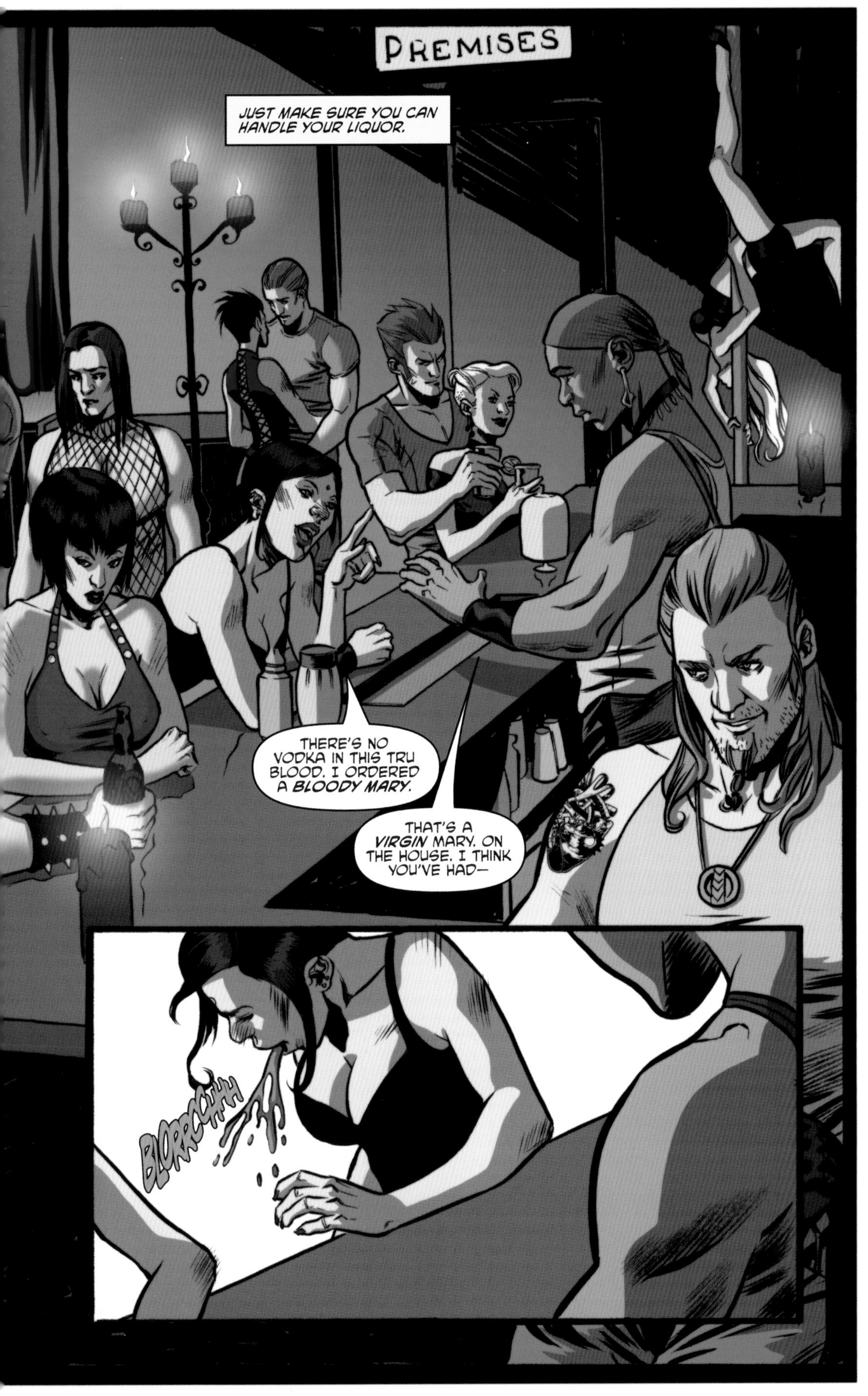
PREMISES
JUST MAKE SURE YOU CAN HANDLE YOUR LIQUOR.
THERE'S NO VODKA IN THIS TRU BLOOD. I ORDERED A *BLOODY MARY*.
THAT'S A *VIRGIN* MARY. ON THE HOUSE. I THINK YOU'VE HAD—
BLORRCHHH

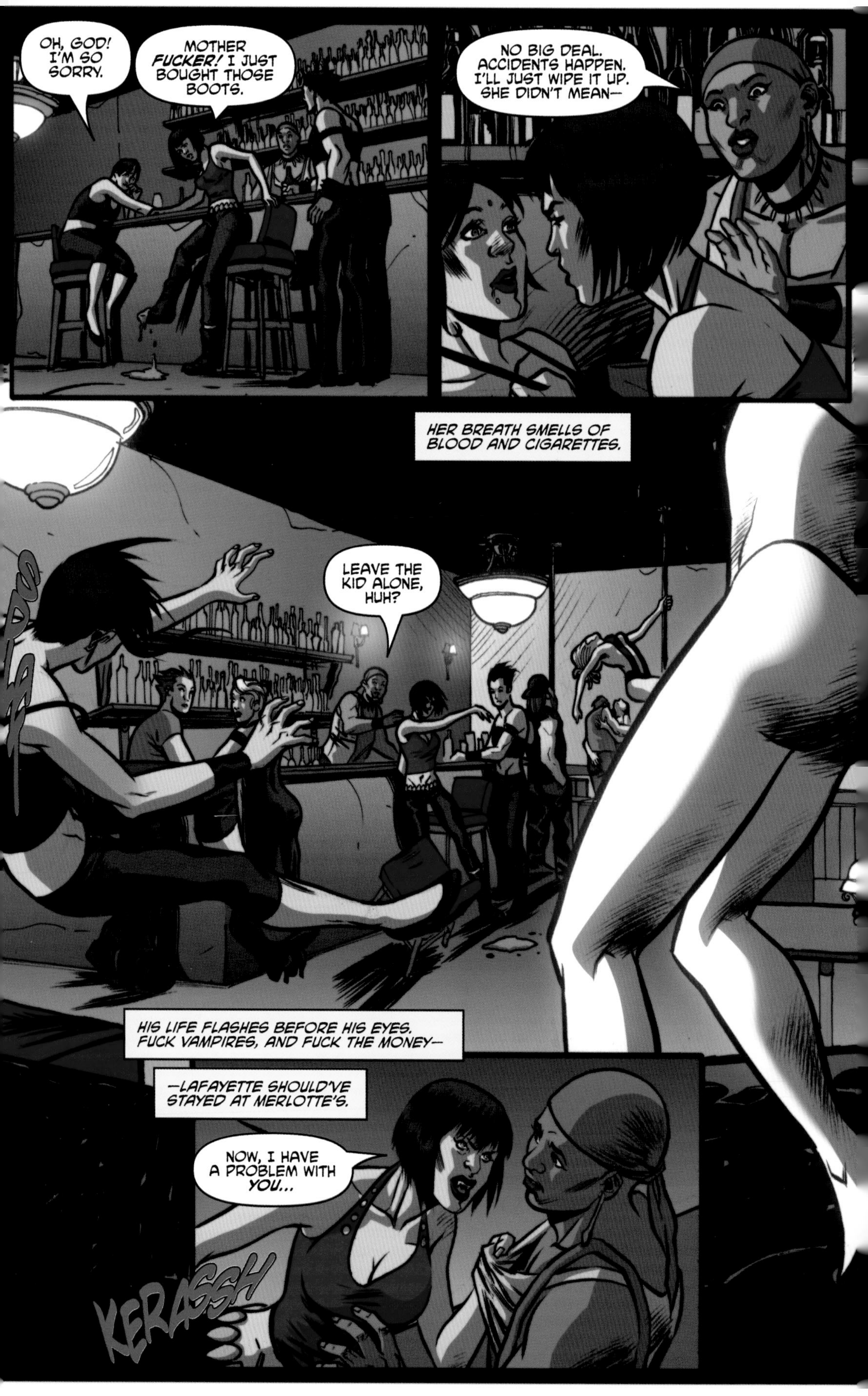
OH, GOD! I'M SO SORRY.
MOTHER FUCKER! I JUST BOUGHT THOSE BOOTS.
NO BIG DEAL. ACCIDENTS HAPPEN. I'LL JUST WIPE IT UP. SHE DIDN'T MEAN—
HER BREATH SMELLS OF BLOOD AND CIGARETTES.
LEAVE THE KID ALONE, HUH?
HIS LIFE FLASHES BEFORE HIS EYES. FUCK VAMPIRES, AND FUCK THE MONEY—
—LAFAYETTE SHOULD'VE STAYED AT MERLOTTE'S.
NOW, I HAVE A PROBLEM WITH YOU...
KERASSH

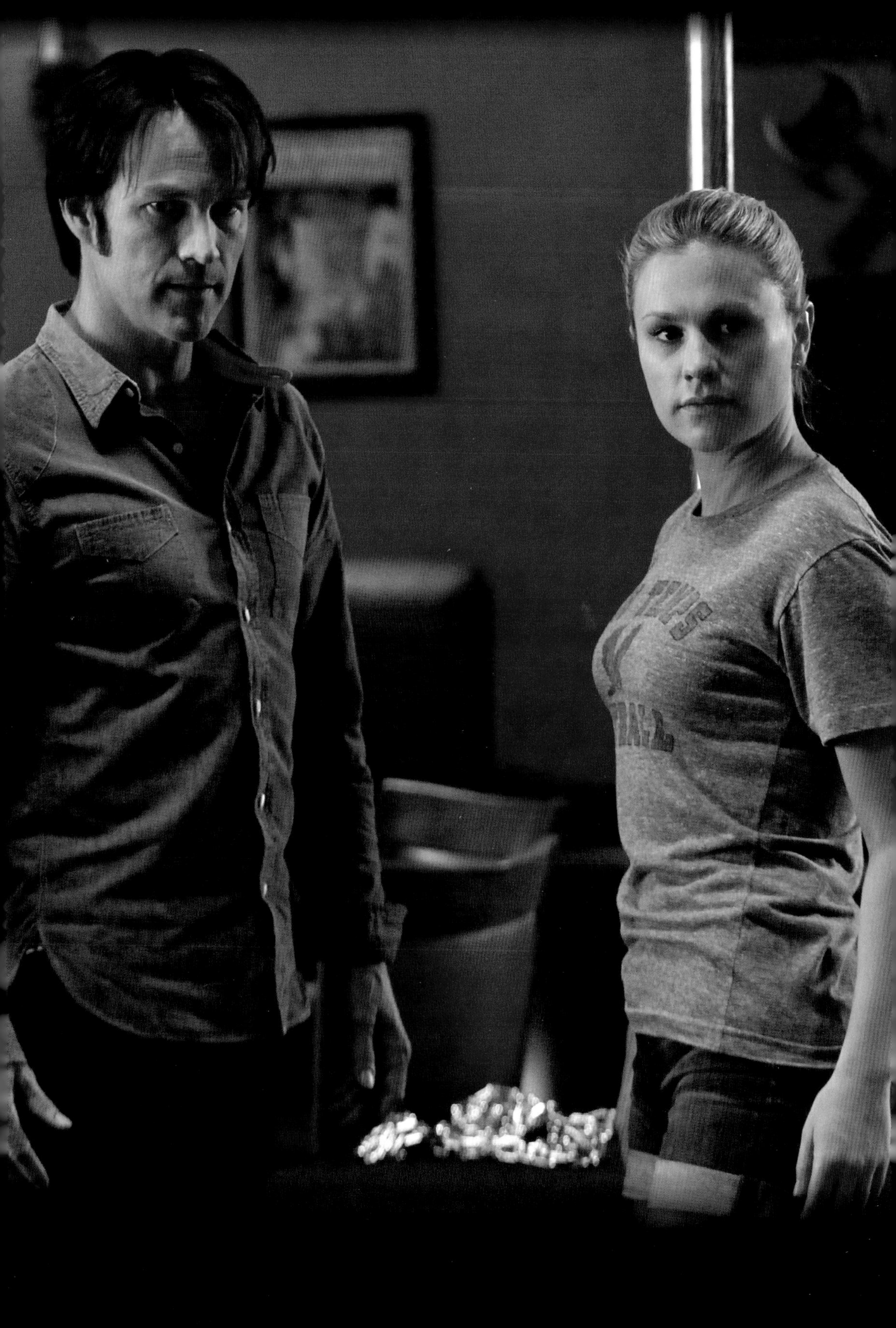

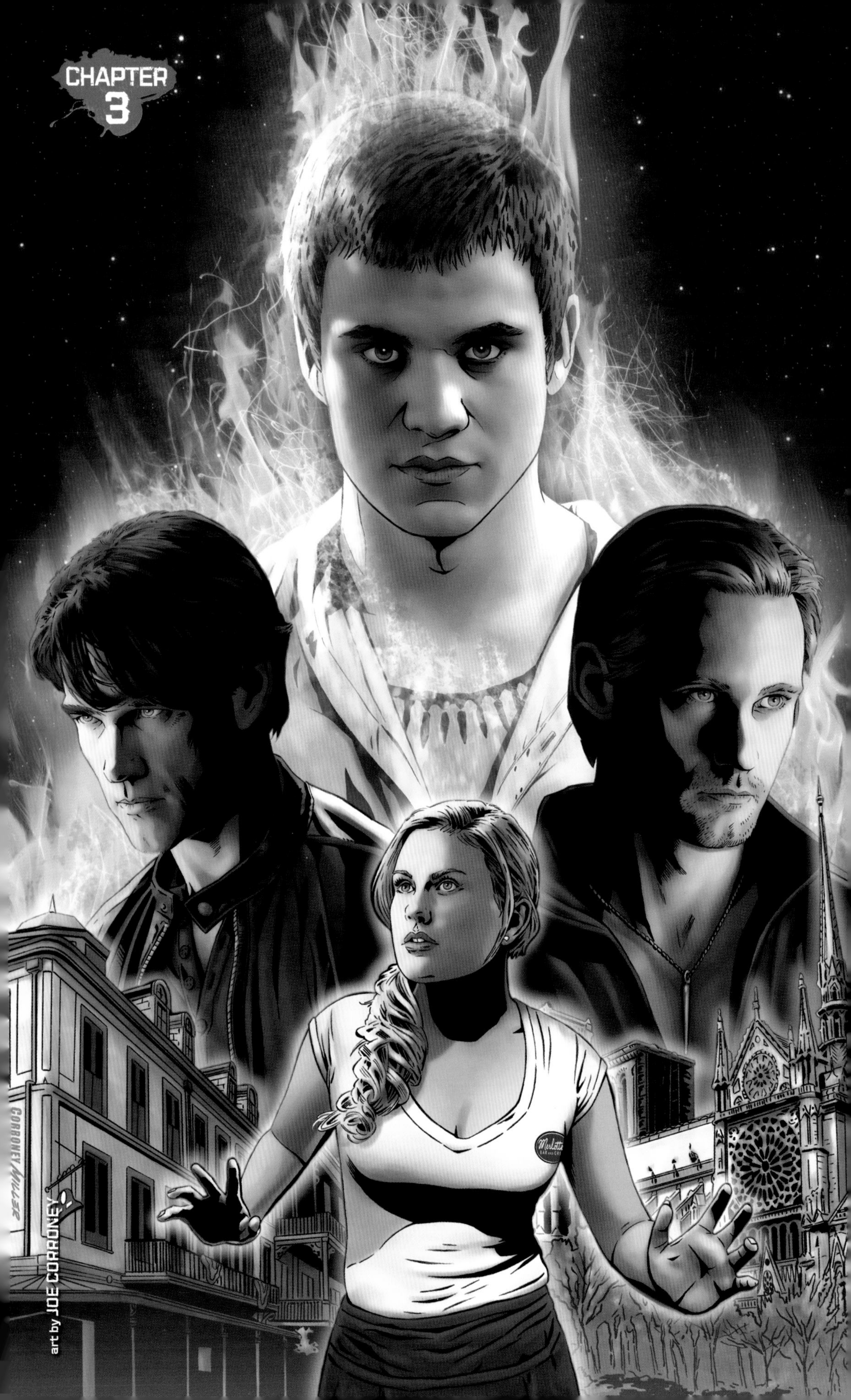
CHAPTER
3
art by JOE CORRONEY

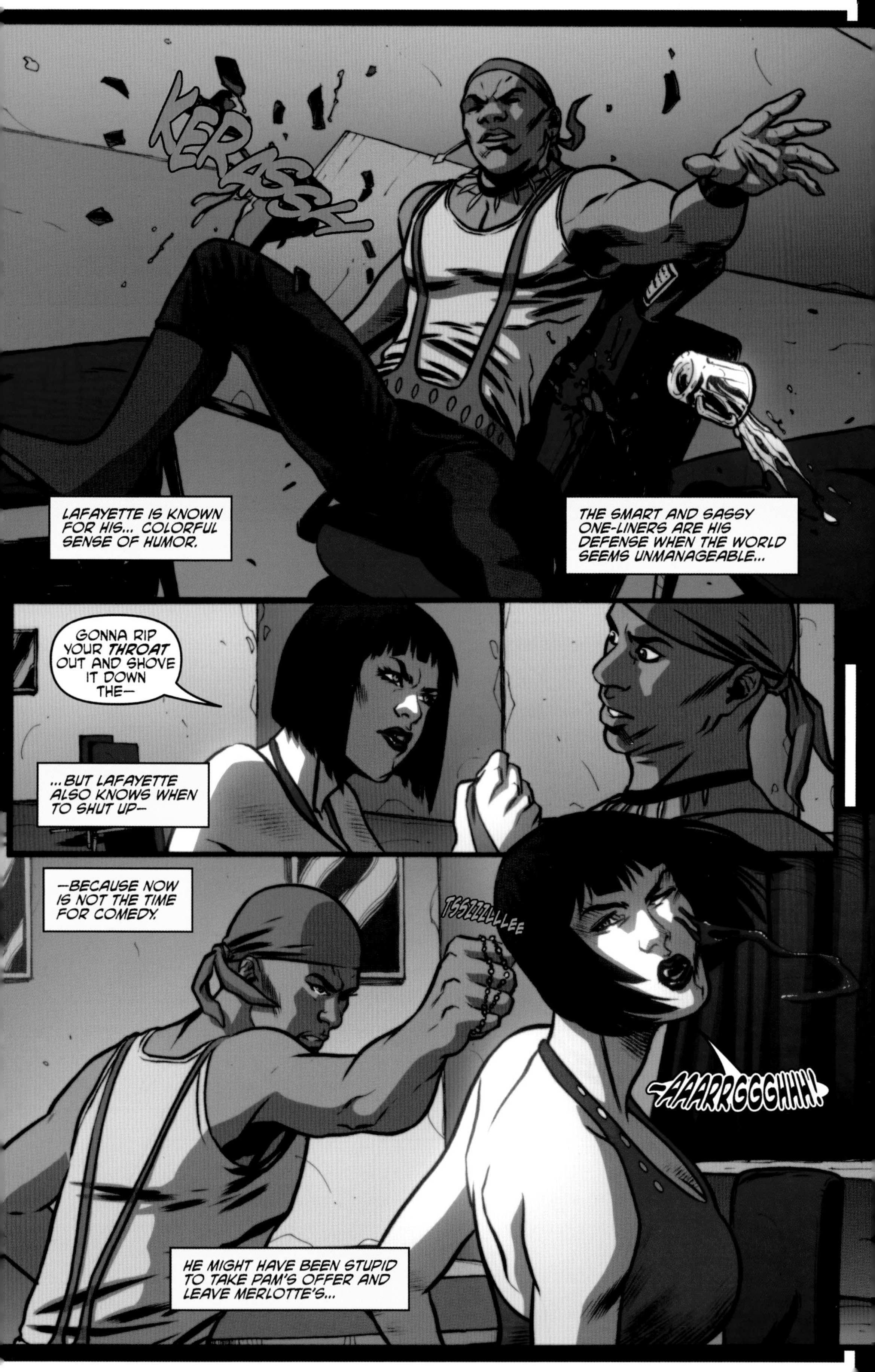
KERASSH
LAFAYETTE IS KNOWN FOR HIS... COLORFUL SENSE OF HUMOR.
THE SMART AND SASSY ONE-LINERS ARE HIS DEFENSE WHEN THE WORLD SEEMS UNMANAGEABLE...
GONNA RIP YOUR THROAT OUT AND SHOVE IT DOWN THE--
...BUT LAFAYETTE ALSO KNOWS WHEN TO SHUT UP--
--BECAUSE NOW IS NOT THE TIME FOR COMEDY.
TSSZZZZLLLEE
--AAARRGGGHHH!
HE MIGHT HAVE BEEN STUPID TO TAKE PAM'S OFFER AND LEAVE MERLOTTE'S...

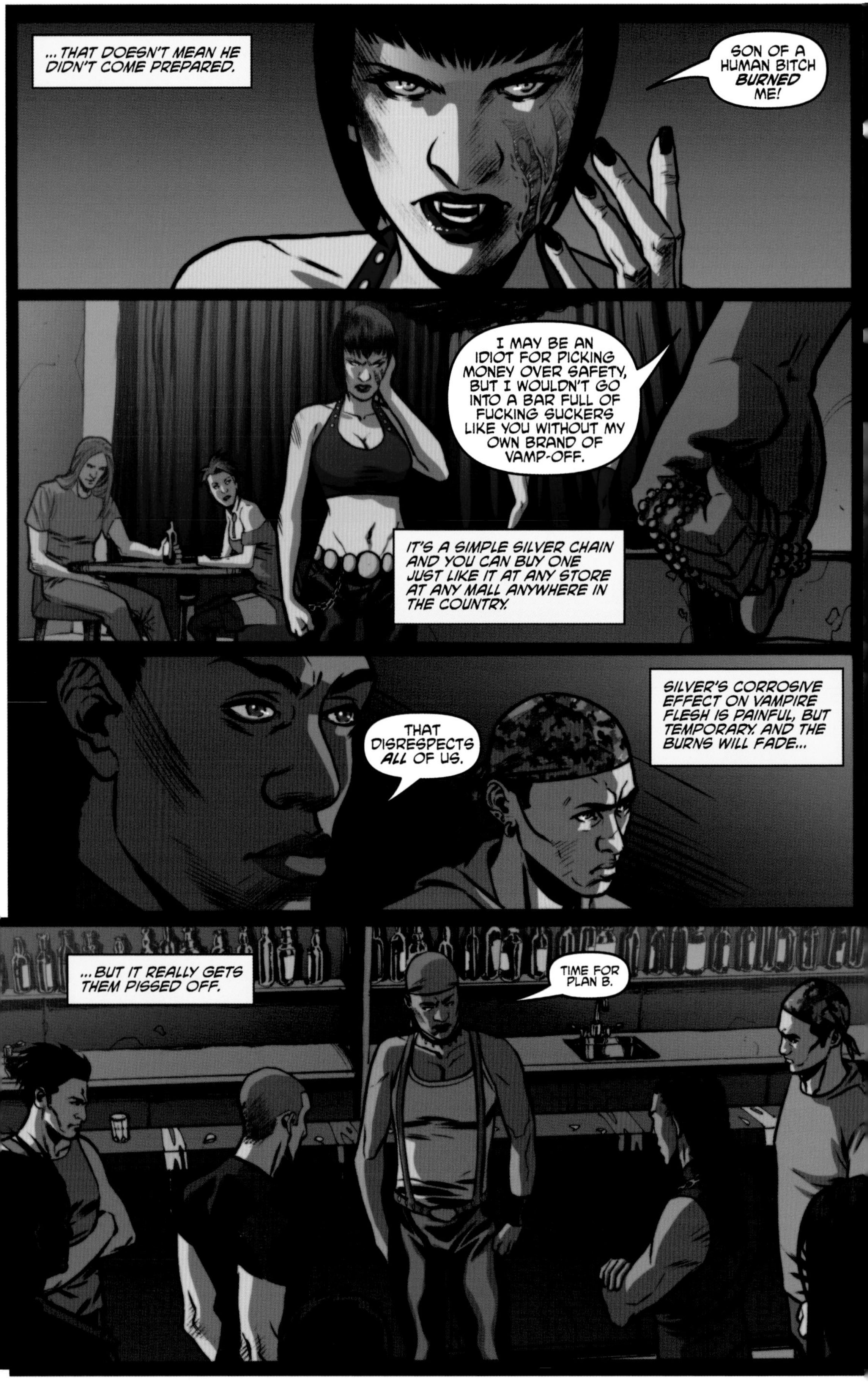
...THAT DOESN'T MEAN HE DIDN'T COME PREPARED.
SON OF A HUMAN BITCH BURNED ME!
I MAY BE AN IDIOT FOR PICKING MONEY OVER SAFETY, BUT I WOULDN'T GO INTO A BAR FULL OF FUCKING SUCKERS LIKE YOU WITHOUT MY OWN BRAND OF VAMP-OFF.
IT'S A SIMPLE SILVER CHAIN AND YOU CAN BUY ONE JUST LIKE IT AT ANY STORE AT ANY MALL ANYWHERE IN THE COUNTRY.
THAT DISRESPECTS ALL OF US.
SILVER'S CORROSIVE EFFECT ON VAMPIRE FLESH IS PAINFUL, BUT TEMPORARY. AND THE BURNS WILL FADE...
...BUT IT REALLY GETS THEM PISSED OFF.
TIME FOR PLAN B.

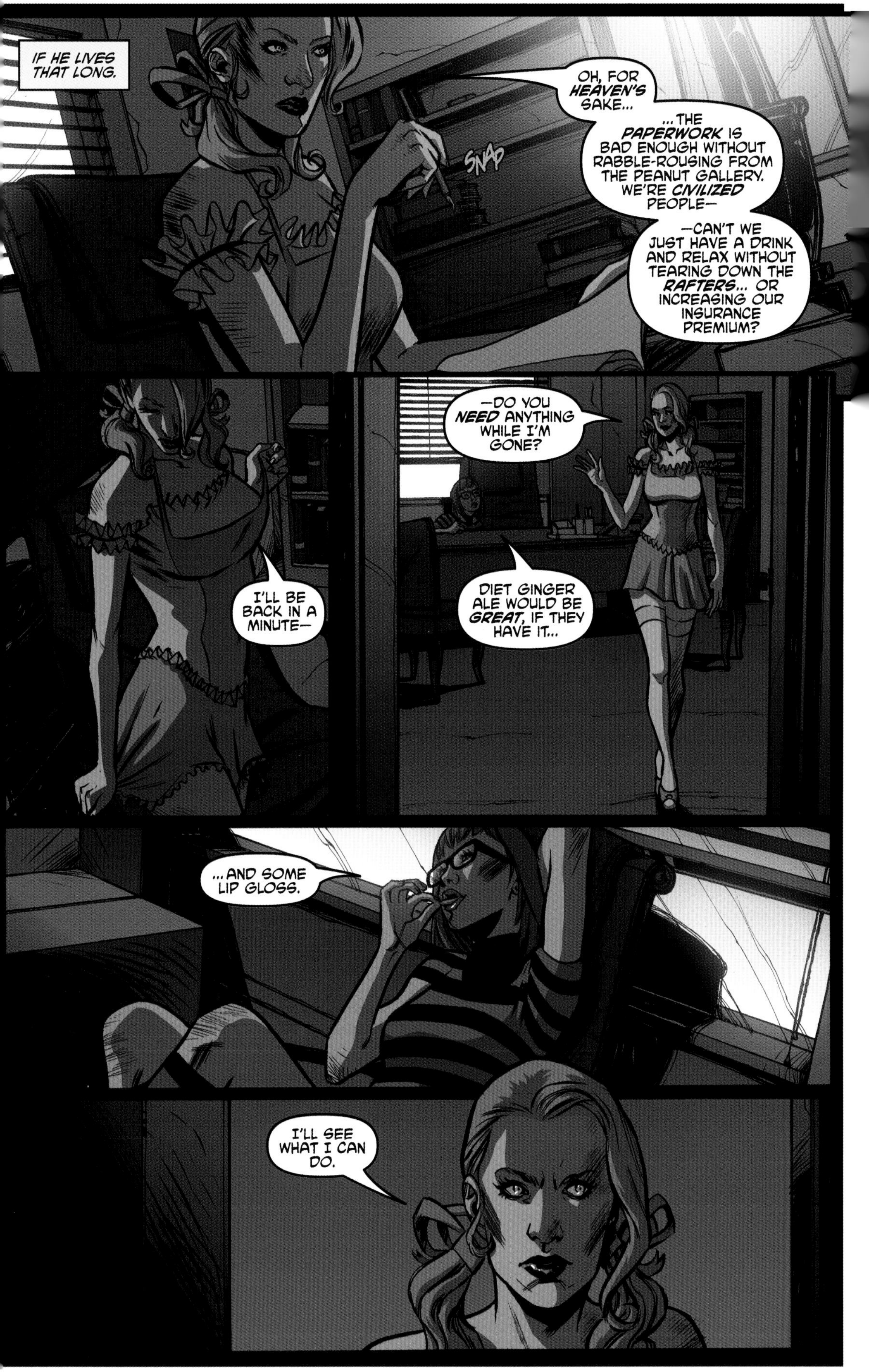
IF HE LIVES THAT LONG.
OH, FOR HEAVEN'S SAKE...
...THE PAPERWORK IS BAD ENOUGH WITHOUT RABBLE-ROUSING FROM THE PEANUT GALLERY. WE'RE CIVILIZED PEOPLE—
—CAN'T WE JUST HAVE A DRINK AND RELAX WITHOUT TEARING DOWN THE RAFTERS... OR INCREASING OUR INSURANCE PREMIUM?
SNAP
I'LL BE BACK IN A MINUTE—
—DO YOU NEED ANYTHING WHILE I'M GONE?
DIET GINGER ALE WOULD BE GREAT, IF THEY HAVE IT...
...AND SOME LIP GLOSS.
I'LL SEE WHAT I CAN DO.

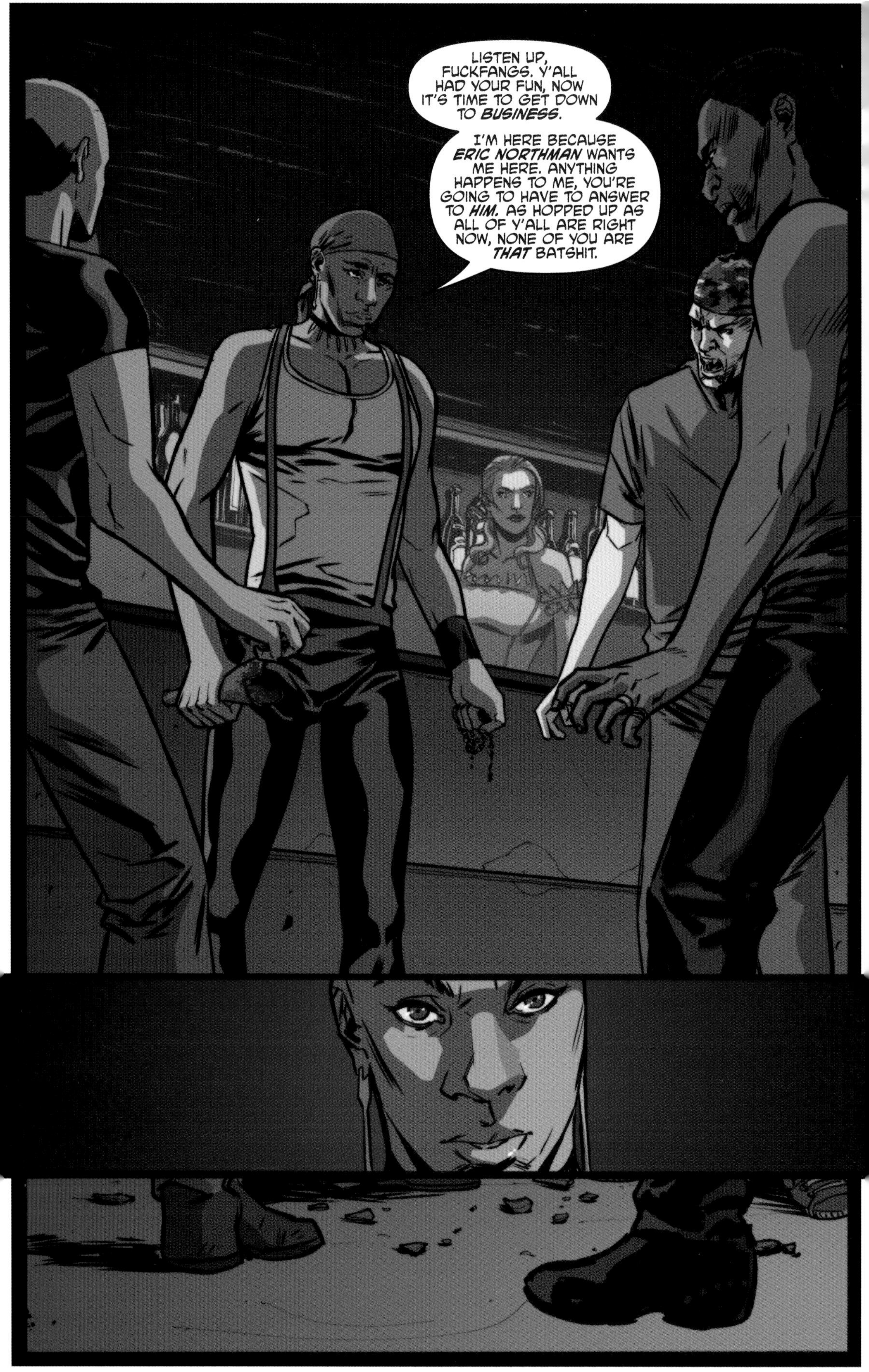
LISTEN UP, FUCKFANGS. Y'ALL HAD YOUR FUN, NOW IT'S TIME TO GET DOWN TO *BUSINESS*.
I'M HERE BECAUSE *ERIC NORTHMAN* WANTS ME HERE. ANYTHING HAPPENS TO ME, YOU'RE GOING TO HAVE TO ANSWER TO *HIM.* AS HOPPED UP AS ALL OF Y'ALL ARE RIGHT NOW, NONE OF YOU ARE *THAT* BATSHIT.

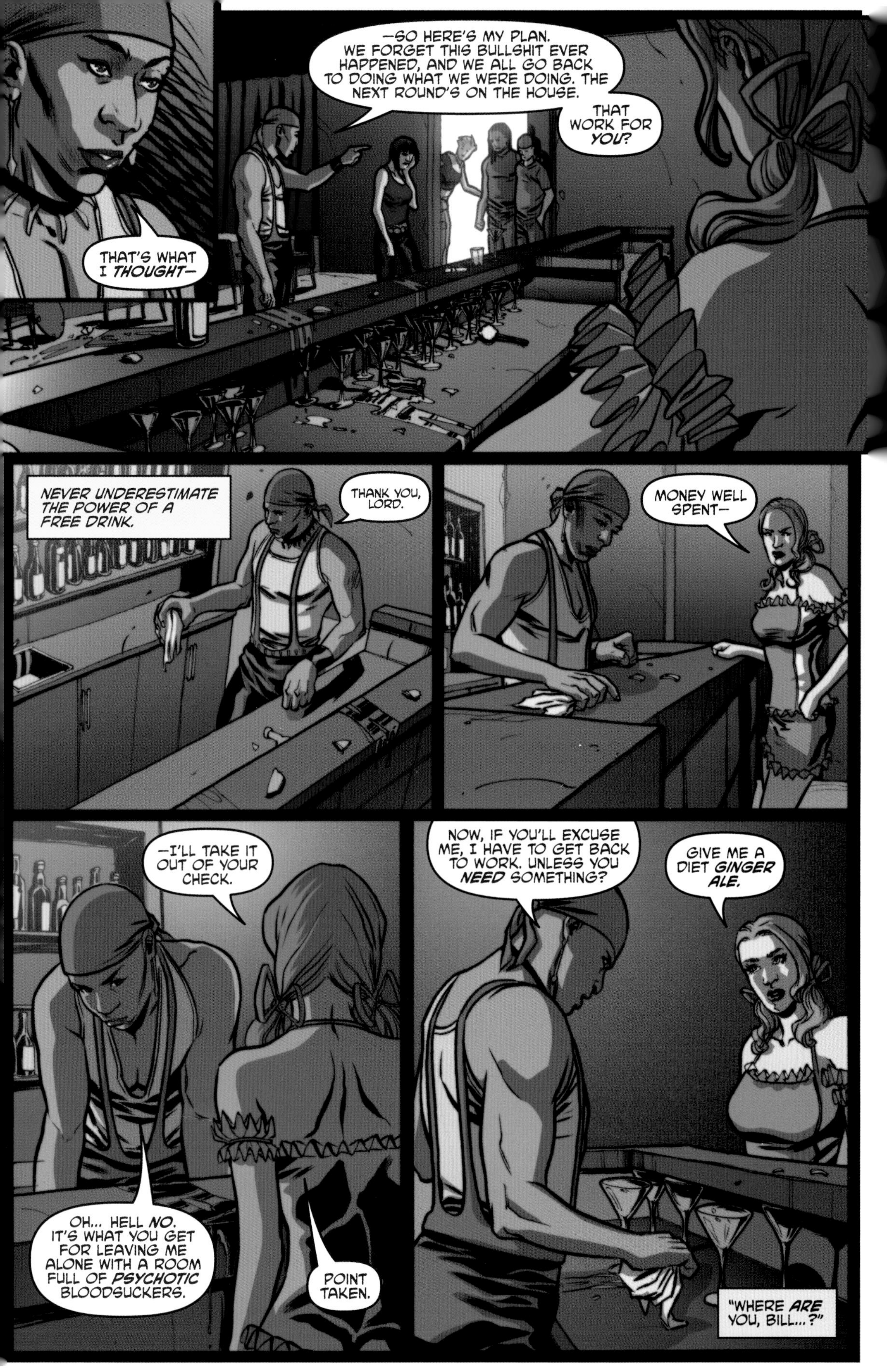

—SO HERE'S MY PLAN. WE FORGET THIS BULLSHIT EVER HAPPENED, AND WE ALL GO BACK TO DOING WHAT WE WERE DOING. THE NEXT ROUND'S ON THE HOUSE.
THAT WORK FOR YOU?
THAT'S WHAT I THOUGHT—
NEVER UNDERESTIMATE THE POWER OF A FREE DRINK.
THANK YOU, LORD.
MONEY WELL SPENT—
—I'LL TAKE IT OUT OF YOUR CHECK.
OH... HELL NO. IT'S WHAT YOU GET FOR LEAVING ME ALONE WITH A ROOM FULL OF PSYCHOTIC BLOODSUCKERS.
POINT TAKEN.
NOW, IF YOU'LL EXCUSE ME, I HAVE TO GET BACK TO WORK. UNLESS YOU NEED SOMETHING?
GIVE ME A DIET GINGER ALE.
"WHERE ARE YOU, BILL...?"

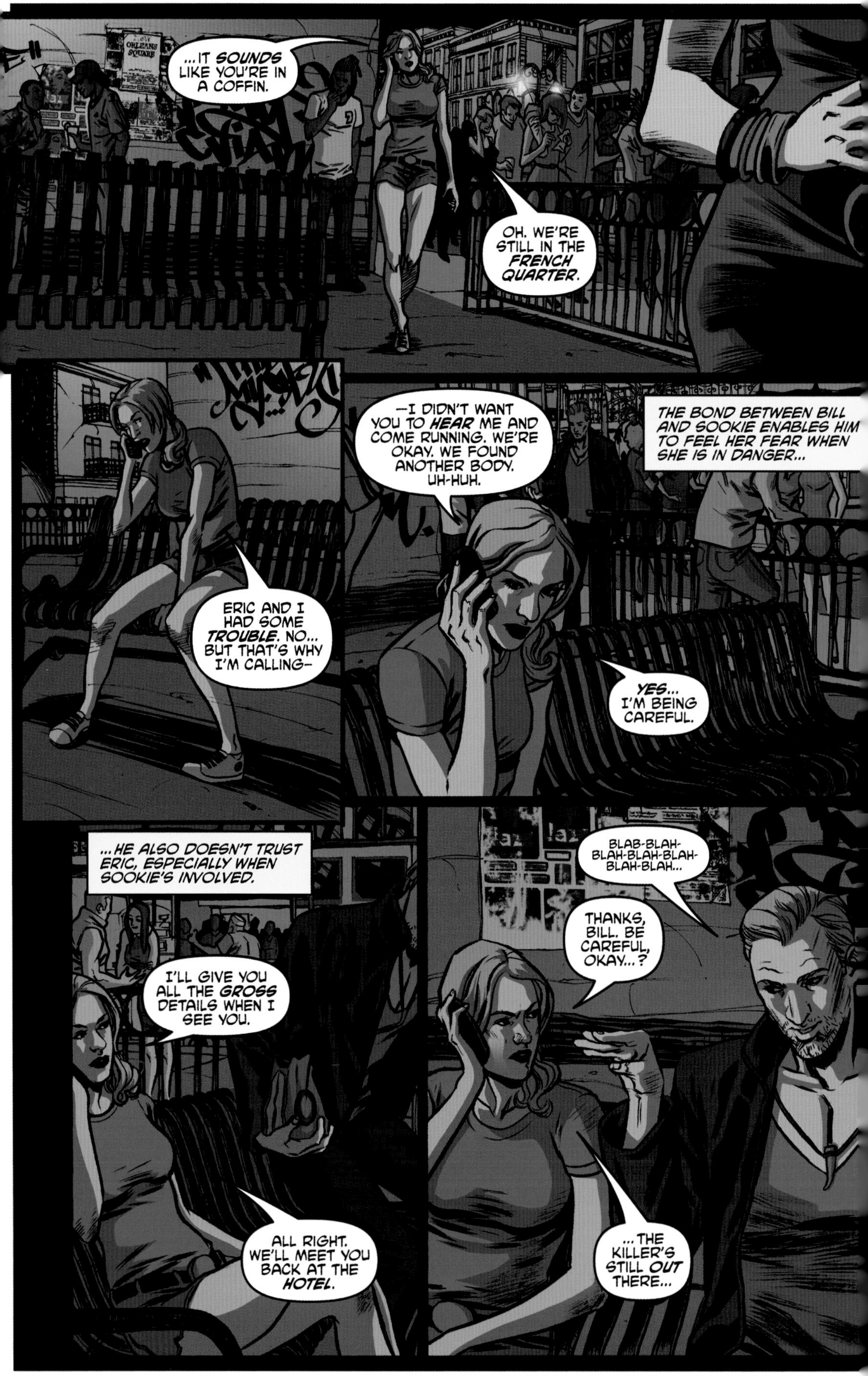
...IT SOUNDS LIKE YOU'RE IN A COFFIN.
OH. WE'RE STILL IN THE FRENCH QUARTER.
ERIC AND I HAD SOME TROUBLE. NO... BUT THAT'S WHY I'M CALLING–
–I DIDN'T WANT YOU TO HEAR ME AND COME RUNNING. WE'RE OKAY. WE FOUND ANOTHER BODY. UH-HUH.
YES... I'M BEING CAREFUL.
THE BOND BETWEEN BILL AND SOOKIE ENABLES HIM TO FEEL HER FEAR WHEN SHE IS IN DANGER...
...HE ALSO DOESN'T TRUST ERIC, ESPECIALLY WHEN SOOKIE'S INVOLVED.
I'LL GIVE YOU ALL THE GROSS DETAILS WHEN I SEE YOU.
ALL RIGHT. WE'LL MEET YOU BACK AT THE HOTEL.
BLAB-BLAH-BLAH-BLAH-BLAH-BLAH-BLAH-BLAH...
THANKS, BILL. BE CAREFUL, OKAY...?
...THE KILLER'S STILL OUT THERE...
NEW ORLEANS SQUARE

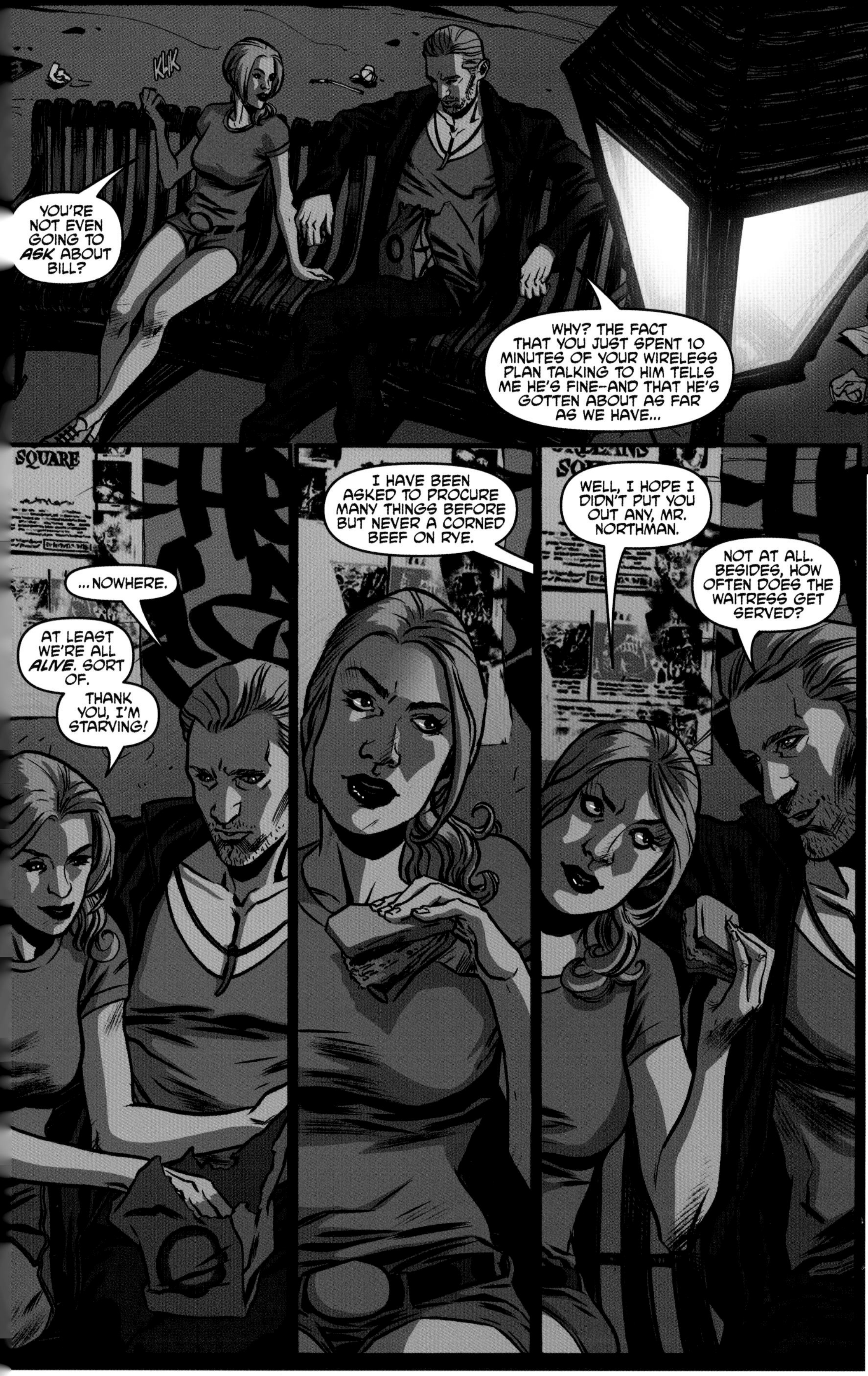
KLIK
YOU'RE NOT EVEN GOING TO *ASK* ABOUT BILL?
WHY? THE FACT THAT YOU JUST SPENT 10 MINUTES OF YOUR WIRELESS PLAN TALKING TO HIM TELLS ME HE'S FINE--AND THAT HE'S GOTTEN ABOUT AS FAR AS WE HAVE...
...NOWHERE.
AT LEAST WE'RE ALL *ALIVE*. SORT OF.
THANK YOU, I'M STARVING!
I HAVE BEEN ASKED TO PROCURE MANY THINGS BEFORE BUT NEVER A CORNED BEEF ON RYE.
WELL, I HOPE I DIDN'T PUT YOU OUT ANY, MR. NORTHMAN.
NOT AT ALL. BESIDES, HOW OFTEN DOES THE WAITRESS GET SERVED?

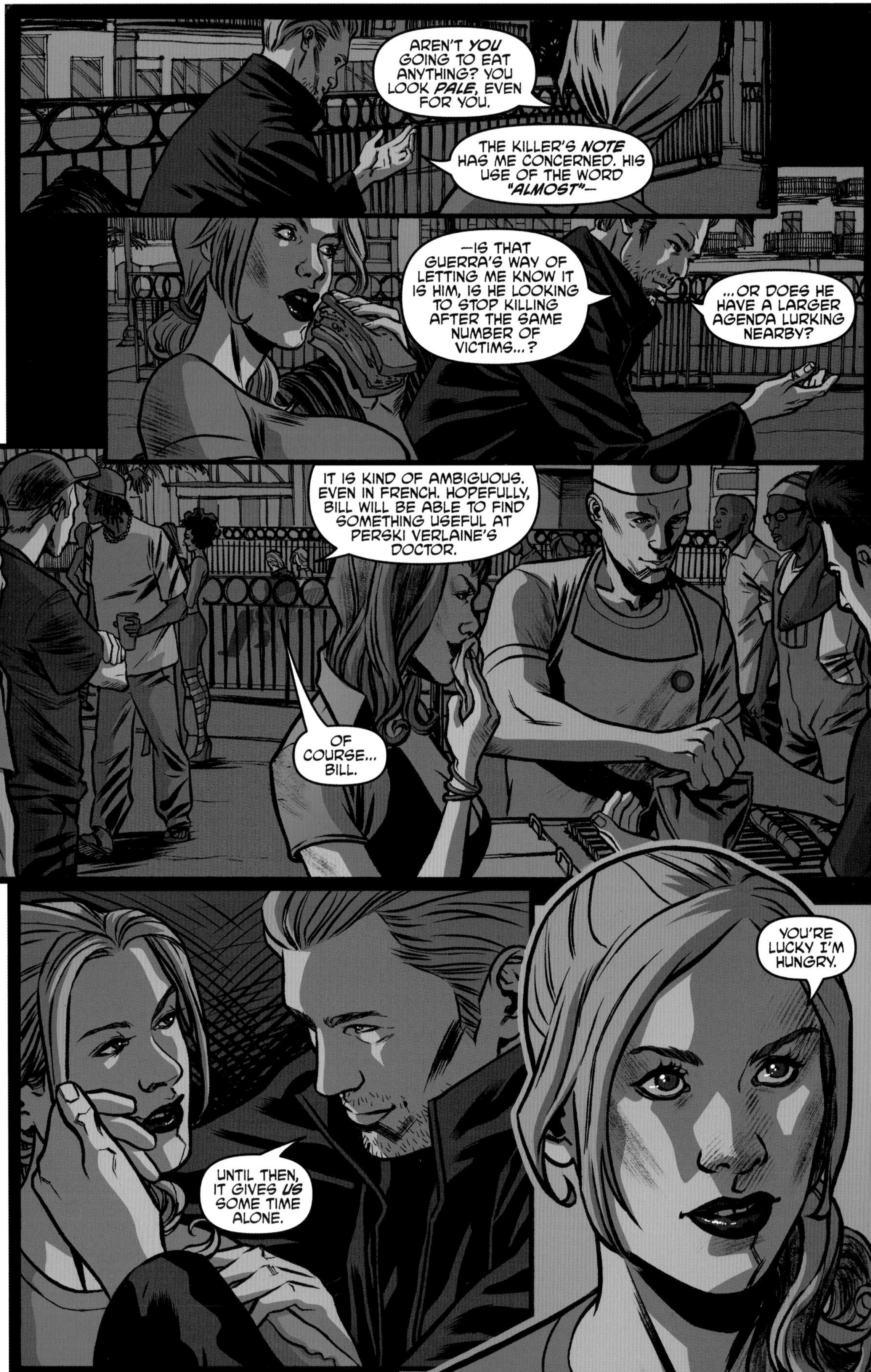
AREN'T YOU GOING TO EAT ANYTHING? YOU LOOK PALE, EVEN FOR YOU.
THE KILLER'S NOTE HAS ME CONCERNED. HIS USE OF THE WORD "ALMOST"—
—IS THAT GUERRA'S WAY OF LETTING ME KNOW IT IS HIM, IS HE LOOKING TO STOP KILLING AFTER THE SAME NUMBER OF VICTIMS...?
...OR DOES HE HAVE A LARGER AGENDA LURKING NEARBY?
IT IS KIND OF AMBIGUOUS. EVEN IN FRENCH. HOPEFULLY, BILL WILL BE ABLE TO FIND SOMETHING USEFUL AT PERSKI VERLAINE'S DOCTOR.
OF COURSE... BILL.
YOU'RE LUCKY I'M HUNGRY.
UNTIL THEN, IT GIVES US SOME TIME ALONE.

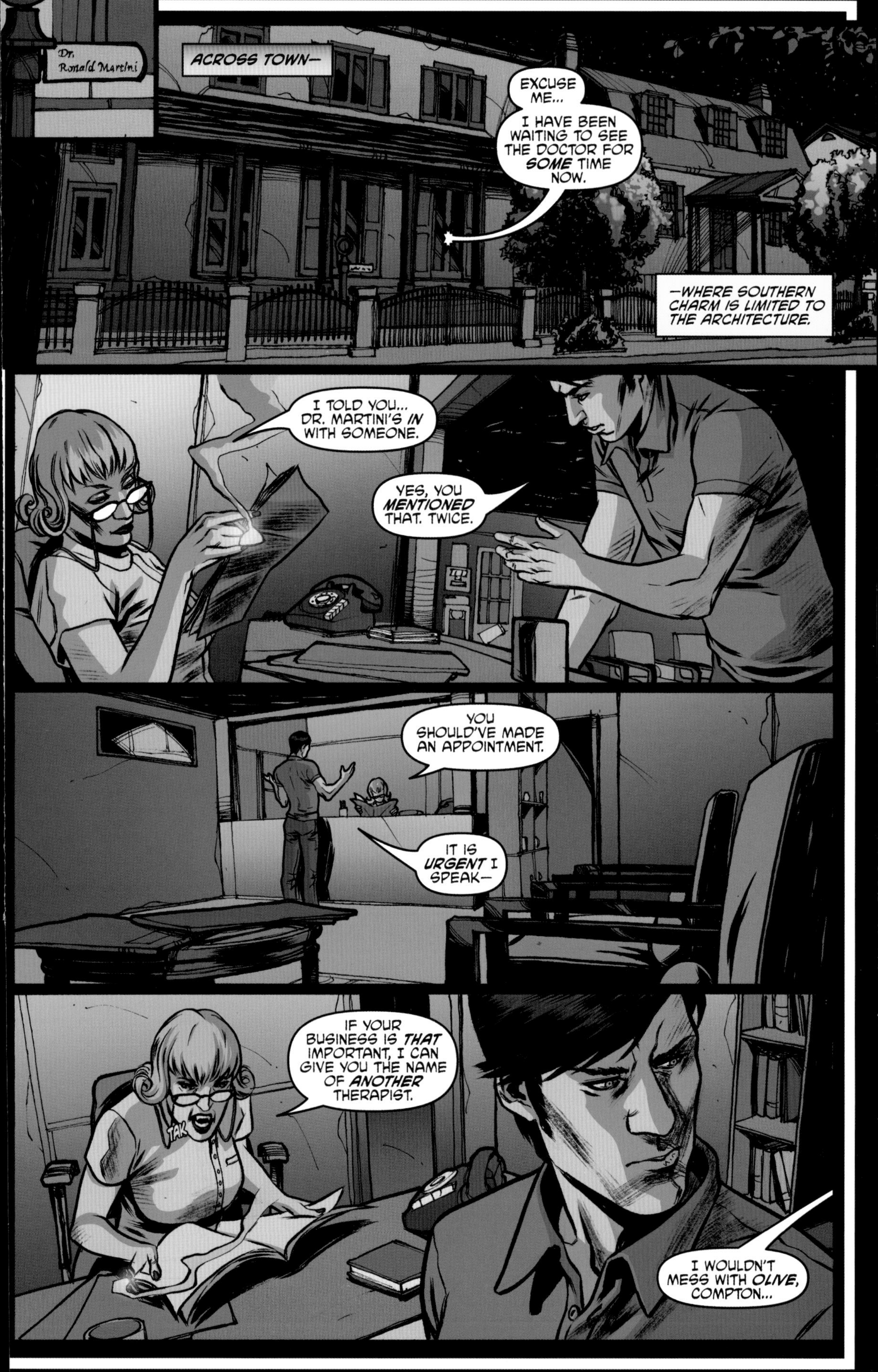

Dr. Ronald Martini
ACROSS TOWN—
EXCUSE ME...
I HAVE BEEN WAITING TO SEE THE DOCTOR FOR SOME TIME NOW.
—WHERE SOUTHERN CHARM IS LIMITED TO THE ARCHITECTURE.
I TOLD YOU... DR. MARTINI'S IN WITH SOMEONE.
YES, YOU MENTIONED THAT. TWICE.
YOU SHOULD'VE MADE AN APPOINTMENT.
IT IS URGENT I SPEAK—
IF YOUR BUSINESS IS THAT IMPORTANT, I CAN GIVE YOU THE NAME OF ANOTHER THERAPIST.
TAK
I WOULDN'T MESS WITH OLIVE, COMPTON...

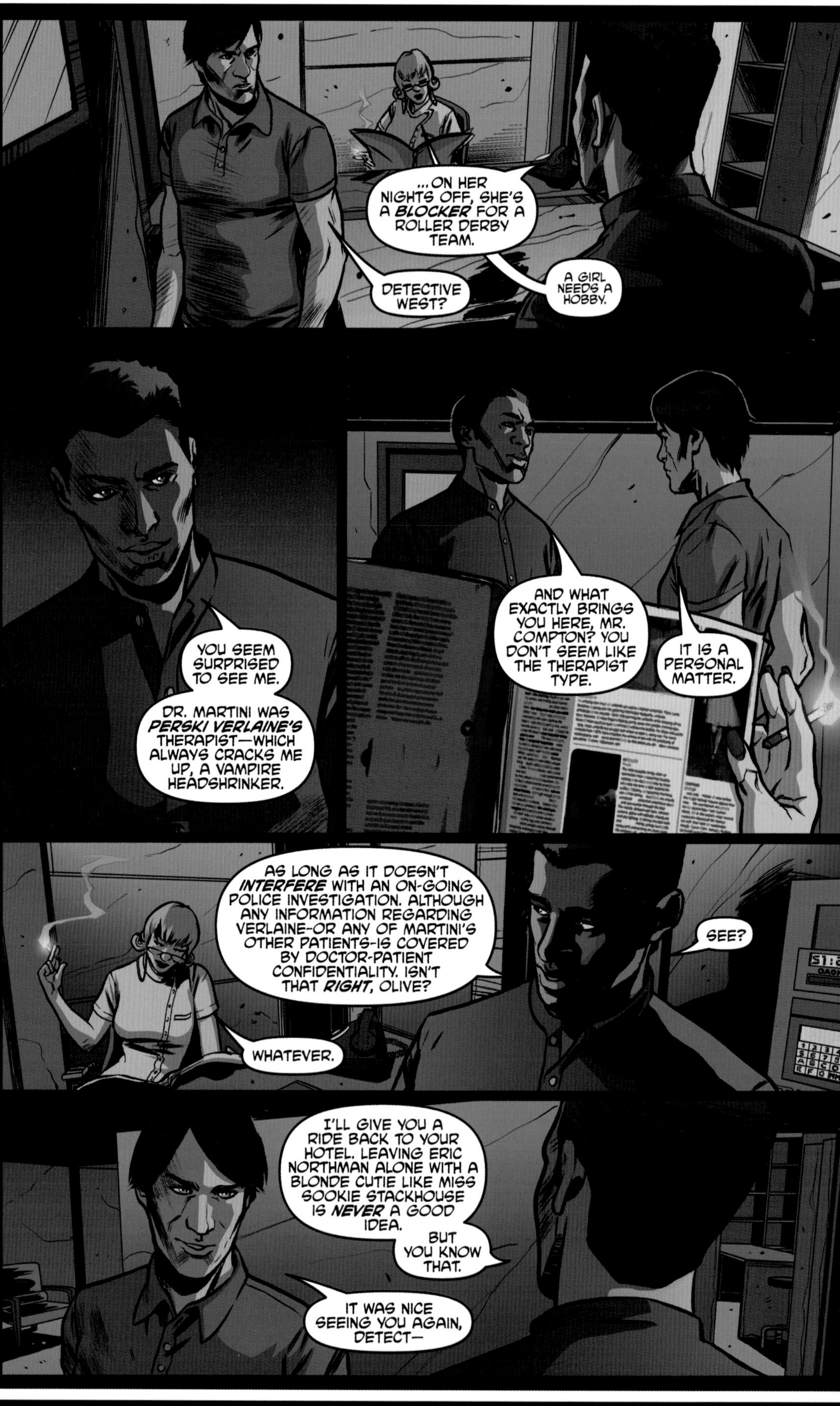
...ON HER NIGHTS OFF, SHE'S A BLOCKER FOR A ROLLER DERBY TEAM.
DETECTIVE WEST?
A GIRL NEEDS A HOBBY.
YOU SEEM SURPRISED TO SEE ME.
DR. MARTINI WAS PERSKI VERLAINE'S THERAPIST—WHICH ALWAYS CRACKS ME UP, A VAMPIRE HEADSHRINKER.
AND WHAT EXACTLY BRINGS YOU HERE, MR. COMPTON? YOU DON'T SEEM LIKE THE THERAPIST TYPE.
IT IS A PERSONAL MATTER.
AS LONG AS IT DOESN'T INTERFERE WITH AN ON-GOING POLICE INVESTIGATION. ALTHOUGH ANY INFORMATION REGARDING VERLAINE-OR ANY OF MARTINI'S OTHER PATIENTS-IS COVERED BY DOCTOR-PATIENT CONFIDENTIALITY. ISN'T THAT RIGHT, OLIVE?
SEE?
WHATEVER.
I'LL GIVE YOU A RIDE BACK TO YOUR HOTEL. LEAVING ERIC NORTHMAN ALONE WITH A BLONDE CUTIE LIKE MISS SOOKIE STACKHOUSE IS NEVER A GOOD IDEA.
BUT YOU KNOW THAT.
IT WAS NICE SEEING YOU AGAIN, DETECT—

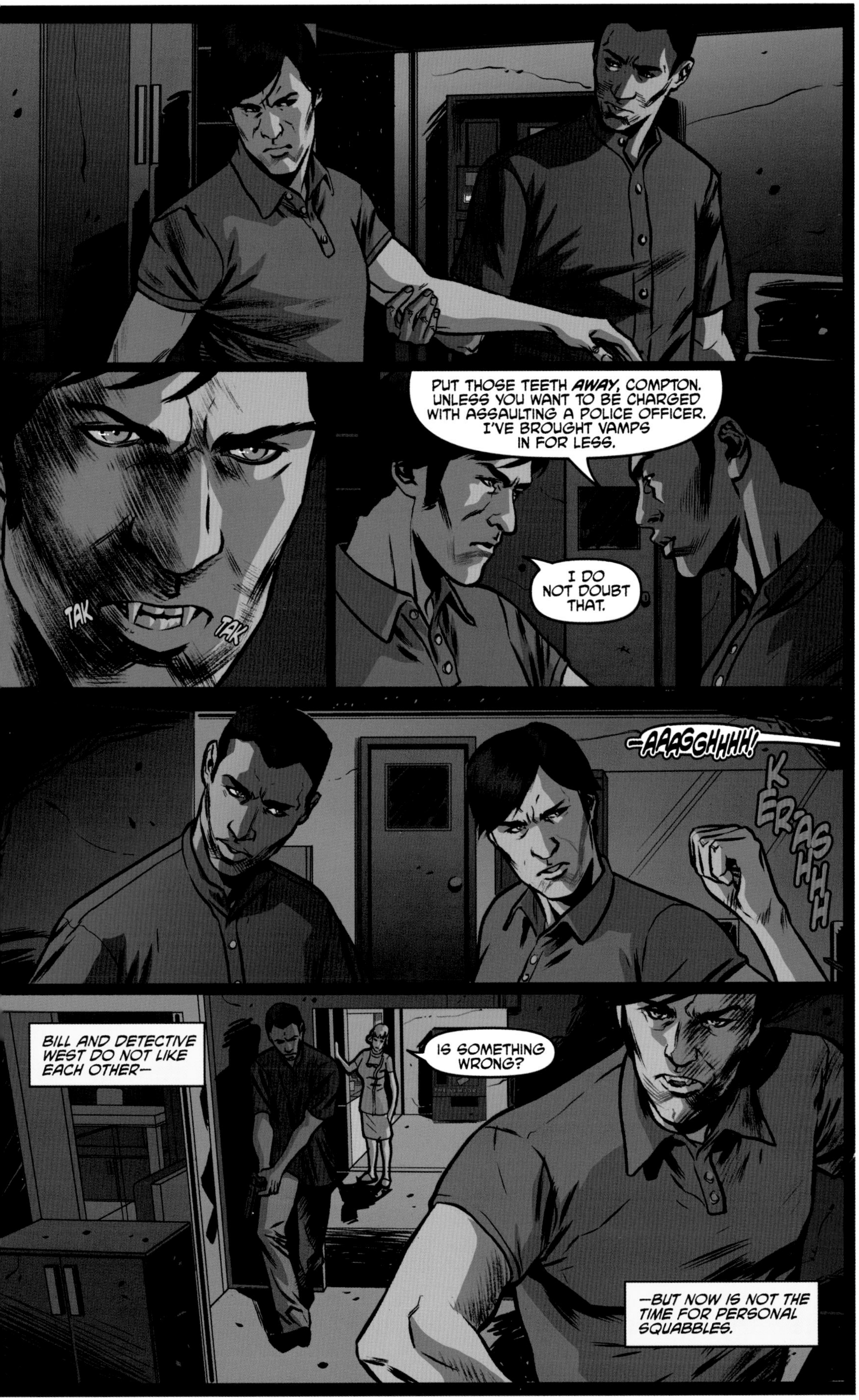

PUT THOSE TEETH AWAY, COMPTON. UNLESS YOU WANT TO BE CHARGED WITH ASSAULTING A POLICE OFFICER. I'VE BROUGHT VAMPS IN FOR LESS.
TAK
TAK
I DO NOT DOUBT THAT.
-AAAGGHHHH!
KER-ASHHH
BILL AND DETECTIVE WEST DO NOT LIKE EACH OTHER--
IS SOMETHING WRONG?
--BUT NOW IS NOT THE TIME FOR PERSONAL SQUABBLES.

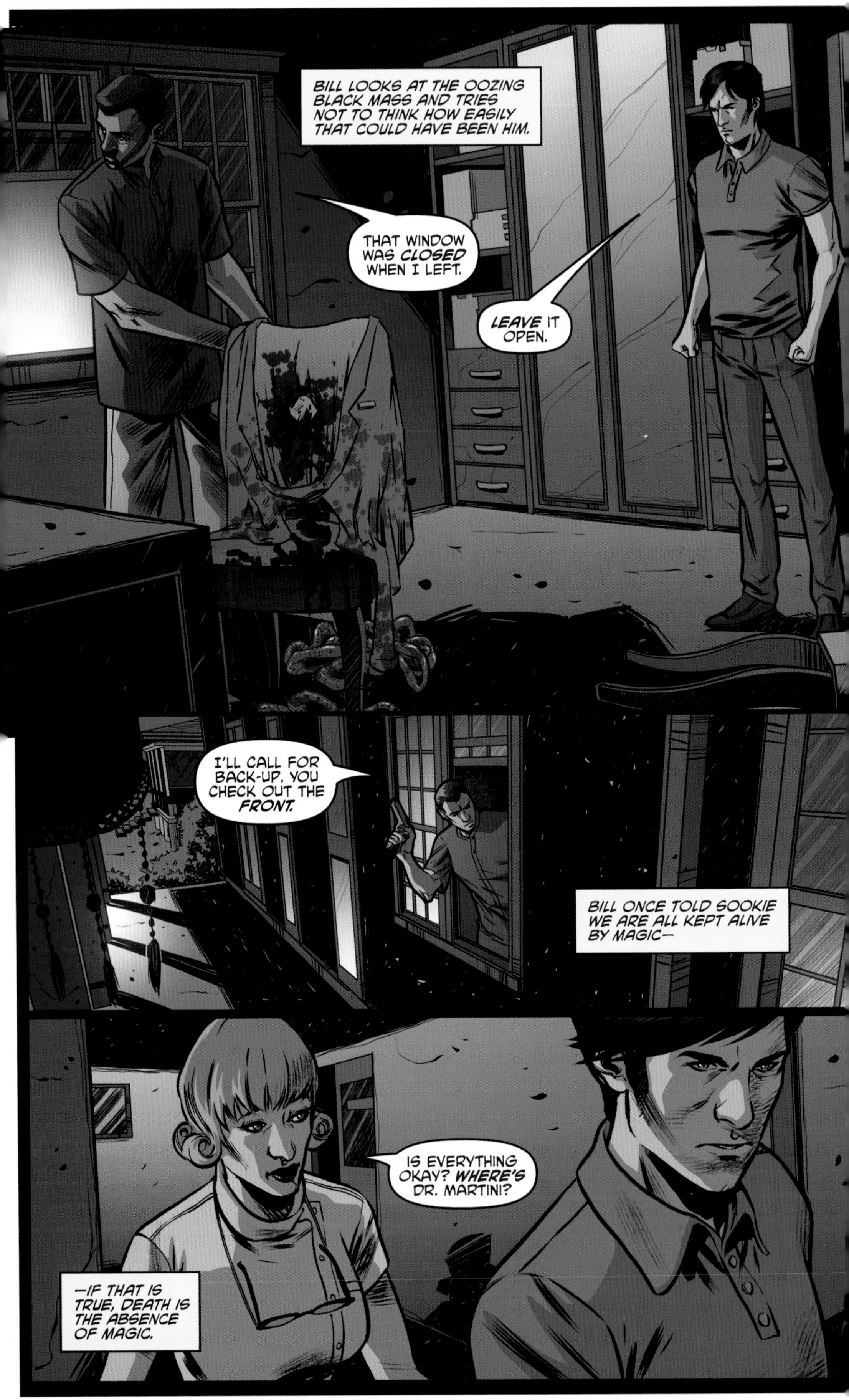
BILL LOOKS AT THE OOZING BLACK MASS AND TRIES NOT TO THINK HOW EASILY THAT COULD HAVE BEEN HIM.
THAT WINDOW WAS CLOSED WHEN I LEFT.
LEAVE IT OPEN.
I'LL CALL FOR BACK-UP. YOU CHECK OUT THE FRONT.
BILL ONCE TOLD SOOKIE WE ARE ALL KEPT ALIVE BY MAGIC—
IS EVERYTHING OKAY? WHERE'S DR. MARTINI?
—IF THAT IS TRUE, DEATH IS THE ABSENCE OF MAGIC.

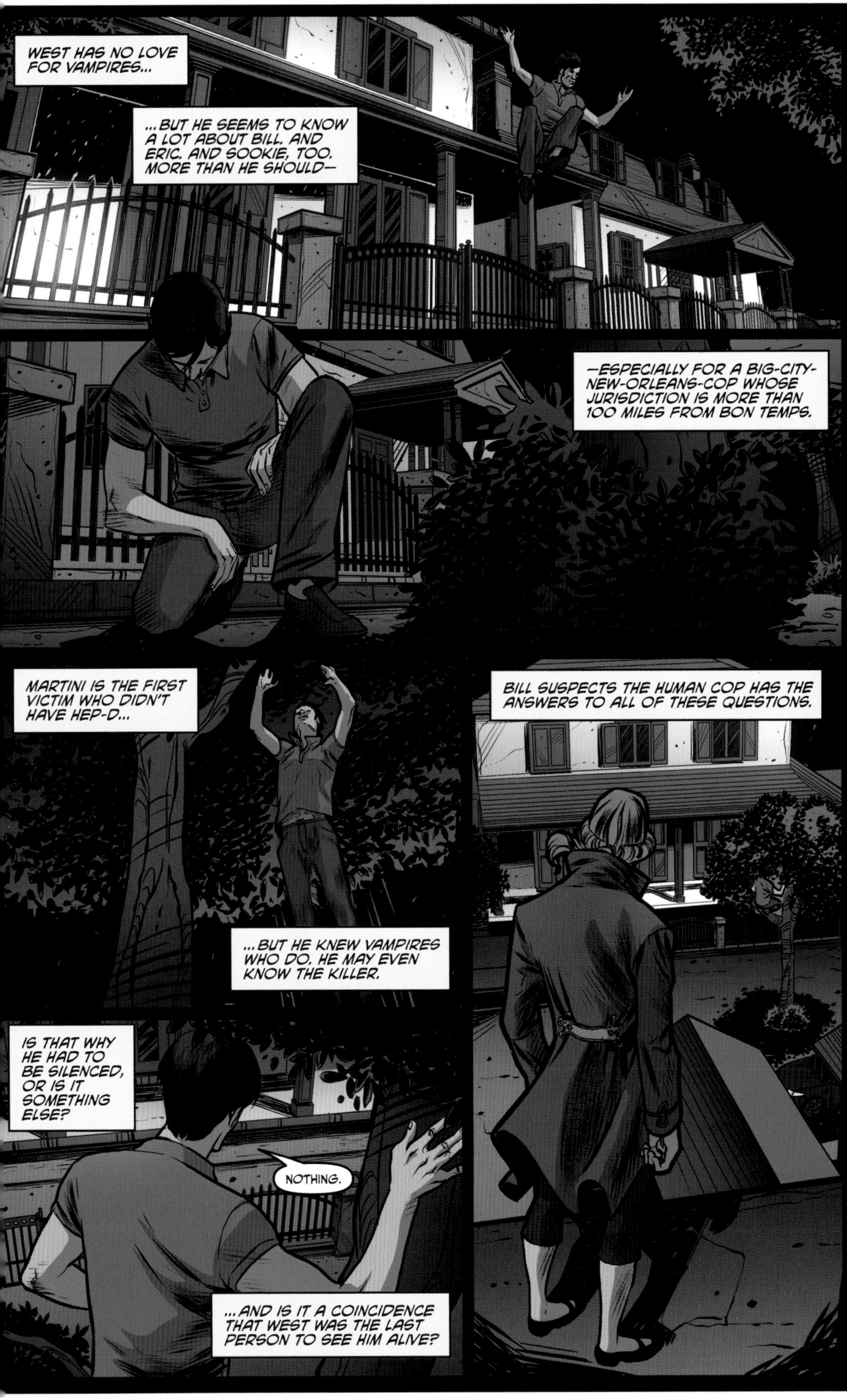
WEST HAS NO LOVE FOR VAMPIRES...
...BUT HE SEEMS TO KNOW A LOT ABOUT BILL. AND ERIC. AND SOOKIE, TOO. MORE THAN HE SHOULD—
—ESPECIALLY FOR A BIG-CITY-NEW-ORLEANS-COP WHOSE JURISDICTION IS MORE THAN 100 MILES FROM BON TEMPS.
MARTINI IS THE FIRST VICTIM WHO DIDN'T HAVE HEP-D...
...BUT HE KNEW VAMPIRES WHO DO. HE MAY EVEN KNOW THE KILLER.
IS THAT WHY HE HAD TO BE SILENCED, OR IS IT SOMETHING ELSE?
NOTHING.
...AND IS IT A COINCIDENCE THAT WEST WAS THE LAST PERSON TO SEE HIM ALIVE?
BILL SUSPECTS THE HUMAN COP HAS THE ANSWERS TO ALL OF THESE QUESTIONS.

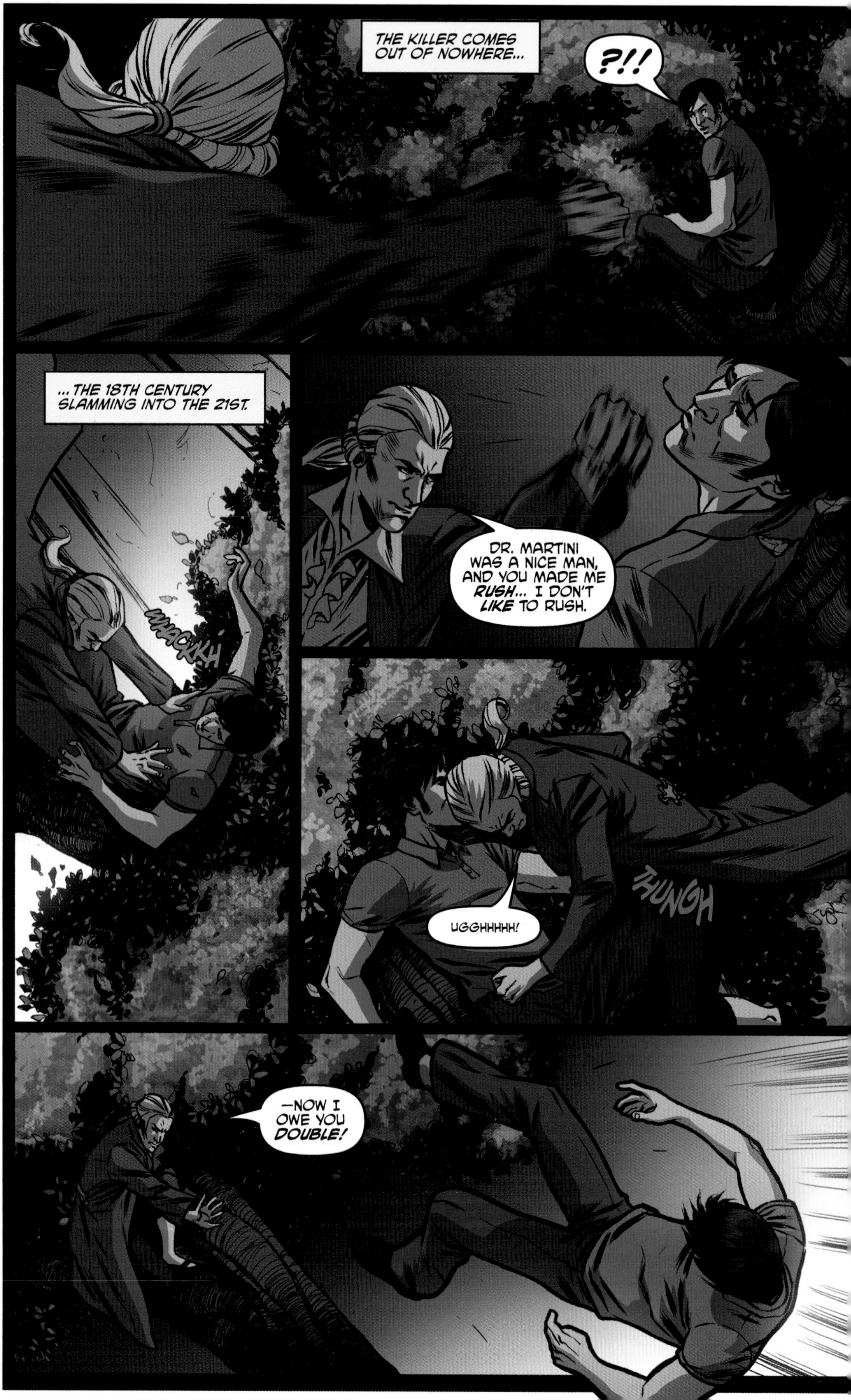

THE KILLER COMES OUT OF NOWHERE...
?!!
...THE 18TH CENTURY SLAMMING INTO THE 21ST.
WHACKKH
DR. MARTINI WAS A NICE MAN, AND YOU MADE ME RUSH... I DON'T LIKE TO RUSH.
THUNGH
UGGHHHHH!
—NOW I OWE YOU DOUBLE!

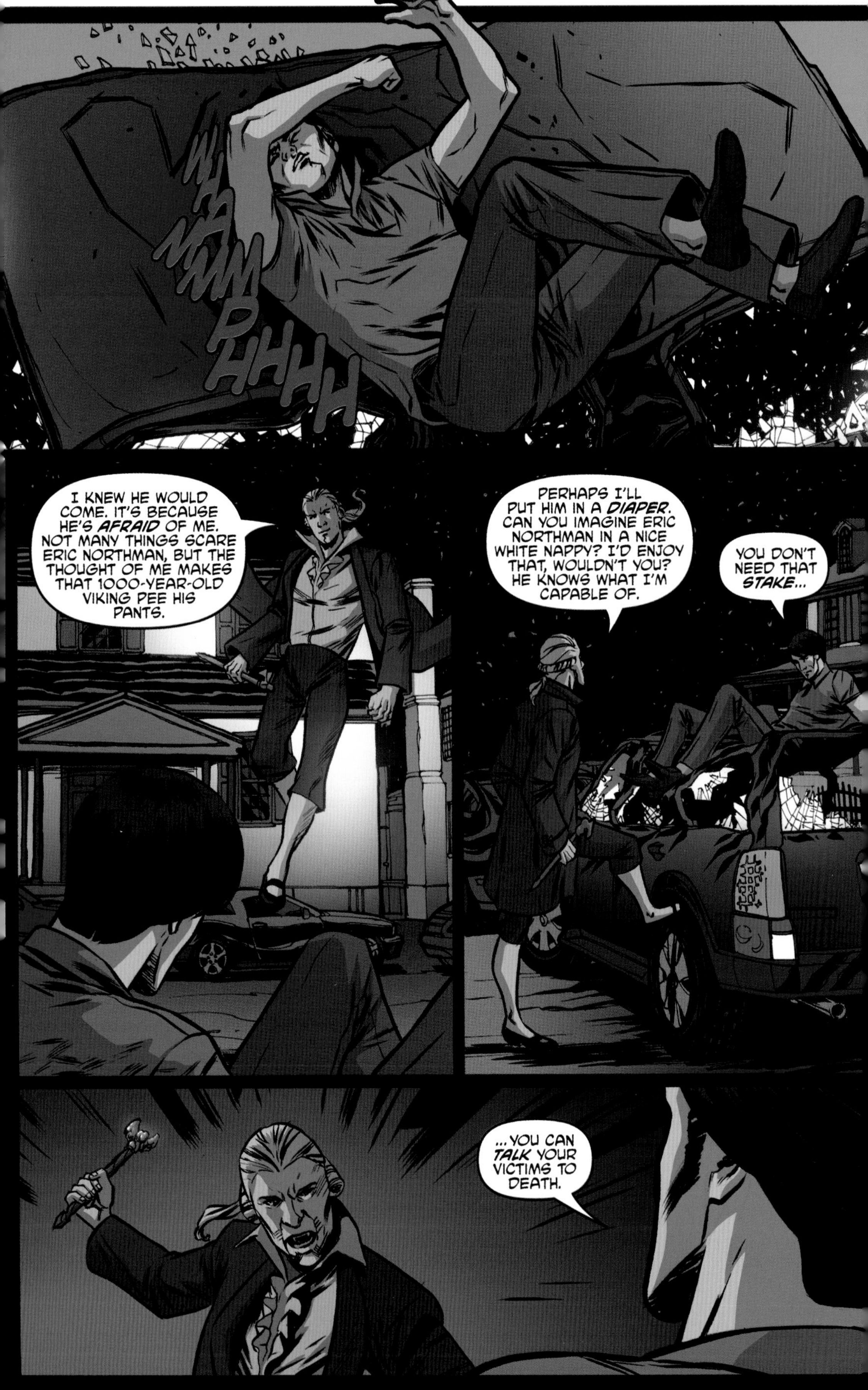
WHAMMMPHHHH
I KNEW HE WOULD COME. IT'S BECAUSE HE'S AFRAID OF ME. NOT MANY THINGS SCARE ERIC NORTHMAN, BUT THE THOUGHT OF ME MAKES THAT 1000-YEAR-OLD VIKING PEE HIS PANTS.
PERHAPS I'LL PUT HIM IN A DIAPER. CAN YOU IMAGINE ERIC NORTHMAN IN A NICE WHITE NAPPY? I'D ENJOY THAT, WOULDN'T YOU? HE KNOWS WHAT I'M CAPABLE OF.
YOU DON'T NEED THAT STAKE...
...YOU CAN TALK YOUR VICTIMS TO DEATH.

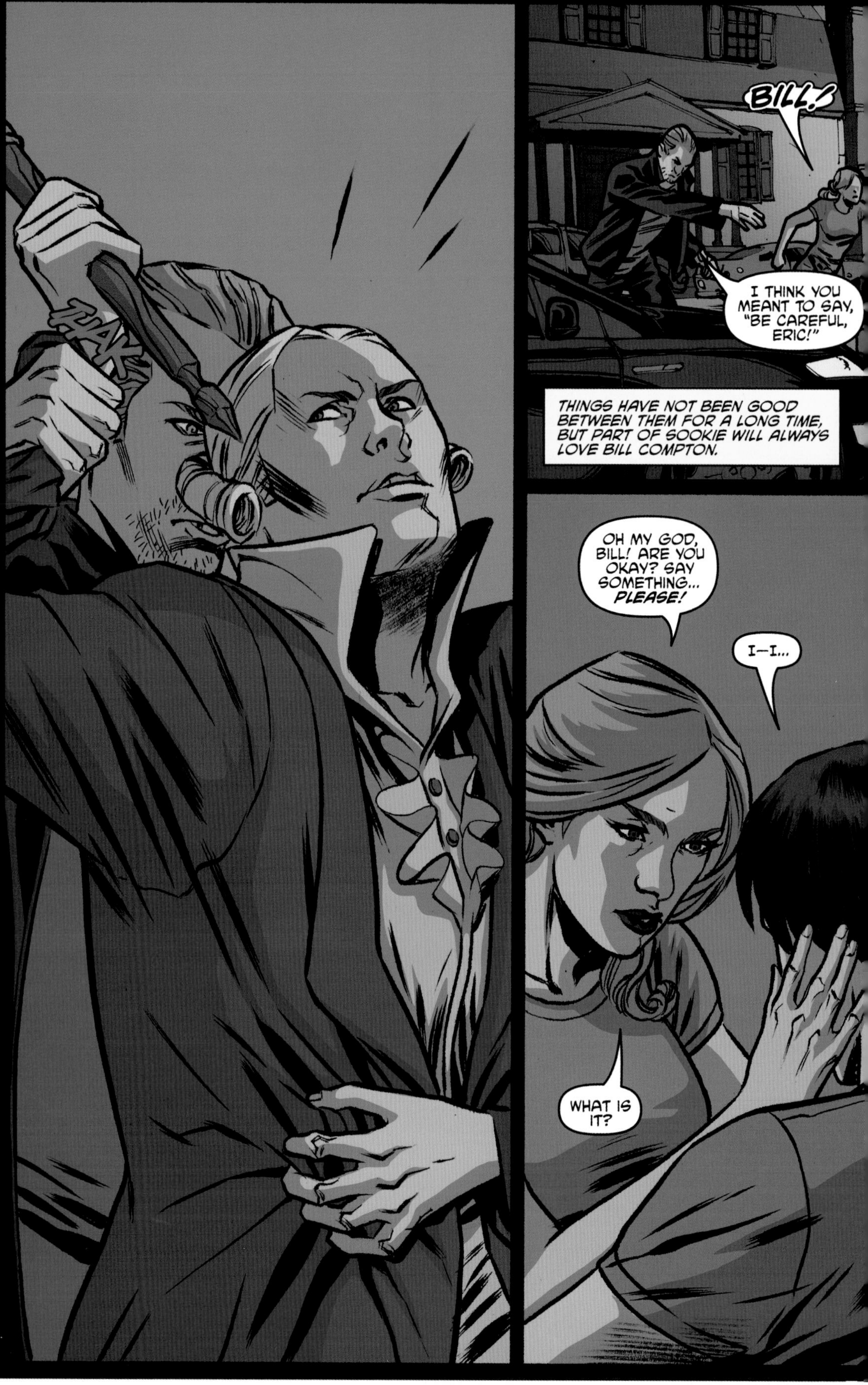
THAK
BILL!
I THINK YOU MEANT TO SAY, "BE CAREFUL, ERIC!"
THINGS HAVE NOT BEEN GOOD BETWEEN THEM FOR A LONG TIME, BUT PART OF SOOKIE WILL ALWAYS LOVE BILL COMPTON.
OH MY GOD, BILL! ARE YOU OKAY? SAY SOMETHING... PLEASE!
I—I...
WHAT IS IT?

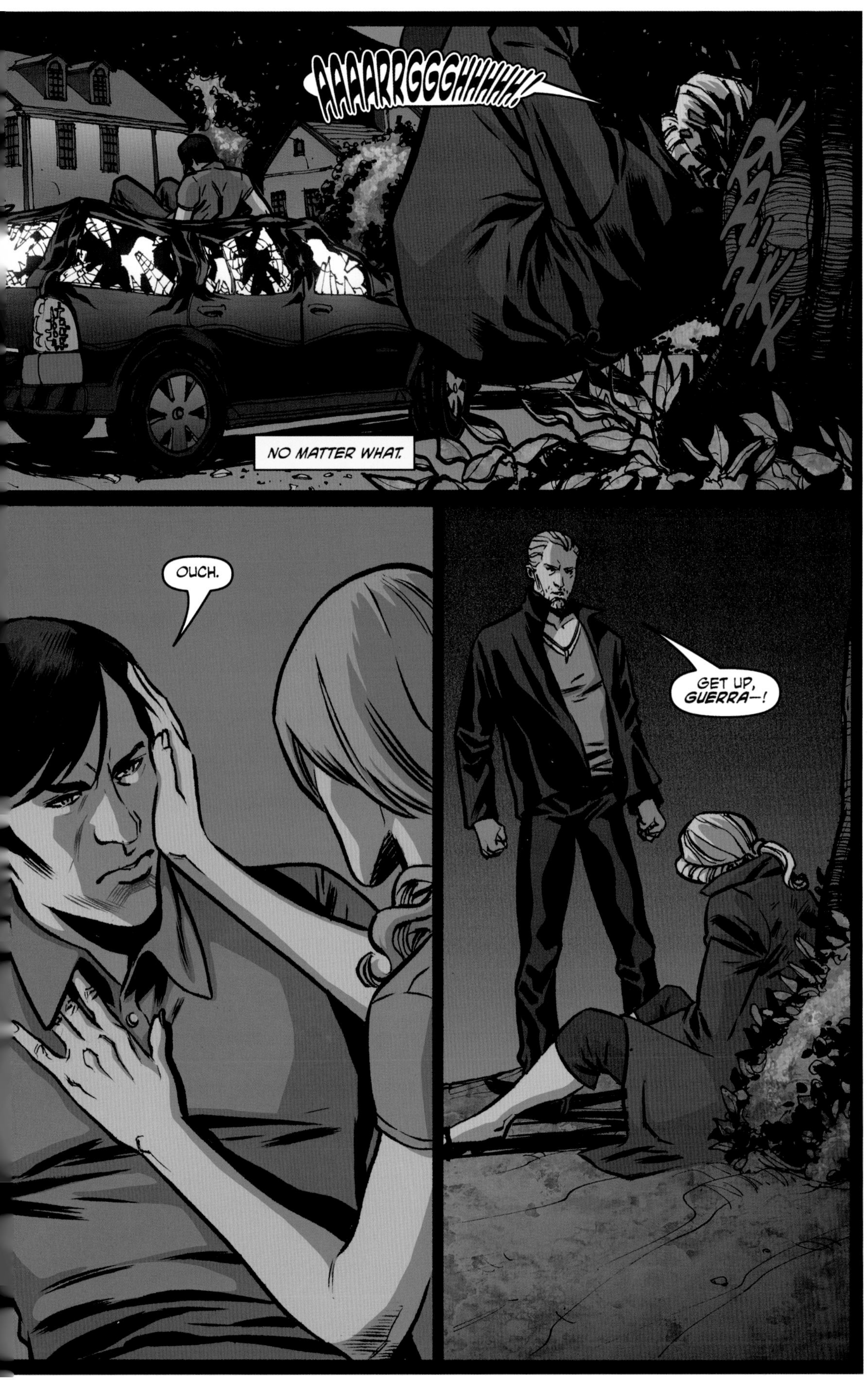
AAAARRGGGHHHHH!
NO MATTER WHAT.
OUCH.
GET UP, GUERRA--!

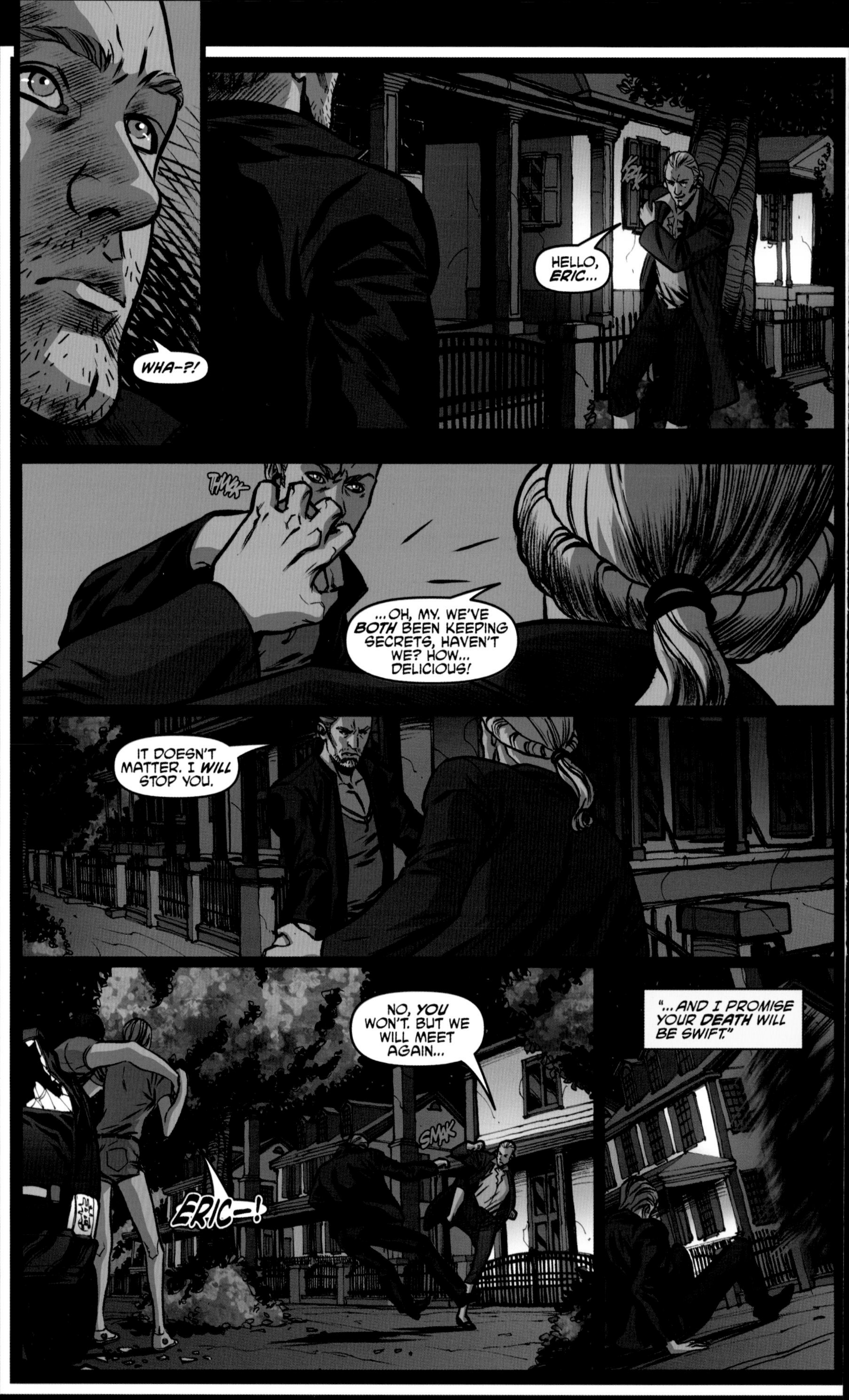
HELLO, ERIC...
WHA-?!
THWAK
...OH, MY. WE'VE BOTH BEEN KEEPING SECRETS, HAVEN'T WE? HOW... DELICIOUS!
IT DOESN'T MATTER. I WILL STOP YOU.
ERIC--!
NO, YOU WON'T. BUT WE WILL MEET AGAIN...
SMAK
"...AND I PROMISE YOUR DEATH WILL BE SWIFT."

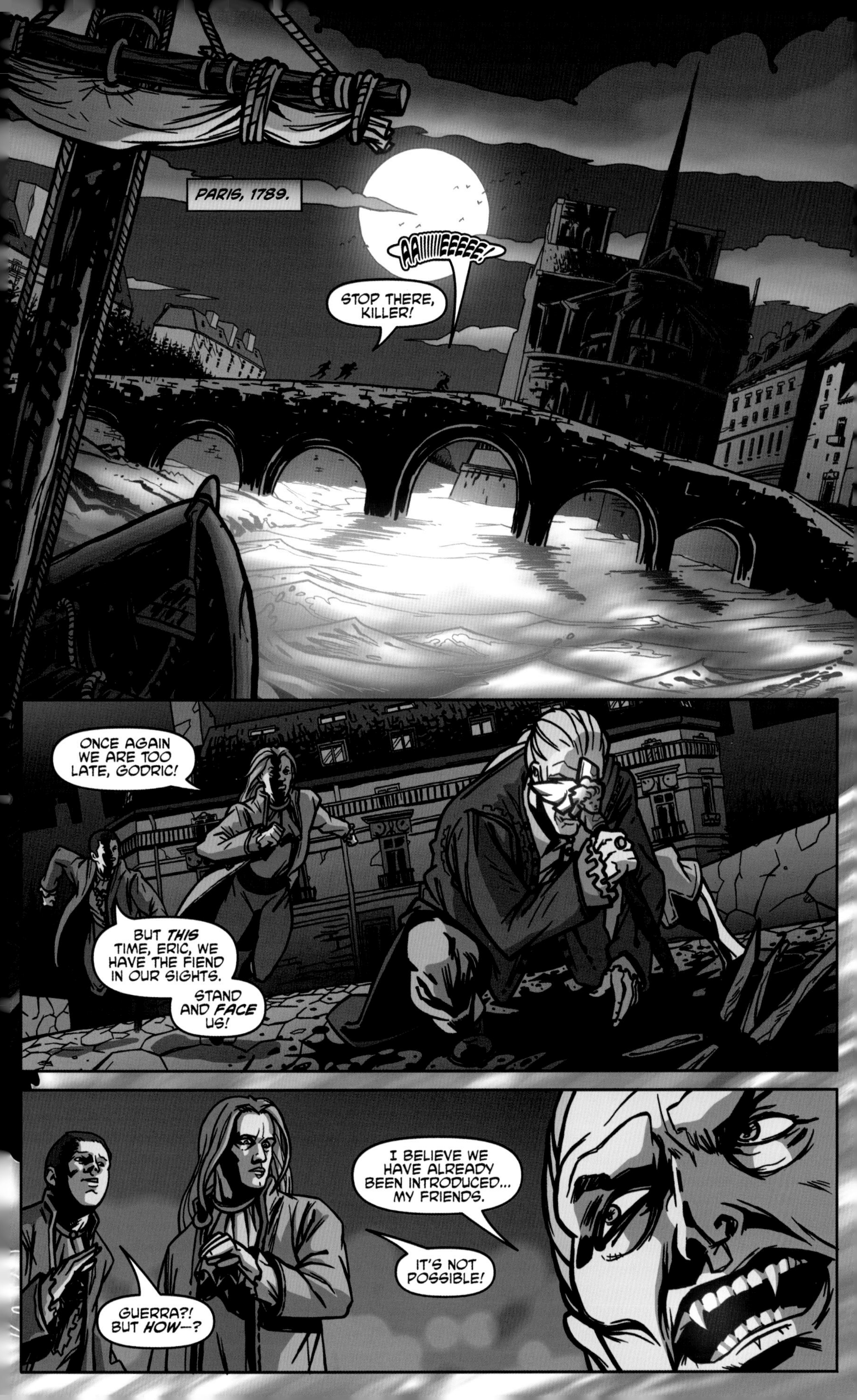
PARIS, 1789.
AAIIIIIEEEEE!
STOP THERE, KILLER!
ONCE AGAIN WE ARE TOO LATE, GODRIC!
BUT THIS TIME, ERIC, WE HAVE THE FIEND IN OUR SIGHTS.
STAND AND FACE US!
I BELIEVE WE HAVE ALREADY BEEN INTRODUCED... MY FRIENDS.
IT'S NOT POSSIBLE!
GUERRA?! BUT HOW--?

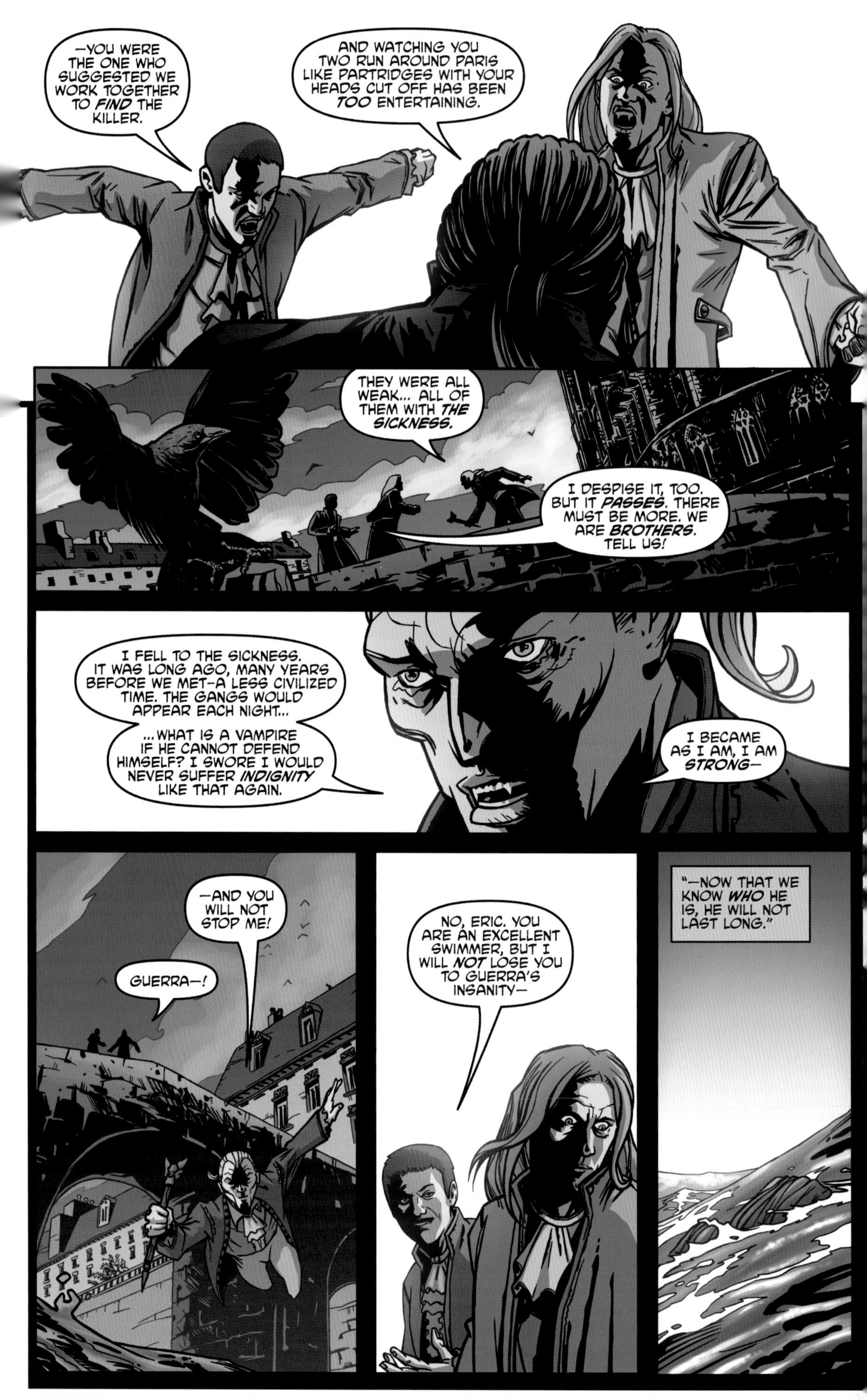

—YOU WERE THE ONE WHO SUGGESTED WE WORK TOGETHER TO *FIND* THE KILLER.
AND WATCHING YOU TWO RUN AROUND PARIS LIKE PARTRIDGES WITH YOUR HEADS CUT OFF HAS BEEN *TOO* ENTERTAINING.
THEY WERE ALL WEAK... ALL OF THEM WITH *THE SICKNESS.*
I DESPISE IT, TOO. BUT IT *PASSES*. THERE MUST BE MORE. WE ARE *BROTHERS*. TELL US!
I FELL TO THE SICKNESS. IT WAS LONG AGO, MANY YEARS BEFORE WE MET—A LESS CIVILIZED TIME. THE GANGS WOULD APPEAR EACH NIGHT...
...WHAT IS A VAMPIRE IF HE CANNOT DEFEND HIMSELF? I SWORE I WOULD NEVER SUFFER *INDIGNITY* LIKE THAT AGAIN.
I BECAME AS I AM, I AM *STRONG*—
—AND YOU WILL NOT STOP ME!
GUERRA—!
NO, ERIC. YOU ARE AN EXCELLENT SWIMMER, BUT I WILL *NOT* LOSE YOU TO GUERRA'S INSANITY—
"—NOW THAT WE KNOW *WHO* HE IS, HE WILL NOT LAST LONG."

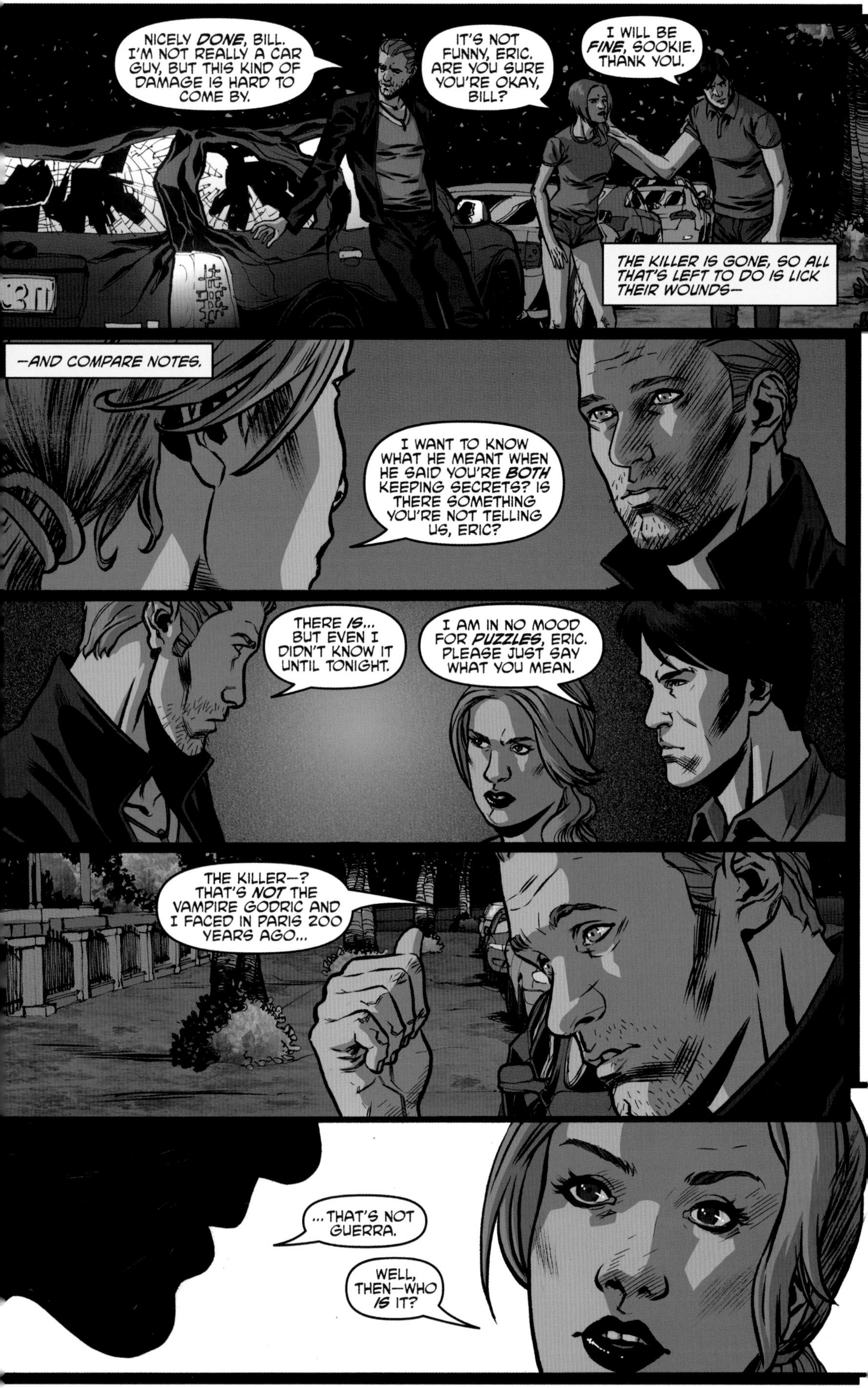
NICELY DONE, BILL. I'M NOT REALLY A CAR GUY, BUT THIS KIND OF DAMAGE IS HARD TO COME BY.
IT'S NOT FUNNY, ERIC. ARE YOU SURE YOU'RE OKAY, BILL?
I WILL BE FINE, SOOKIE. THANK YOU.
THE KILLER IS GONE, SO ALL THAT'S LEFT TO DO IS LICK THEIR WOUNDS—
—AND COMPARE NOTES.
I WANT TO KNOW WHAT HE MEANT WHEN HE SAID YOU'RE BOTH KEEPING SECRETS? IS THERE SOMETHING YOU'RE NOT TELLING US, ERIC?
THERE IS... BUT EVEN I DIDN'T KNOW IT UNTIL TONIGHT.
I AM IN NO MOOD FOR PUZZLES, ERIC. PLEASE JUST SAY WHAT YOU MEAN.
THE KILLER—? THAT'S NOT THE VAMPIRE GODRIC AND I FACED IN PARIS 200 YEARS AGO...
...THAT'S NOT GUERRA.
WELL, THEN—WHO IS IT?

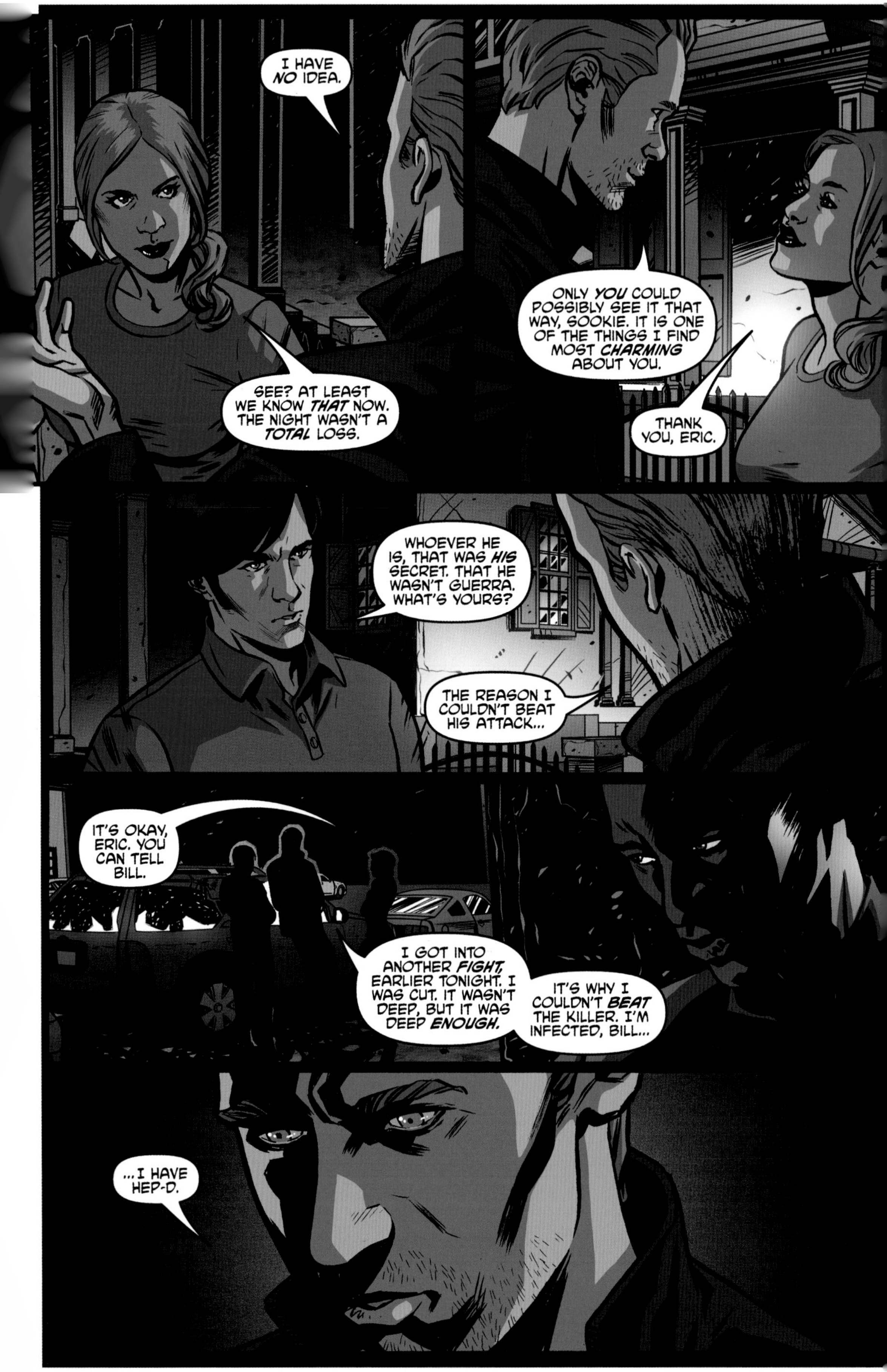
I HAVE NO IDEA.
SEE? AT LEAST WE KNOW THAT NOW. THE NIGHT WASN'T A TOTAL LOSS.
ONLY YOU COULD POSSIBLY SEE IT THAT WAY, SOOKIE. IT IS ONE OF THE THINGS I FIND MOST CHARMING ABOUT YOU.
THANK YOU, ERIC.
WHOEVER HE IS, THAT WAS HIS SECRET. THAT HE WASN'T GUERRA. WHAT'S YOURS?
THE REASON I COULDN'T BEAT HIS ATTACK...
IT'S OKAY, ERIC. YOU CAN TELL BILL.
I GOT INTO ANOTHER FIGHT, EARLIER TONIGHT. I WAS CUT. IT WASN'T DEEP, BUT IT WAS DEEP ENOUGH.
IT'S WHY I COULDN'T BEAT THE KILLER. I'M INFECTED, BILL...
...I HAVE HEP-D.

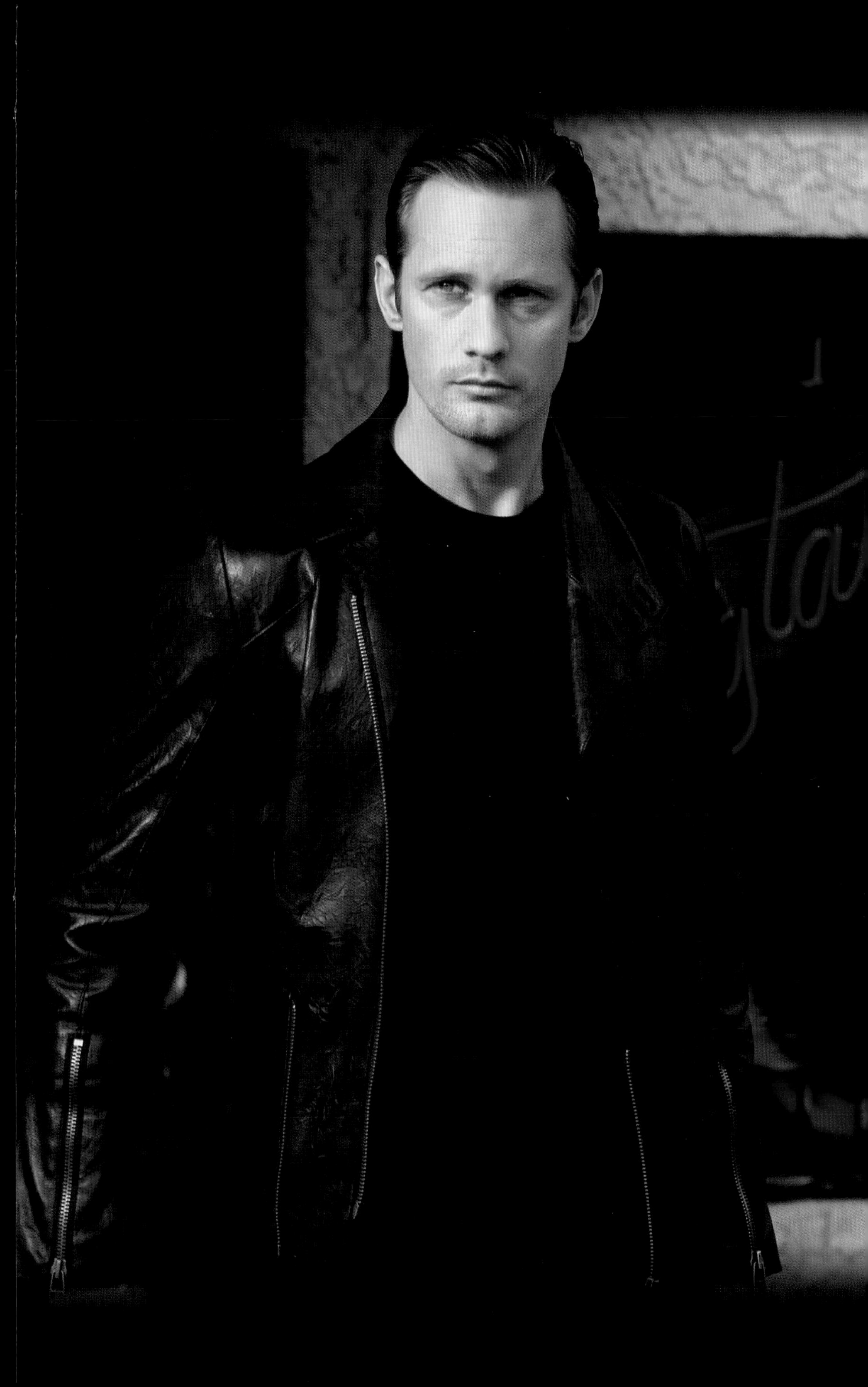

# CHAPTER 4

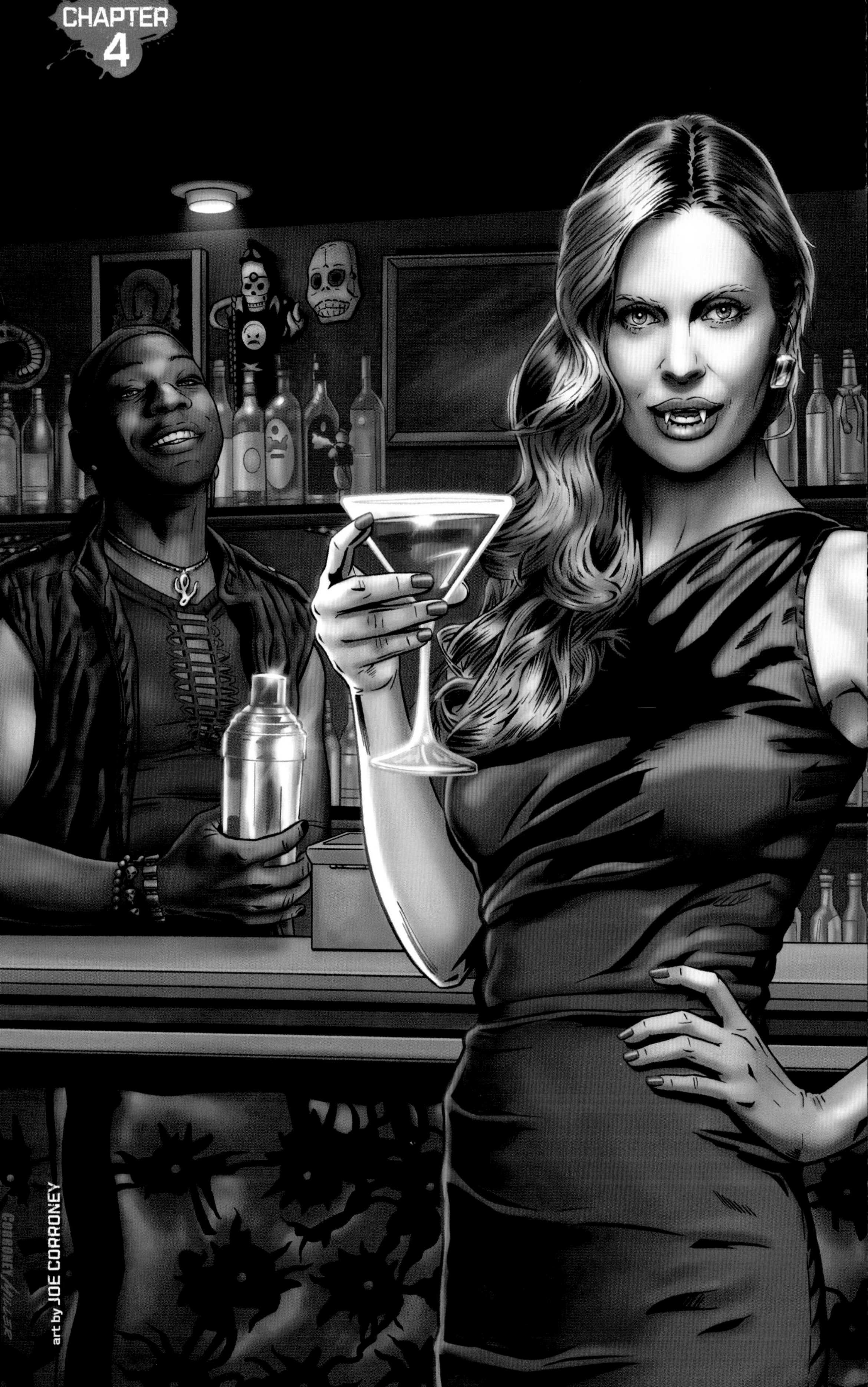

art by JOE CORRONEY

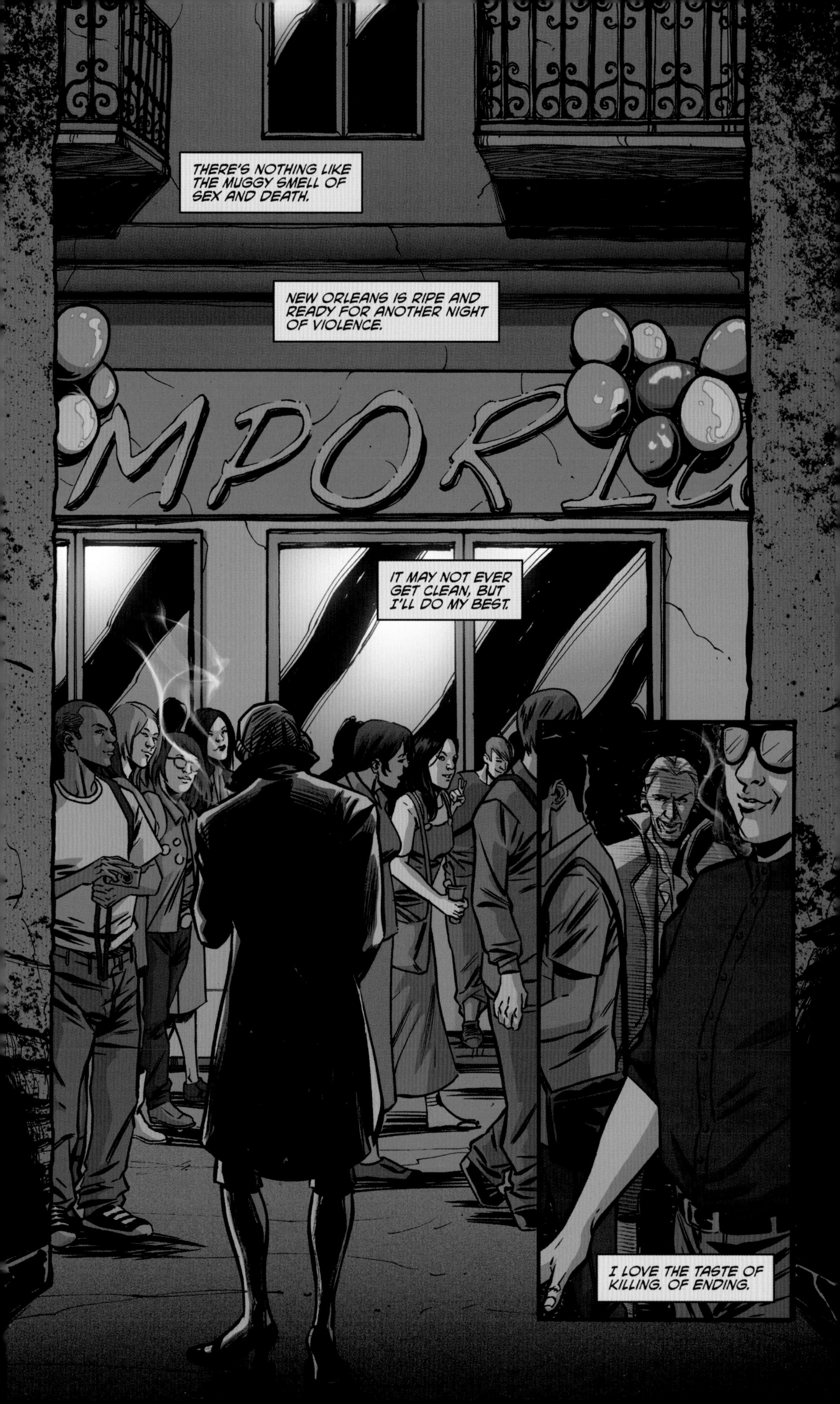
THERE'S NOTHING LIKE THE MUGGY SMELL OF SEX AND DEATH.
NEW ORLEANS IS RIPE AND READY FOR ANOTHER NIGHT OF VIOLENCE.
IT MAY NOT EVER GET CLEAN, BUT I'LL DO MY BEST.
I LOVE THE TASTE OF KILLING. OF ENDING.

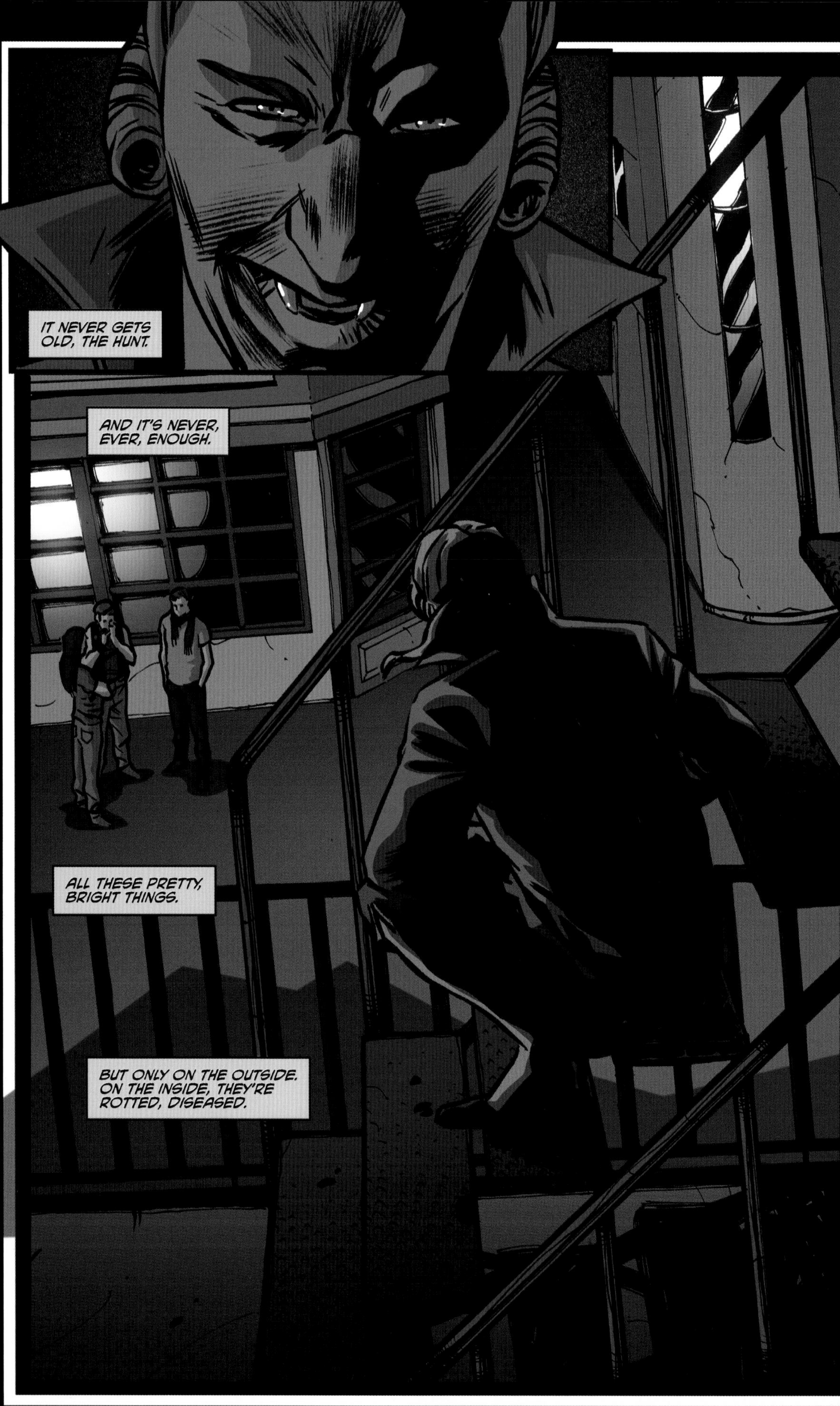

IT NEVER GETS OLD, THE HUNT.
AND IT'S NEVER, EVER, ENOUGH.
ALL THESE PRETTY, BRIGHT THINGS.
BUT ONLY ON THE OUTSIDE. ON THE INSIDE, THEY'RE ROTTED, DISEASED.

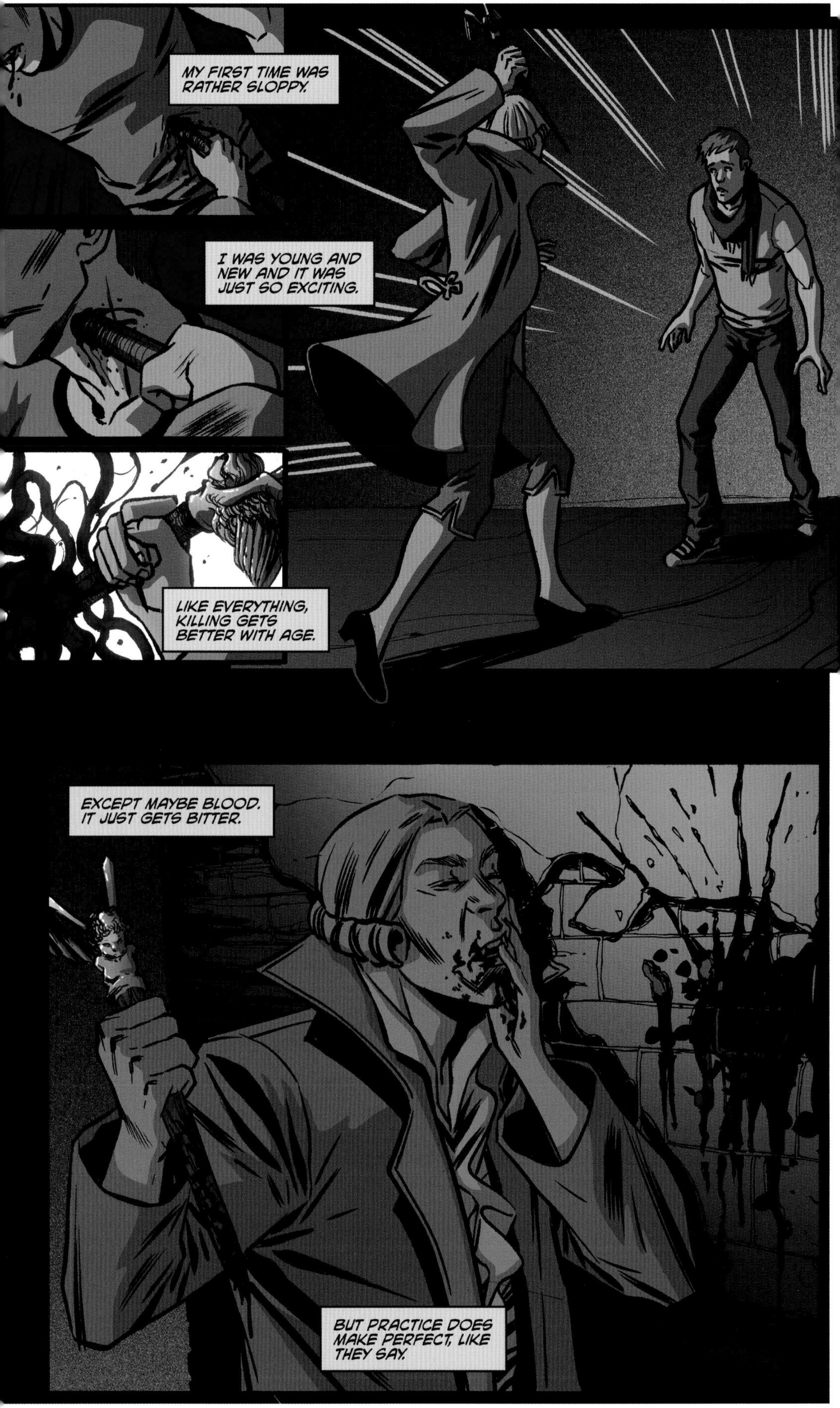
MY FIRST TIME WAS RATHER SLOPPY.
I WAS YOUNG AND NEW AND IT WAS JUST SO EXCITING.
LIKE EVERYTHING, KILLING GETS BETTER WITH AGE.
EXCEPT MAYBE BLOOD. IT JUST GETS BITTER.
BUT PRACTICE DOES MAKE PERFECT, LIKE THEY SAY.

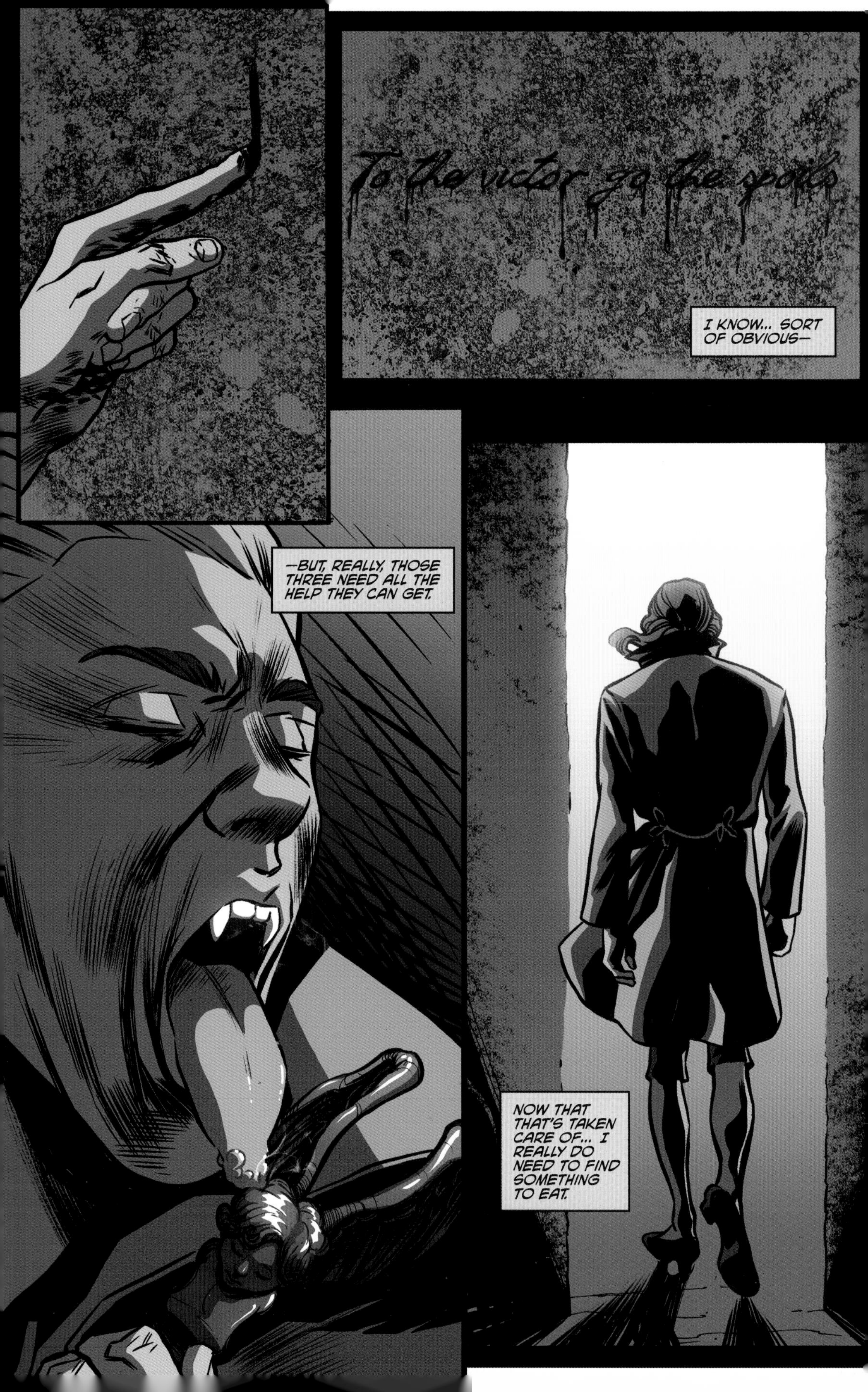
To the victor go the spoils
I KNOW... SORT OF OBVIOUS—
—BUT, REALLY, THOSE THREE NEED ALL THE HELP THEY CAN GET.
NOW THAT THAT'S TAKEN CARE OF... I REALLY DO NEED TO FIND SOMETHING TO EAT.

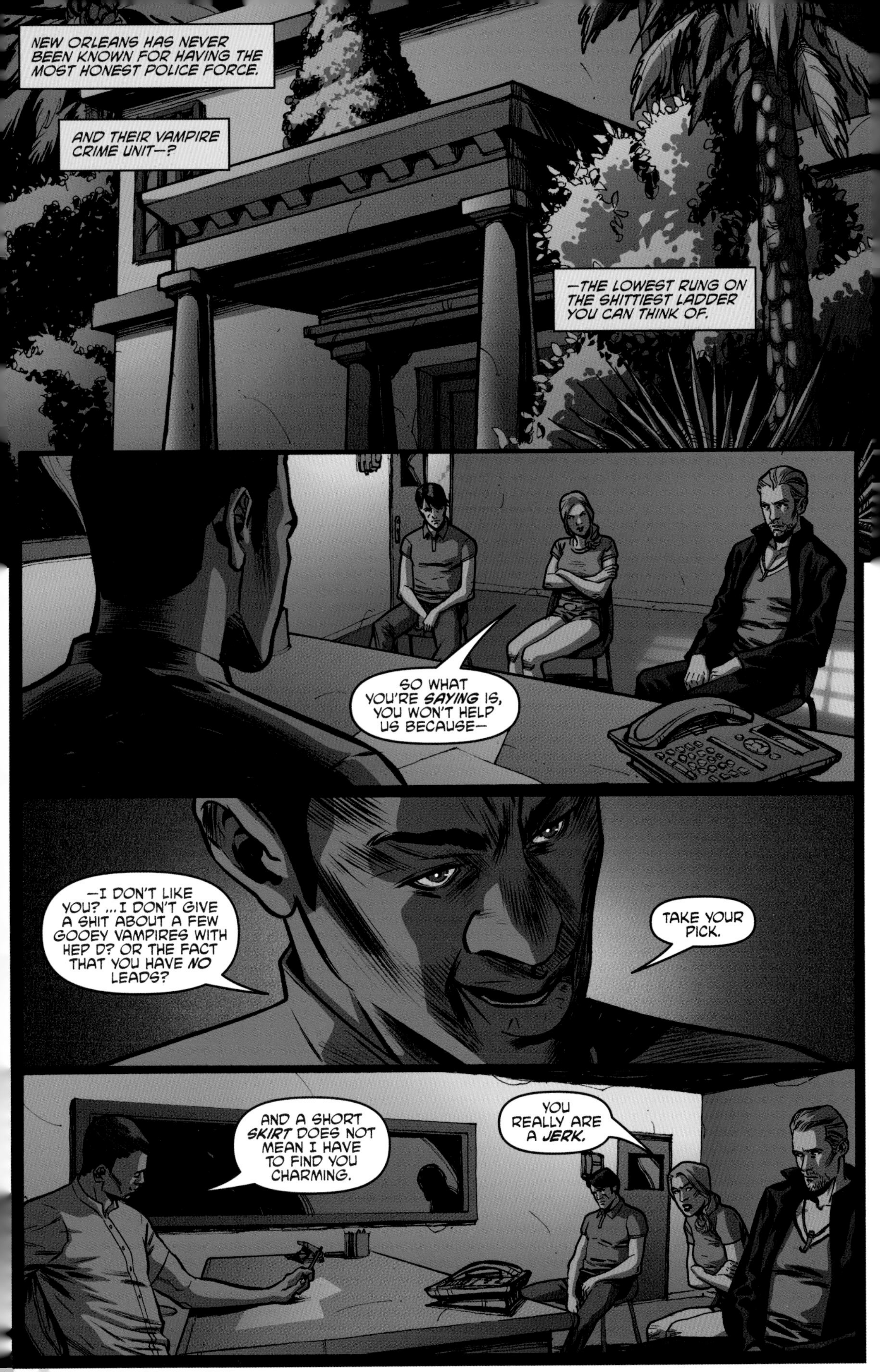
NEW ORLEANS HAS NEVER BEEN KNOWN FOR HAVING THE MOST HONEST POLICE FORCE.
AND THEIR VAMPIRE CRIME UNIT—?
—THE LOWEST RUNG ON THE SHITTIEST LADDER YOU CAN THINK OF.
SO WHAT YOU'RE SAYING IS, YOU WON'T HELP US BECAUSE—
—I DON'T LIKE YOU? ...I DON'T GIVE A SHIT ABOUT A FEW GOOEY VAMPIRES WITH HEP D? OR THE FACT THAT YOU HAVE NO LEADS?
TAKE YOUR PICK.
AND A SHORT SKIRT DOES NOT MEAN I HAVE TO FIND YOU CHARMING.
YOU REALLY ARE A JERK.

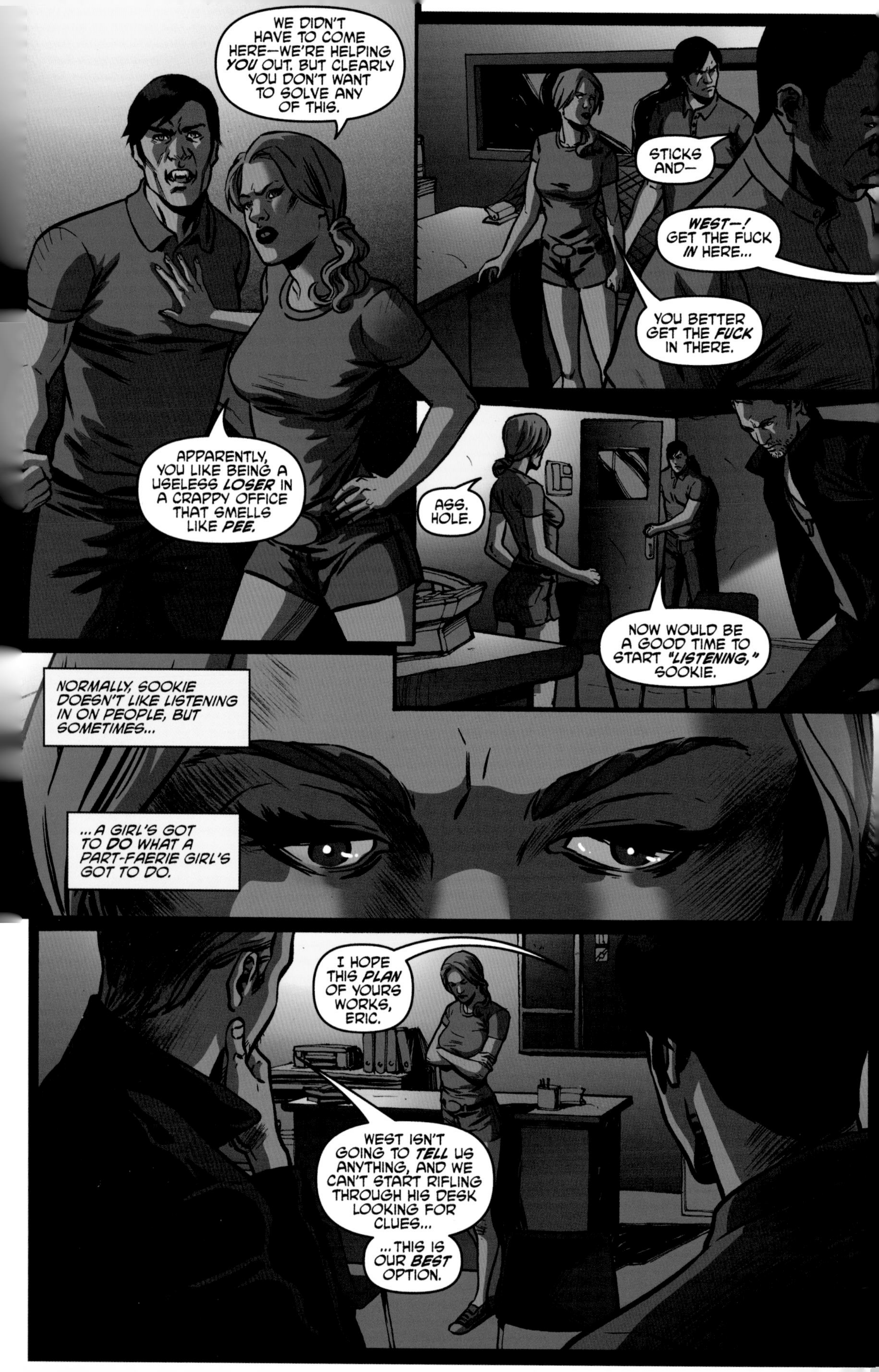
WE DIDN'T HAVE TO COME HERE—WE'RE HELPING YOU OUT. BUT CLEARLY YOU DON'T WANT TO SOLVE ANY OF THIS.
APPARENTLY, YOU LIKE BEING A USELESS LOSER IN A CRAPPY OFFICE THAT SMELLS LIKE PEE.
STICKS AND—
WEST—! GET THE FUCK IN HERE...
YOU BETTER GET THE FUCK IN THERE.
ASS. HOLE.
NOW WOULD BE A GOOD TIME TO START "LISTENING," SOOKIE.
NORMALLY, SOOKIE DOESN'T LIKE LISTENING IN ON PEOPLE, BUT SOMETIMES...
...A GIRL'S GOT TO DO WHAT A PART-FAERIE GIRL'S GOT TO DO.
I HOPE THIS PLAN OF YOURS WORKS, ERIC.
WEST ISN'T GOING TO TELL US ANYTHING, AND WE CAN'T START RIFLING THROUGH HIS DESK LOOKING FOR CLUES...
...THIS IS OUR BEST OPTION.

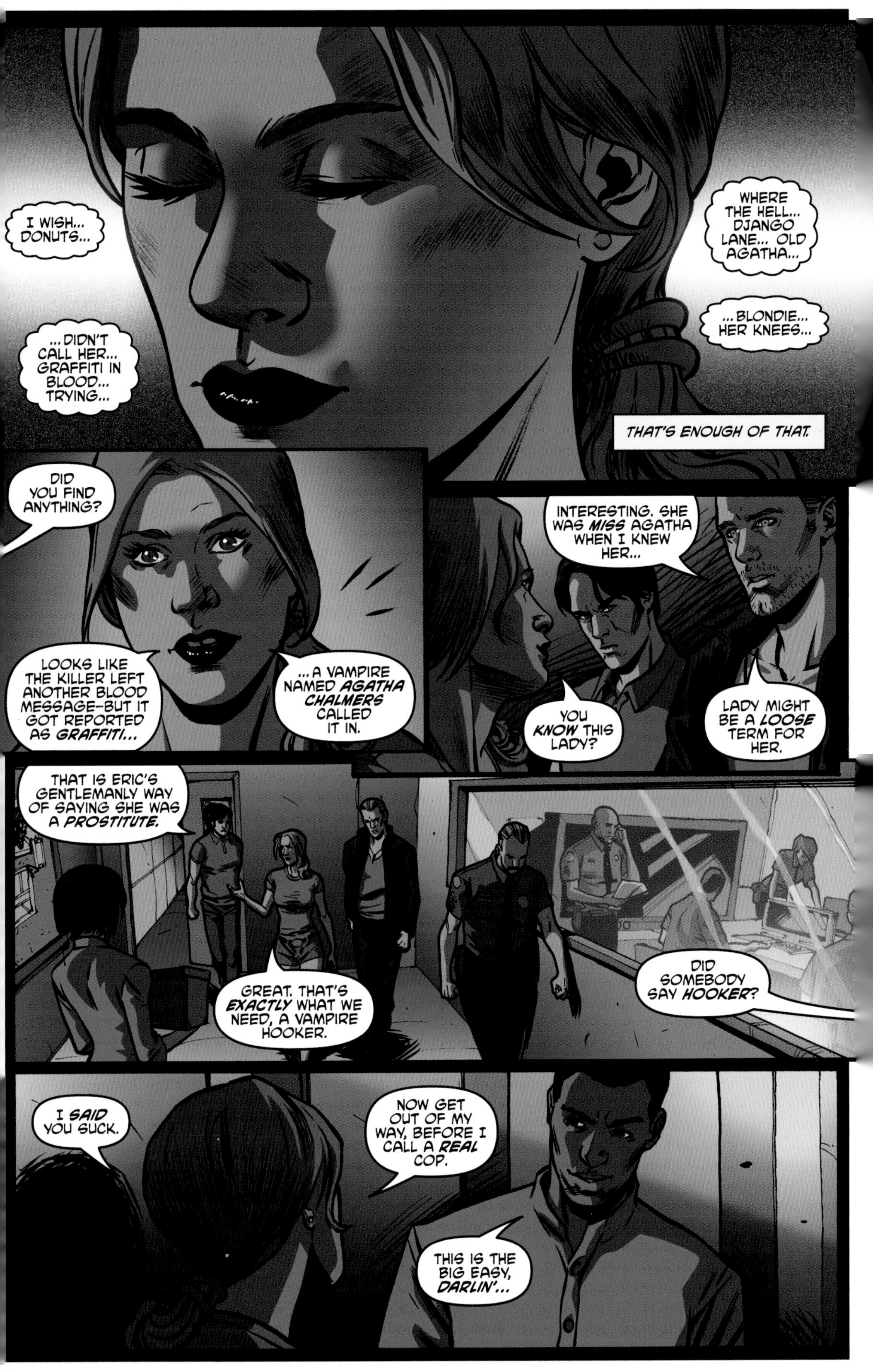
I WISH... DONUTS...
...DIDN'T CALL HER... GRAFFITI IN BLOOD... TRYING...
WHERE THE HELL... DJANGO LANE... OLD AGATHA...
...BLONDIE... HER KNEES...
THAT'S ENOUGH OF THAT.
DID YOU FIND ANYTHING?
LOOKS LIKE THE KILLER LEFT ANOTHER BLOOD MESSAGE--BUT IT GOT REPORTED AS GRAFFITI...
...A VAMPIRE NAMED AGATHA CHALMERS CALLED IT IN.
INTERESTING. SHE WAS MISS AGATHA WHEN I KNEW HER...
YOU KNOW THIS LADY?
LADY MIGHT BE A LOOSE TERM FOR HER.
THAT IS ERIC'S GENTLEMANLY WAY OF SAYING SHE WAS A PROSTITUTE.
GREAT. THAT'S EXACTLY WHAT WE NEED, A VAMPIRE HOOKER.
DID SOMEBODY SAY HOOKER?
I SAID YOU SUCK.
NOW GET OUT OF MY WAY, BEFORE I CALL A REAL COP.
THIS IS THE BIG EASY, DARLIN'...

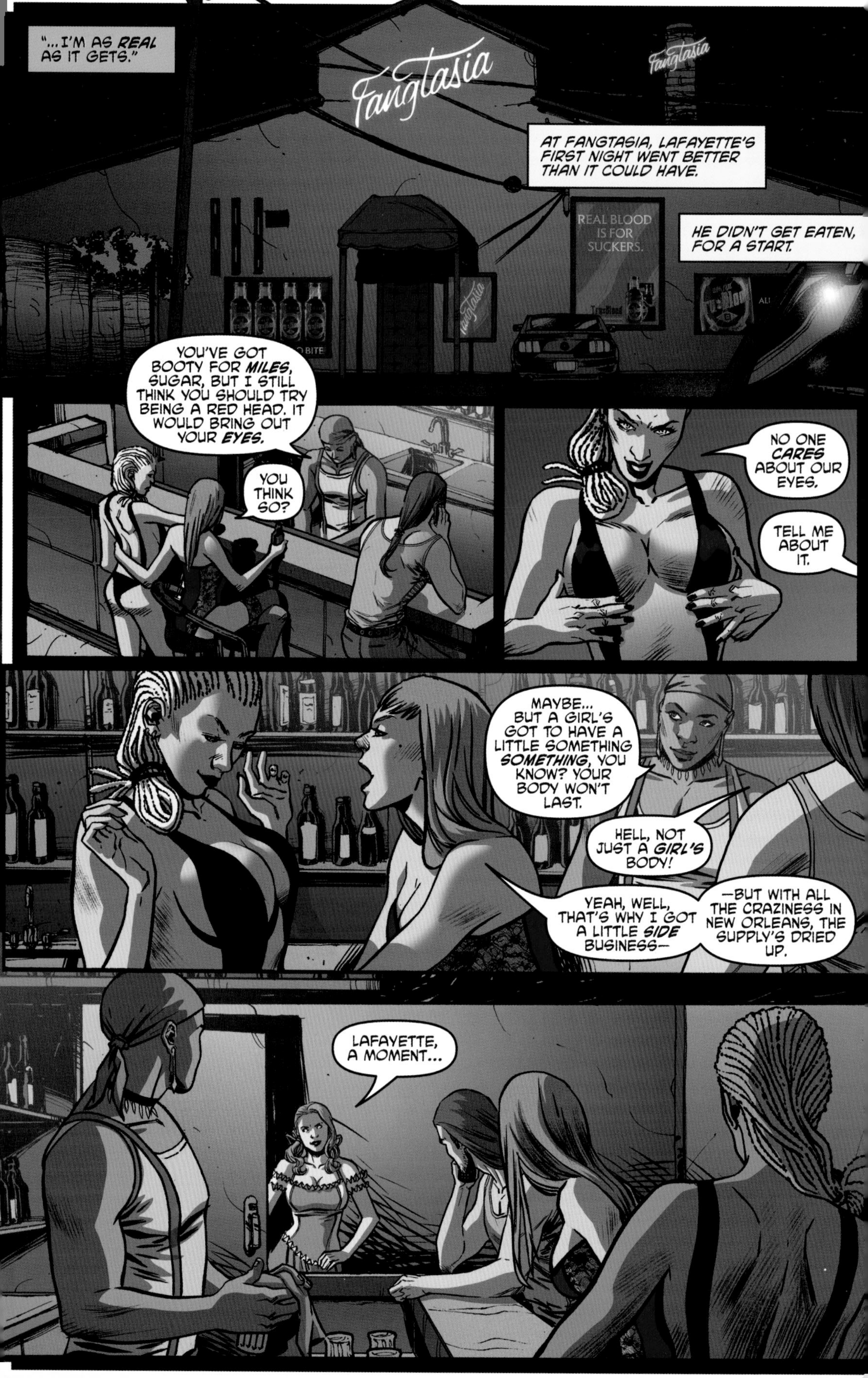
"...I'M AS REAL AS IT GETS."
Fangtasia
Fangtasia
AT FANGTASIA, LAFAYETTE'S FIRST NIGHT WENT BETTER THAN IT COULD HAVE.
REAL BLOOD IS FOR SUCKERS.
HE DIDN'T GET EATEN, FOR A START.
YOU'VE GOT BOOTY FOR MILES, SUGAR, BUT I STILL THINK YOU SHOULD TRY BEING A RED HEAD. IT WOULD BRING OUT YOUR EYES.
YOU THINK SO?
NO ONE CARES ABOUT OUR EYES.
TELL ME ABOUT IT.
MAYBE... BUT A GIRL'S GOT TO HAVE A LITTLE SOMETHING SOMETHING, YOU KNOW? YOUR BODY WON'T LAST.
HELL, NOT JUST A GIRL'S BODY!
YEAH, WELL, THAT'S WHY I GOT A LITTLE SIDE BUSINESS—
—BUT WITH ALL THE CRAZINESS IN NEW ORLEANS, THE SUPPLY'S DRIED UP.
LAFAYETTE, A MOMENT...

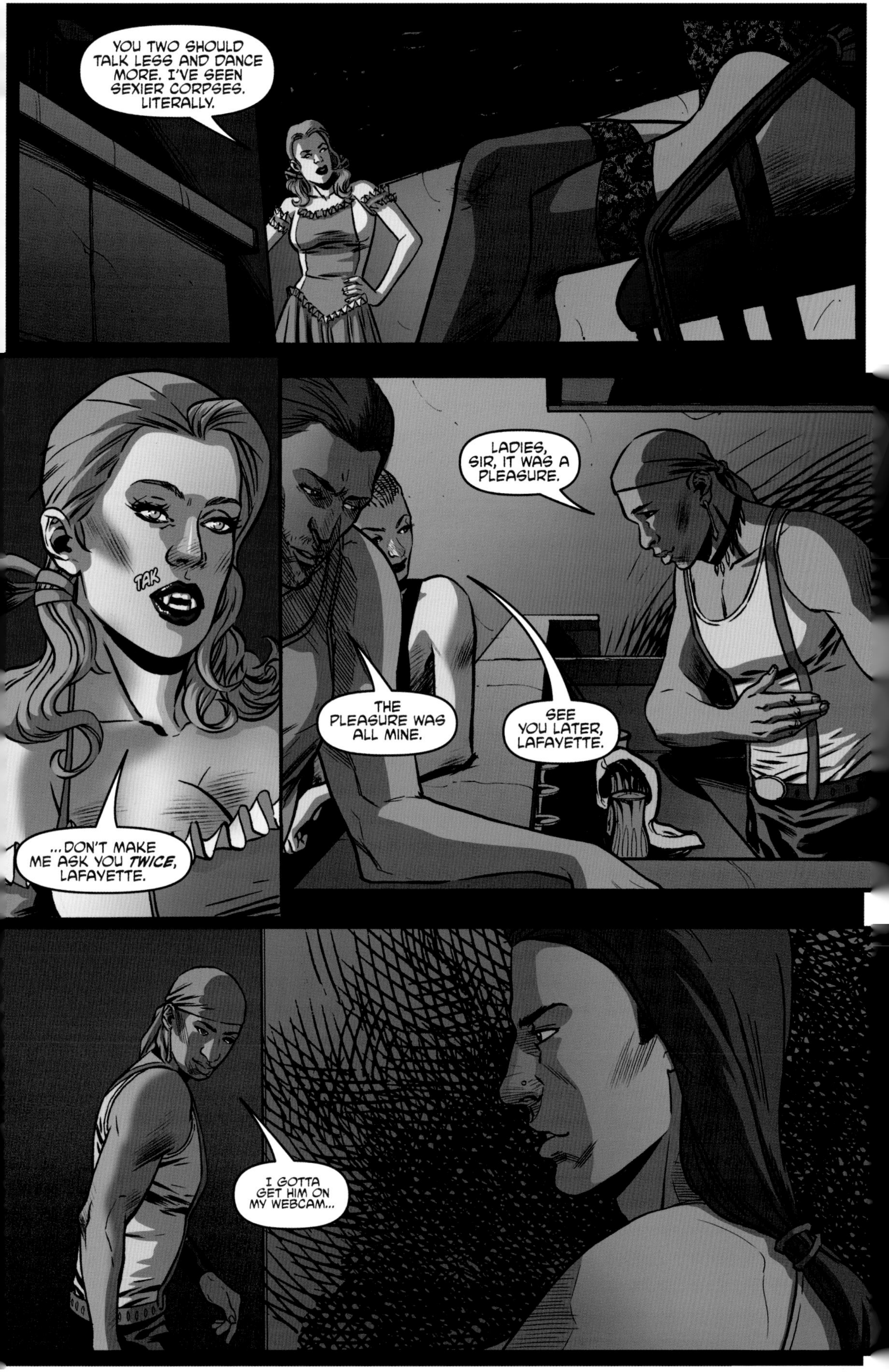

YOU TWO SHOULD TALK LESS AND DANCE MORE. I'VE SEEN SEXIER CORPSES. LITERALLY.
TAK
...DON'T MAKE ME ASK YOU *TWICE*, LAFAYETTE.
LADIES, SIR, IT WAS A PLEASURE.
THE PLEASURE WAS ALL MINE.
SEE YOU LATER, LAFAYETTE.
I GOTTA GET HIM ON MY WEBCAM...

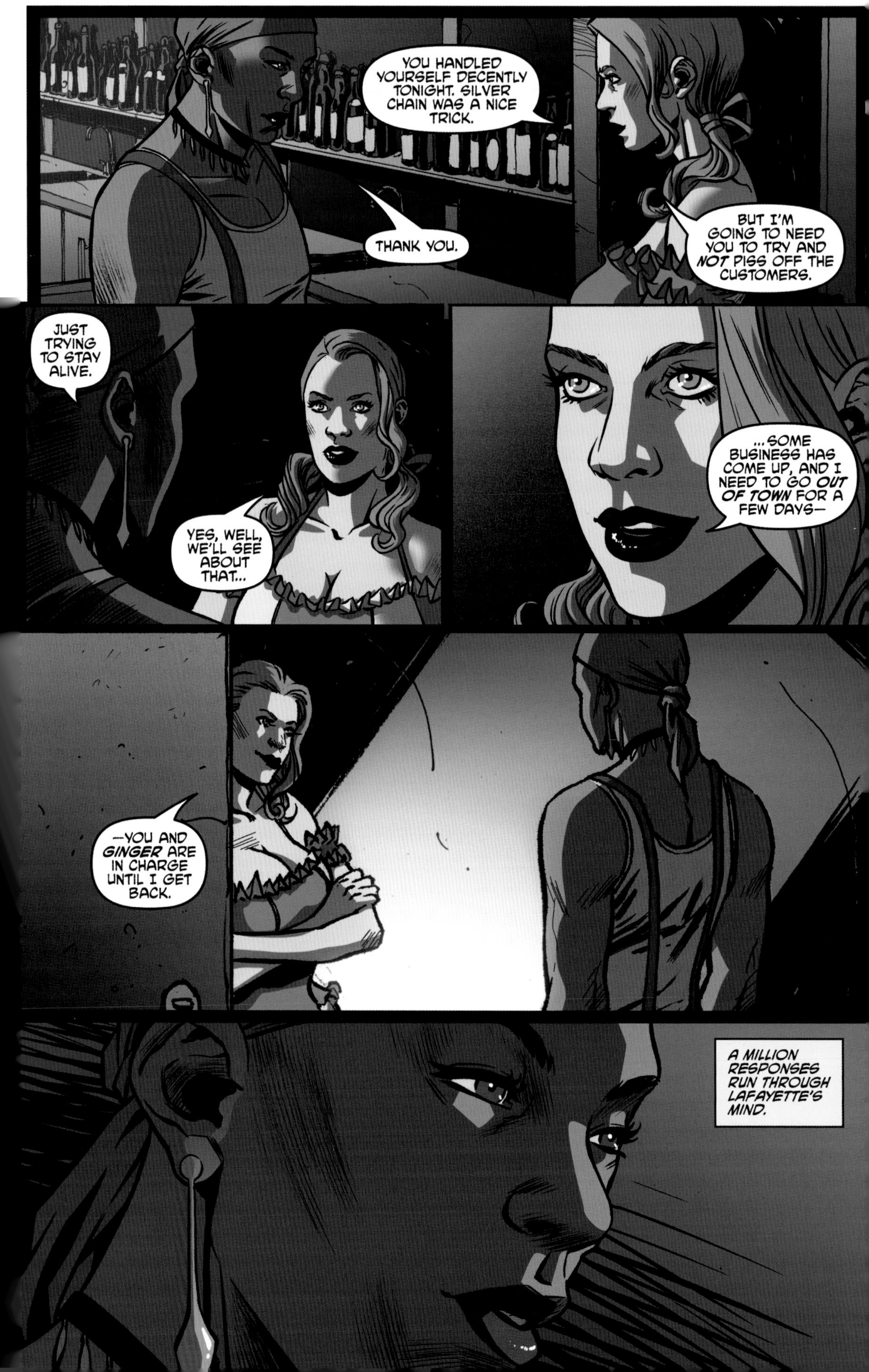
YOU HANDLED YOURSELF DECENTLY TONIGHT. SILVER CHAIN WAS A NICE TRICK.
THANK YOU.
BUT I'M GOING TO NEED YOU TO TRY AND *NOT* PISS OFF THE CUSTOMERS.
JUST TRYING TO STAY ALIVE.
YES, WELL, WE'LL SEE ABOUT THAT...
...SOME BUSINESS HAS COME UP, AND I NEED TO GO *OUT OF TOWN* FOR A FEW DAYS—
—YOU AND *GINGER* ARE IN CHARGE UNTIL I GET BACK.
*A MILLION RESPONSES RUN THROUGH LAFAYETTE'S MIND.*

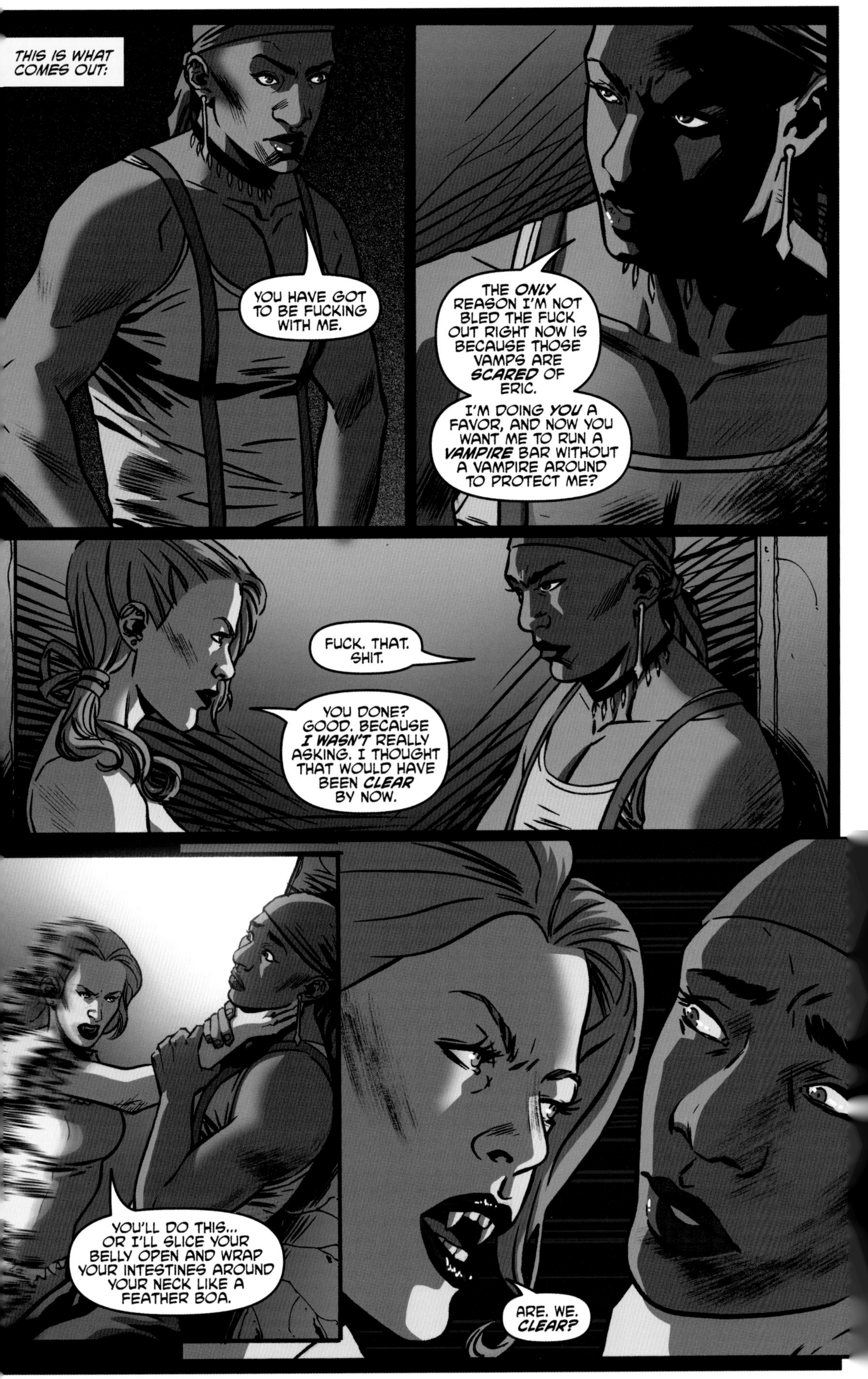
THIS IS WHAT COMES OUT:
YOU HAVE GOT TO BE FUCKING WITH ME.
THE *ONLY* REASON I'M NOT BLED THE FUCK OUT RIGHT NOW IS BECAUSE THOSE VAMPS ARE *SCARED* OF ERIC.
I'M DOING *YOU* A FAVOR, AND NOW YOU WANT ME TO RUN A *VAMPIRE* BAR WITHOUT A VAMPIRE AROUND TO PROTECT ME?
FUCK. THAT. SHIT.
YOU DONE? GOOD. BECAUSE *I WASN'T* REALLY ASKING. I THOUGHT THAT WOULD HAVE BEEN *CLEAR* BY NOW.
YOU'LL DO THIS... OR I'LL SLICE YOUR BELLY OPEN AND WRAP YOUR INTESTINES AROUND YOUR NECK LIKE A FEATHER BOA.
ARE. WE. *CLEAR?*

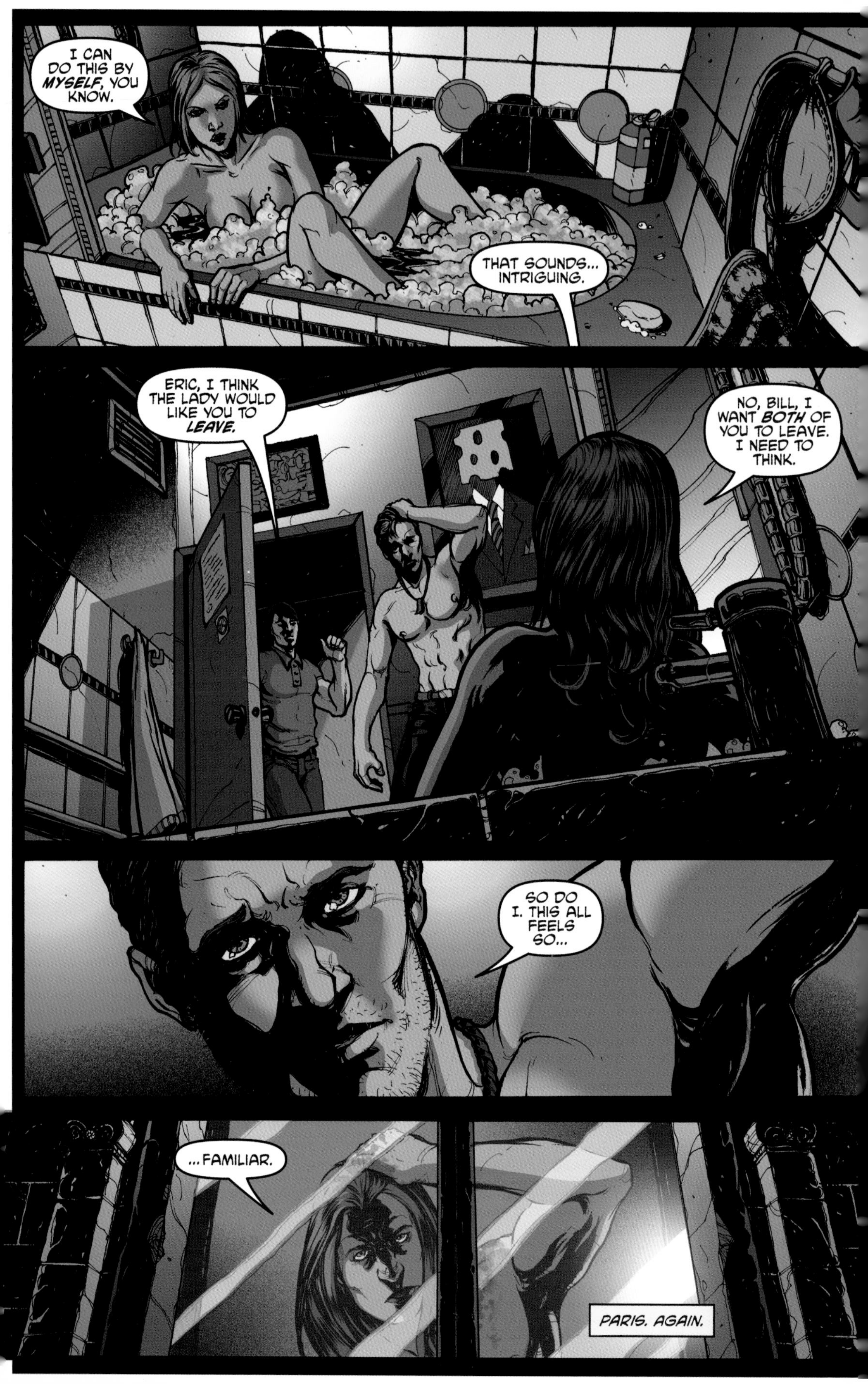
I CAN DO THIS BY *MYSELF*, YOU KNOW.
THAT SOUNDS... INTRIGUING.
ERIC, I THINK THE LADY WOULD LIKE YOU TO *LEAVE.*
NO, BILL, I WANT *BOTH* OF YOU TO LEAVE. I NEED TO THINK.
SO DO I. THIS ALL FEELS SO...
...FAMILIAR.
PARIS. AGAIN.

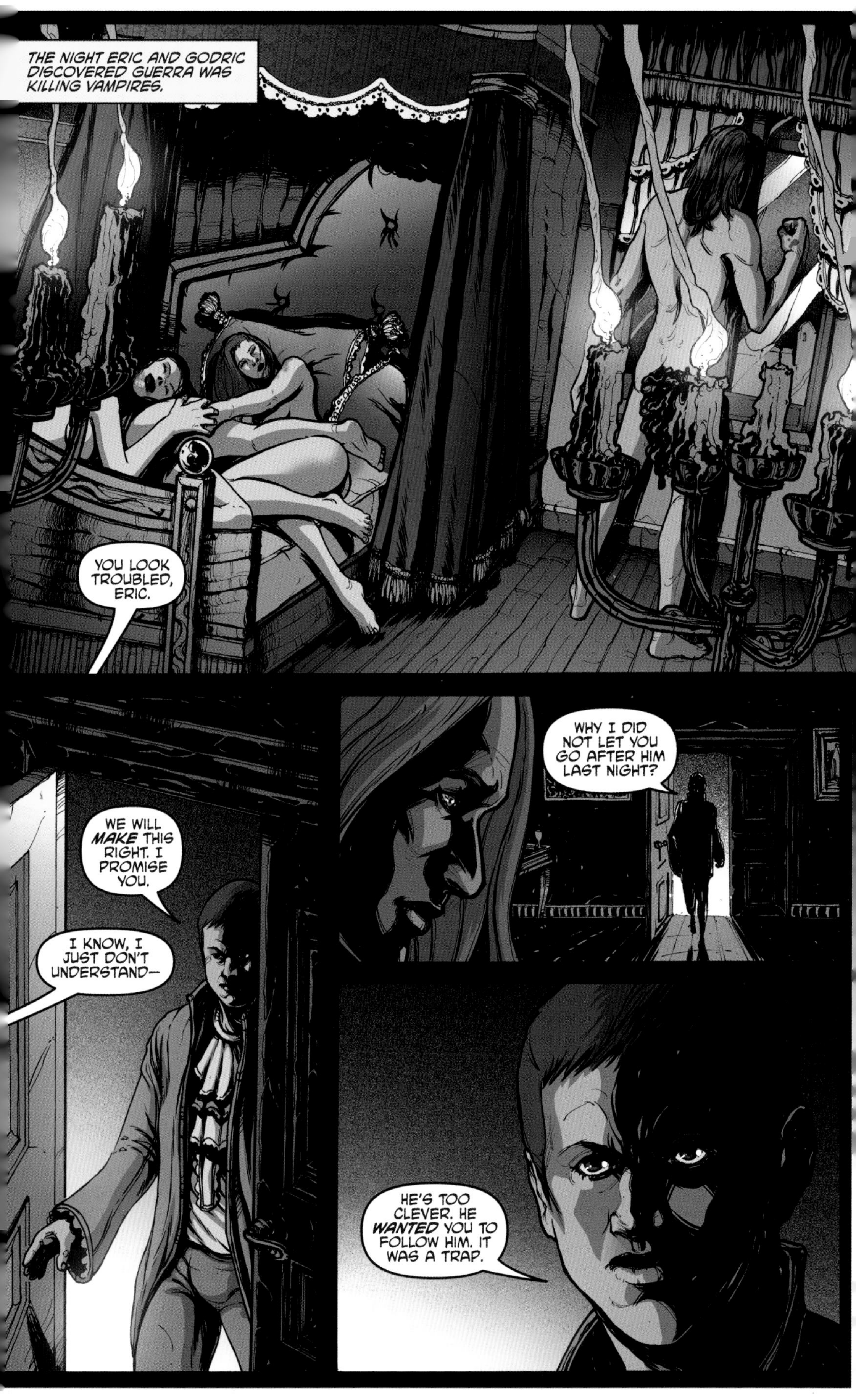
THE NIGHT ERIC AND GODRIC DISCOVERED GUERRA WAS KILLING VAMPIRES.
YOU LOOK TROUBLED, ERIC.
WE WILL *MAKE* THIS RIGHT. I PROMISE YOU.
I KNOW, I JUST DON'T UNDERSTAND—
WHY I DID NOT LET YOU GO AFTER HIM LAST NIGHT?
HE'S TOO CLEVER. HE *WANTED* YOU TO FOLLOW HIM. IT WAS A TRAP.

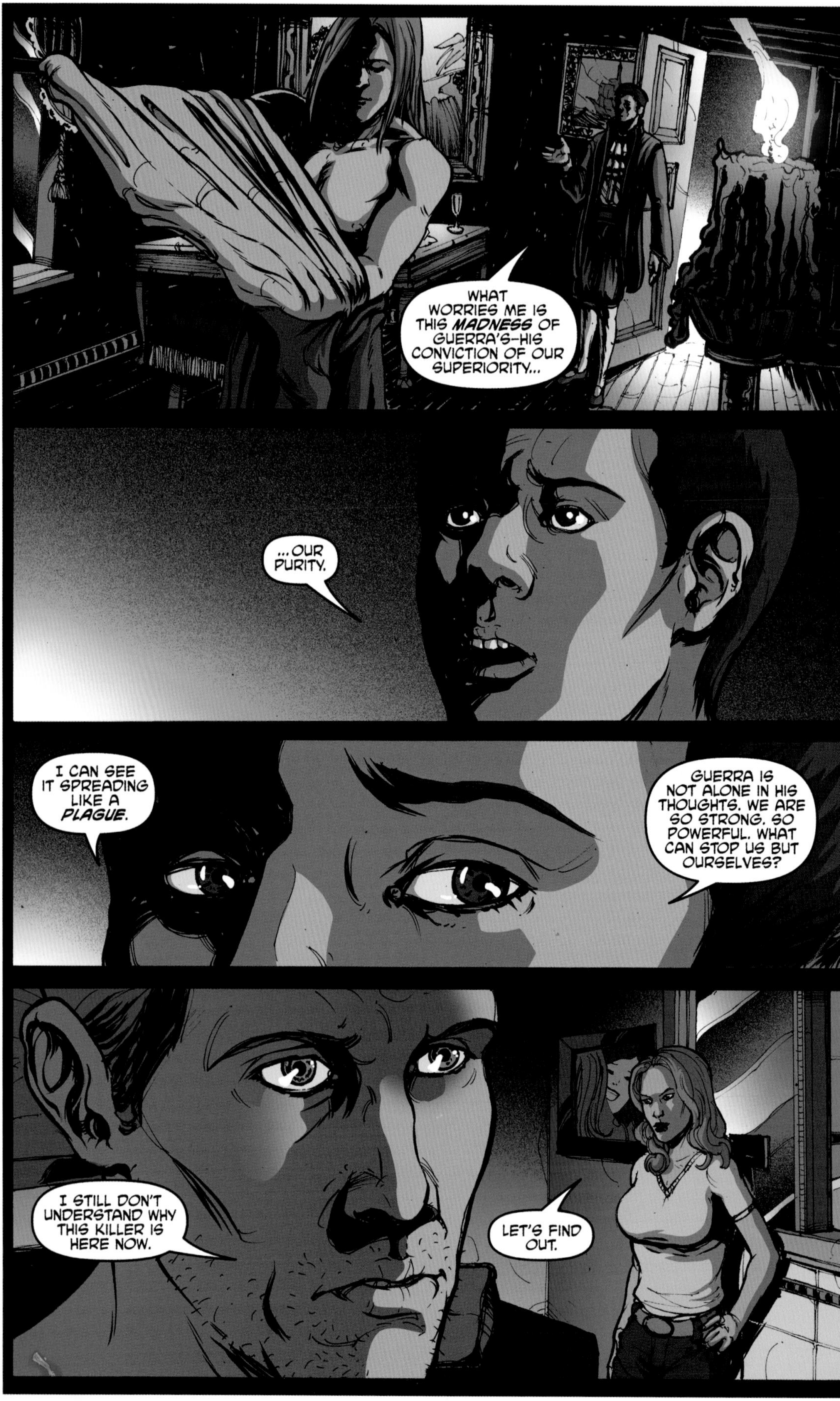
WHAT WORRIES ME IS THIS MADNESS OF GUERRA'S–HIS CONVICTION OF OUR SUPERIORITY...
...OUR PURITY.
I CAN SEE IT SPREADING LIKE A PLAGUE.
GUERRA IS NOT ALONE IN HIS THOUGHTS. WE ARE SO STRONG. SO POWERFUL. WHAT CAN STOP US BUT OURSELVES?
I STILL DON'T UNDERSTAND WHY THIS KILLER IS HERE NOW.
LET'S FIND OUT.

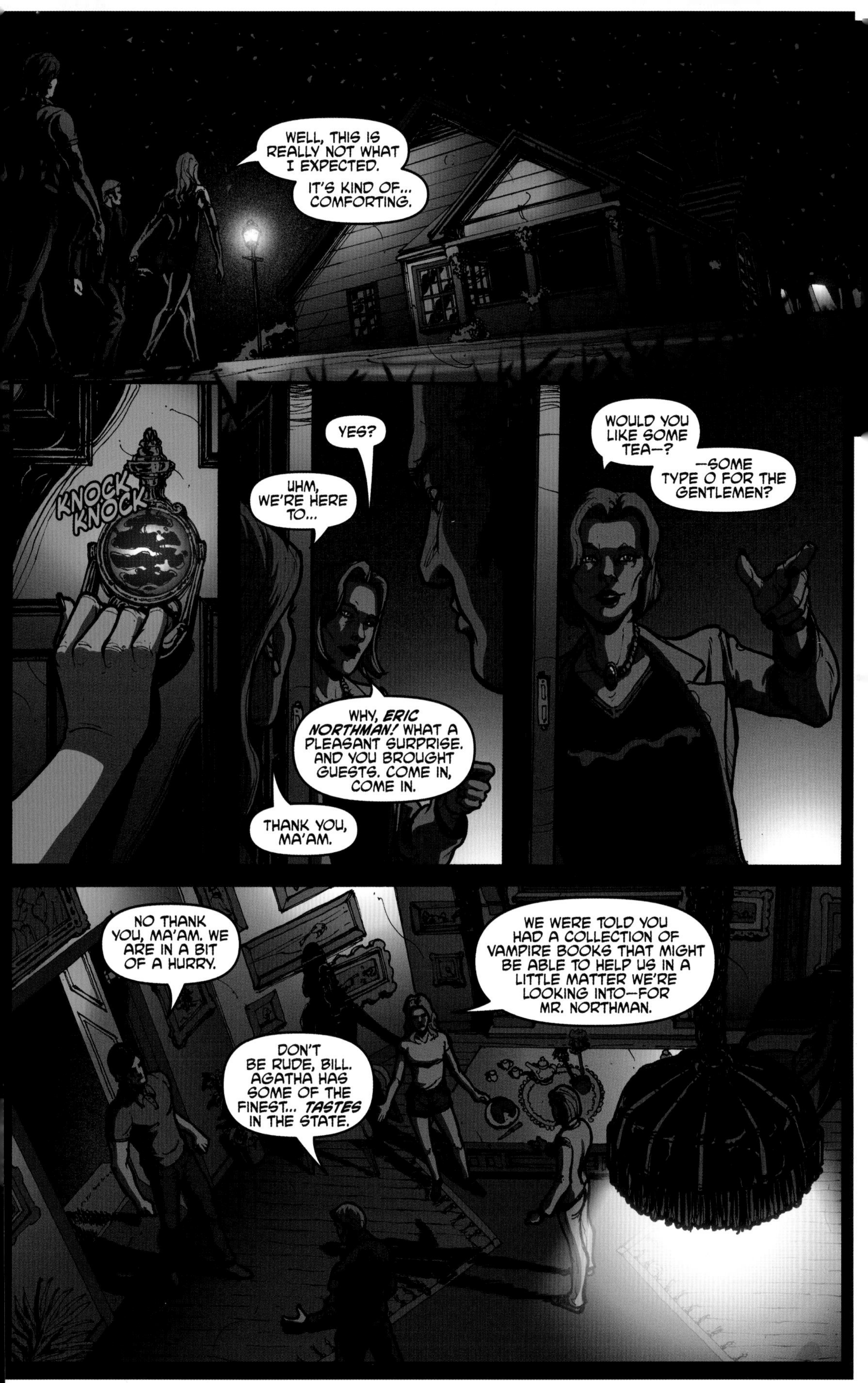
WELL, THIS IS REALLY NOT WHAT I EXPECTED.
IT'S KIND OF... COMFORTING.
KNOCK KNOCK
YES?
UHM, WE'RE HERE TO...
WHY, *ERIC NORTHMAN!* WHAT A PLEASANT SURPRISE. AND YOU BROUGHT GUESTS. COME IN, COME IN.
THANK YOU, MA'AM.
WOULD YOU LIKE SOME TEA--?
--SOME TYPE O FOR THE GENTLEMEN?
NO THANK YOU, MA'AM. WE ARE IN A BIT OF A HURRY.
WE WERE TOLD YOU HAD A COLLECTION OF VAMPIRE BOOKS THAT MIGHT BE ABLE TO HELP US IN A LITTLE MATTER WE'RE LOOKING INTO--FOR MR. NORTHMAN.
DON'T BE RUDE, BILL. AGATHA HAS SOME OF THE FINEST... *TASTES* IN THE STATE.

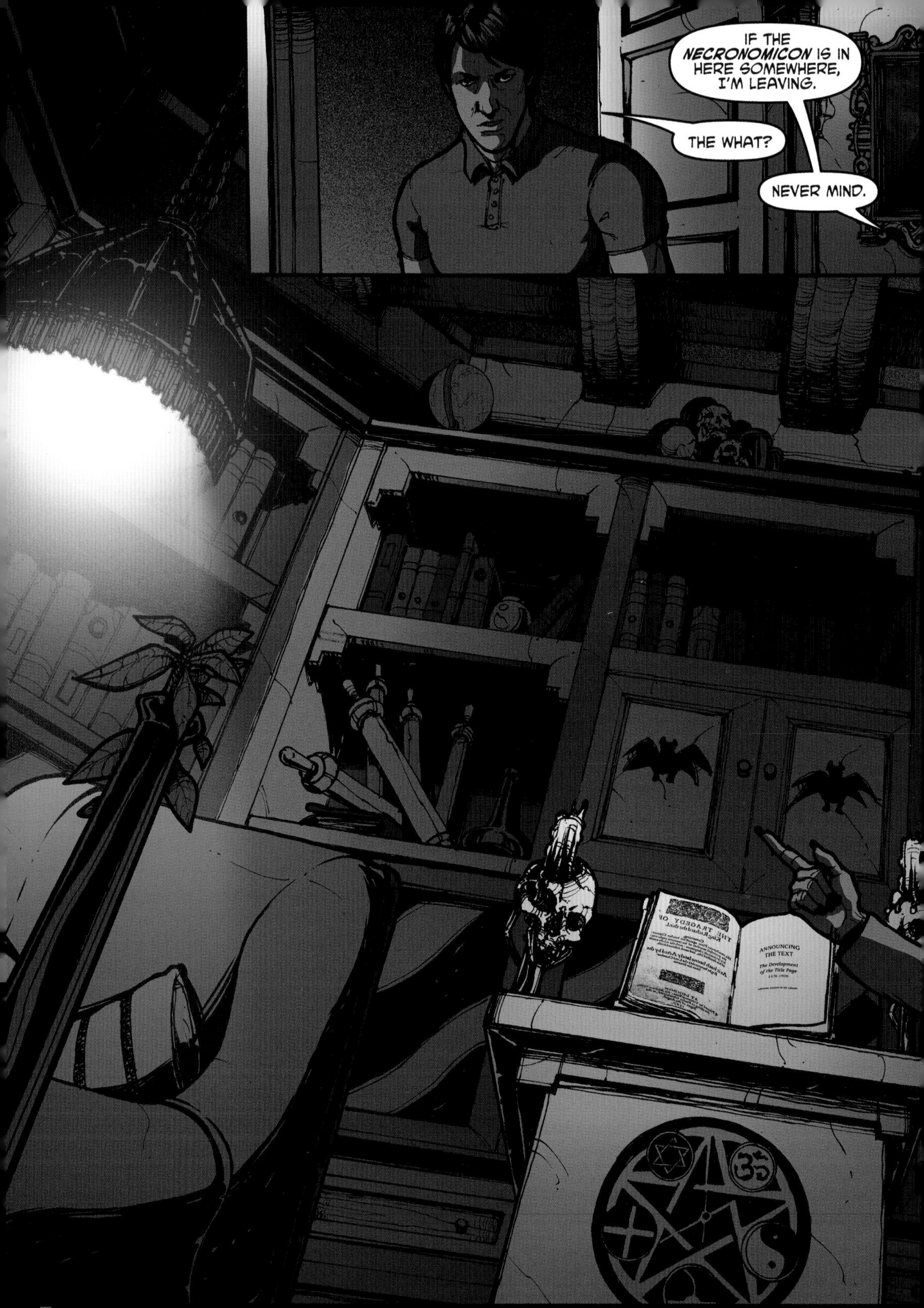
IF THE NECRONOMICON IS IN HERE SOMEWHERE, I'M LEAVING.
THE WHAT?
NEVER MIND.
ANNOUNCING THE TEXT
The Development of the Title Page

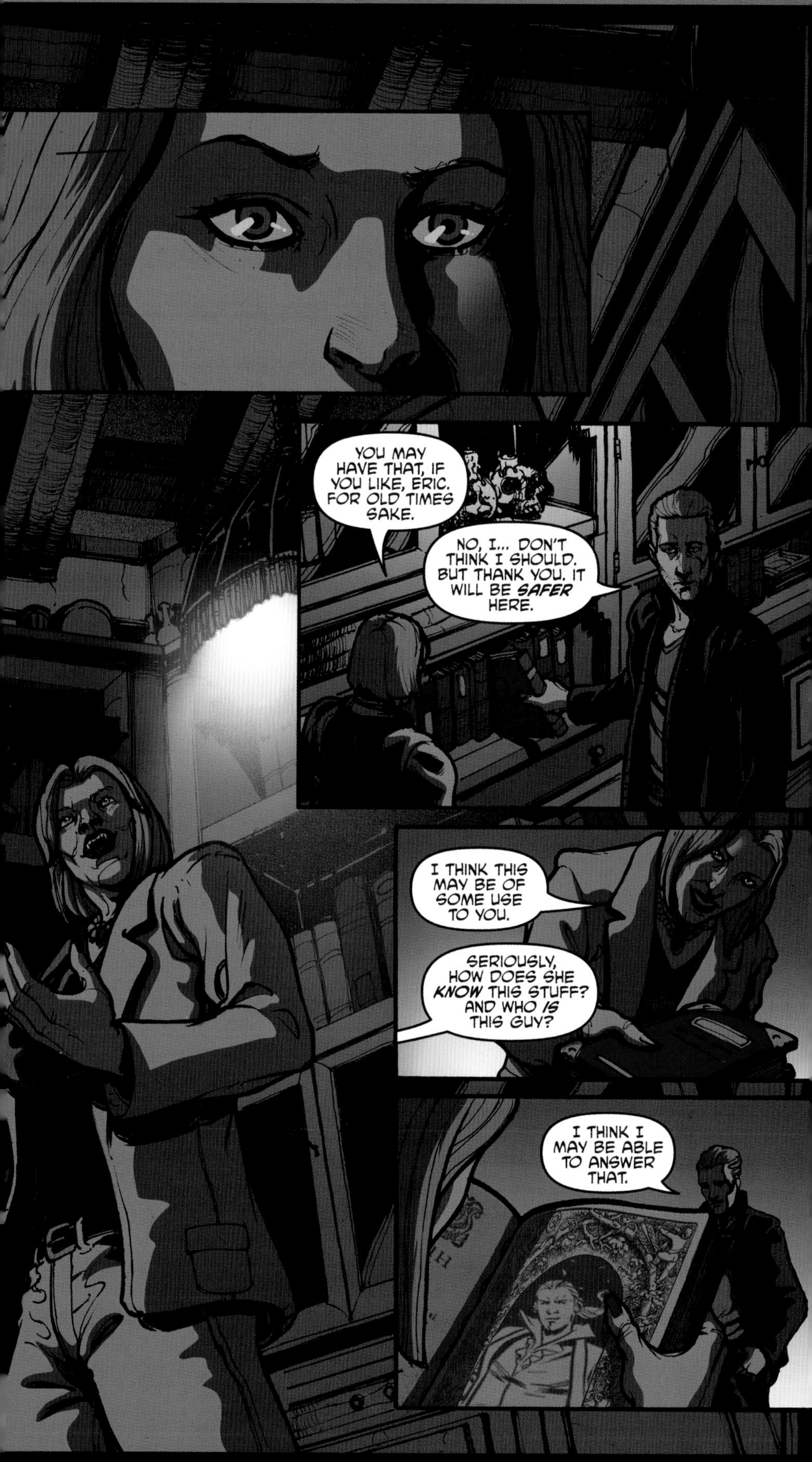
YOU MAY HAVE THAT, IF YOU LIKE, ERIC. FOR OLD TIMES SAKE.
NO, I... DON'T THINK I SHOULD. BUT THANK YOU. IT WILL BE *SAFER* HERE.
I THINK THIS MAY BE OF SOME USE TO YOU.
SERIOUSLY, HOW DOES SHE *KNOW* THIS STUFF? AND WHO *IS* THIS GUY?
I THINK I MAY BE ABLE TO ANSWER THAT.

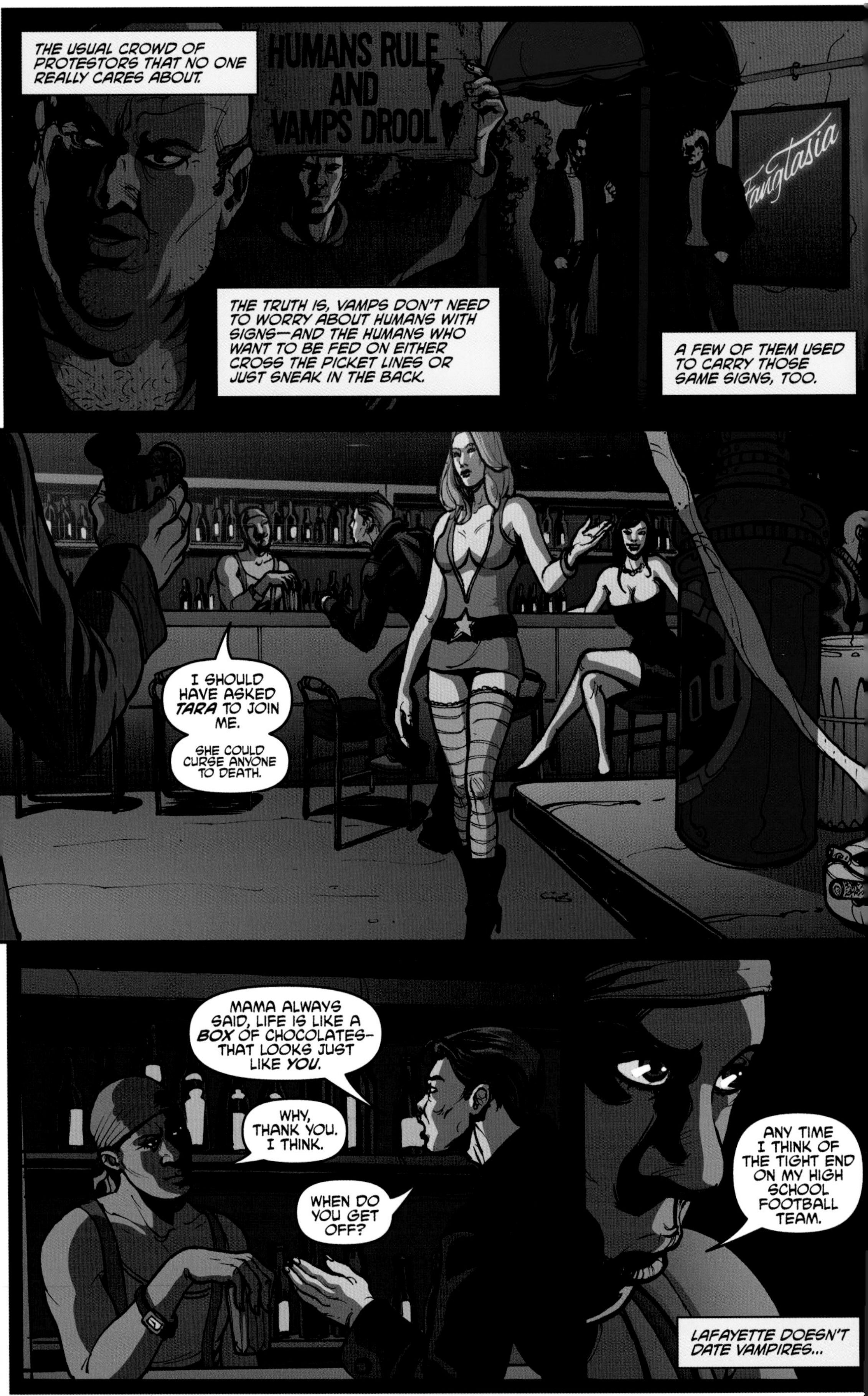
THE USUAL CROWD OF PROTESTORS THAT NO ONE REALLY CARES ABOUT.
HUMANS RULE AND VAMPS DROOL
Fangtasia
THE TRUTH IS, VAMPS DON'T NEED TO WORRY ABOUT HUMANS WITH SIGNS—AND THE HUMANS WHO WANT TO BE FED ON EITHER CROSS THE PICKET LINES OR JUST SNEAK IN THE BACK.
A FEW OF THEM USED TO CARRY THOSE SAME SIGNS, TOO.
I SHOULD HAVE ASKED TARA TO JOIN ME.
SHE COULD CURSE ANYONE TO DEATH.
MAMA ALWAYS SAID, LIFE IS LIKE A BOX OF CHOCOLATES-THAT LOOKS JUST LIKE YOU.
WHY, THANK YOU. I THINK.
WHEN DO YOU GET OFF?
ANY TIME I THINK OF THE TIGHT END ON MY HIGH SCHOOL FOOTBALL TEAM.
LAFAYETTE DOESN'T DATE VAMPIRES...

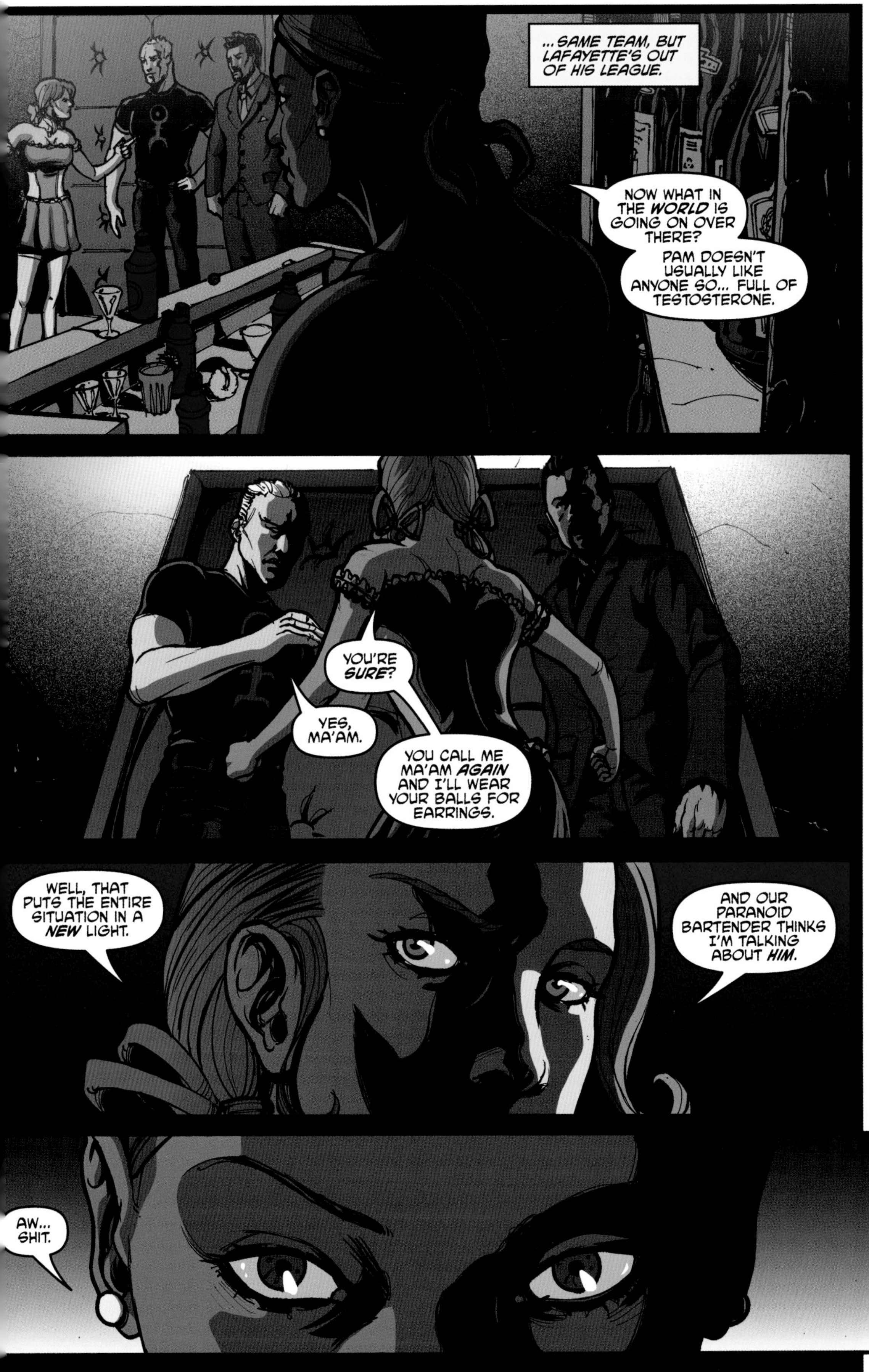
...SAME TEAM, BUT LAFAYETTE'S OUT OF HIS LEAGUE.
NOW WHAT IN THE WORLD IS GOING ON OVER THERE?
PAM DOESN'T USUALLY LIKE ANYONE SO... FULL OF TESTOSTERONE.
YOU'RE SURE?
YES, MA'AM.
YOU CALL ME MA'AM AGAIN AND I'LL WEAR YOUR BALLS FOR EARRINGS.
WELL, THAT PUTS THE ENTIRE SITUATION IN A NEW LIGHT.
AND OUR PARANOID BARTENDER THINKS I'M TALKING ABOUT HIM.
AW... SHIT.

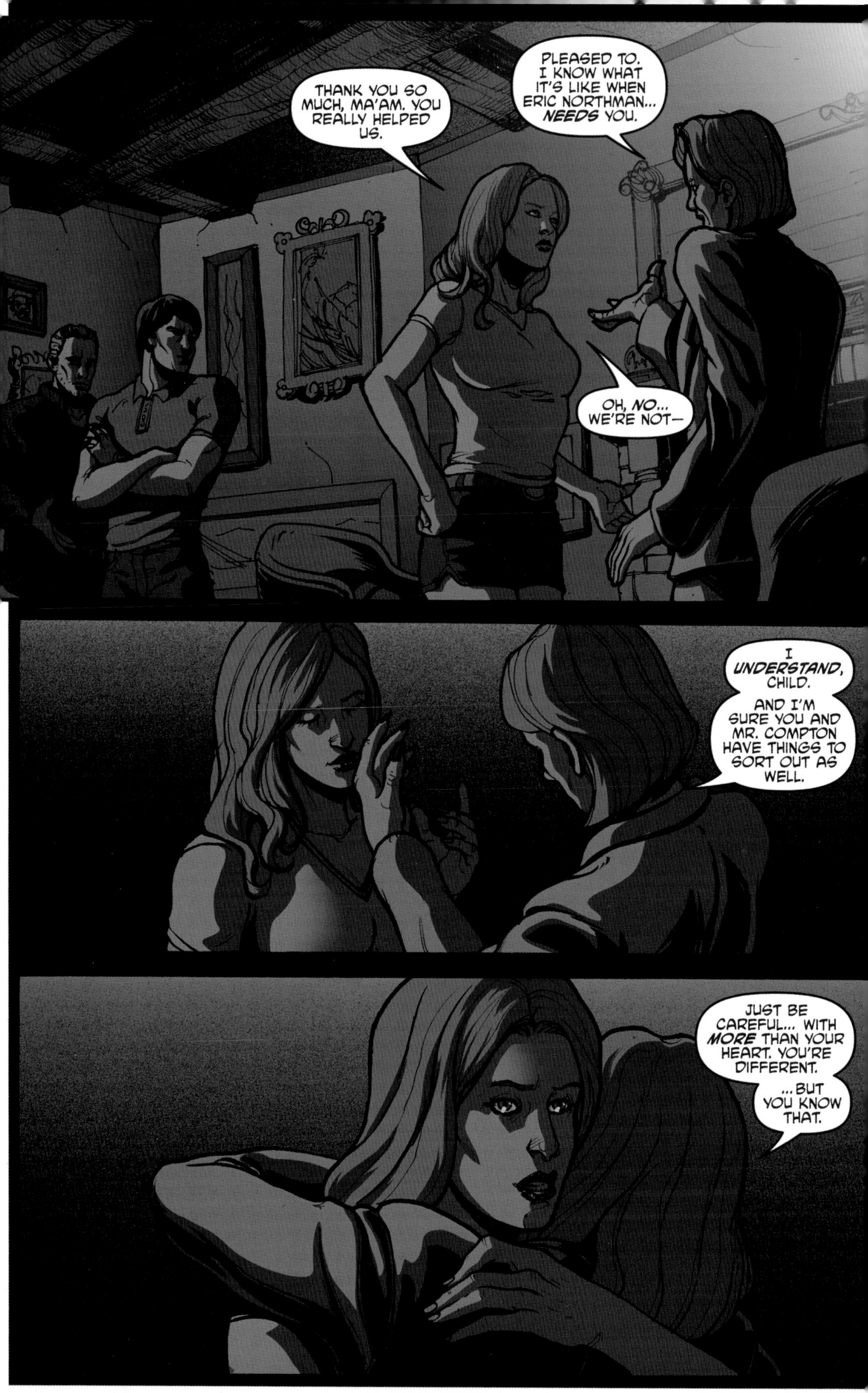
THANK YOU SO MUCH, MA'AM. YOU REALLY HELPED US.
PLEASED TO. I KNOW WHAT IT'S LIKE WHEN ERIC NORTHMAN... NEEDS YOU.
OH, NO... WE'RE NOT—
I UNDERSTAND, CHILD.
AND I'M SURE YOU AND MR. COMPTON HAVE THINGS TO SORT OUT AS WELL.
JUST BE CAREFUL... WITH MORE THAN YOUR HEART. YOU'RE DIFFERENT.
...BUT YOU KNOW THAT.

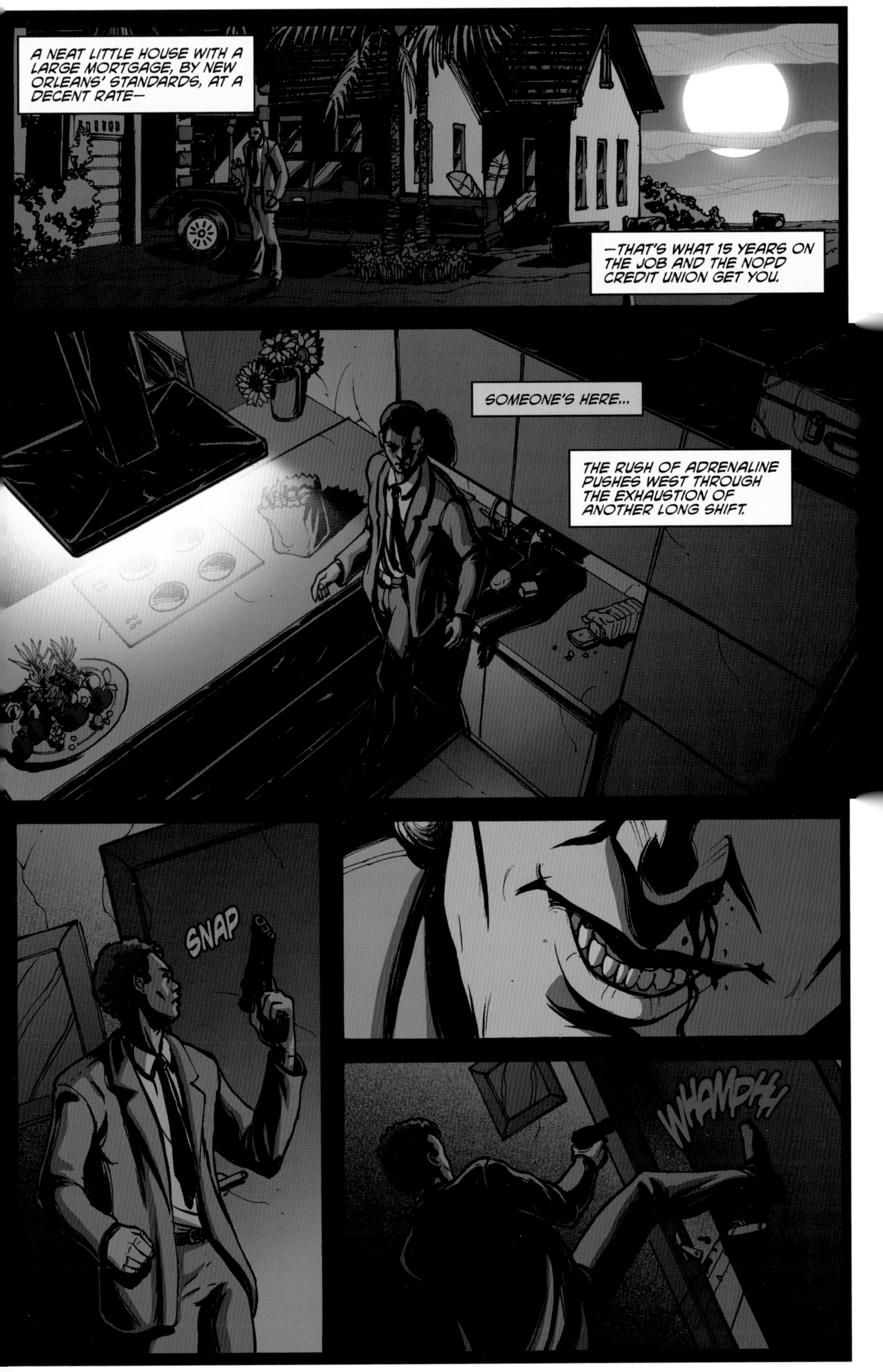
A NEAT LITTLE HOUSE WITH A LARGE MORTGAGE, BY NEW ORLEANS' STANDARDS, AT A DECENT RATE—
—THAT'S WHAT 15 YEARS ON THE JOB AND THE NOPD CREDIT UNION GET YOU.
SOMEONE'S HERE...
THE RUSH OF ADRENALINE PUSHES WEST THROUGH THE EXHAUSTION OF ANOTHER LONG SHIFT.
SNAP
WHAMPH

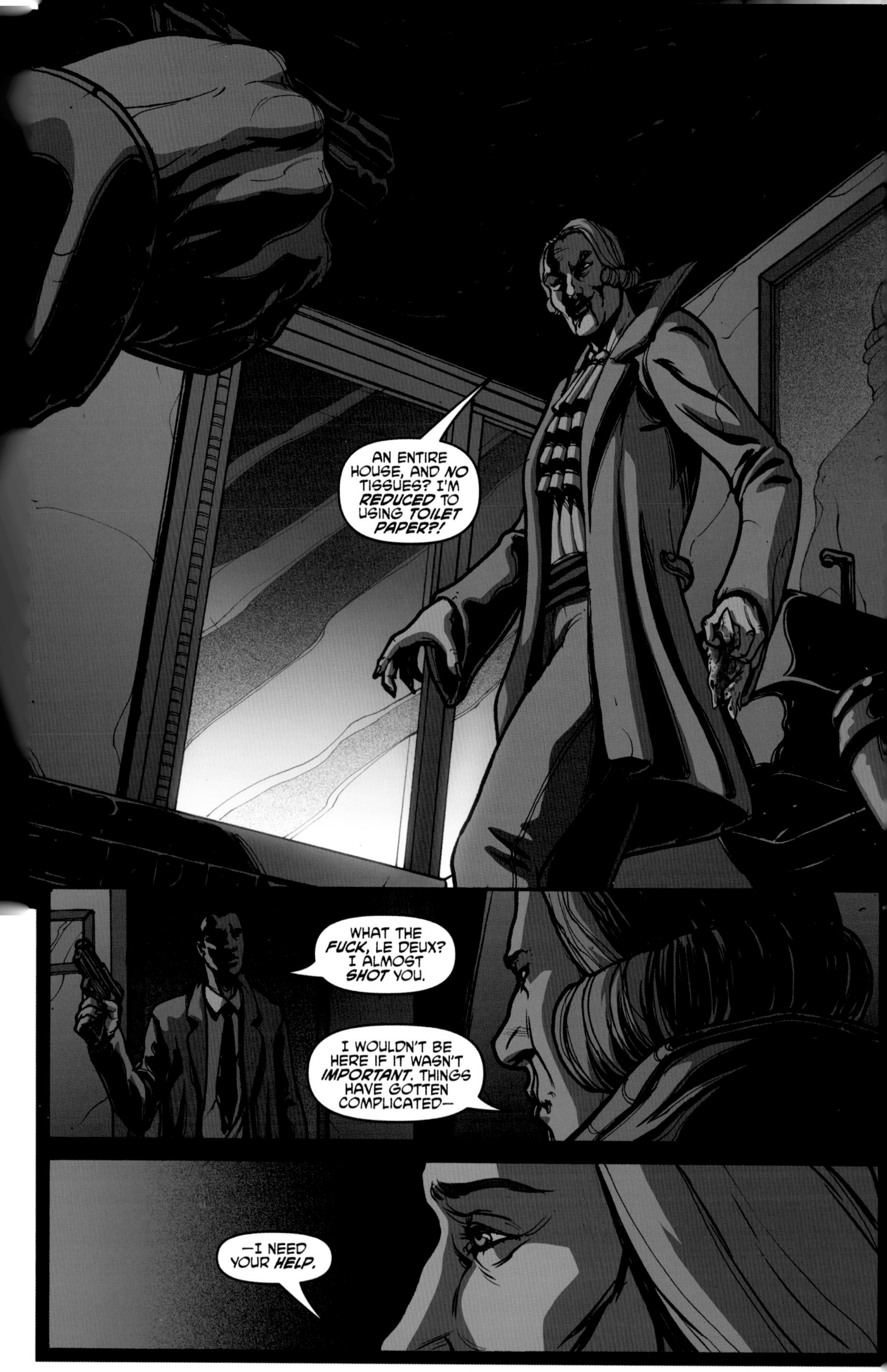
AN ENTIRE HOUSE, AND NO TISSUES? I'M REDUCED TO USING TOILET PAPER?!
WHAT THE FUCK, LE DEUX? I ALMOST SHOT YOU.
I WOULDN'T BE HERE IF IT WASN'T IMPORTANT. THINGS HAVE GOTTEN COMPLICATED—
—I NEED YOUR HELP.

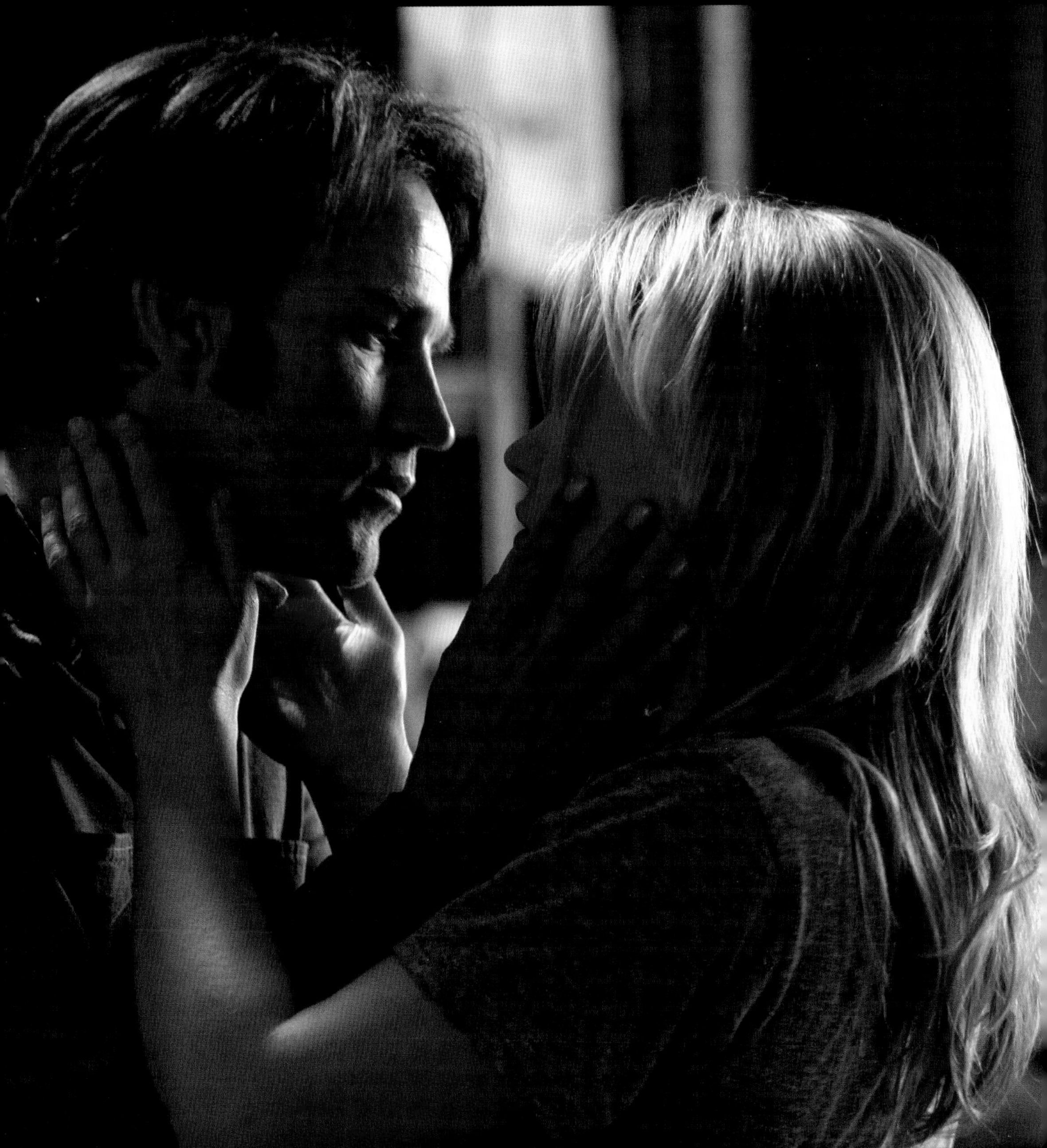

# CHAPTER 5

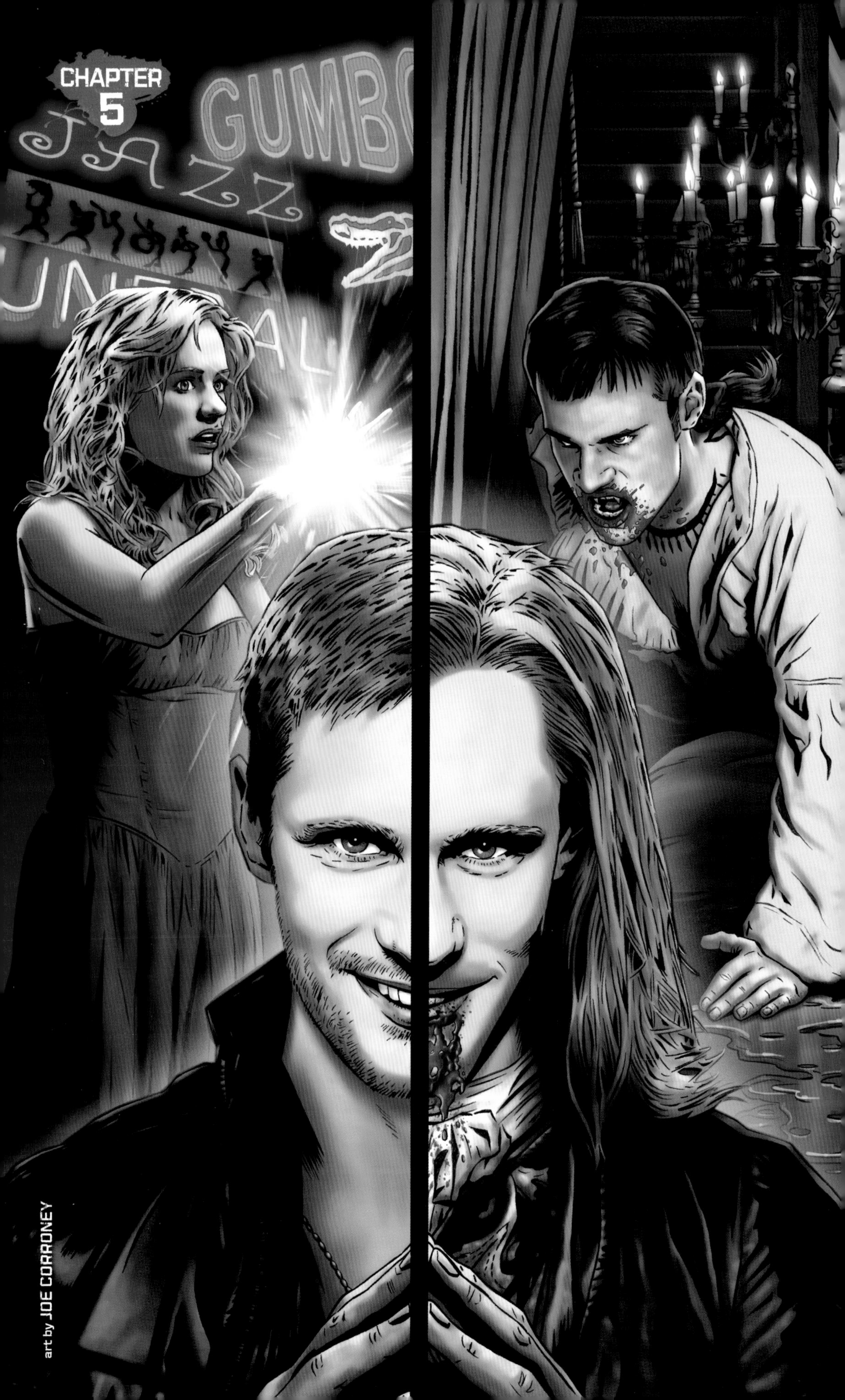
GUMBO
JAZZ
UNERAL

art by JOE CORRONEY

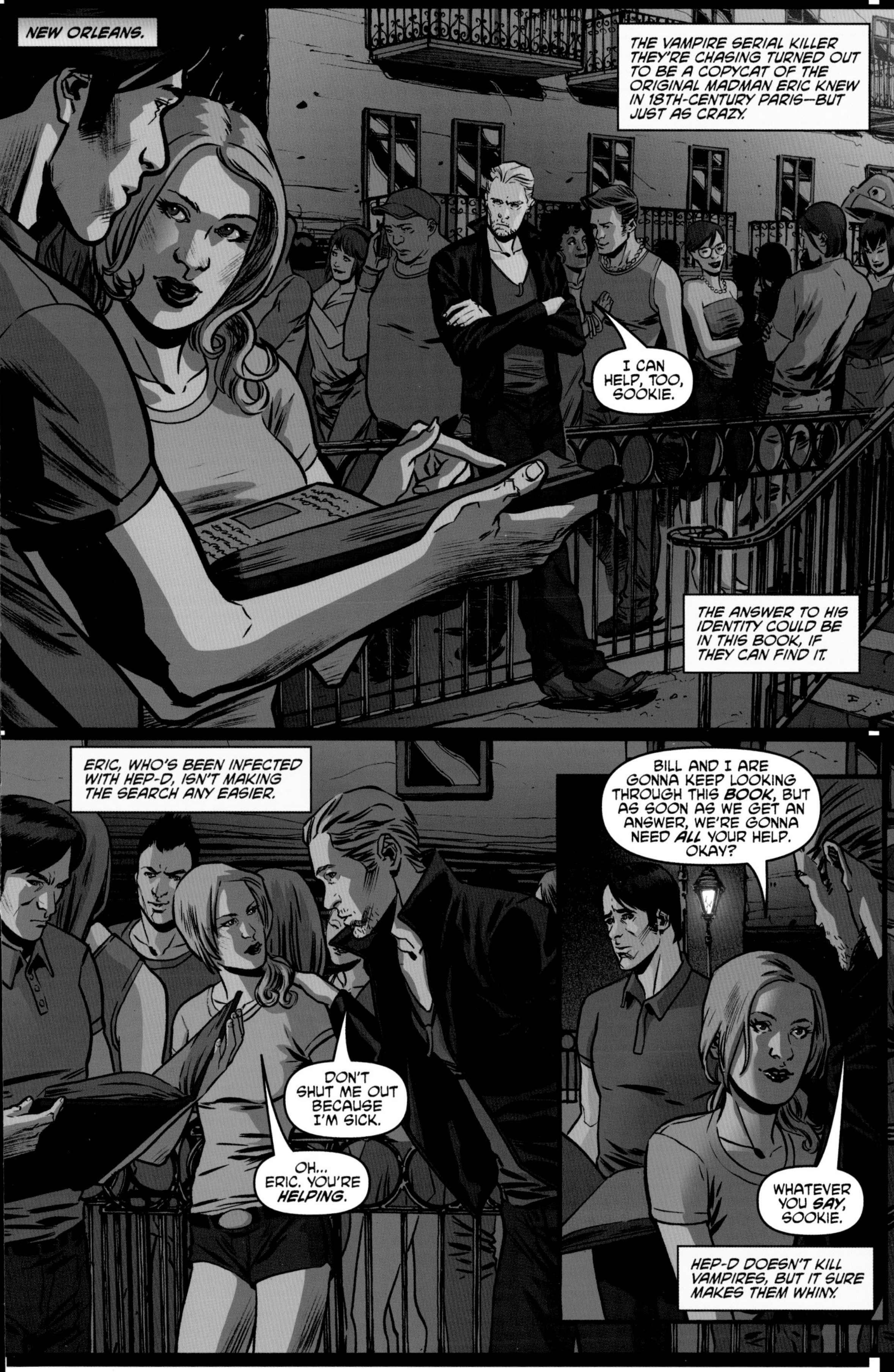
NEW ORLEANS.
THE VAMPIRE SERIAL KILLER THEY'RE CHASING TURNED OUT TO BE A COPYCAT OF THE ORIGINAL MADMAN ERIC KNEW IN 18TH-CENTURY PARIS--BUT JUST AS CRAZY.
I CAN HELP, TOO, SOOKIE.
THE ANSWER TO HIS IDENTITY COULD BE IN THIS BOOK, IF THEY CAN FIND IT.
ERIC, WHO'S BEEN INFECTED WITH HEP-D, ISN'T MAKING THE SEARCH ANY EASIER.
DON'T SHUT ME OUT BECAUSE I'M SICK.
OH... ERIC. YOU'RE *HELPING*.
BILL AND I ARE GONNA KEEP LOOKING THROUGH THIS *BOOK*, BUT AS SOON AS WE GET AN ANSWER, WE'RE GONNA NEED *ALL* YOUR HELP. OKAY?
WHATEVER YOU *SAY*, SOOKIE.
HEP-D DOESN'T KILL VAMPIRES, BUT IT SURE MAKES THEM WHINY.

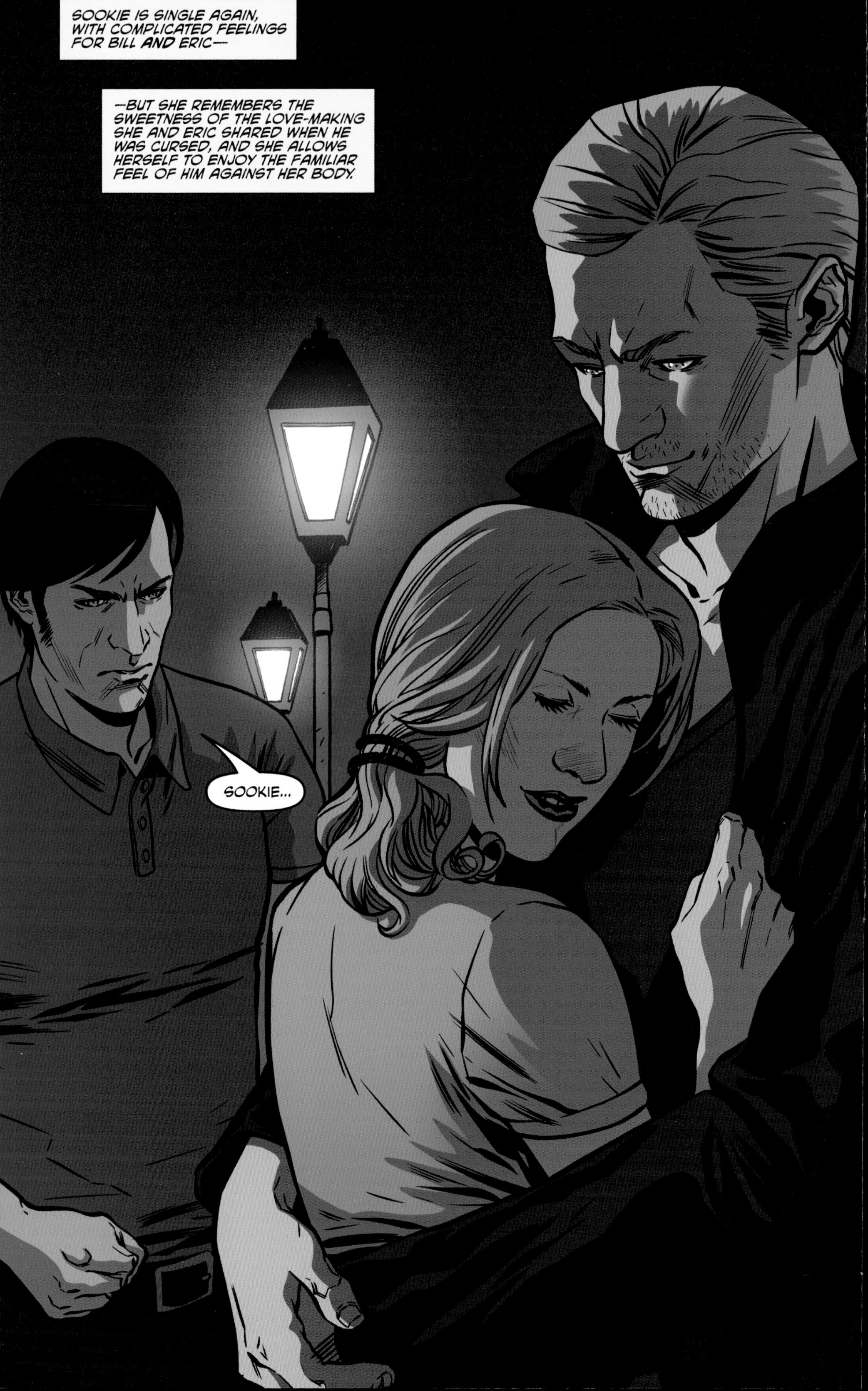
SOOKIE IS SINGLE AGAIN, WITH COMPLICATED FEELINGS FOR BILL **AND** ERIC—
—BUT SHE REMEMBERS THE SWEETNESS OF THE LOVE-MAKING SHE AND ERIC SHARED WHEN HE WAS CURSED, AND SHE ALLOWS HERSELF TO ENJOY THE FAMILIAR FEEL OF HIM AGAINST HER BODY.
SOOKIE...

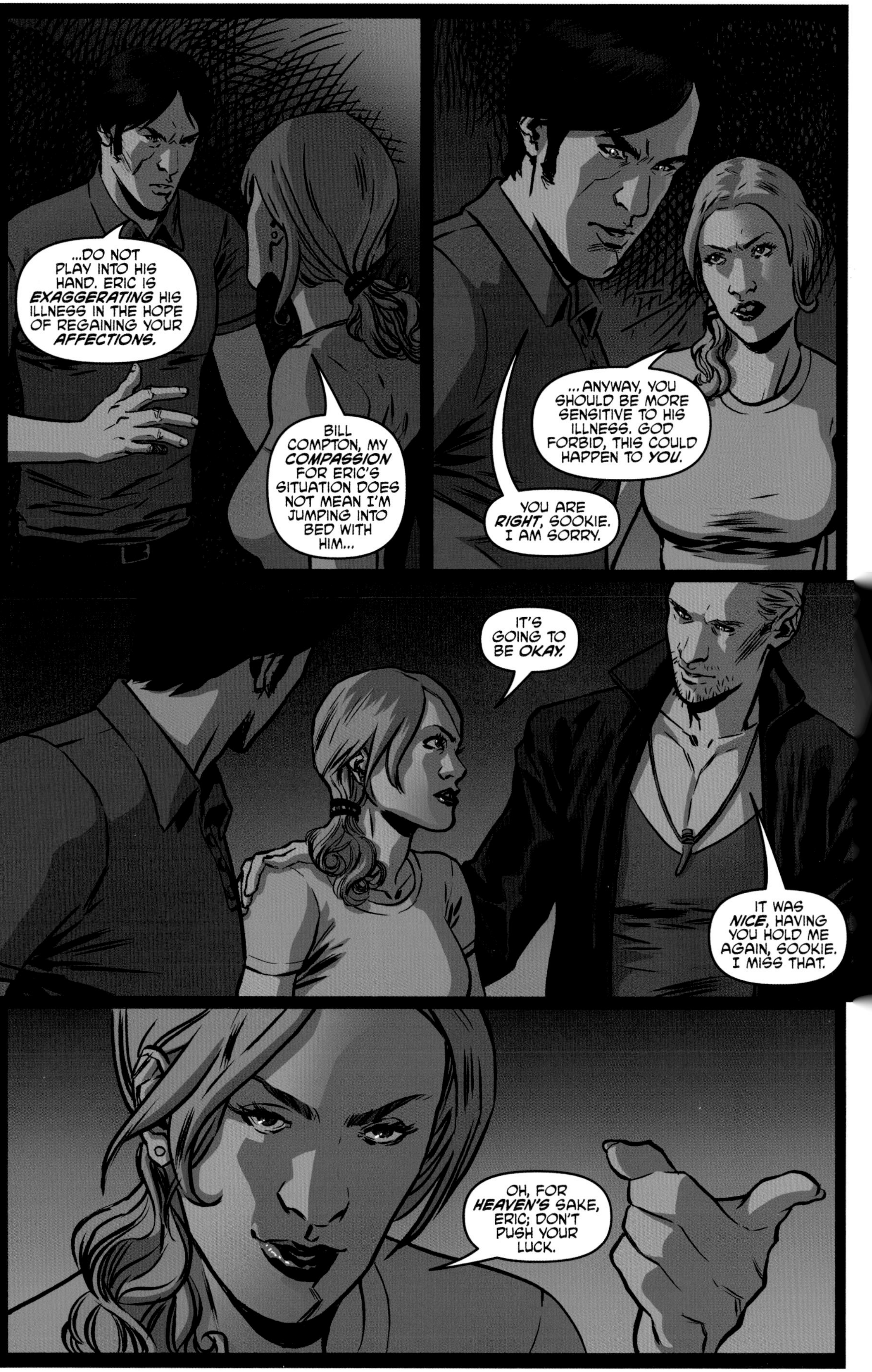
...DO NOT PLAY INTO HIS HAND. ERIC IS *EXAGGERATING* HIS ILLNESS IN THE HOPE OF REGAINING YOUR *AFFECTIONS.*
BILL COMPTON, MY *COMPASSION* FOR ERIC'S SITUATION DOES NOT MEAN I'M JUMPING INTO BED WITH HIM...
...ANYWAY, YOU SHOULD BE MORE SENSITIVE TO HIS ILLNESS. GOD FORBID, THIS COULD HAPPEN TO *YOU.*
YOU ARE *RIGHT,* SOOKIE. I AM SORRY.
IT'S GOING TO BE *OKAY.*
IT WAS *NICE,* HAVING YOU HOLD ME AGAIN, SOOKIE. I MISS THAT.
OH, FOR *HEAVEN'S* SAKE, ERIC; DON'T PUSH YOUR LUCK.

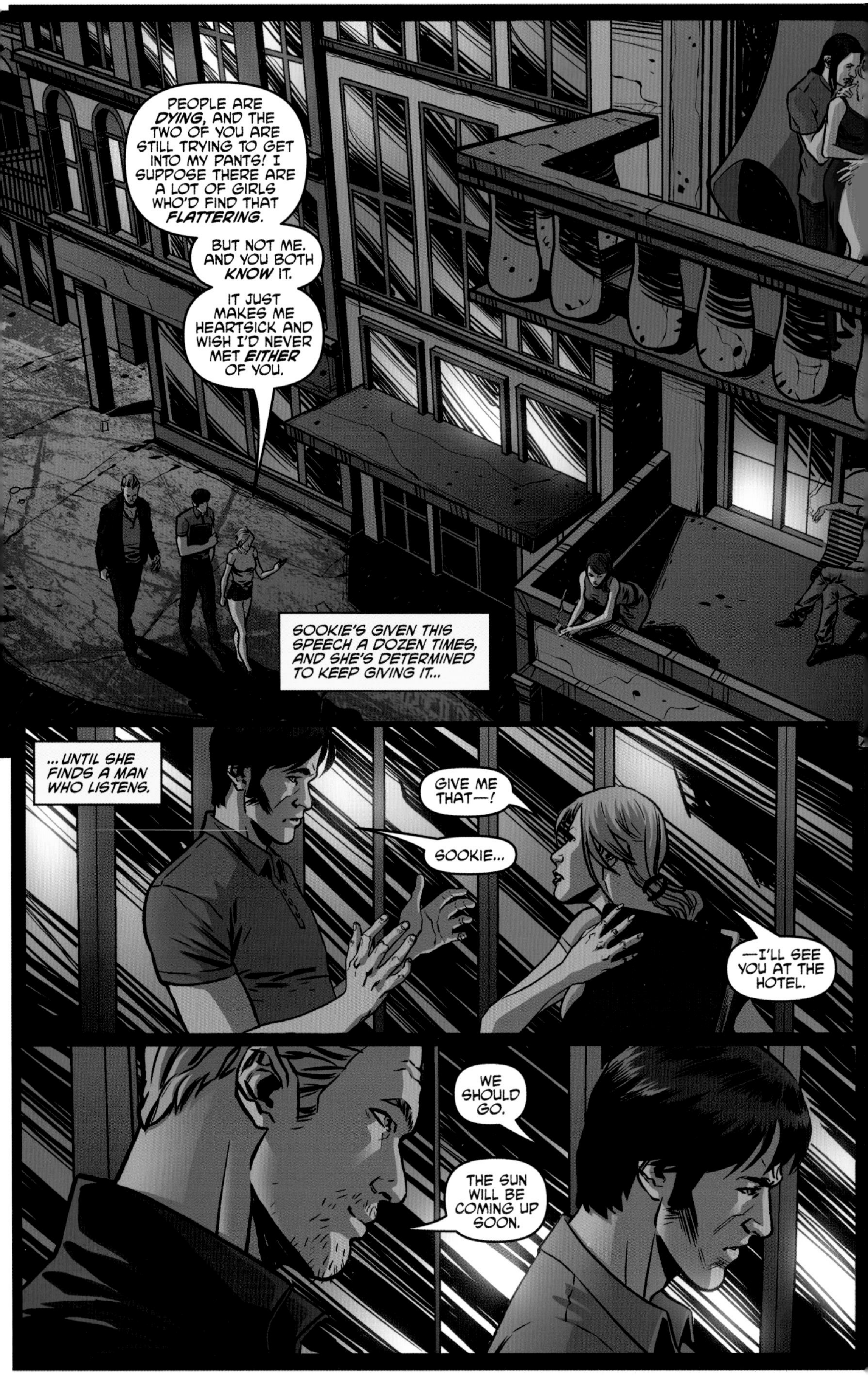
PEOPLE ARE DYING, AND THE TWO OF YOU ARE STILL TRYING TO GET INTO MY PANTS! I SUPPOSE THERE ARE A LOT OF GIRLS WHO'D FIND THAT FLATTERING.
BUT NOT ME. AND YOU BOTH KNOW IT.
IT JUST MAKES ME HEARTSICK AND WISH I'D NEVER MET EITHER OF YOU.
SOOKIE'S GIVEN THIS SPEECH A DOZEN TIMES, AND SHE'S DETERMINED TO KEEP GIVING IT...
...UNTIL SHE FINDS A MAN WHO LISTENS.
GIVE ME THAT—!
SOOKIE...
—I'LL SEE YOU AT THE HOTEL.
WE SHOULD GO.
THE SUN WILL BE COMING UP SOON.

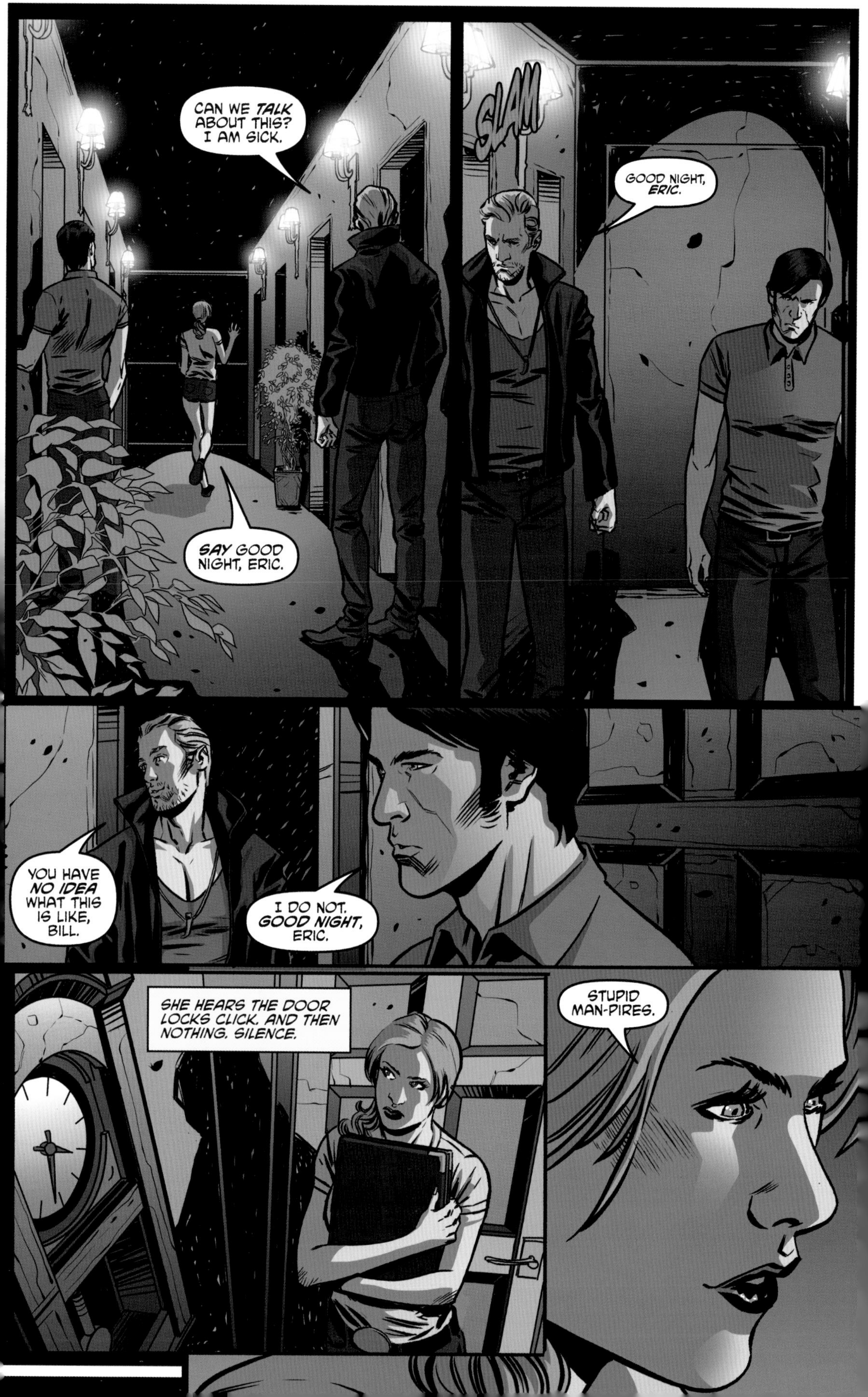
CAN WE TALK ABOUT THIS? I AM SICK.
SAY GOOD NIGHT, ERIC.
SLAM
GOOD NIGHT, ERIC.
YOU HAVE NO IDEA WHAT THIS IS LIKE, BILL.
I DO NOT. GOOD NIGHT, ERIC.
SHE HEARS THE DOOR LOCKS CLICK. AND THEN NOTHING. SILENCE.
STUPID MAN-PIRES.

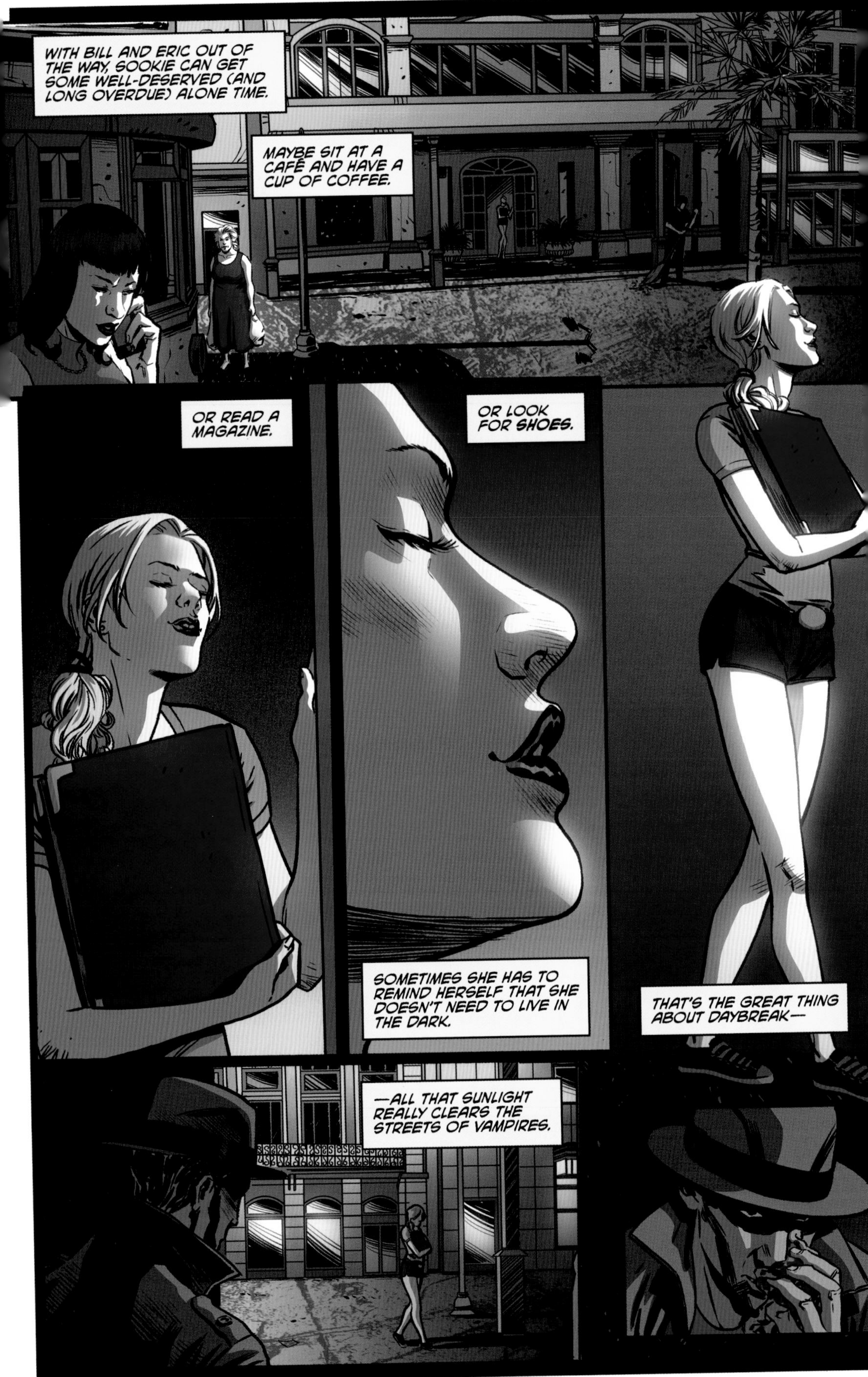
WITH BILL AND ERIC OUT OF THE WAY, SOOKIE CAN GET SOME WELL-DESERVED (AND LONG OVERDUE) ALONE TIME.
MAYBE SIT AT A CAFÉ AND HAVE A CUP OF COFFEE.
OR READ A MAGAZINE.
OR LOOK FOR SHOES.
SOMETIMES SHE HAS TO REMIND HERSELF THAT SHE DOESN'T NEED TO LIVE IN THE DARK.
THAT'S THE GREAT THING ABOUT DAYBREAK—
—ALL THAT SUNLIGHT REALLY CLEARS THE STREETS OF VAMPIRES.

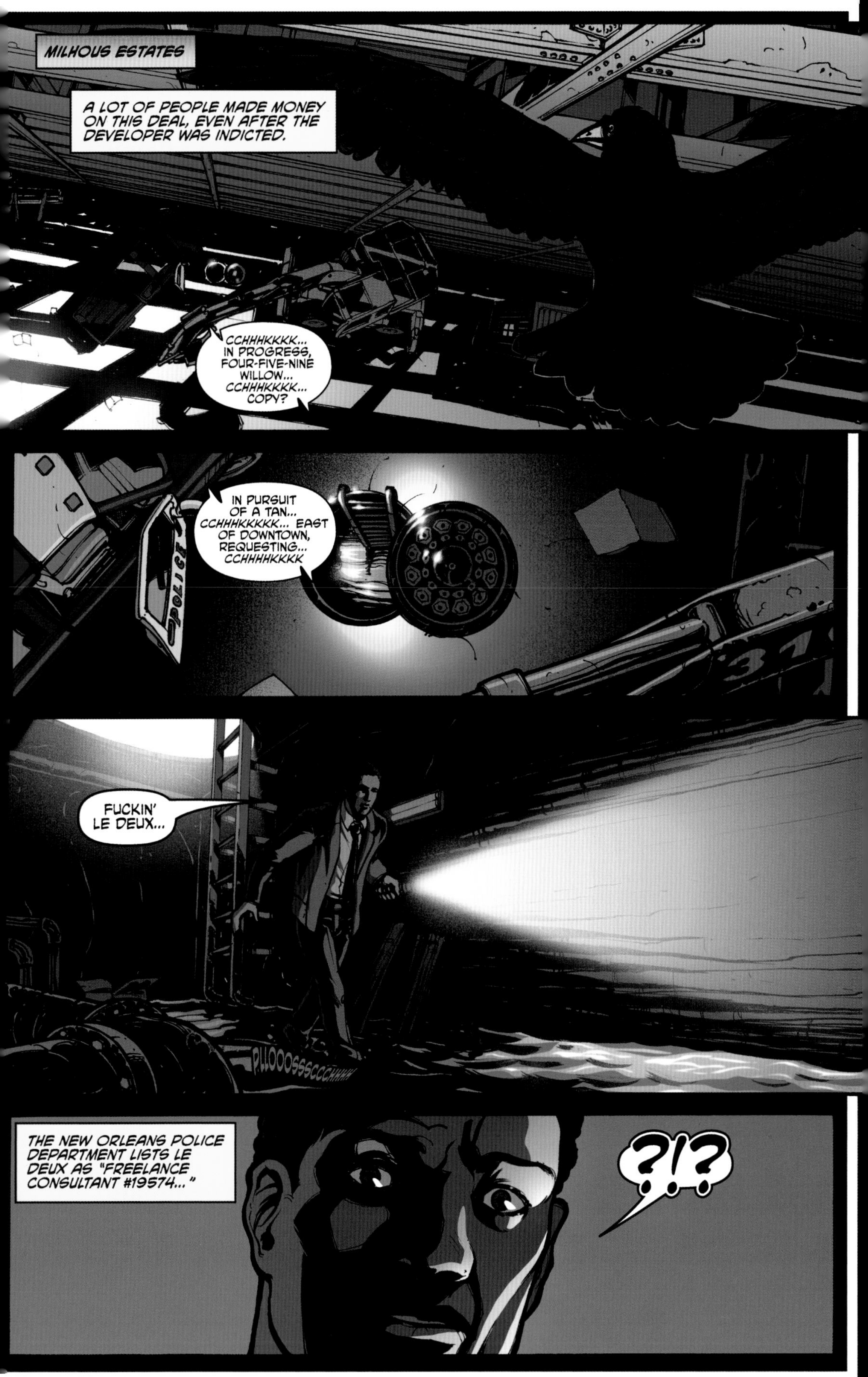
MILHOUS ESTATES
A LOT OF PEOPLE MADE MONEY ON THIS DEAL, EVEN AFTER THE DEVELOPER WAS INDICTED.
CCHHHKKKK... IN PROGRESS, FOUR-FIVE-NINE WILLOW... CCHHKKKKK... COPY?
IN PURSUIT OF A TAN... CCHHHKKKKK... EAST OF DOWNTOWN, REQUESTING... CCHHHHKKKK
POLICE
FUCKIN' LE DEUX...
PLLOOOSSSCCCHHHH
THE NEW ORLEANS POLICE DEPARTMENT LISTS LE DEUX AS "FREELANCE CONSULTANT #19574..."
?!?

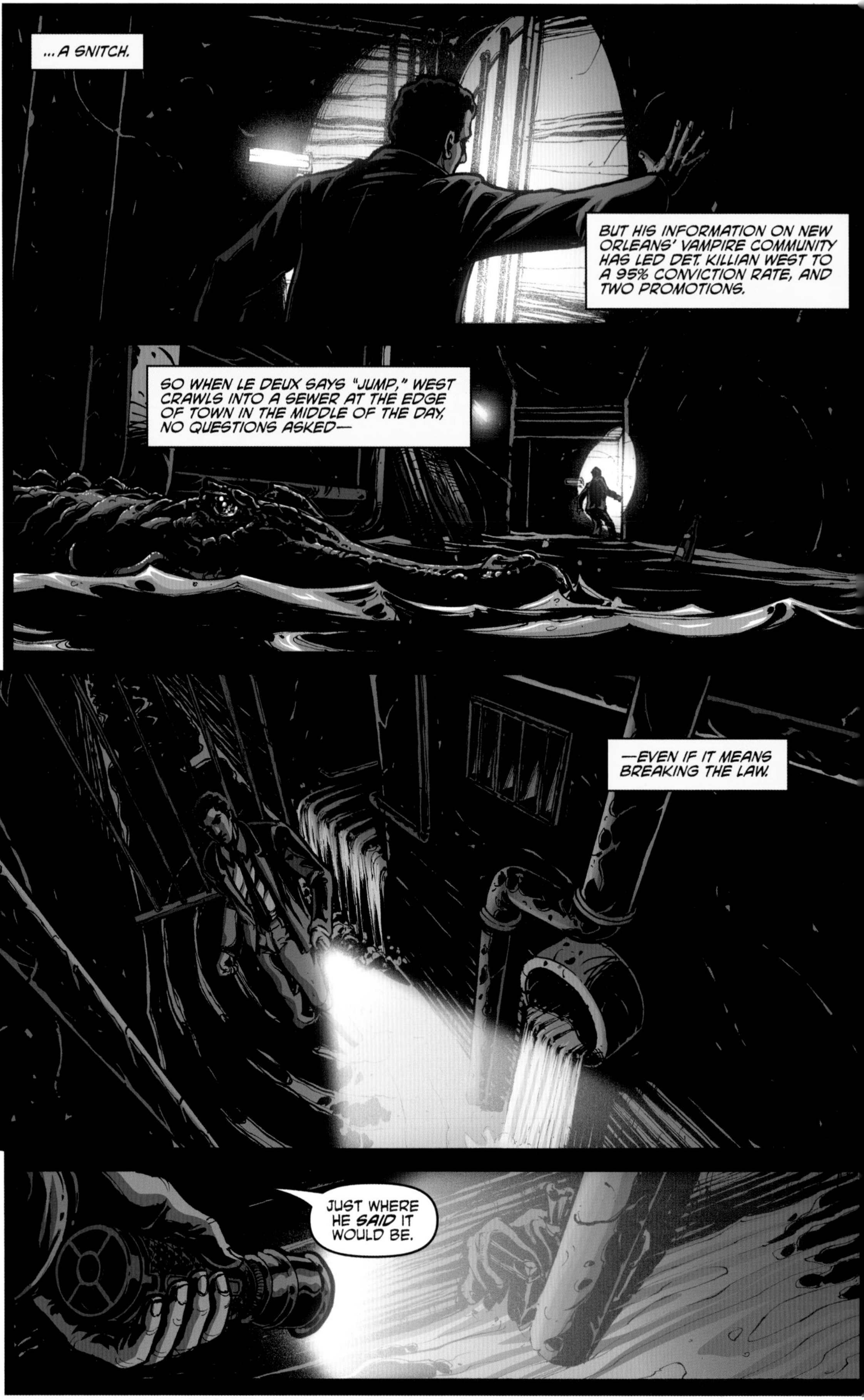

...A SNITCH.
BUT HIS INFORMATION ON NEW ORLEANS' VAMPIRE COMMUNITY HAS LED DET. KILLIAN WEST TO A 95% CONVICTION RATE, AND TWO PROMOTIONS.
SO WHEN LE DEUX SAYS "JUMP," WEST CRAWLS INTO A SEWER AT THE EDGE OF TOWN IN THE MIDDLE OF THE DAY, NO QUESTIONS ASKED—
—EVEN IF IT MEANS BREAKING THE LAW.
JUST WHERE HE *SAID* IT WOULD BE.

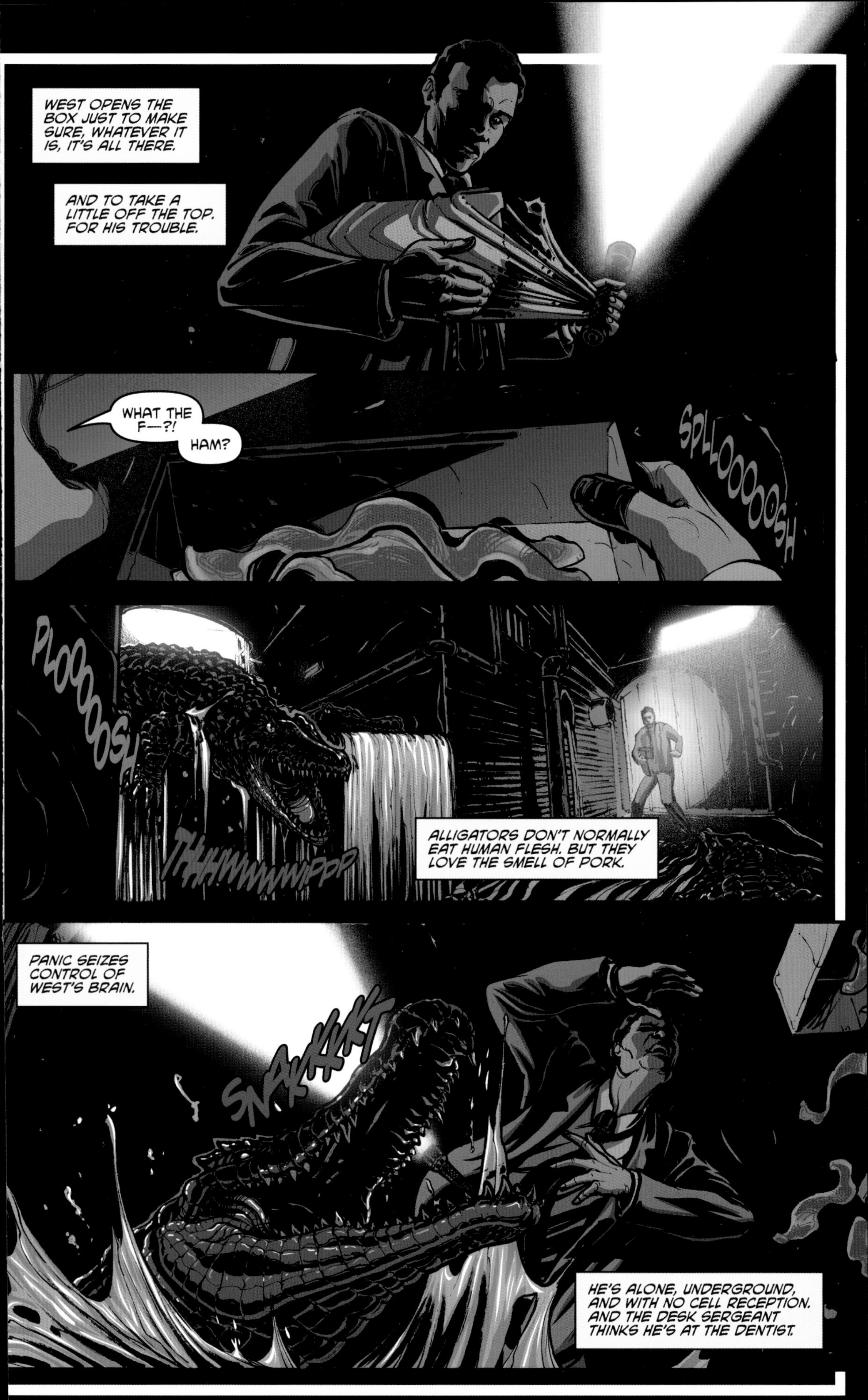
WEST OPENS THE BOX JUST TO MAKE SURE, WHATEVER IT IS, IT'S ALL THERE.
AND TO TAKE A LITTLE OFF THE TOP. FOR HIS TROUBLE.
WHAT THE F--?! HAM?
SPLLOOOOOOSH
PLOOOOOOSH
THHWWWWIPPP
ALLIGATORS DON'T NORMALLY EAT HUMAN FLESH. BUT THEY LOVE THE SMELL OF PORK.
PANIC SEIZES CONTROL OF WEST'S BRAIN.
SNAKKKKKT
HE'S ALONE, UNDERGROUND, AND WITH NO CELL RECEPTION. AND THE DESK SERGEANT THINKS HE'S AT THE DENTIST.

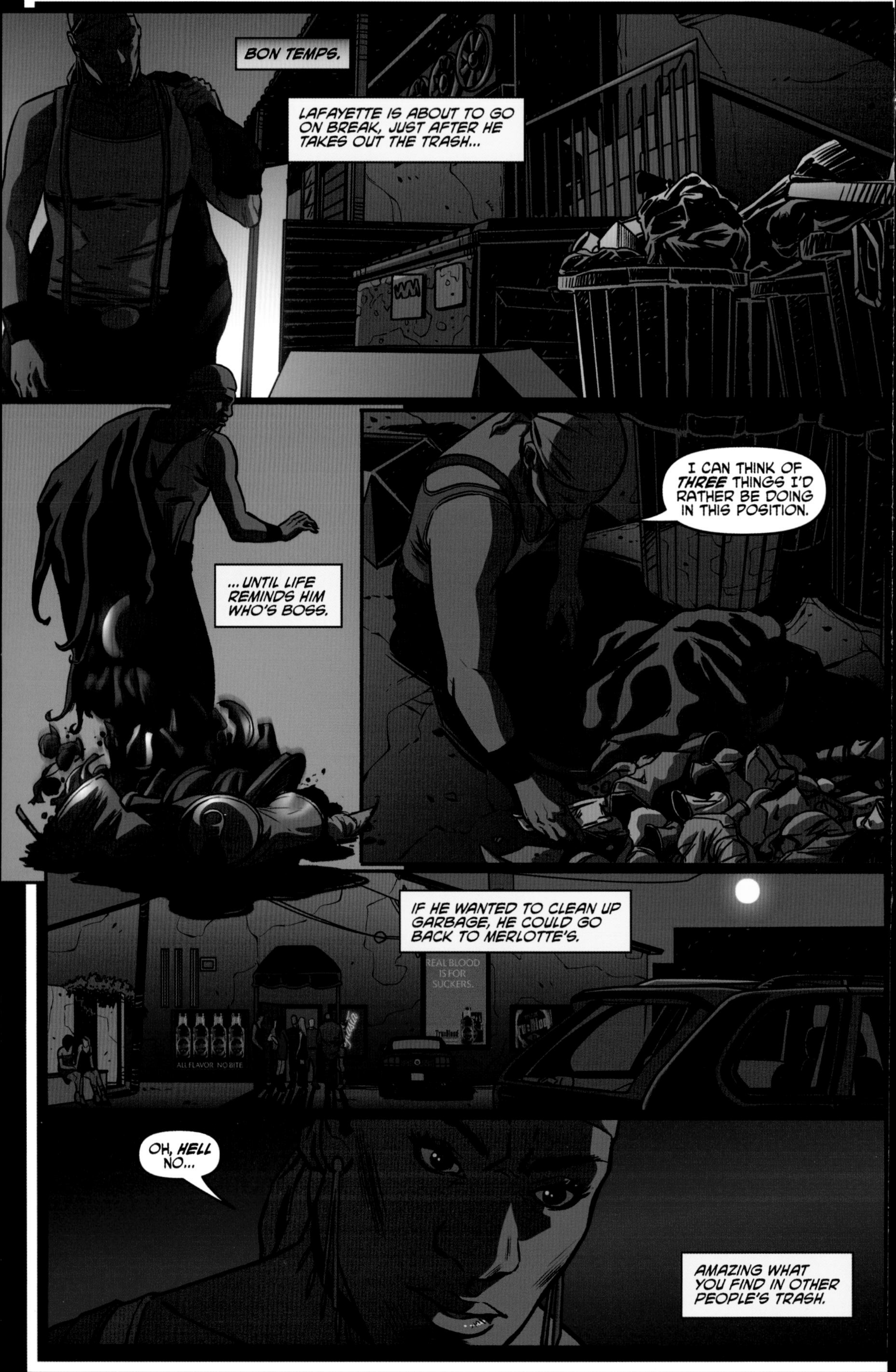
BON TEMPS.
LAFAYETTE IS ABOUT TO GO ON BREAK, JUST AFTER HE TAKES OUT THE TRASH...
...UNTIL LIFE REMINDS HIM WHO'S BOSS.
I CAN THINK OF THREE THINGS I'D RATHER BE DOING IN THIS POSITION.
IF HE WANTED TO CLEAN UP GARBAGE, HE COULD GO BACK TO MERLOTTE'S.
REAL BLOOD IS FOR SUCKERS.
ALL FLAVOR NO BITE
OH, HELL NO...
AMAZING WHAT YOU FIND IN OTHER PEOPLE'S TRASH.

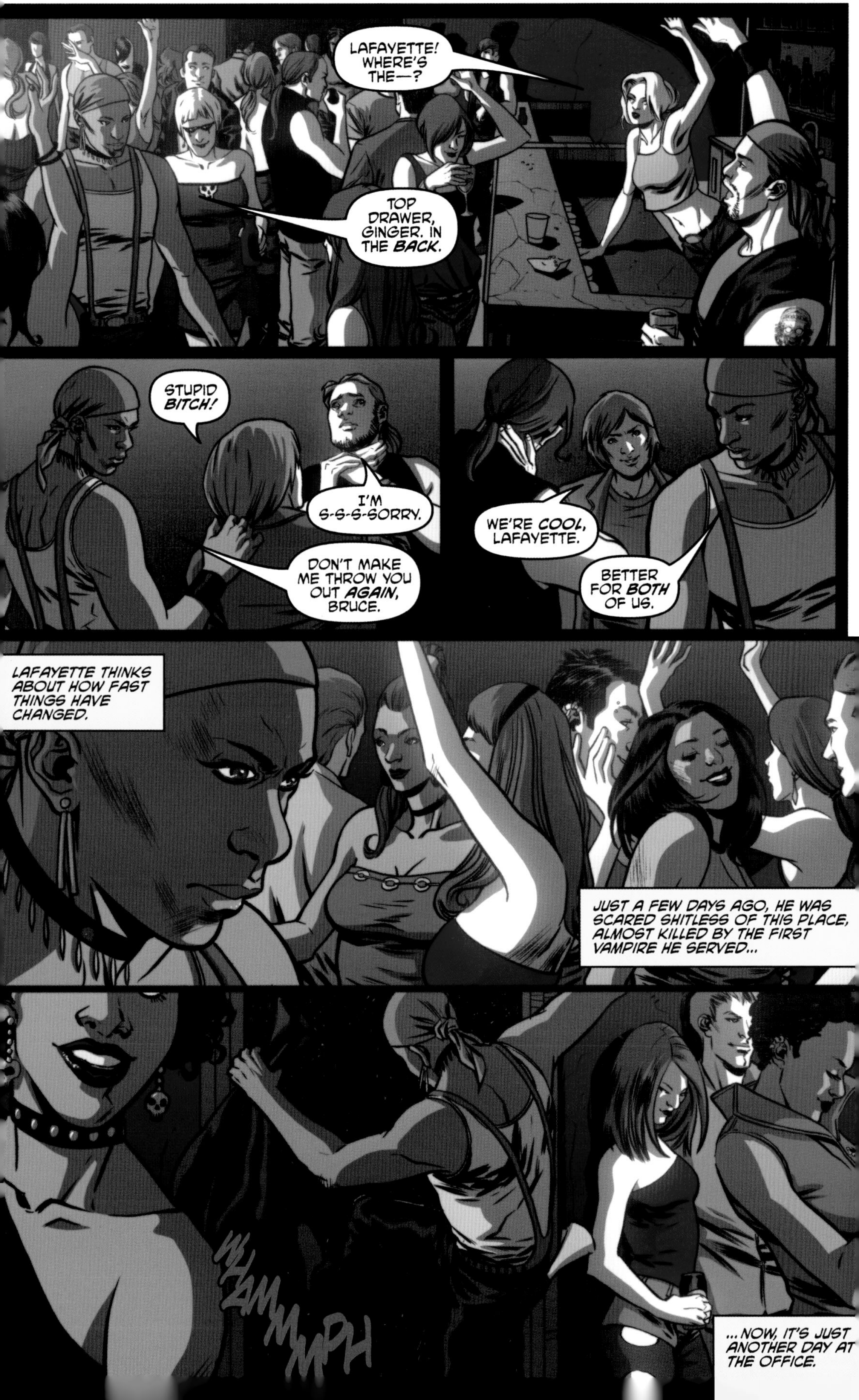
LAFAYETTE! WHERE'S THE—?
TOP DRAWER, GINGER. IN THE BACK.
STUPID BITCH!
I'M S-S-S-SORRY.
DON'T MAKE ME THROW YOU OUT AGAIN, BRUCE.
WE'RE COOL, LAFAYETTE.
BETTER FOR BOTH OF US.
LAFAYETTE THINKS ABOUT HOW FAST THINGS HAVE CHANGED.
JUST A FEW DAYS AGO, HE WAS SCARED SHITLESS OF THIS PLACE, ALMOST KILLED BY THE FIRST VAMPIRE HE SERVED...
WHAMMMPH
...NOW, IT'S JUST ANOTHER DAY AT THE OFFICE.

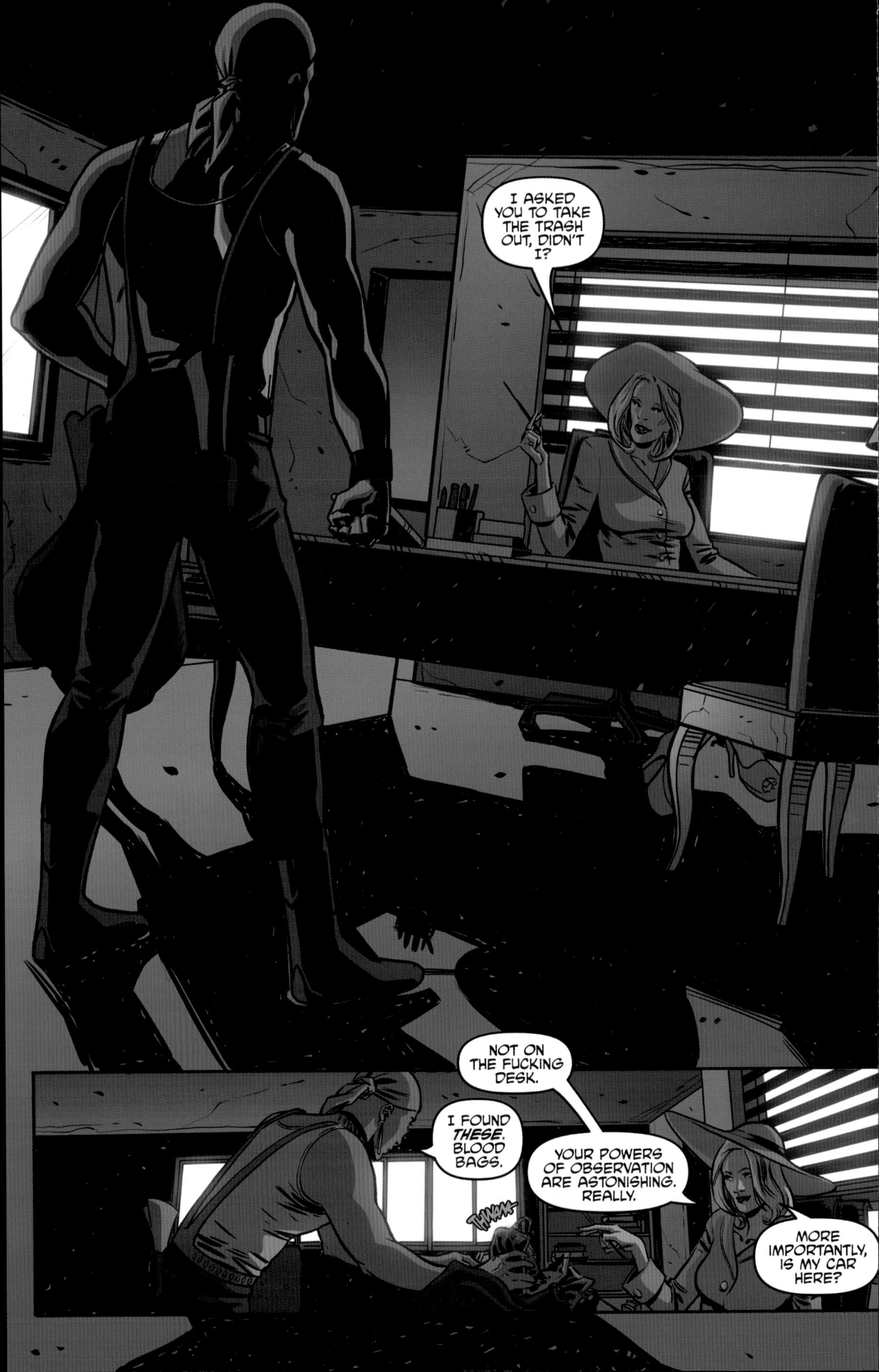

I ASKED YOU TO TAKE THE TRASH OUT, DIDN'T I?
I FOUND *THESE*. BLOOD BAGS.
THWAAK
NOT ON THE FUCKING DESK.
YOUR POWERS OF OBSERVATION ARE ASTONISHING. REALLY.
MORE IMPORTANTLY, IS MY CAR HERE?

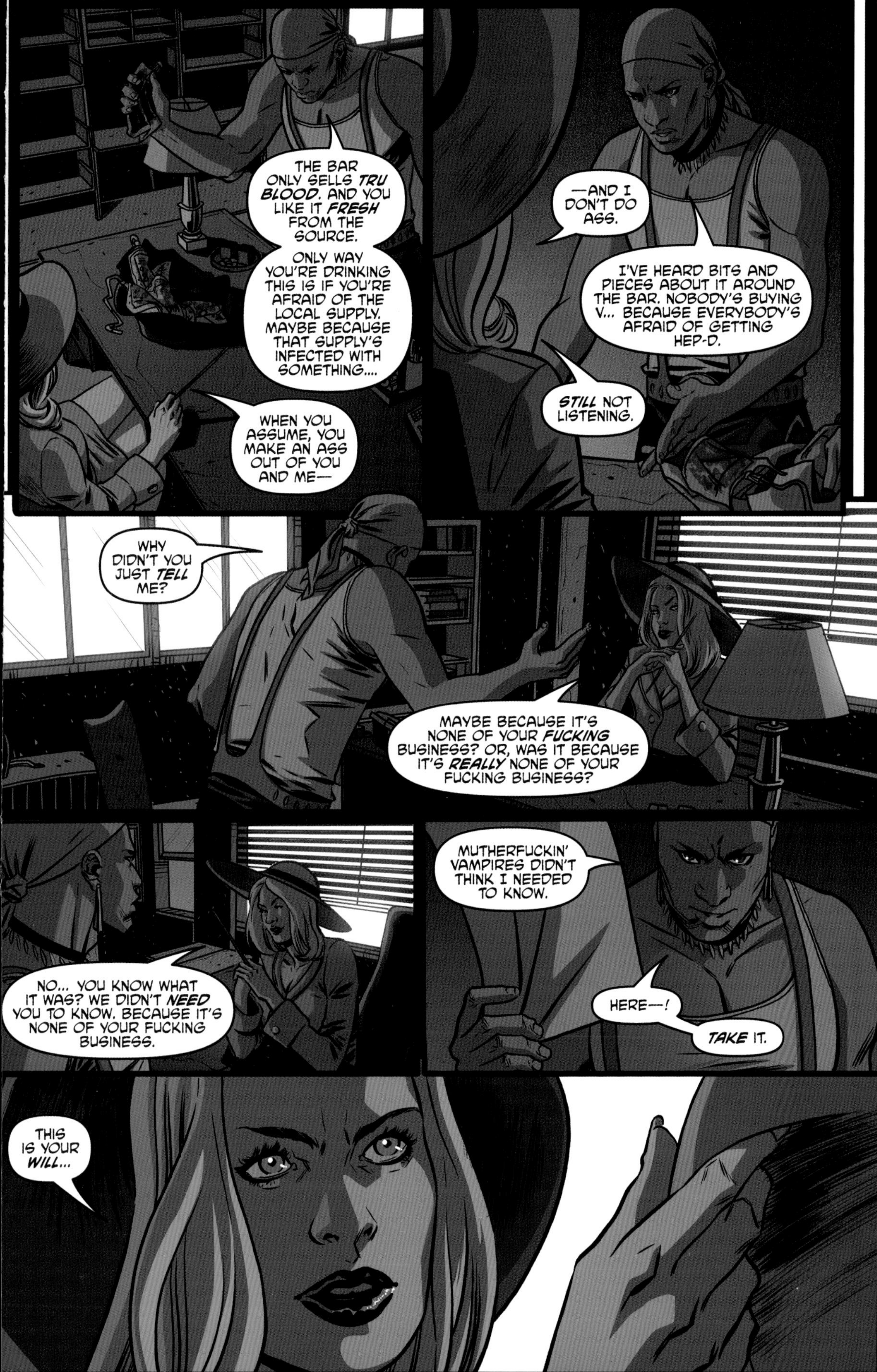

THE BAR ONLY SELLS TRU BLOOD. AND YOU LIKE IT FRESH FROM THE SOURCE.
ONLY WAY YOU'RE DRINKING THIS IS IF YOU'RE AFRAID OF THE LOCAL SUPPLY. MAYBE BECAUSE THAT SUPPLY'S INFECTED WITH SOMETHING....
WHEN YOU ASSUME, YOU MAKE AN ASS OUT OF YOU AND ME—
—AND I DON'T DO ASS.
I'VE HEARD BITS AND PIECES ABOUT IT AROUND THE BAR. NOBODY'S BUYING V... BECAUSE EVERYBODY'S AFRAID OF GETTING HEP-D.
STILL NOT LISTENING.
WHY DIDN'T YOU JUST TELL ME?
MAYBE BECAUSE IT'S NONE OF YOUR FUCKING BUSINESS? OR, WAS IT BECAUSE IT'S REALLY NONE OF YOUR FUCKING BUSINESS?
NO... YOU KNOW WHAT IT WAS? WE DIDN'T NEED YOU TO KNOW. BECAUSE IT'S NONE OF YOUR FUCKING BUSINESS.
MUTHERFUCKIN' VAMPIRES DIDN'T THINK I NEEDED TO KNOW.
HERE—!
TAKE IT.
THIS IS YOUR WILL...

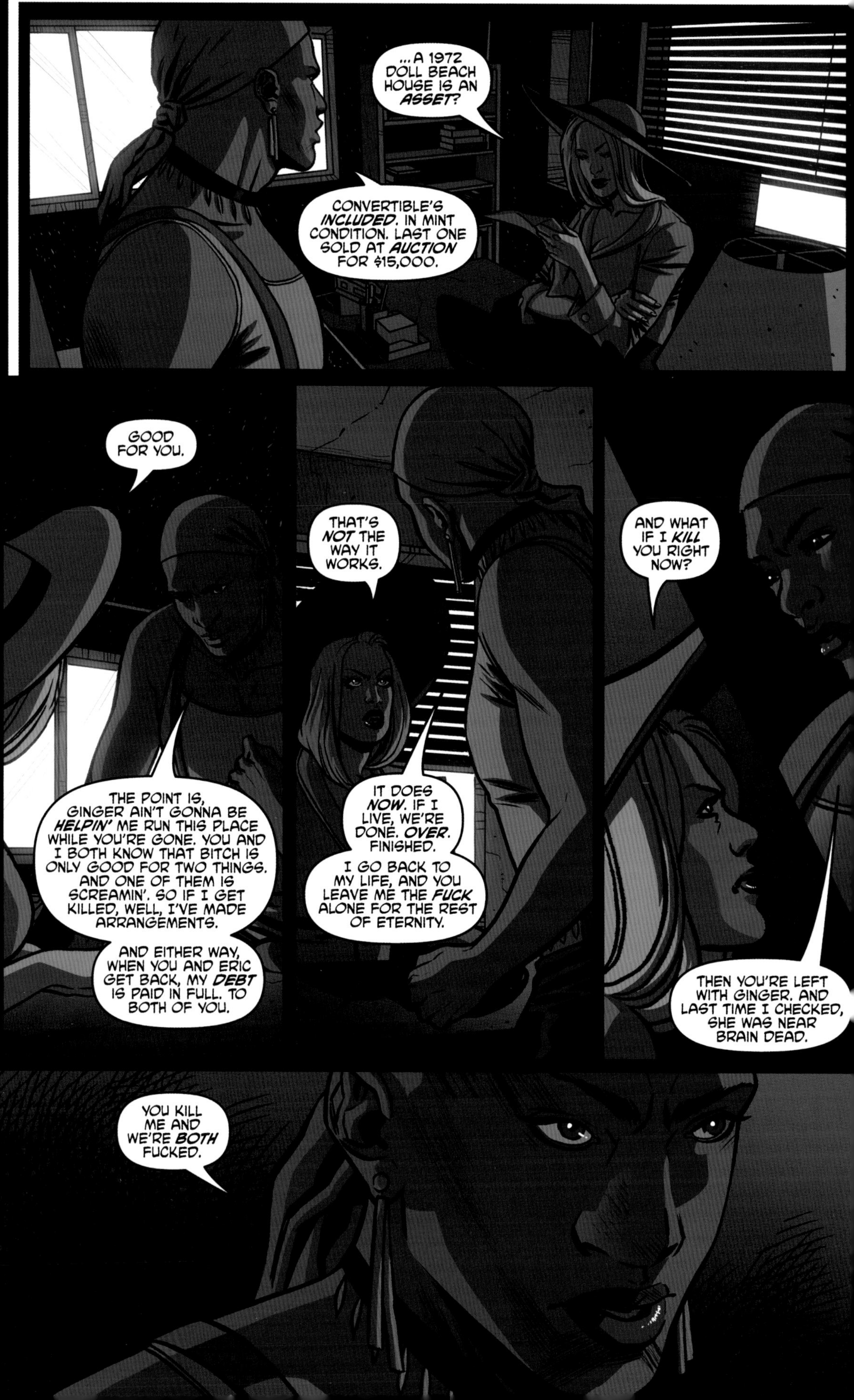
...A 1972 DOLL BEACH HOUSE IS AN ASSET?
CONVERTIBLE'S INCLUDED. IN MINT CONDITION. LAST ONE SOLD AT AUCTION FOR $15,000.
GOOD FOR YOU.
THE POINT IS, GINGER AIN'T GONNA BE HELPIN' ME RUN THIS PLACE WHILE YOU'RE GONE. YOU AND I BOTH KNOW THAT BITCH IS ONLY GOOD FOR TWO THINGS. AND ONE OF THEM IS SCREAMIN'. SO IF I GET KILLED, WELL, I'VE MADE ARRANGEMENTS.
AND EITHER WAY, WHEN YOU AND ERIC GET BACK, MY DEBT IS PAID IN FULL. TO BOTH OF YOU.
THAT'S NOT THE WAY IT WORKS.
IT DOES NOW. IF I LIVE, WE'RE DONE. OVER. FINISHED.
I GO BACK TO MY LIFE, AND YOU LEAVE ME THE FUCK ALONE FOR THE REST OF ETERNITY.
AND WHAT IF I KILL YOU RIGHT NOW?
THEN YOU'RE LEFT WITH GINGER. AND LAST TIME I CHECKED, SHE WAS NEAR BRAIN DEAD.
YOU KILL ME AND WE'RE BOTH FUCKED.

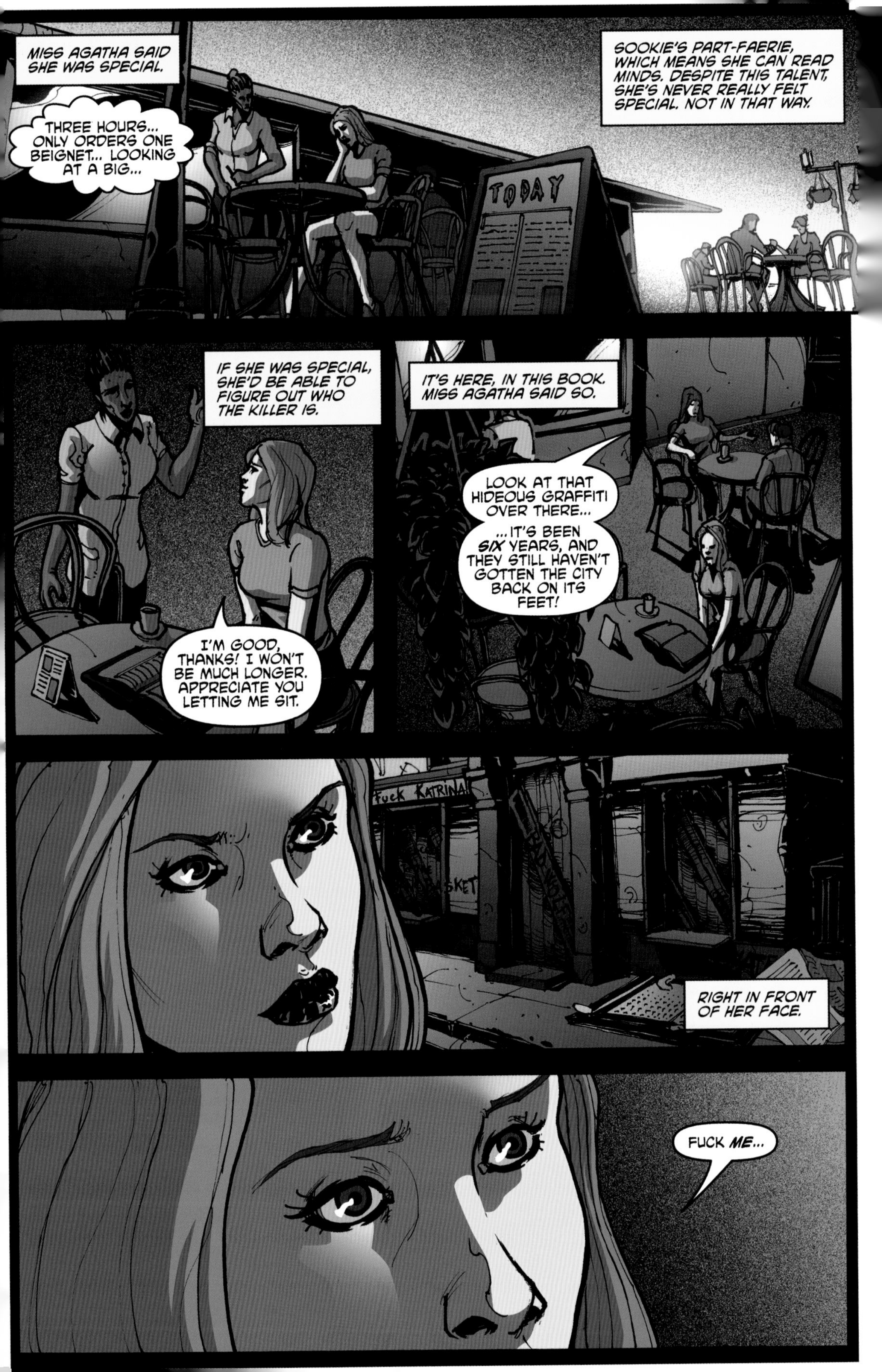
MISS AGATHA SAID SHE WAS SPECIAL.
THREE HOURS... ONLY ORDERS ONE BEIGNET... LOOKING AT A BIG...
SOOKIE'S PART-FAERIE, WHICH MEANS SHE CAN READ MINDS. DESPITE THIS TALENT, SHE'S NEVER REALLY FELT SPECIAL. NOT IN THAT WAY.
TODAY
IF SHE WAS SPECIAL, SHE'D BE ABLE TO FIGURE OUT WHO THE KILLER IS.
I'M GOOD, THANKS! I WON'T BE MUCH LONGER. APPRECIATE YOU LETTING ME SIT.
IT'S HERE, IN THIS BOOK. MISS AGATHA SAID SO.
LOOK AT THAT HIDEOUS GRAFFITI OVER THERE...
...IT'S BEEN SIX YEARS, AND THEY STILL HAVEN'T GOTTEN THE CITY BACK ON ITS FEET!
Fuck Katrina
RIGHT IN FRONT OF HER FACE.
FUCK ME...

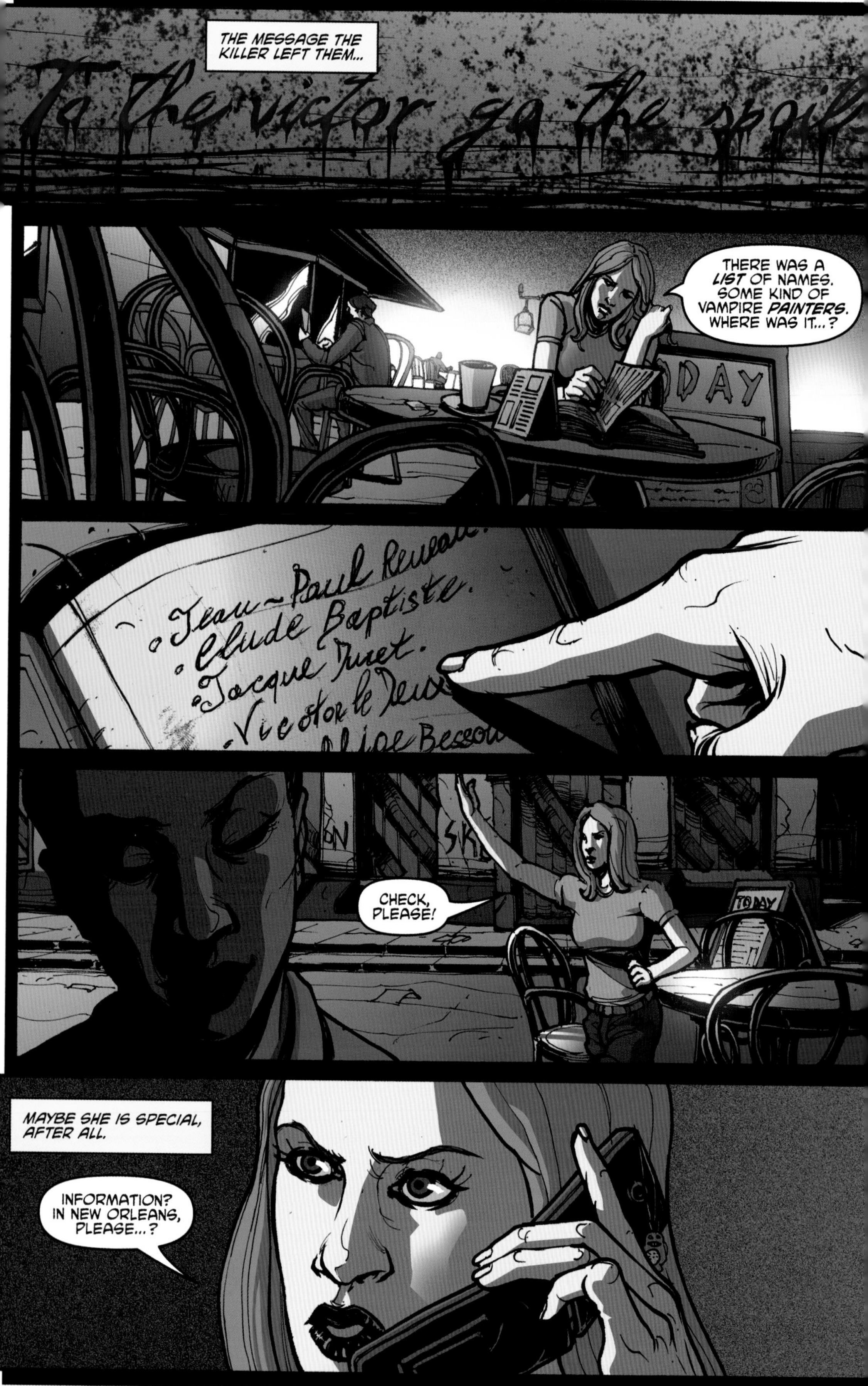
THE MESSAGE THE KILLER LEFT THEM...
To the victor go the spoil
THERE WAS A LIST OF NAMES. SOME KIND OF VAMPIRE PAINTERS. WHERE WAS IT...?
Baptiste
CHECK, PLEASE!
TODAY
MAYBE SHE IS SPECIAL, AFTER ALL.
INFORMATION? IN NEW ORLEANS, PLEASE...?

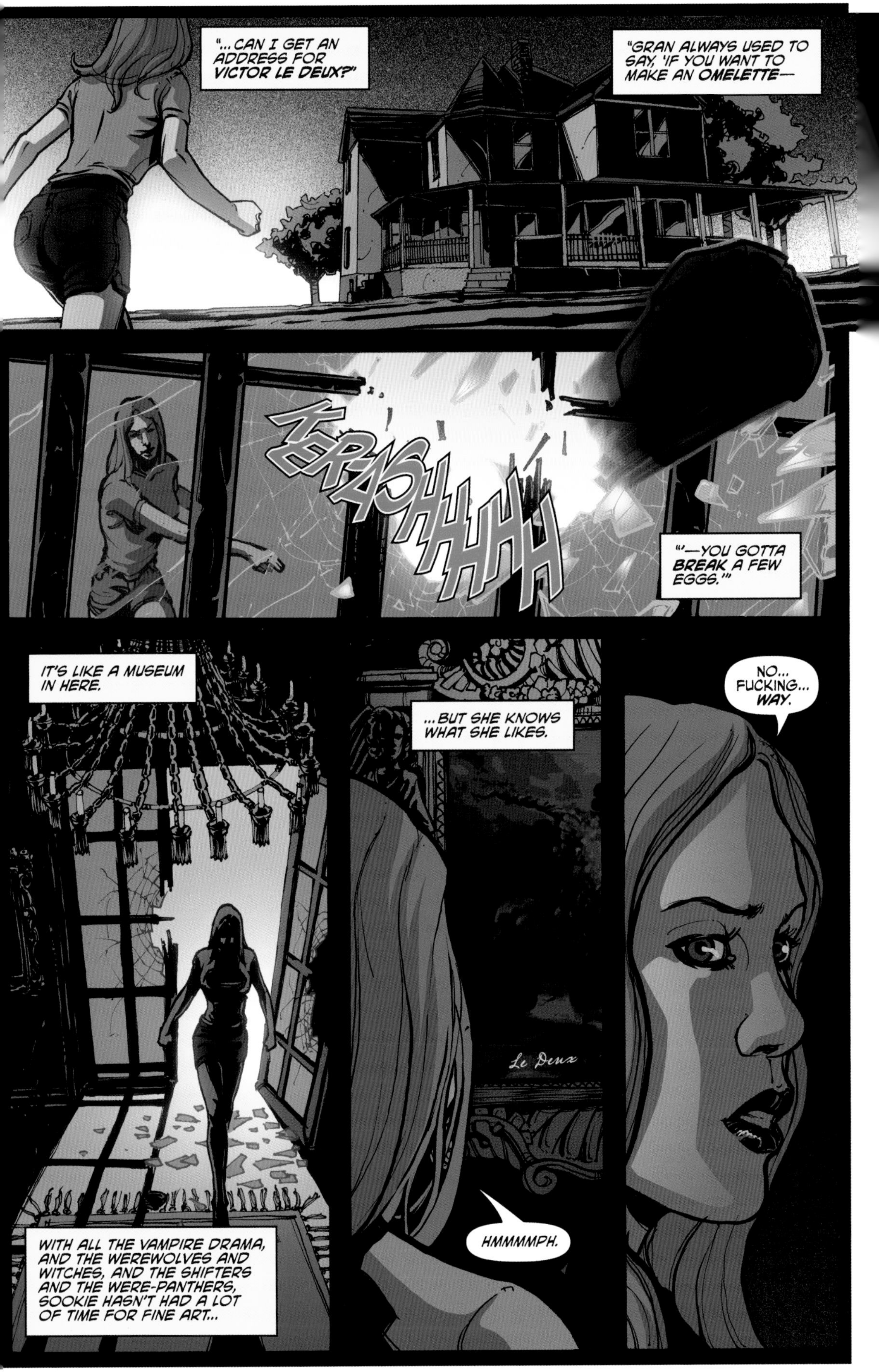
"...CAN I GET AN ADDRESS FOR VICTOR LE DEUX?"
"GRAN ALWAYS USED TO SAY, 'IF YOU WANT TO MAKE AN OMELETTE—
KERASHHHHH
"'—YOU GOTTA BREAK A FEW EGGS.'"
IT'S LIKE A MUSEUM IN HERE.
WITH ALL THE VAMPIRE DRAMA, AND THE WEREWOLVES AND WITCHES, AND THE SHIFTERS AND THE WERE-PANTHERS, SOOKIE HASN'T HAD A LOT OF TIME FOR FINE ART...
...BUT SHE KNOWS WHAT SHE LIKES.
Le Deux
HMMMMPH.
NO... FUCKING... WAY.

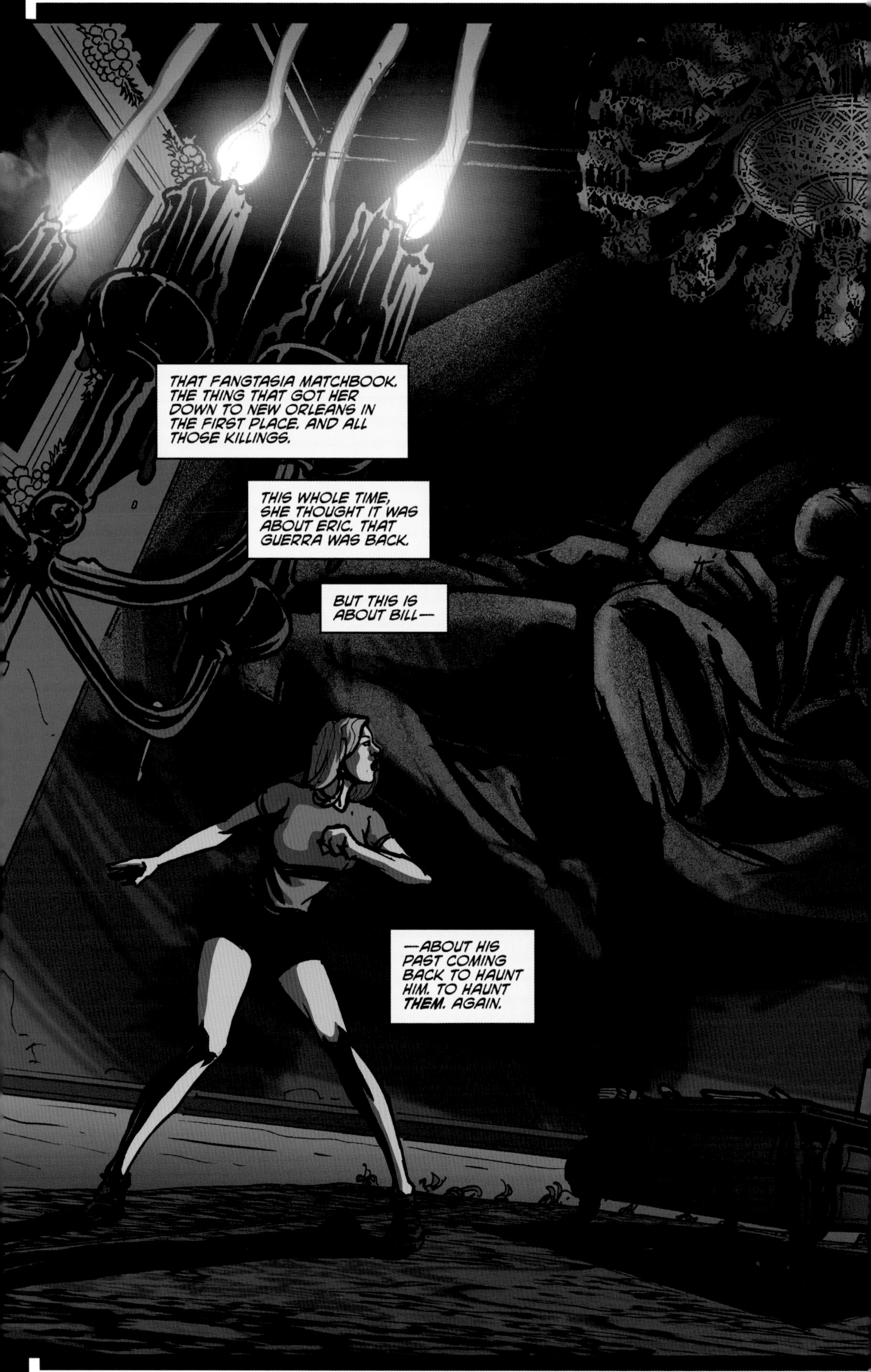
THAT FANGTASIA MATCHBOOK. THE THING THAT GOT HER DOWN TO NEW ORLEANS IN THE FIRST PLACE. AND ALL THOSE KILLINGS.
THIS WHOLE TIME, SHE THOUGHT IT WAS ABOUT ERIC. THAT GUERRA WAS BACK.
BUT THIS IS ABOUT BILL—
—ABOUT HIS PAST COMING BACK TO HAUNT HIM. TO HAUNT THEM. AGAIN.

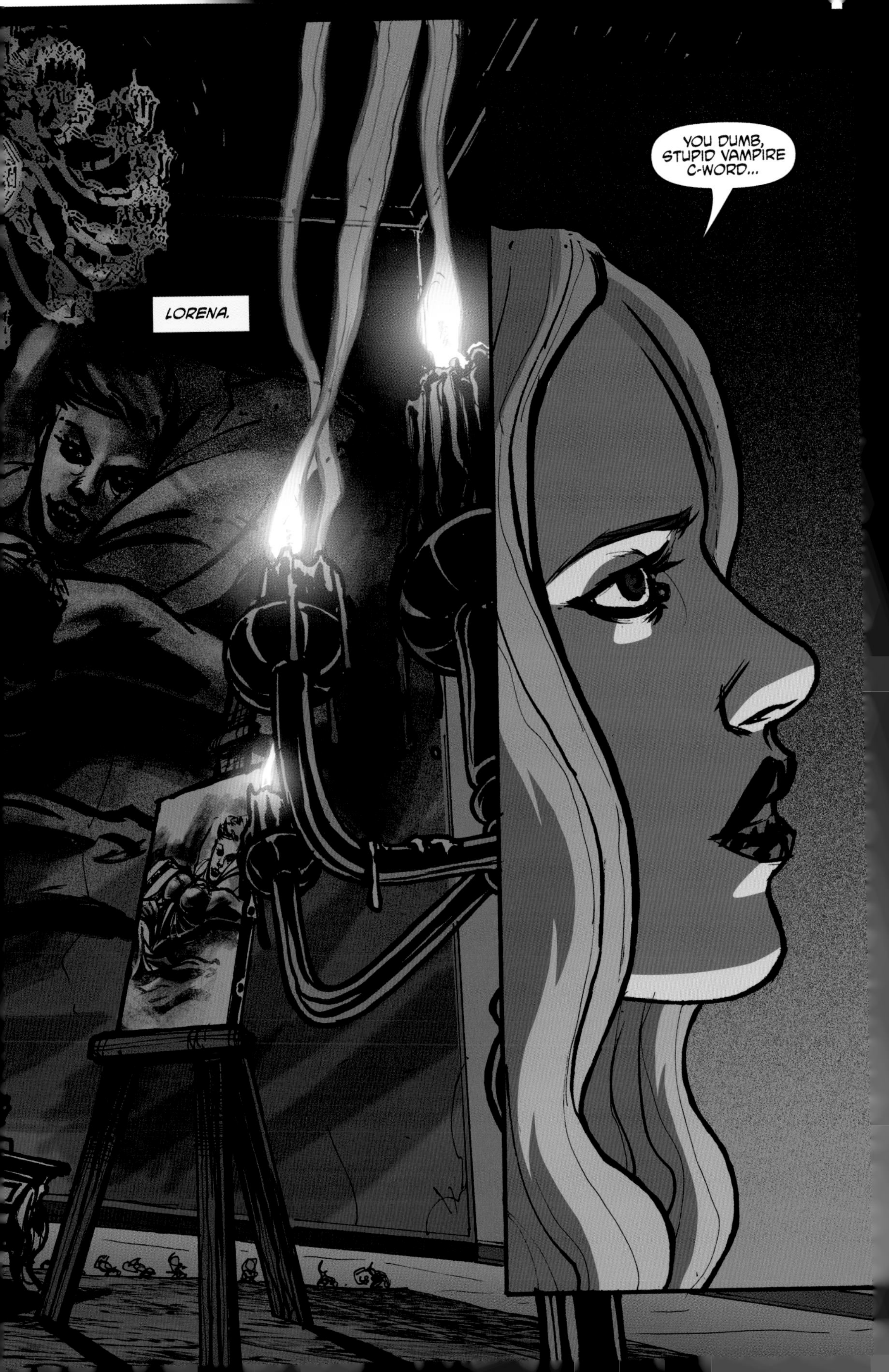
LORENA.
YOU DUMB, STUPID VAMPIRE C-WORD...

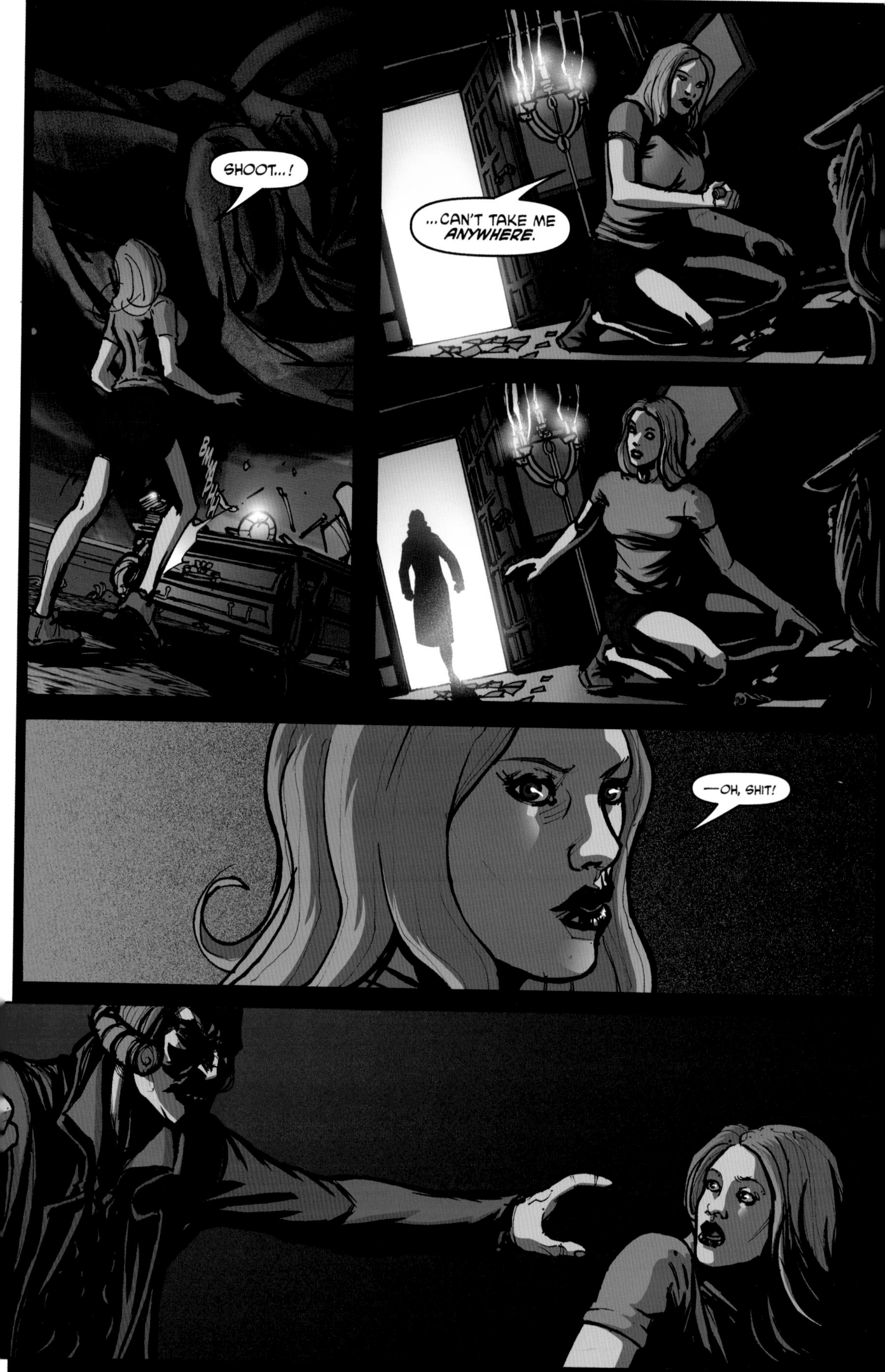
SHOOT...!
...CAN'T TAKE ME ANYWHERE.
—OH, SHIT!

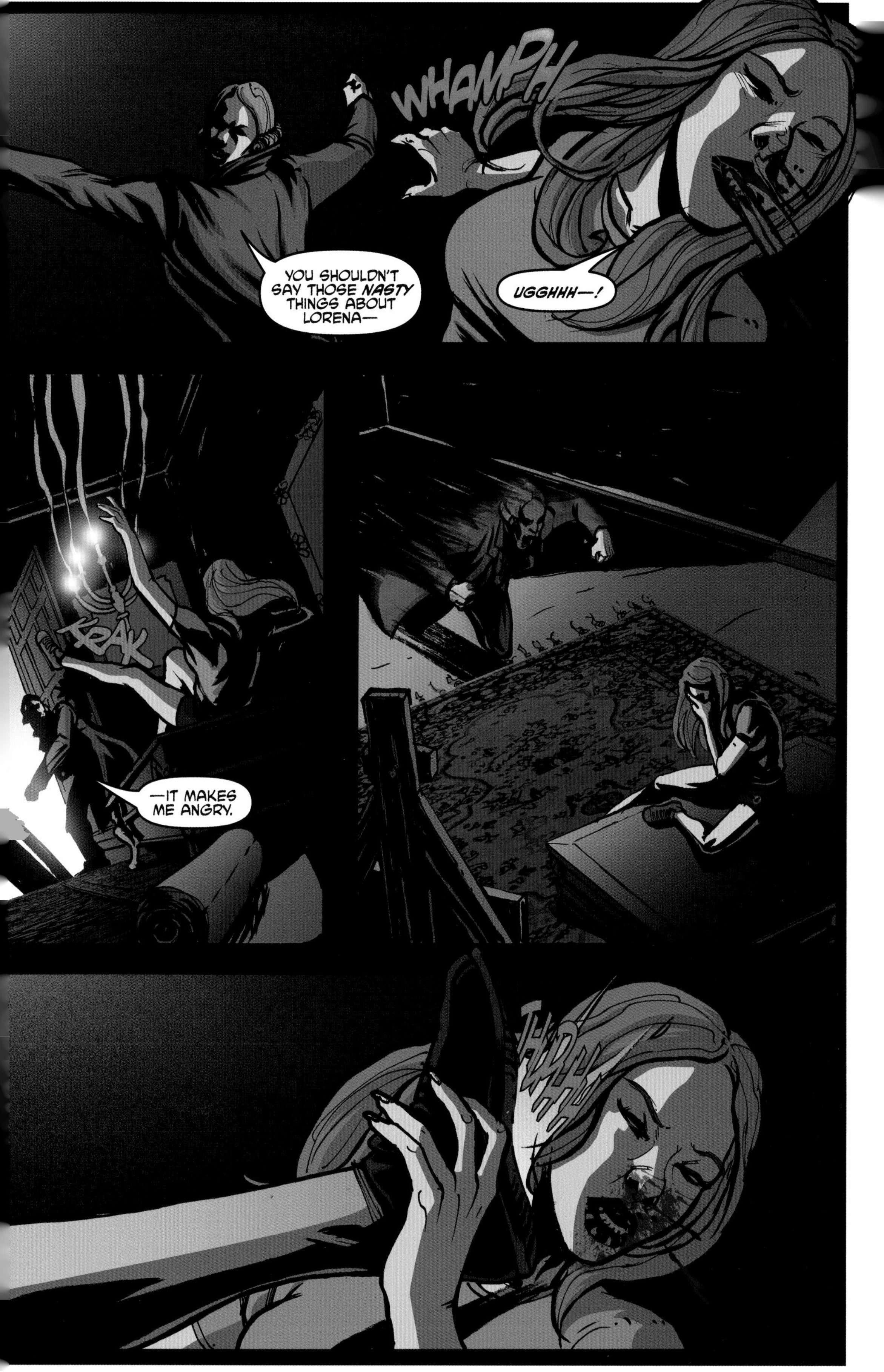
WHAMPH
YOU SHOULDN'T SAY THOSE *NASTY* THINGS ABOUT LORENA—
*UGGHHH—!*
KRAK
—IT MAKES ME ANGRY.

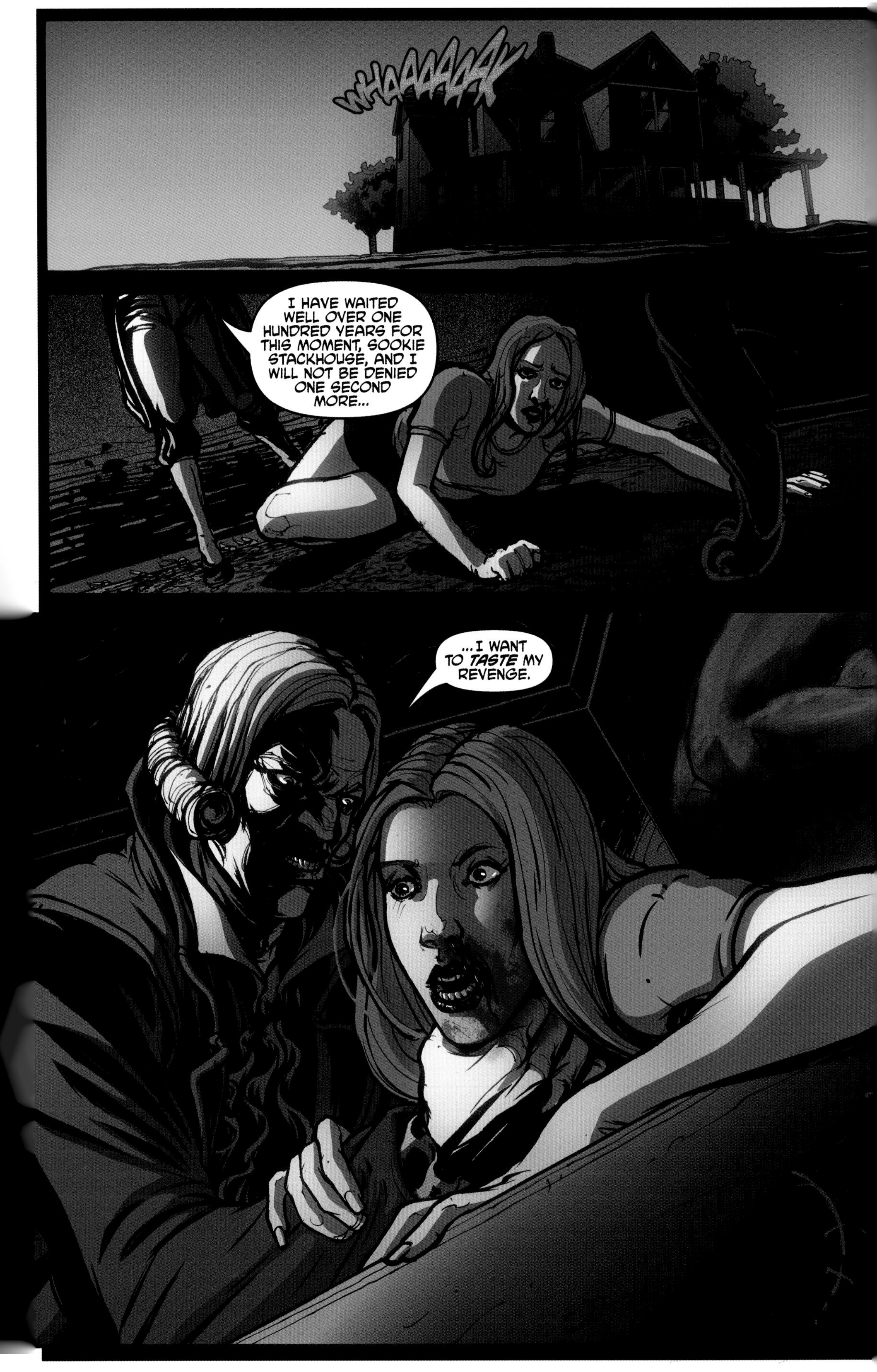
WHOAAAAAA!
I HAVE WAITED WELL OVER ONE HUNDRED YEARS FOR THIS MOMENT, SOOKIE STACKHOUSE, AND I WILL NOT BE DENIED ONE SECOND MORE...
...I WANT TO TASTE MY REVENGE.

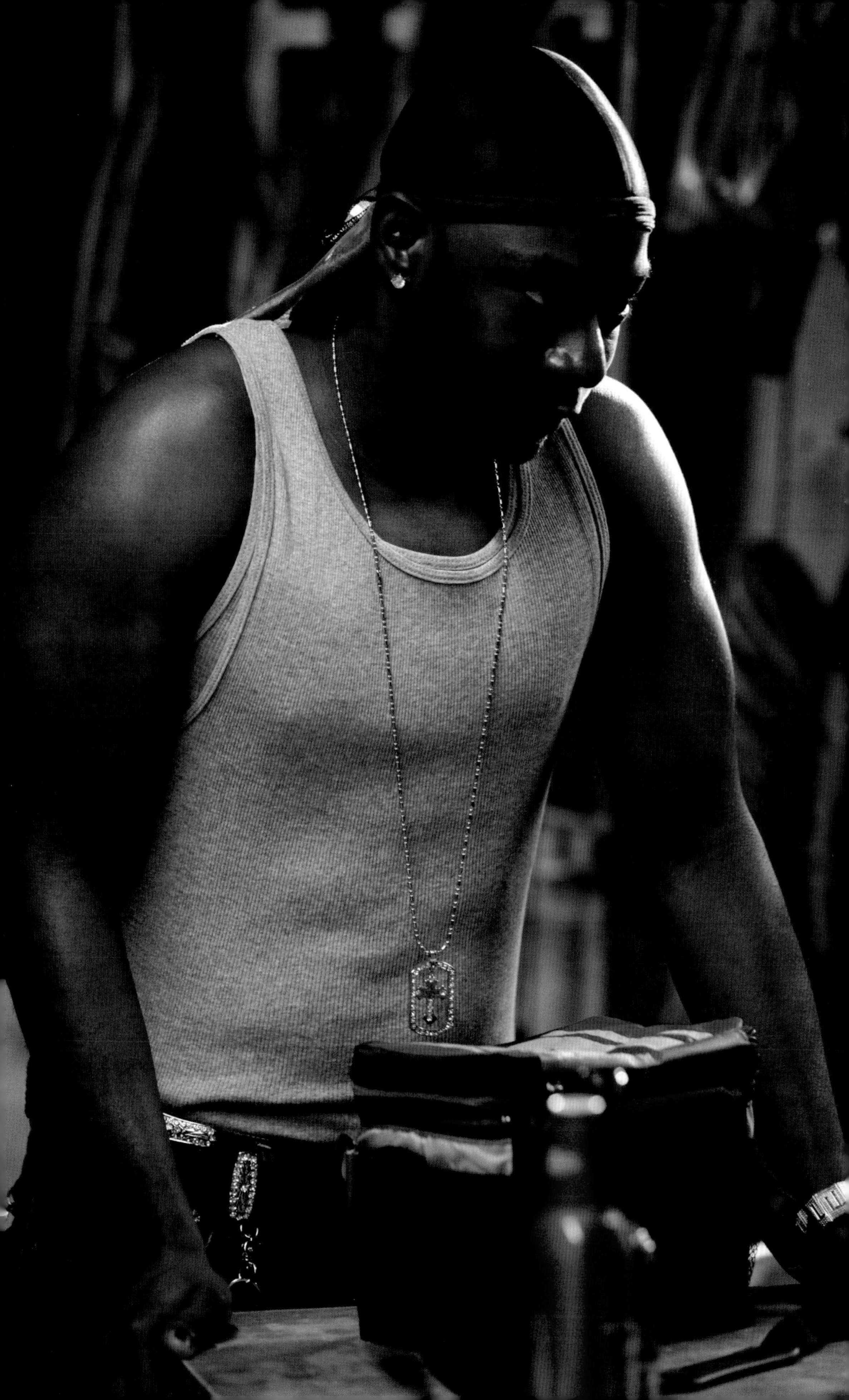

# CHAPTER 6

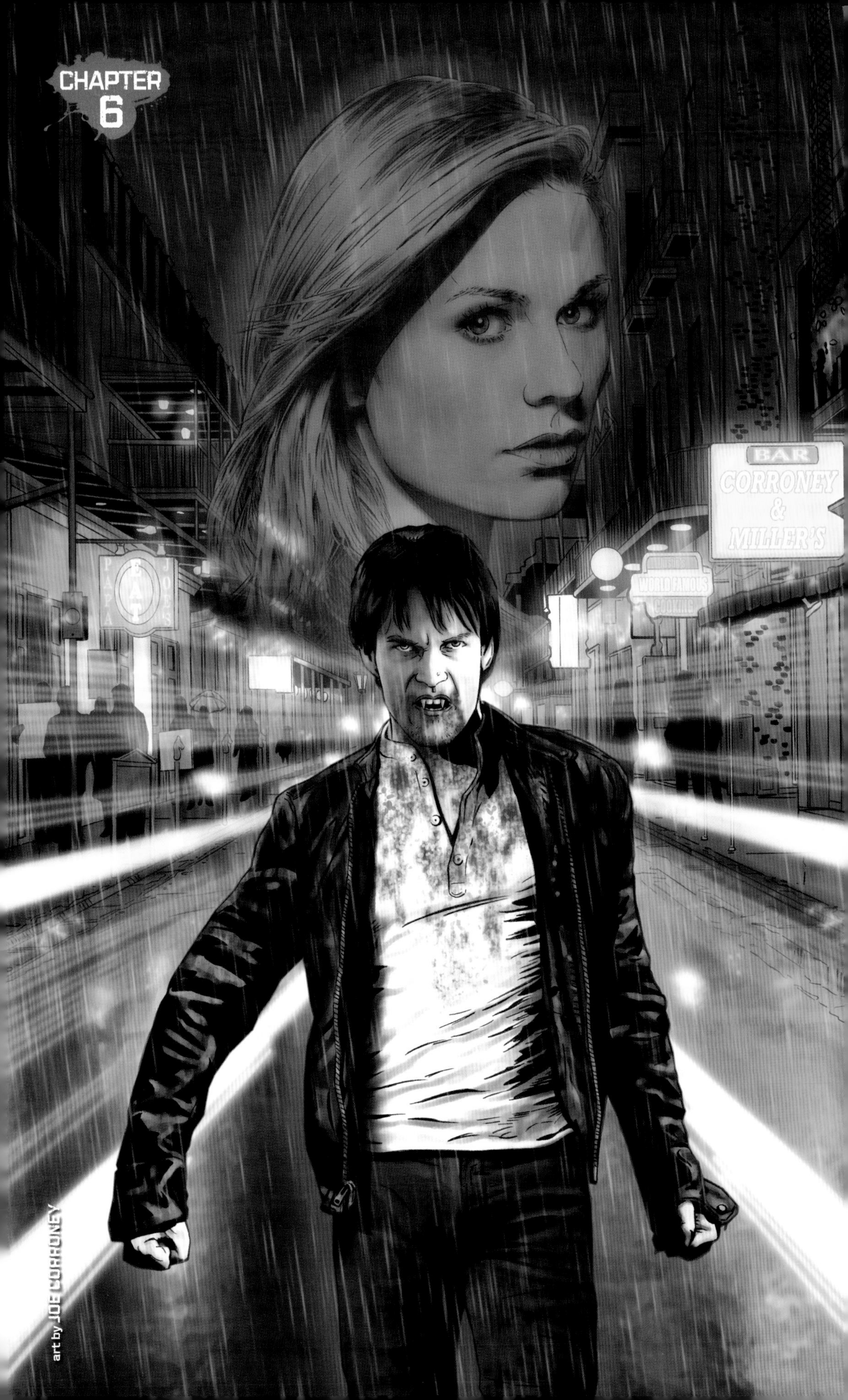
BAR
CORRONEY & MILLER'S
WORLD FAMOUS COOKING
PAPA
EAT
JOE'S

art by JOE CORRONEY

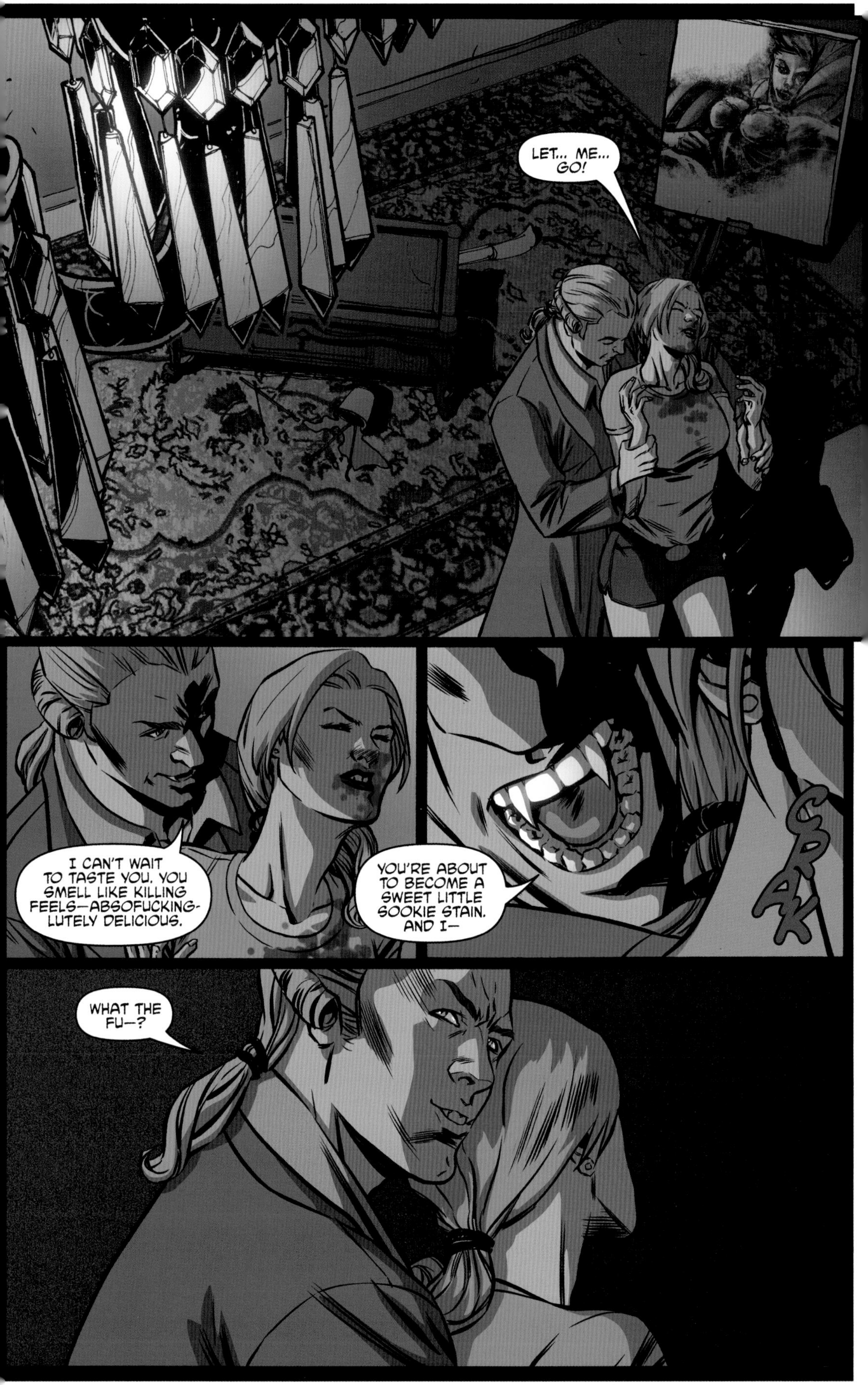
LET... ME... GO!
I CAN'T WAIT TO TASTE YOU. YOU SMELL LIKE KILLING FEELS—ABSOFUCKING-LUTELY DELICIOUS.
YOU'RE ABOUT TO BECOME A SWEET LITTLE SOOKIE STAIN. AND I—
CRAK
WHAT THE FU—?

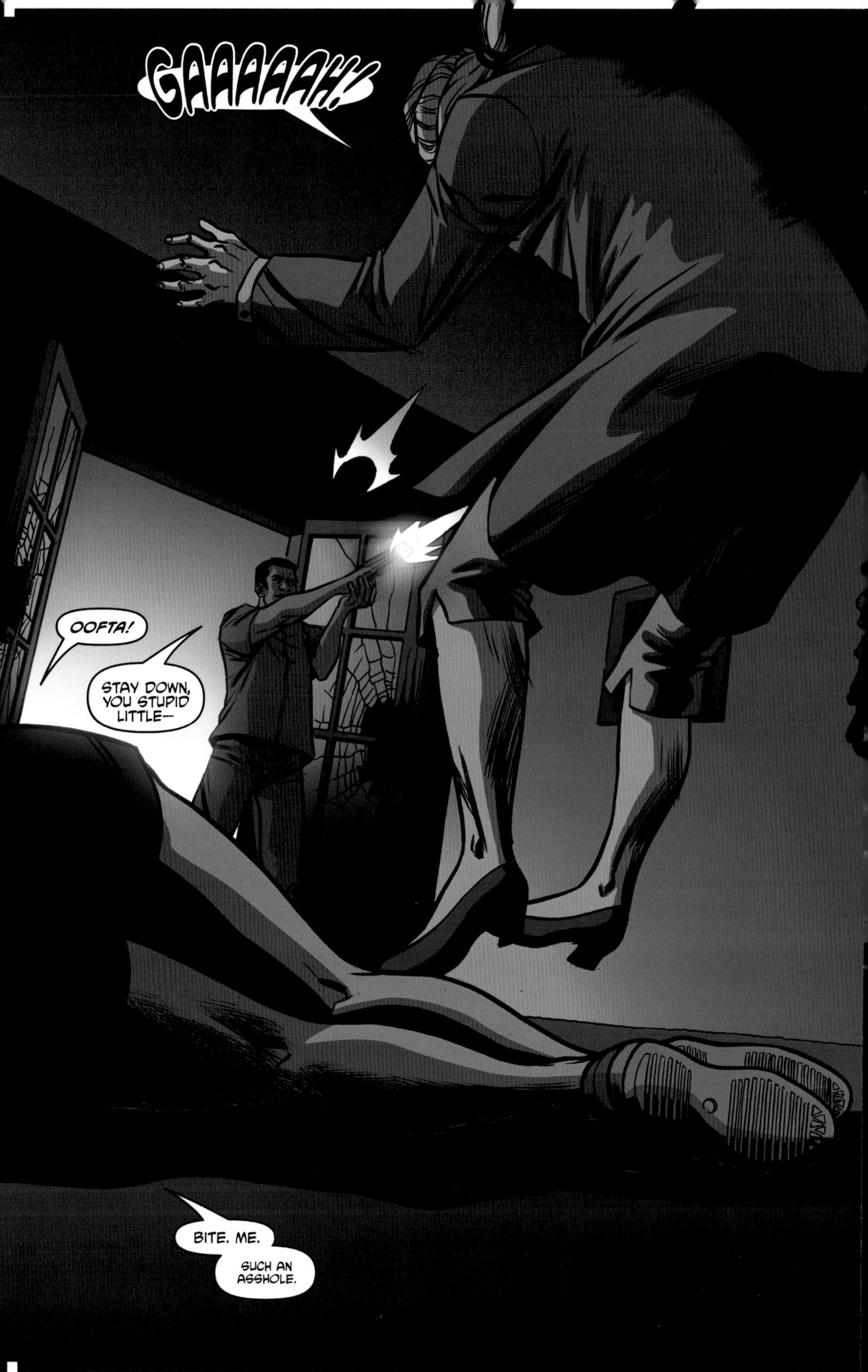
GAAAAAH!
OOFTA!
STAY DOWN, YOU STUPID LITTLE--
BITE. ME.
SUCH AN ASSHOLE.

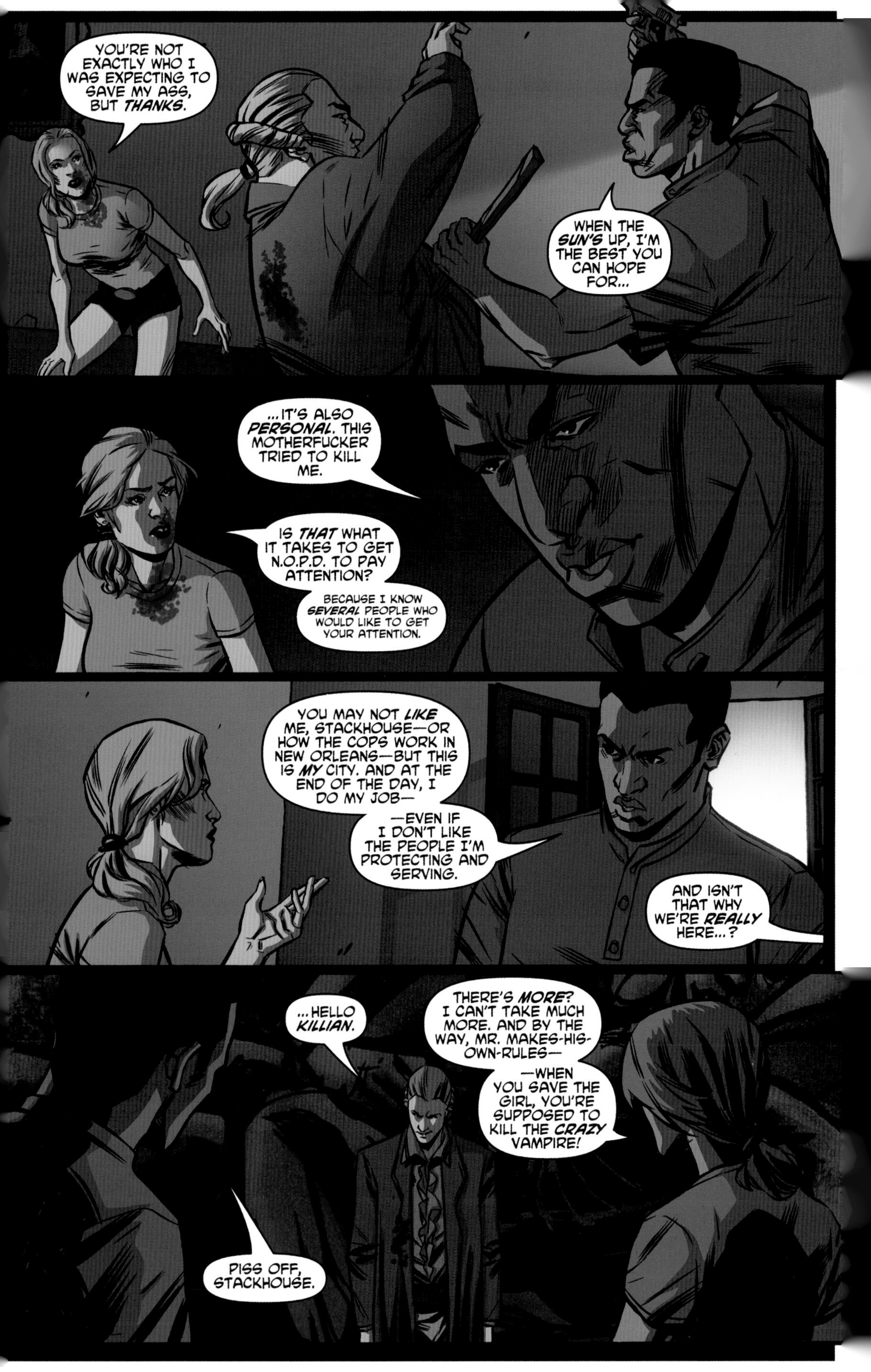
YOU'RE NOT EXACTLY WHO I WAS EXPECTING TO SAVE MY ASS, BUT *THANKS*.
WHEN THE *SUN'S* UP, I'M THE BEST YOU CAN HOPE FOR...
...IT'S ALSO *PERSONAL*. THIS MOTHERFUCKER TRIED TO KILL ME.
IS *THAT* WHAT IT TAKES TO GET N.O.P.D. TO PAY ATTENTION?
BECAUSE I KNOW *SEVERAL* PEOPLE WHO WOULD LIKE TO GET YOUR ATTENTION.
YOU MAY NOT *LIKE* ME, STACKHOUSE—OR HOW THE COPS WORK IN NEW ORLEANS—BUT THIS IS *MY* CITY. AND AT THE END OF THE DAY, I DO MY JOB—
—EVEN IF I DON'T LIKE THE PEOPLE I'M PROTECTING AND SERVING.
AND ISN'T THAT WHY WE'RE *REALLY* HERE...?
...HELLO *KILLIAN*.
THERE'S *MORE*? I CAN'T TAKE MUCH MORE. AND BY THE WAY, MR. MAKES-HIS-OWN-RULES—
—WHEN YOU SAVE THE GIRL, YOU'RE SUPPOSED TO KILL THE *CRAZY* VAMPIRE!
PISS OFF, STACKHOUSE.

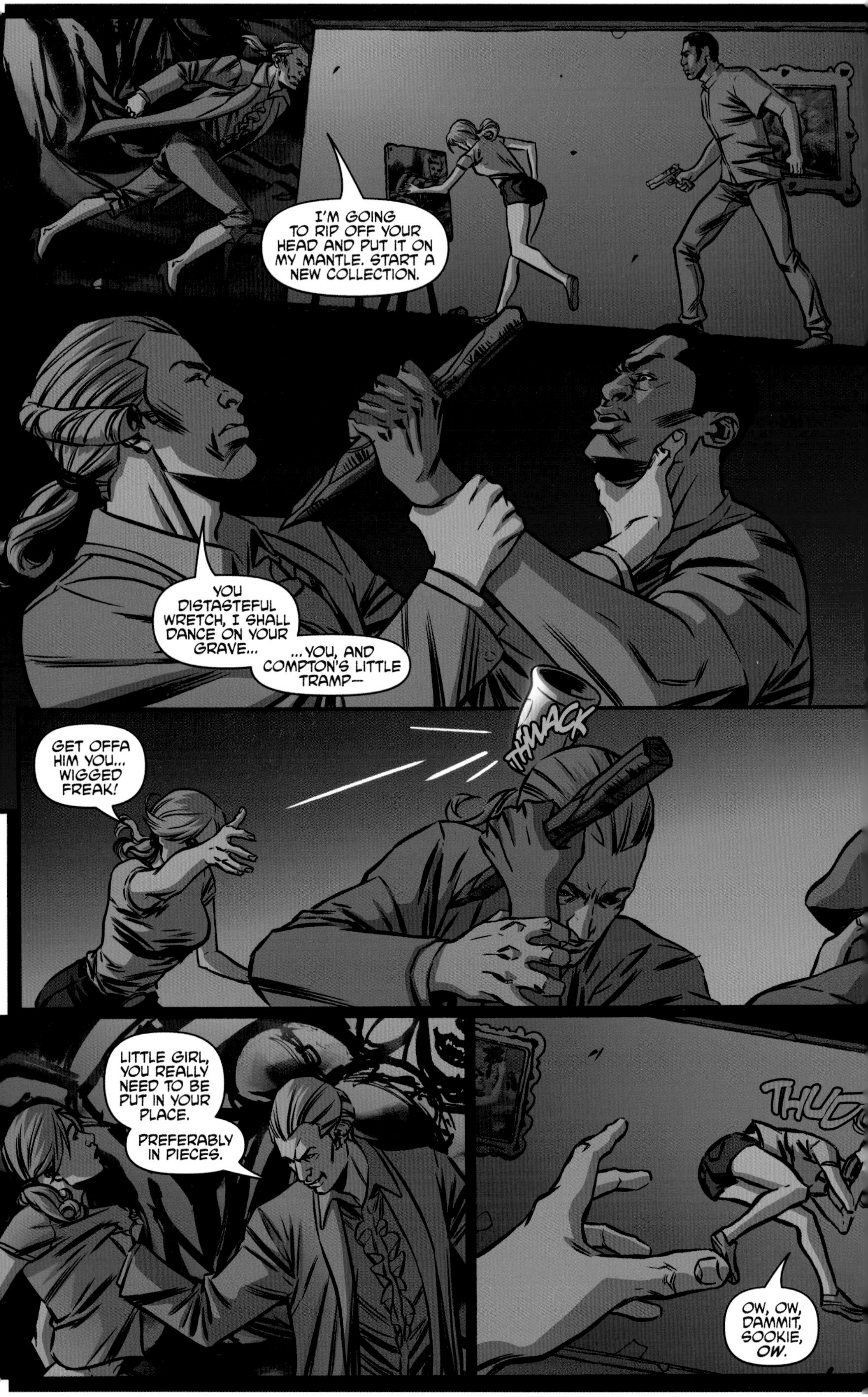
I'M GOING TO RIP OFF YOUR HEAD AND PUT IT ON MY MANTLE. START A NEW COLLECTION.
YOU DISTASTEFUL WRETCH, I SHALL DANCE ON YOUR GRAVE...
...YOU, AND COMPTON'S LITTLE TRAMP—
GET OFFA HIM YOU... WIGGED FREAK!
THWACK
LITTLE GIRL, YOU REALLY NEED TO BE PUT IN YOUR PLACE.
PREFERABLY IN PIECES.
OW, OW, DAMMIT, SOOKIE, OW.

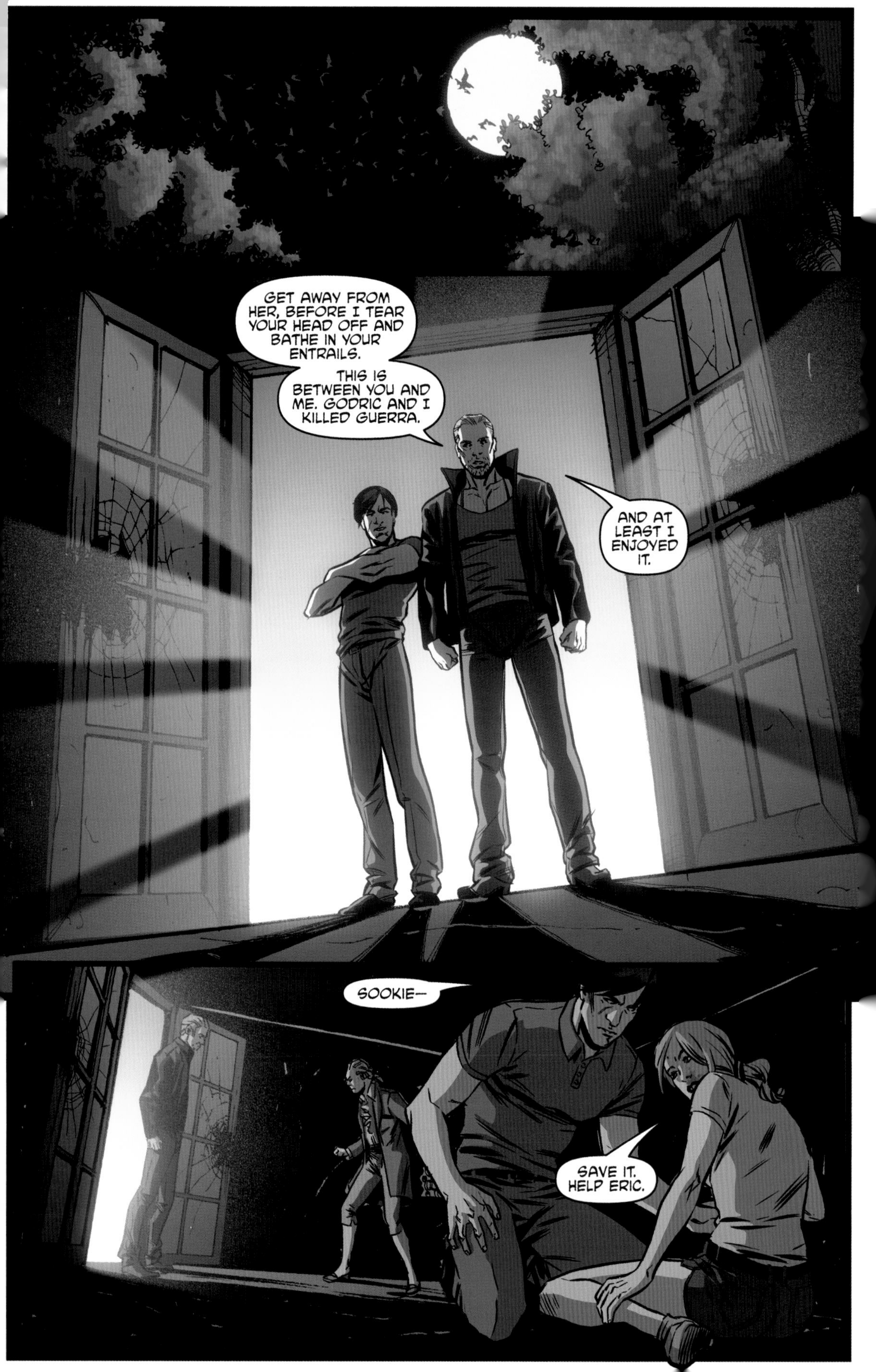
GET AWAY FROM HER, BEFORE I TEAR YOUR HEAD OFF AND BATHE IN YOUR ENTRAILS.
THIS IS BETWEEN YOU AND ME. GODRIC AND I KILLED GUERRA.
AND AT LEAST I ENJOYED IT.
SOOKIE--
SAVE IT. HELP ERIC.

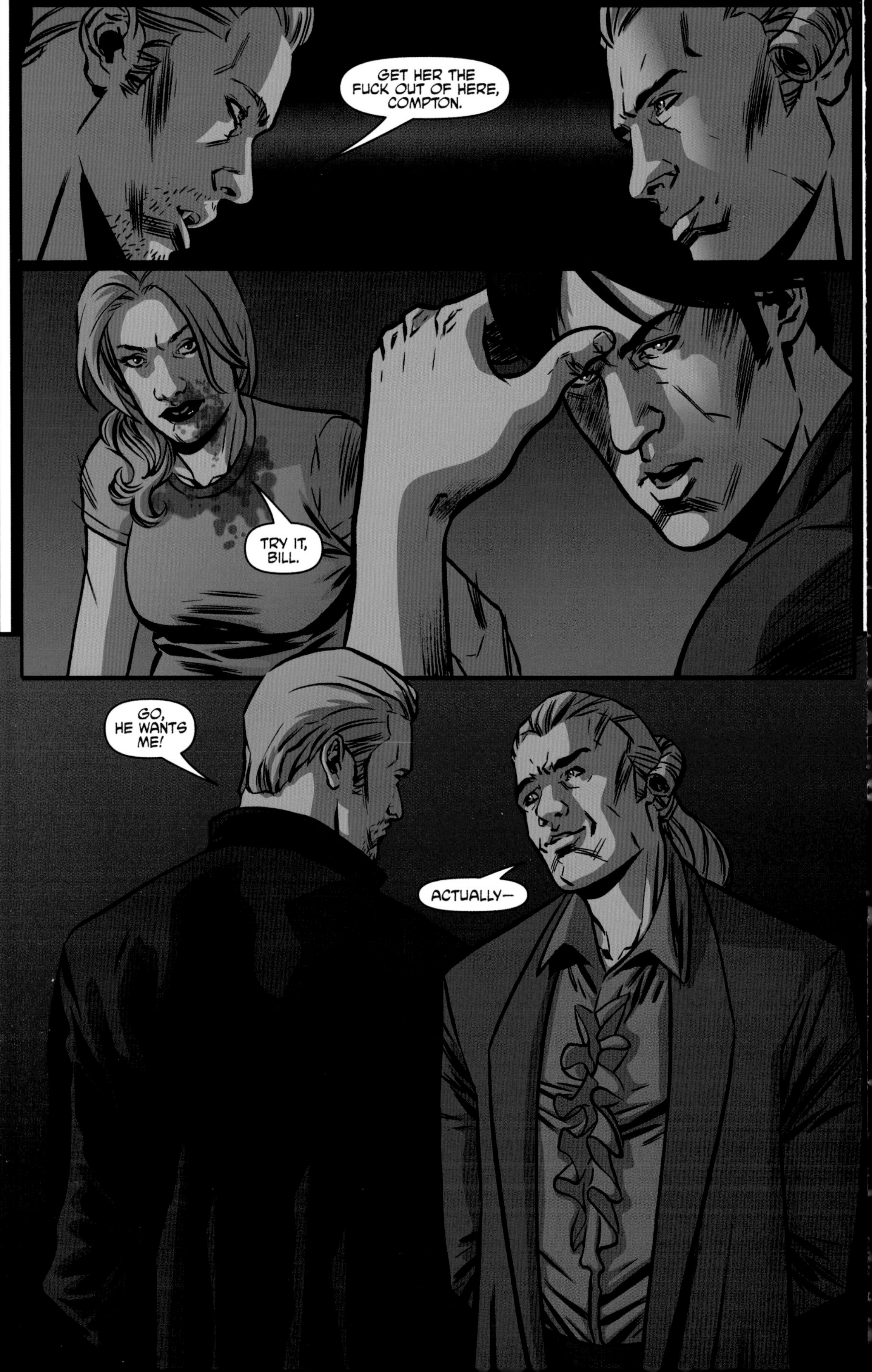
GET HER THE FUCK OUT OF HERE, COMPTON.
TRY IT, BILL.
GO, HE WANTS ME!
ACTUALLY—

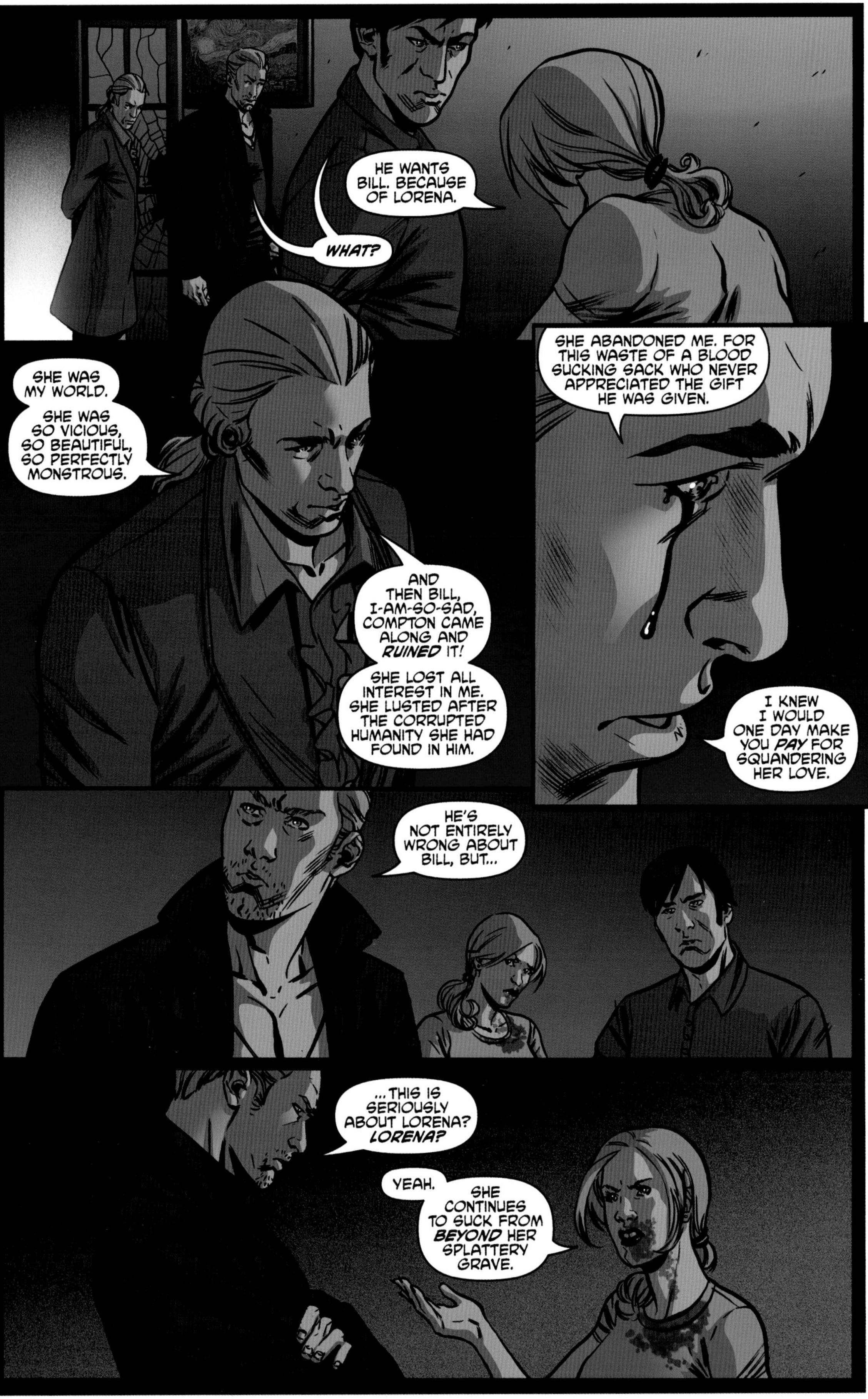
HE WANTS BILL. BECAUSE OF LORENA.
WHAT?
SHE WAS MY WORLD.
SHE WAS SO VICIOUS, SO BEAUTIFUL, SO PERFECTLY MONSTROUS.
AND THEN BILL, I-AM-SO-SAD, COMPTON CAME ALONG AND RUINED IT!
SHE LOST ALL INTEREST IN ME. SHE LUSTED AFTER THE CORRUPTED HUMANITY SHE HAD FOUND IN HIM.
SHE ABANDONED ME. FOR THIS WASTE OF A BLOOD SUCKING SACK WHO NEVER APPRECIATED THE GIFT HE WAS GIVEN.
I KNEW I WOULD ONE DAY MAKE YOU PAY FOR SQUANDERING HER LOVE.
HE'S NOT ENTIRELY WRONG ABOUT BILL, BUT...
...THIS IS SERIOUSLY ABOUT LORENA? LORENA?
YEAH.
SHE CONTINUES TO SUCK FROM BEYOND HER SPLATTERY GRAVE.

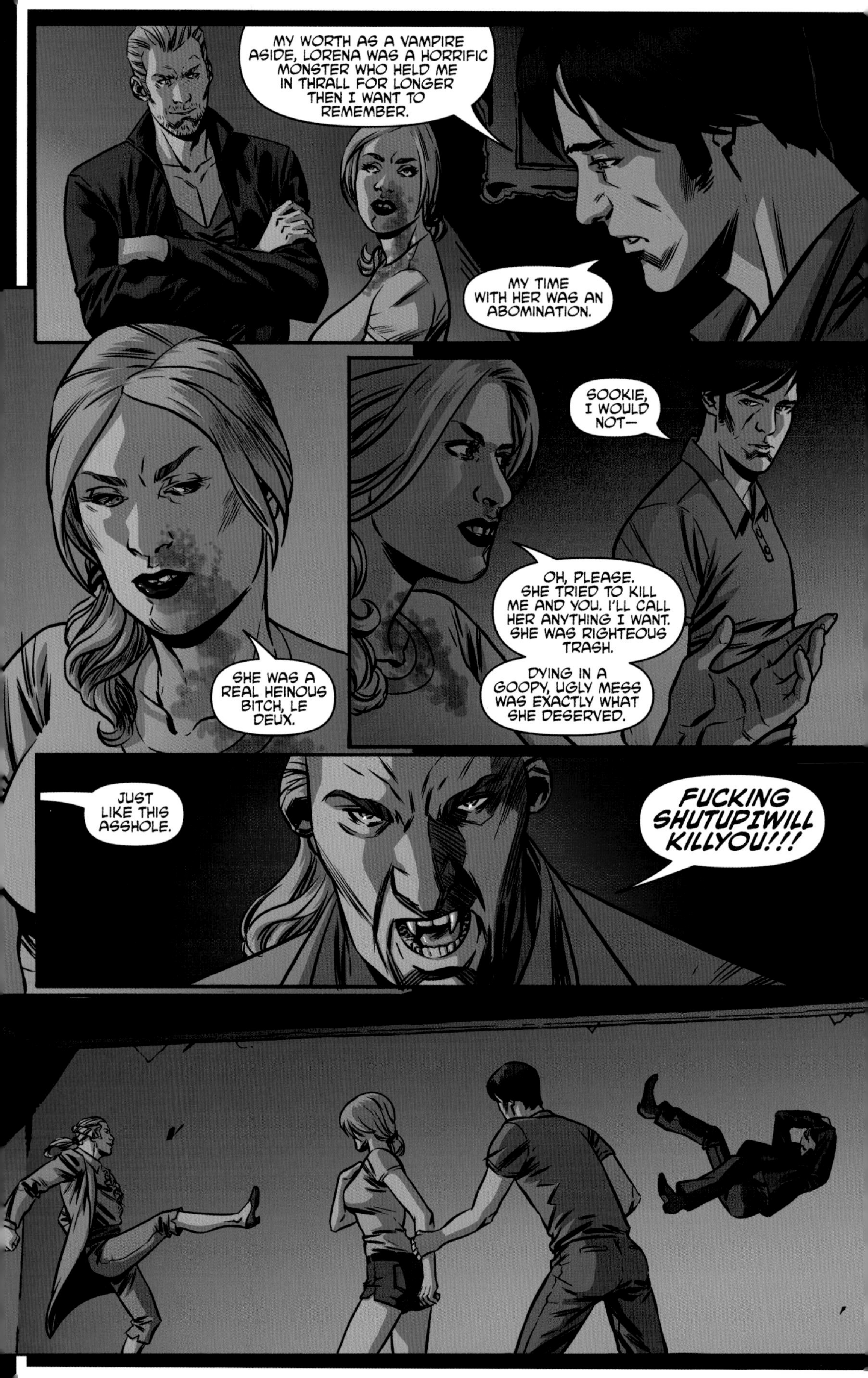
MY WORTH AS A VAMPIRE ASIDE, LORENA WAS A HORRIFIC MONSTER WHO HELD ME IN THRALL FOR LONGER THEN I WANT TO REMEMBER.
MY TIME WITH HER WAS AN ABOMINATION.
SHE WAS A REAL HEINOUS BITCH, LE DEUX.
SOOKIE, I WOULD NOT--
OH, PLEASE. SHE TRIED TO KILL ME AND YOU. I'LL CALL HER ANYTHING I WANT. SHE WAS RIGHTEOUS TRASH.
DYING IN A GOOPY, UGLY MESS WAS EXACTLY WHAT SHE DESERVED.
JUST LIKE THIS ASSHOLE.
FUCKING SHUTUPIWILL KILLYOU!!!

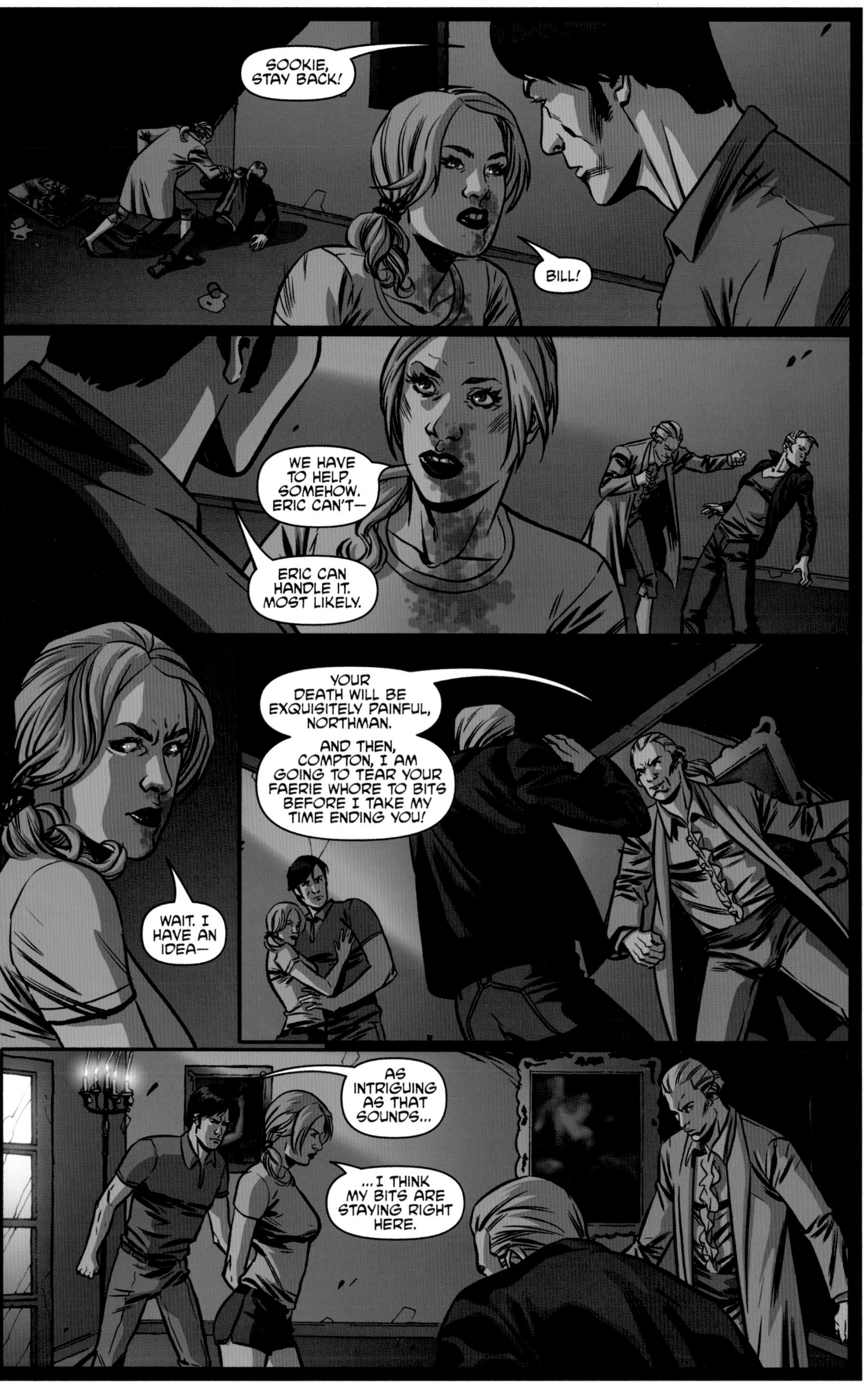
SOOKIE, STAY BACK!
BILL!
WE HAVE TO HELP, SOMEHOW. ERIC CAN'T--
ERIC CAN HANDLE IT. MOST LIKELY.
WAIT. I HAVE AN IDEA--
YOUR DEATH WILL BE EXQUISITELY PAINFUL, NORTHMAN.
AND THEN, COMPTON, I AM GOING TO TEAR YOUR FAERIE WHORE TO BITS BEFORE I TAKE MY TIME ENDING YOU!
AS INTRIGUING AS THAT SOUNDS...
...I THINK MY BITS ARE STAYING RIGHT HERE.

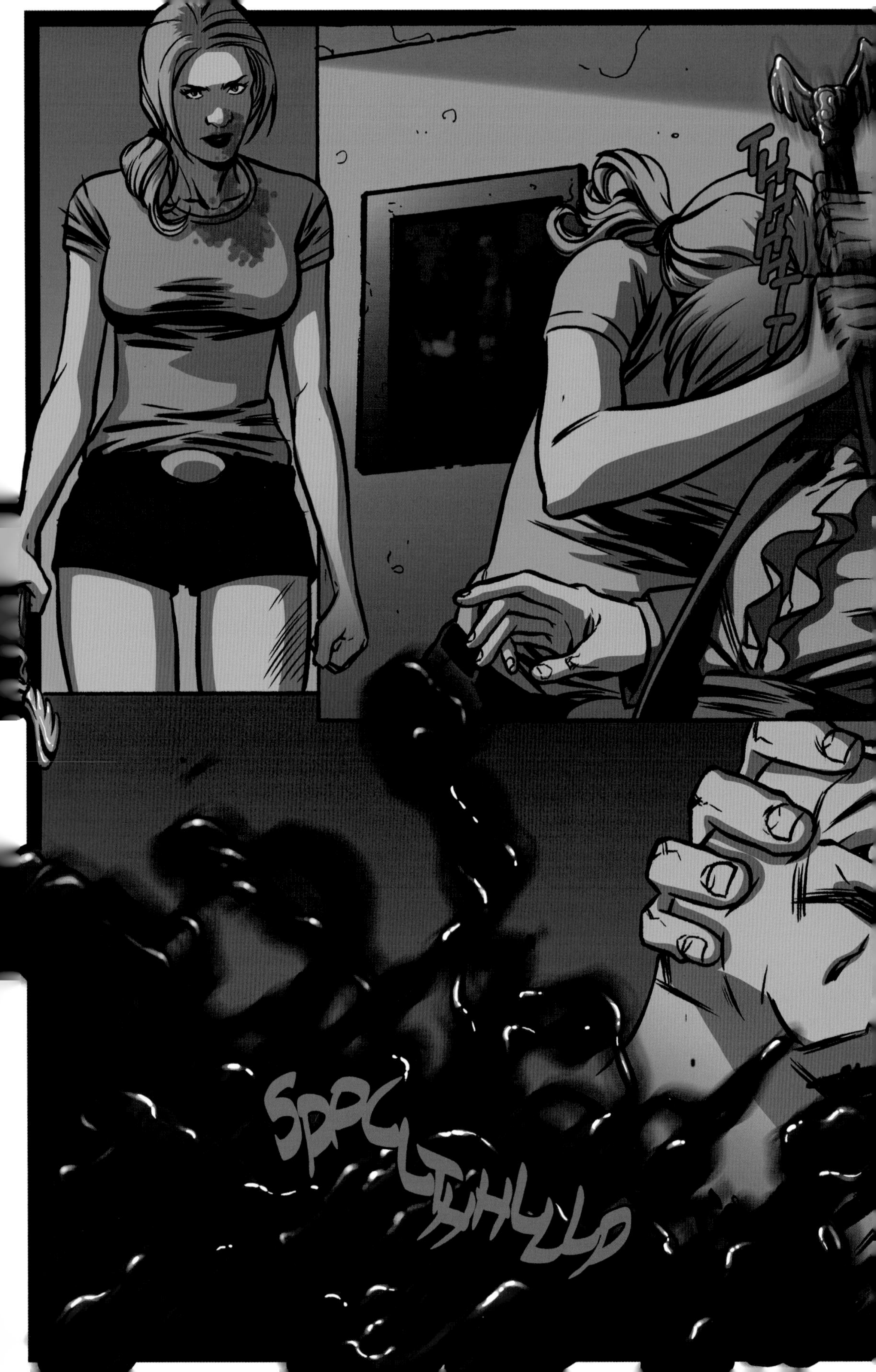
THHHTT
SPCLTHHLLD

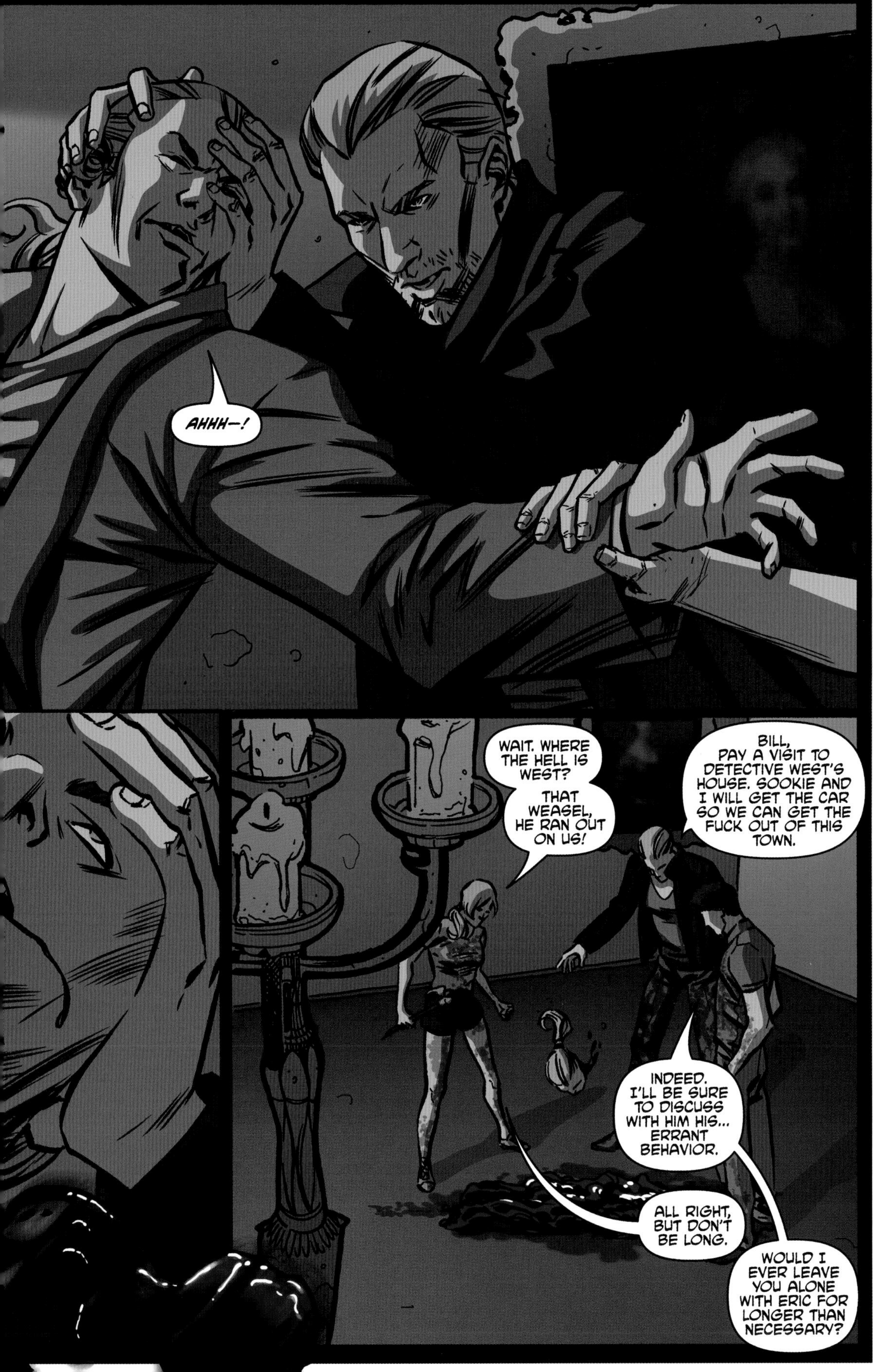
AHHH-!
WAIT. WHERE THE HELL IS WEST?
THAT WEASEL, HE RAN OUT ON US!
BILL, PAY A VISIT TO DETECTIVE WEST'S HOUSE. SOOKIE AND I WILL GET THE CAR SO WE CAN GET THE FUCK OUT OF THIS TOWN.
INDEED. I'LL BE SURE TO DISCUSS WITH HIM HIS... ERRANT BEHAVIOR.
ALL RIGHT, BUT DON'T BE LONG.
WOULD I EVER LEAVE YOU ALONE WITH ERIC FOR LONGER THAN NECESSARY?

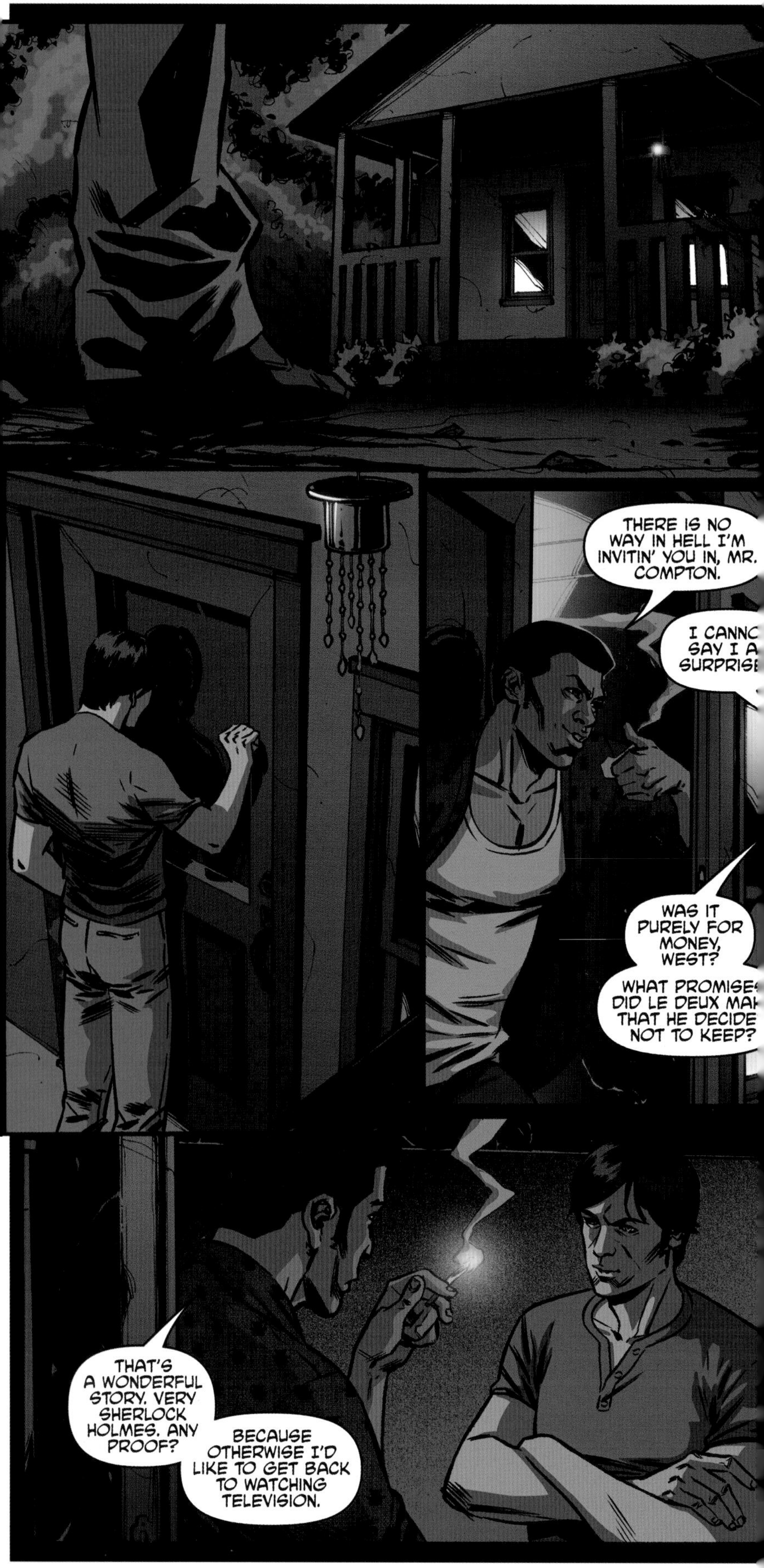
THERE IS NO WAY IN HELL I'M INVITIN' YOU IN, MR. COMPTON.
I CANNO SAY I A SURPRISE
WAS IT PURELY FOR MONEY, WEST?
WHAT PROMISE DID LE DEUX MA THAT HE DECIDE NOT TO KEEP?
THAT'S A WONDERFUL STORY. VERY SHERLOCK HOLMES. ANY PROOF?
BECAUSE OTHERWISE I'D LIKE TO GET BACK TO WATCHING TELEVISION.

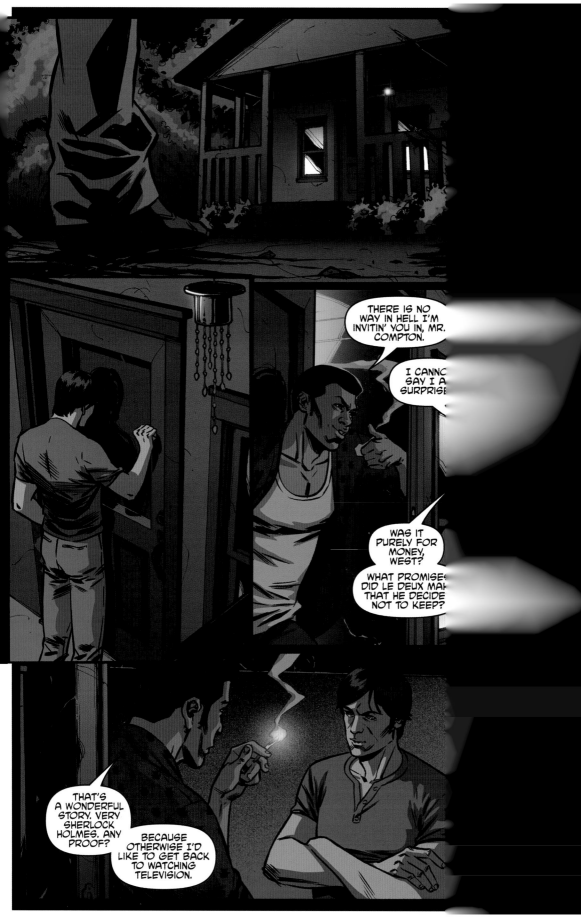

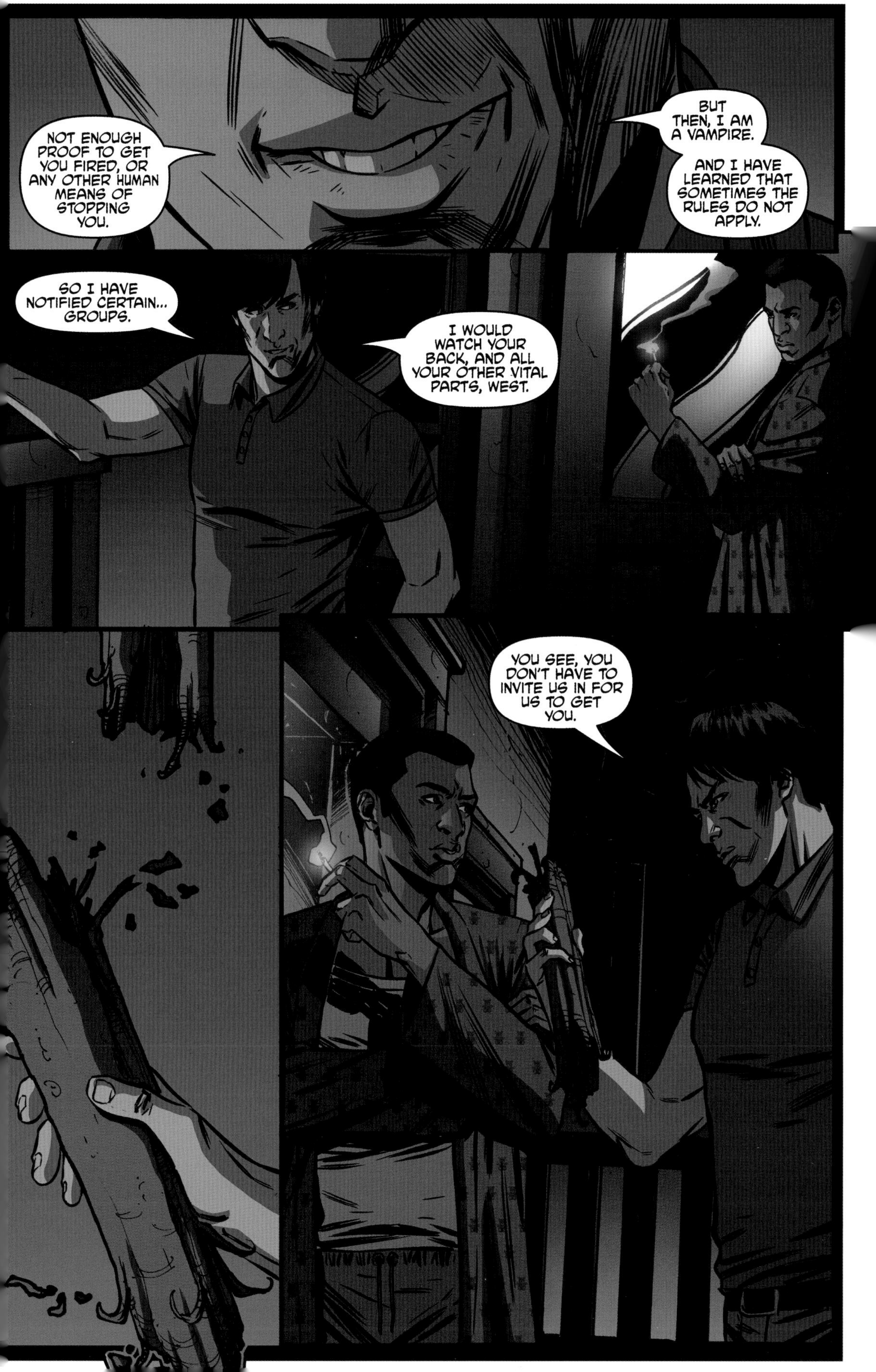
NOT ENOUGH PROOF TO GET YOU FIRED, OR ANY OTHER HUMAN MEANS OF STOPPING YOU.
BUT THEN, I AM A VAMPIRE.
AND I HAVE LEARNED THAT SOMETIMES THE RULES DO NOT APPLY.
SO I HAVE NOTIFIED CERTAIN... GROUPS.
I WOULD WATCH YOUR BACK, AND ALL YOUR OTHER VITAL PARTS, WEST.
YOU SEE, YOU DON'T HAVE TO INVITE US IN FOR US TO GET YOU.

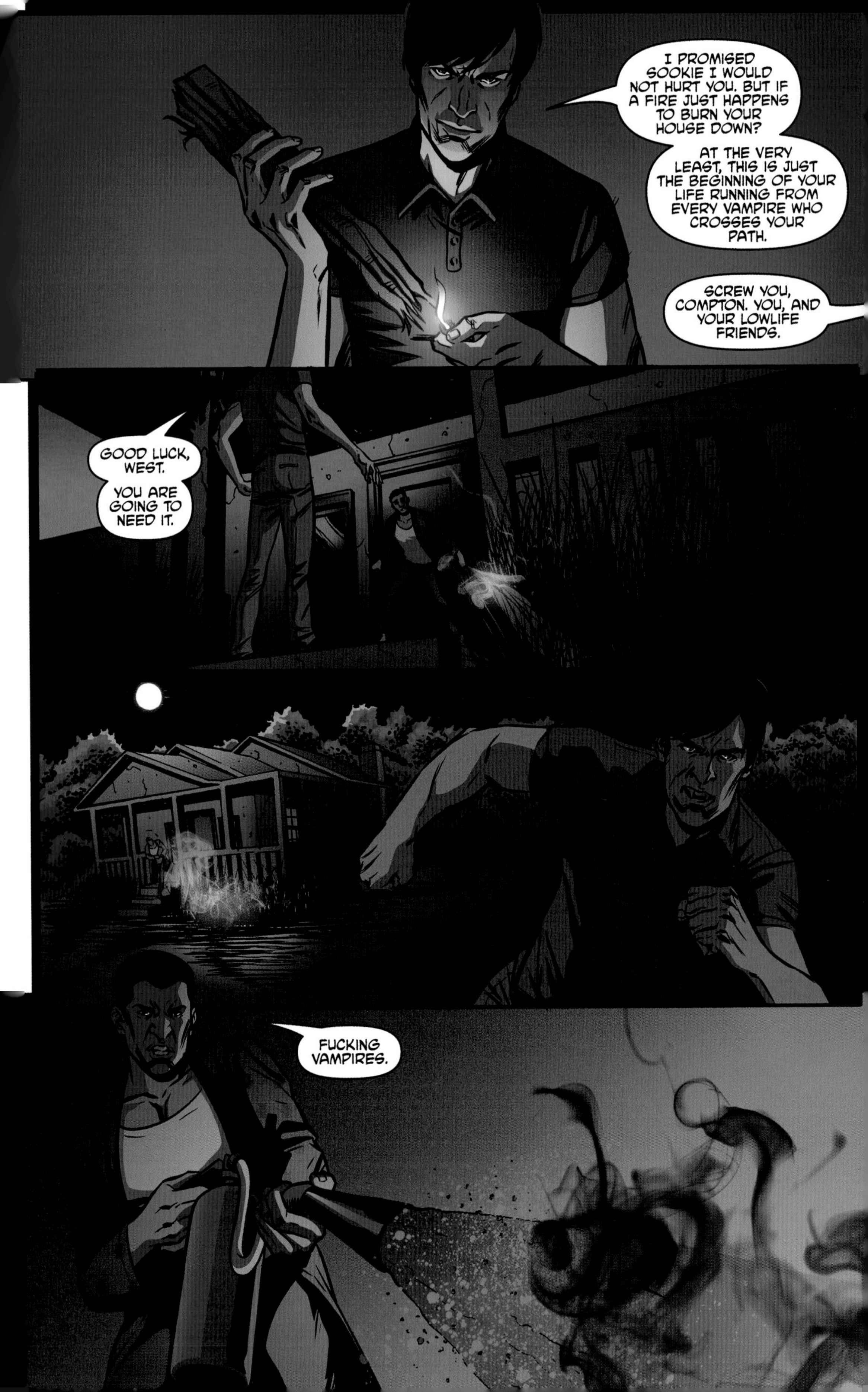
I PROMISED SOOKIE I WOULD NOT HURT YOU. BUT IF A FIRE JUST HAPPENS TO BURN YOUR HOUSE DOWN?
AT THE VERY LEAST, THIS IS JUST THE BEGINNING OF YOUR LIFE RUNNING FROM EVERY VAMPIRE WHO CROSSES YOUR PATH.
SCREW YOU, COMPTON. YOU, AND YOUR LOWLIFE FRIENDS.
GOOD LUCK, WEST.
YOU ARE GOING TO NEED IT.
FUCKING VAMPIRES.

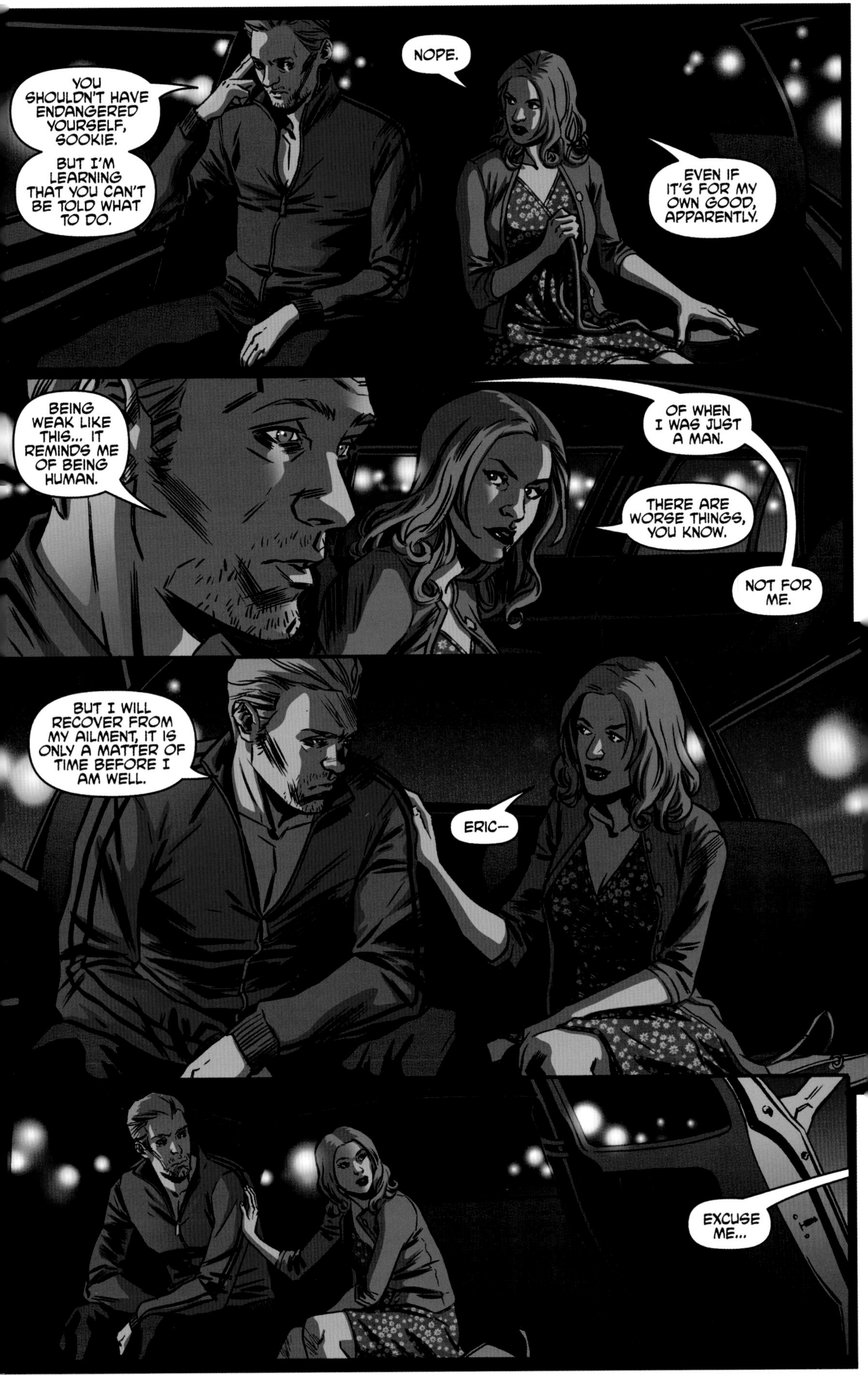
YOU SHOULDN'T HAVE ENDANGERED YOURSELF, SOOKIE.
BUT I'M LEARNING THAT YOU CAN'T BE TOLD WHAT TO DO.
NOPE.
EVEN IF IT'S FOR MY OWN GOOD, APPARENTLY.
BEING WEAK LIKE THIS... IT REMINDS ME OF BEING HUMAN.
OF WHEN I WAS JUST A MAN.
THERE ARE WORSE THINGS, YOU KNOW.
NOT FOR ME.
BUT I WILL RECOVER FROM MY AILMENT, IT IS ONLY A MATTER OF TIME BEFORE I AM WELL.
ERIC--
EXCUSE ME...

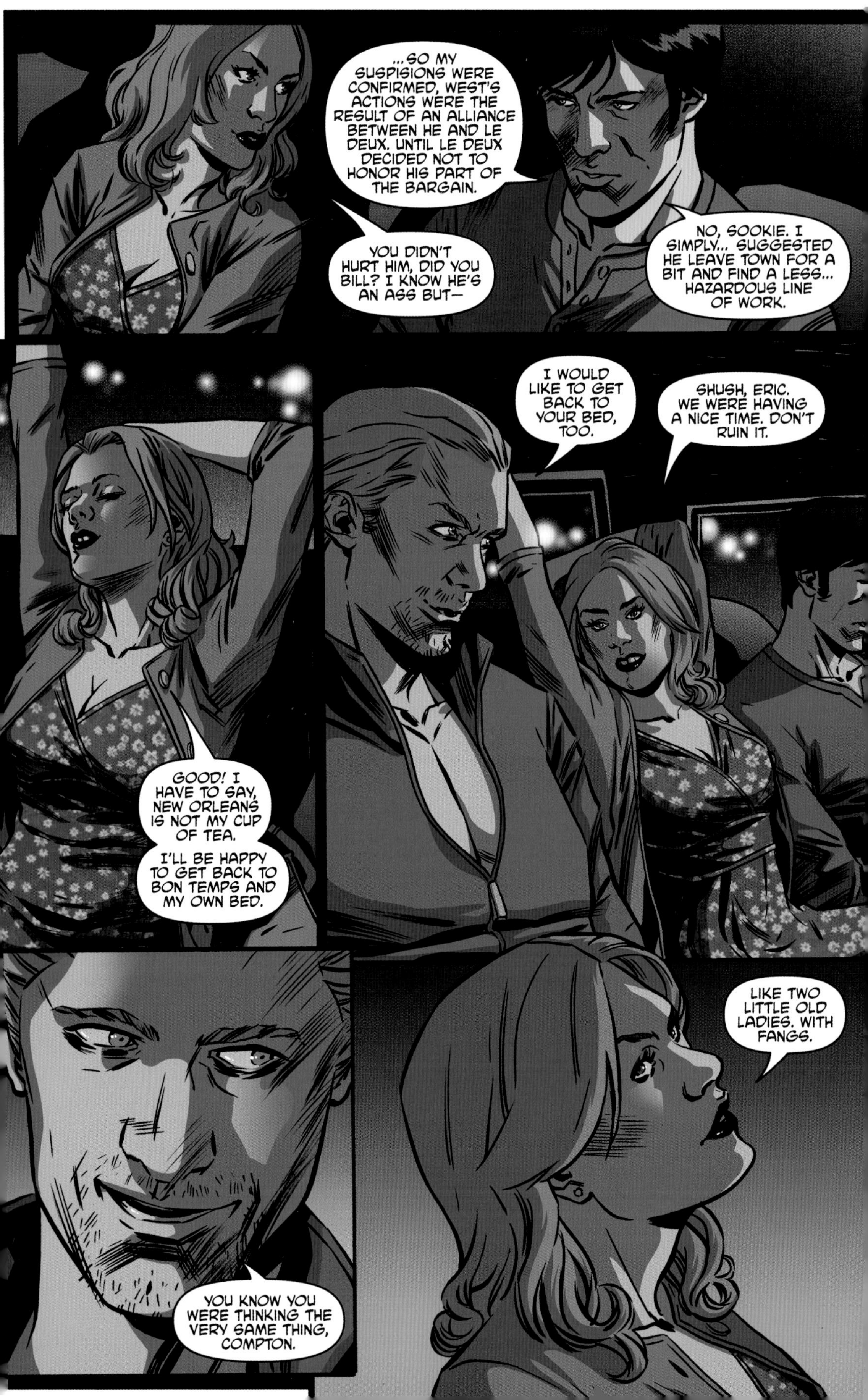

...SO MY SUSPISIONS WERE CONFIRMED, WEST'S ACTIONS WERE THE RESULT OF AN ALLIANCE BETWEEN HE AND LE DEUX. UNTIL LE DEUX DECIDED NOT TO HONOR HIS PART OF THE BARGAIN.
YOU DIDN'T HURT HIM, DID YOU BILL? I KNOW HE'S AN ASS BUT—
NO, SOOKIE. I SIMPLY... SUGGESTED HE LEAVE TOWN FOR A BIT AND FIND A LESS... HAZARDOUS LINE OF WORK.
GOOD! I HAVE TO SAY, NEW ORLEANS IS NOT MY CUP OF TEA.
I'LL BE HAPPY TO GET BACK TO BON TEMPS AND MY OWN BED.
I WOULD LIKE TO GET BACK TO YOUR BED, TOO.
SHUSH, ERIC. WE WERE HAVING A NICE TIME. DON'T RUIN IT.
YOU KNOW YOU WERE THINKING THE VERY SAME THING, COMPTON.
LIKE TWO LITTLE OLD LADIES. WITH FANGS.

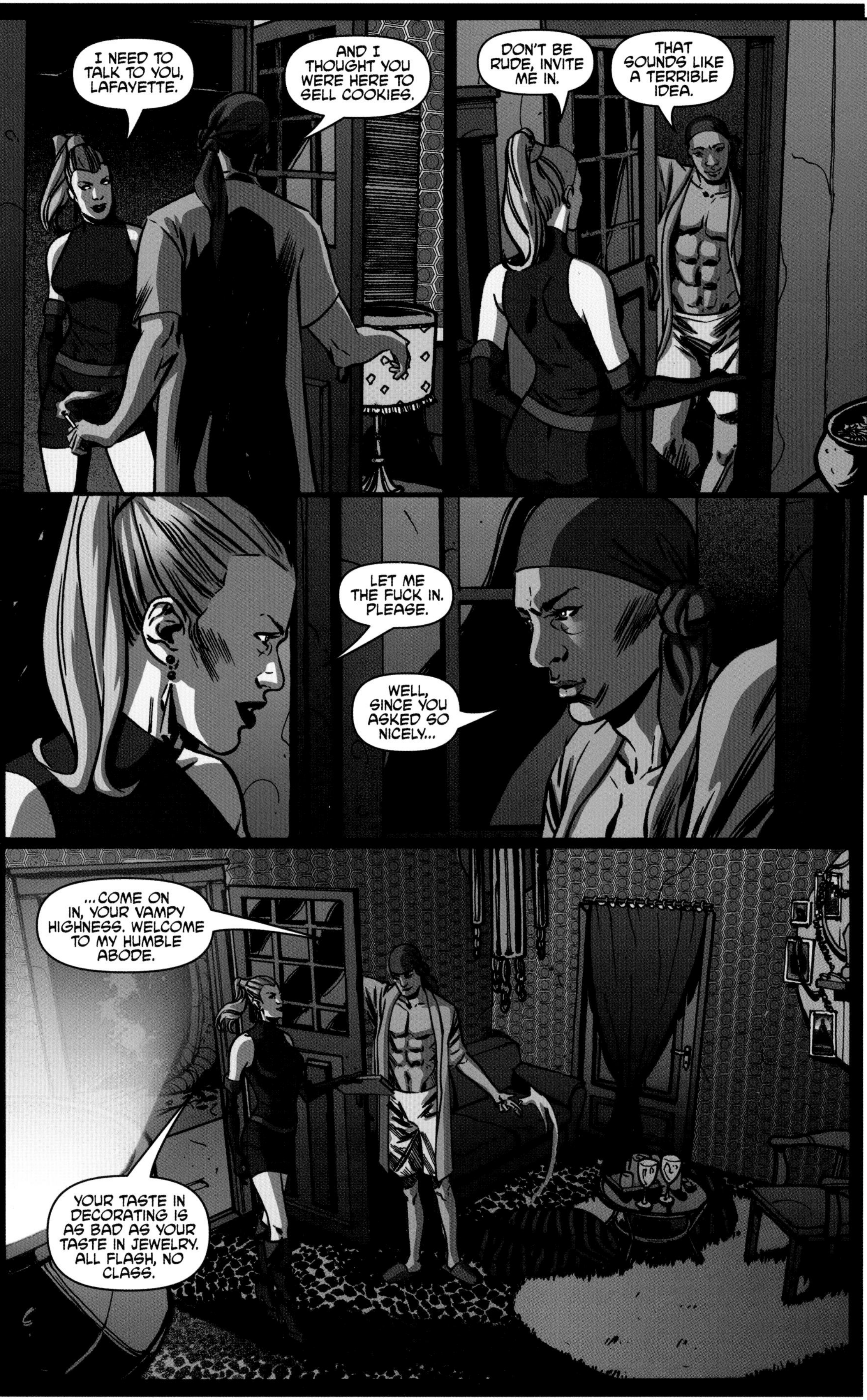
I NEED TO TALK TO YOU, LAFAYETTE.
AND I THOUGHT YOU WERE HERE TO SELL COOKIES.
DON'T BE RUDE, INVITE ME IN.
THAT SOUNDS LIKE A TERRIBLE IDEA.
LET ME THE FUCK IN. PLEASE.
WELL, SINCE YOU ASKED SO NICELY...
...COME ON IN, YOUR VAMPY HIGHNESS. WELCOME TO MY HUMBLE ABODE.
YOUR TASTE IN DECORATING IS AS BAD AS YOUR TASTE IN JEWELRY. ALL FLASH, NO CLASS.

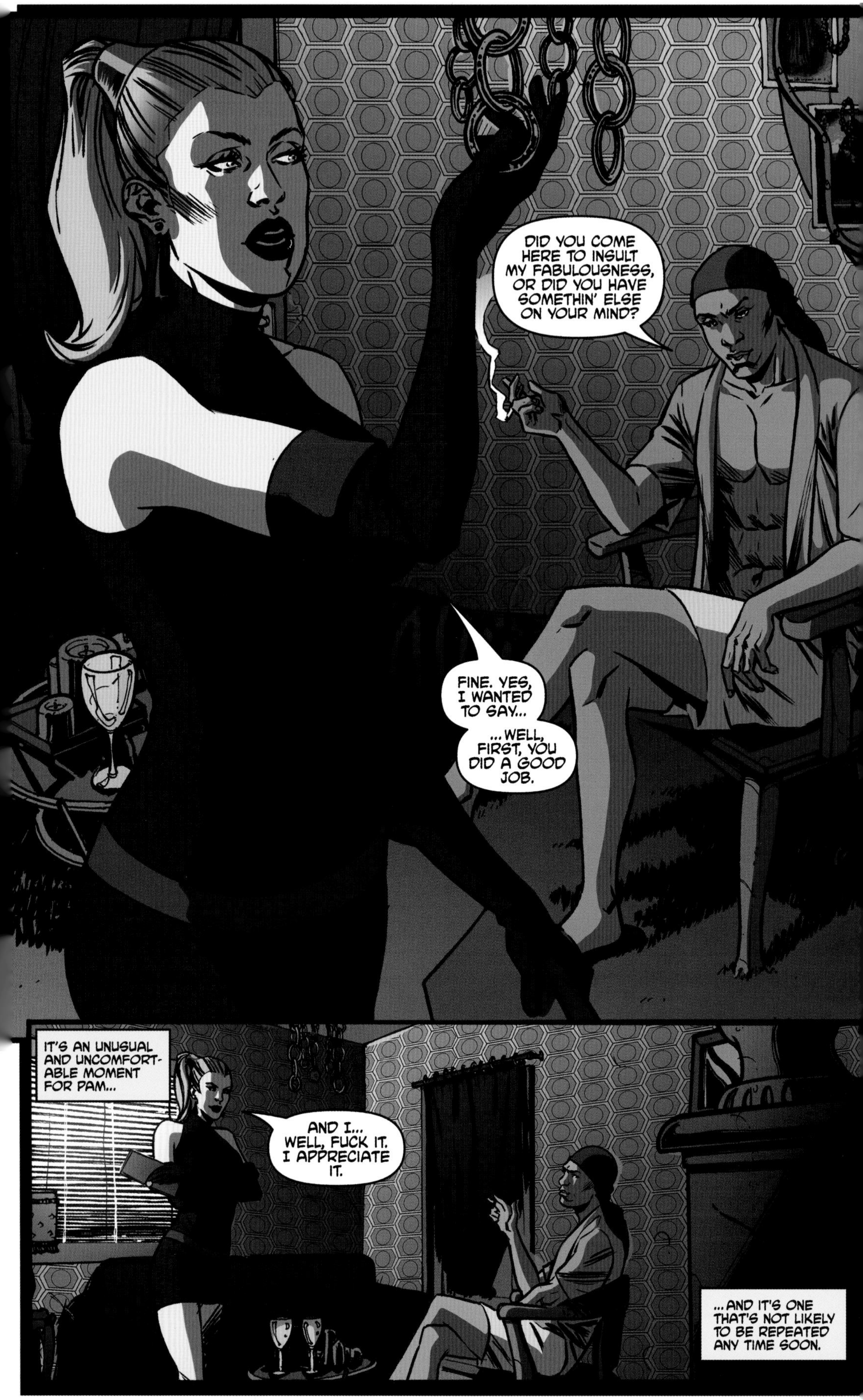
DID YOU COME HERE TO INSULT MY FABULOUSNESS, OR DID YOU HAVE SOMETHIN' ELSE ON YOUR MIND?
FINE. YES, I WANTED TO SAY...
...WELL, FIRST, YOU DID A GOOD JOB.
IT'S AN UNUSUAL AND UNCOMFORT-ABLE MOMENT FOR PAM...
AND I... WELL, FUCK IT. I APPRECIATE IT.
...AND IT'S ONE THAT'S NOT LIKELY TO BE REPEATED ANY TIME SOON.

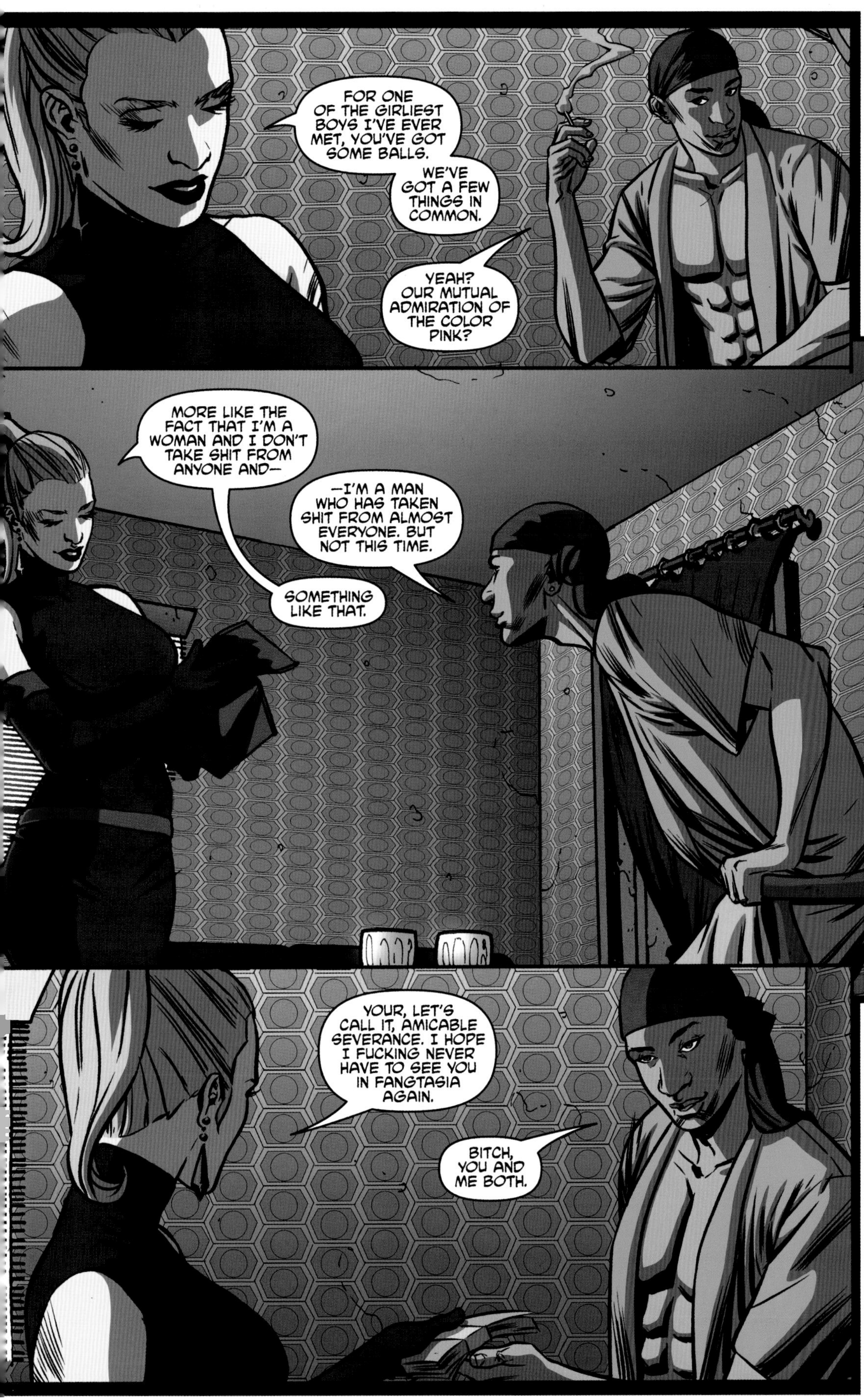
FOR ONE OF THE GIRLIEST BOYS I'VE EVER MET, YOU'VE GOT SOME BALLS.
WE'VE GOT A FEW THINGS IN COMMON.
YEAH? OUR MUTUAL ADMIRATION OF THE COLOR PINK?
MORE LIKE THE FACT THAT I'M A WOMAN AND I DON'T TAKE SHIT FROM ANYONE AND—
—I'M A MAN WHO HAS TAKEN SHIT FROM ALMOST EVERYONE. BUT NOT THIS TIME.
SOMETHING LIKE THAT.
YOUR, LET'S CALL IT, AMICABLE SEVERANCE. I HOPE I FUCKING NEVER HAVE TO SEE YOU IN FANGTASIA AGAIN.
BITCH, YOU AND ME BOTH.

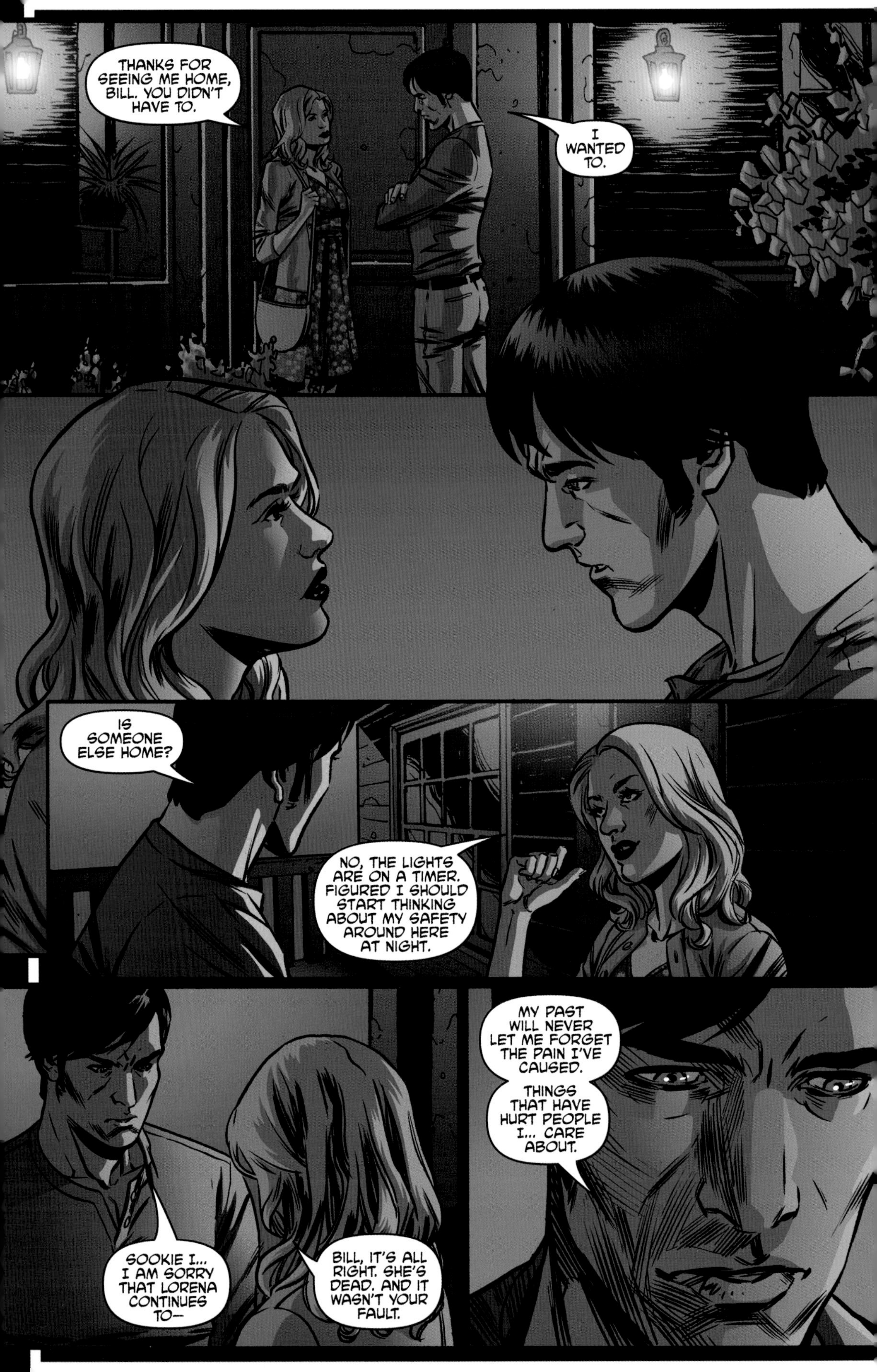
THANKS FOR SEEING ME HOME, BILL. YOU DIDN'T HAVE TO.
I WANTED TO.
IS SOMEONE ELSE HOME?
NO, THE LIGHTS ARE ON A TIMER. FIGURED I SHOULD START THINKING ABOUT MY SAFETY AROUND HERE AT NIGHT.
SOOKIE I... I AM SORRY THAT LORENA CONTINUES TO—
BILL, IT'S ALL RIGHT. SHE'S DEAD. AND IT WASN'T YOUR FAULT.
MY PAST WILL NEVER LET ME FORGET THE PAIN I'VE CAUSED.
THINGS THAT HAVE HURT PEOPLE I... CARE ABOUT.

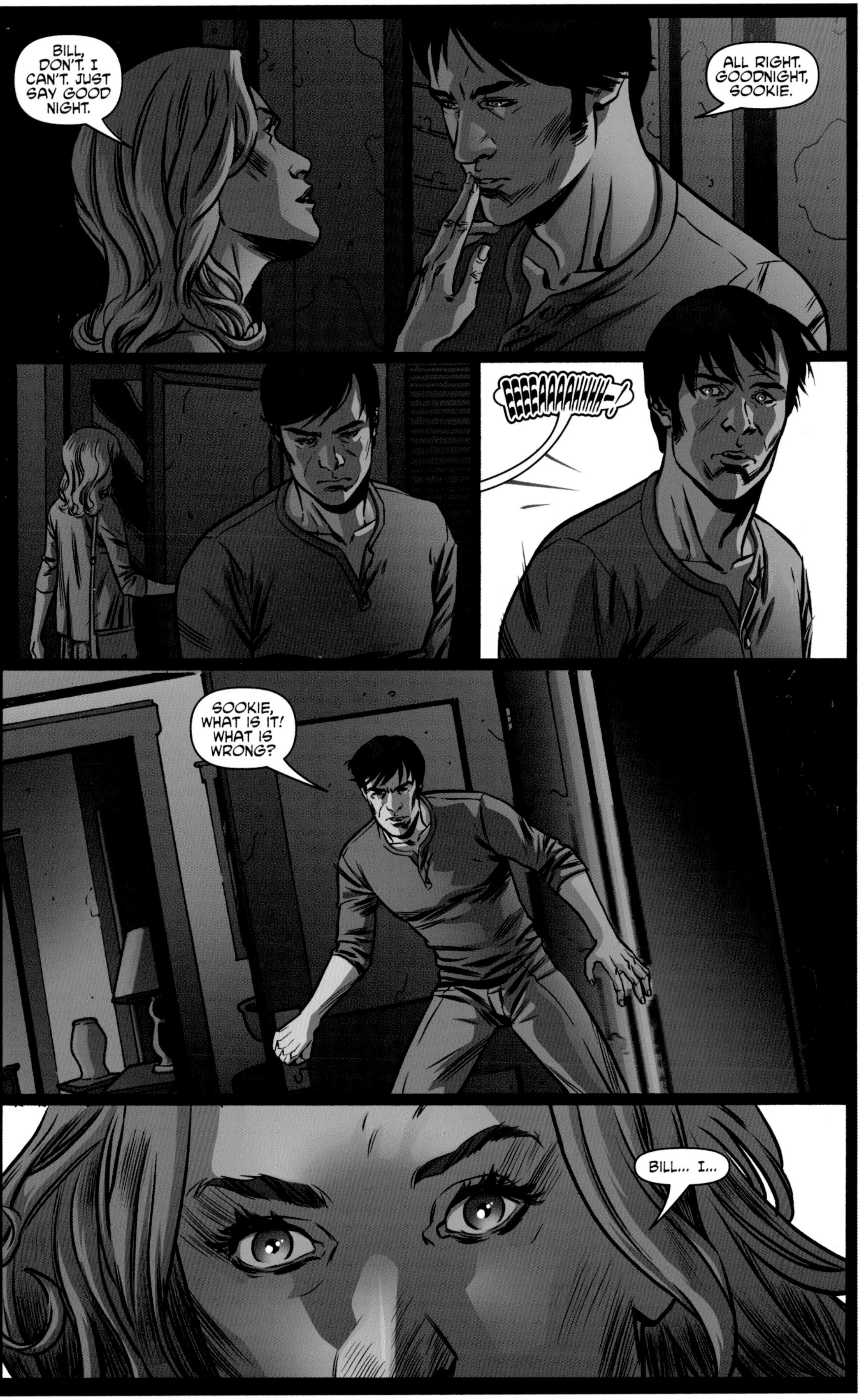
BILL, DON'T. I CAN'T. JUST SAY GOOD NIGHT.
ALL RIGHT. GOODNIGHT, SOOKIE.
EEEEAAAAHHHH-!
SOOKIE, WHAT IS IT! WHAT IS WRONG?
BILL... I...

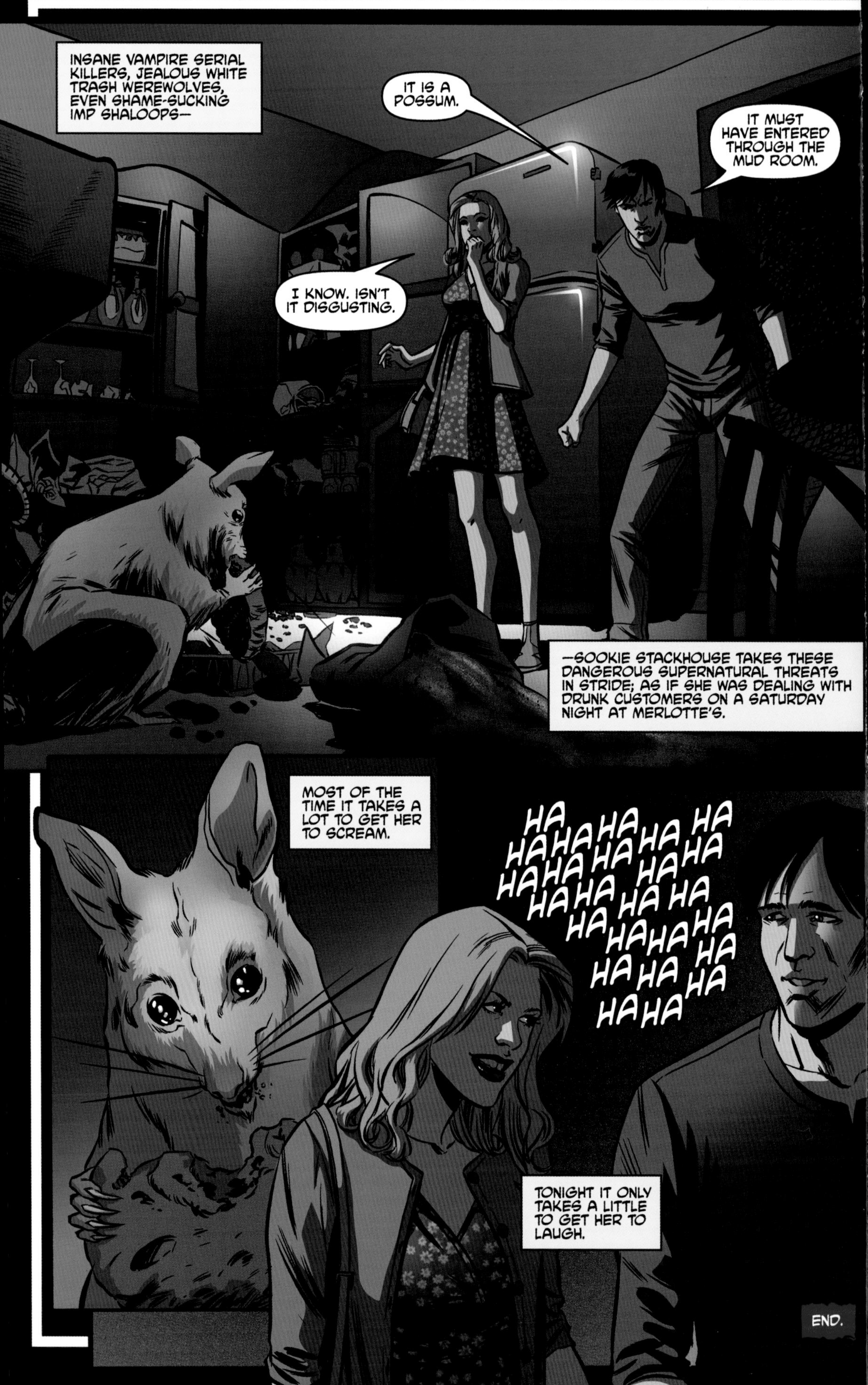

INSANE VAMPIRE SERIAL KILLERS, JEALOUS WHITE TRASH WEREWOLVES, EVEN SHAME-SUCKING IMP SHALOOPS—
IT IS A POSSUM.
IT MUST HAVE ENTERED THROUGH THE MUD ROOM.
I KNOW. ISN'T IT DISGUSTING.
—SOOKIE STACKHOUSE TAKES THESE DANGEROUS SUPERNATURAL THREATS IN STRIDE; AS IF SHE WAS DEALING WITH DRUNK CUSTOMERS ON A SATURDAY NIGHT AT MERLOTTE'S.
MOST OF THE TIME IT TAKES A LOT TO GET HER TO SCREAM.
HA HA HA HA HA HA HA HA HA HA HA HA HA HA HA HA HA HA HA HA HA HA HA HA HA HA HA HA HA HA HA HA HA HA HA HA
TONIGHT IT ONLY TAKES A LITTLE TO GET HER TO LAUGH.
END.

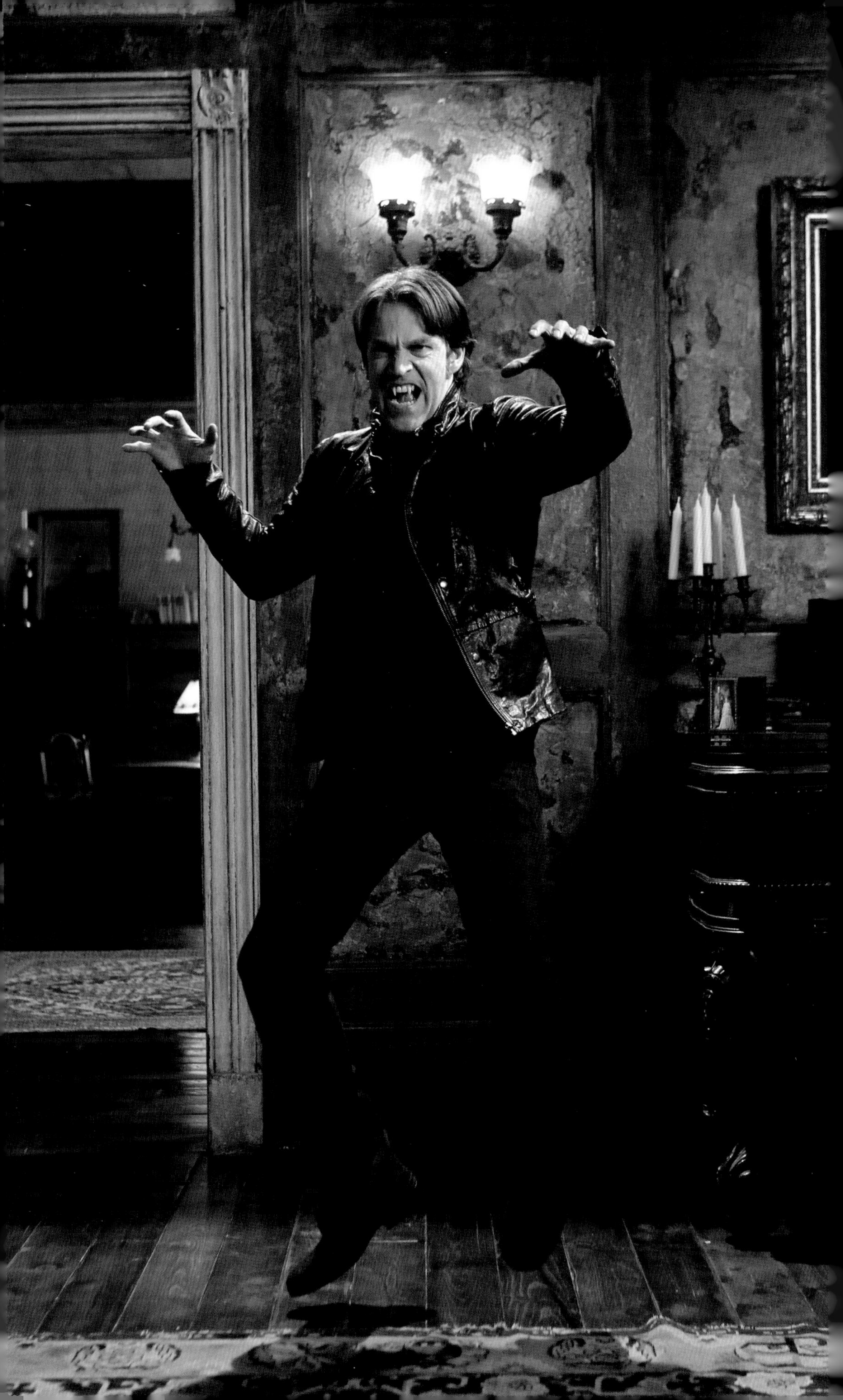

# ART GALLERY

art by DAVID MESSINA
colors by GIOVANNA NIRO

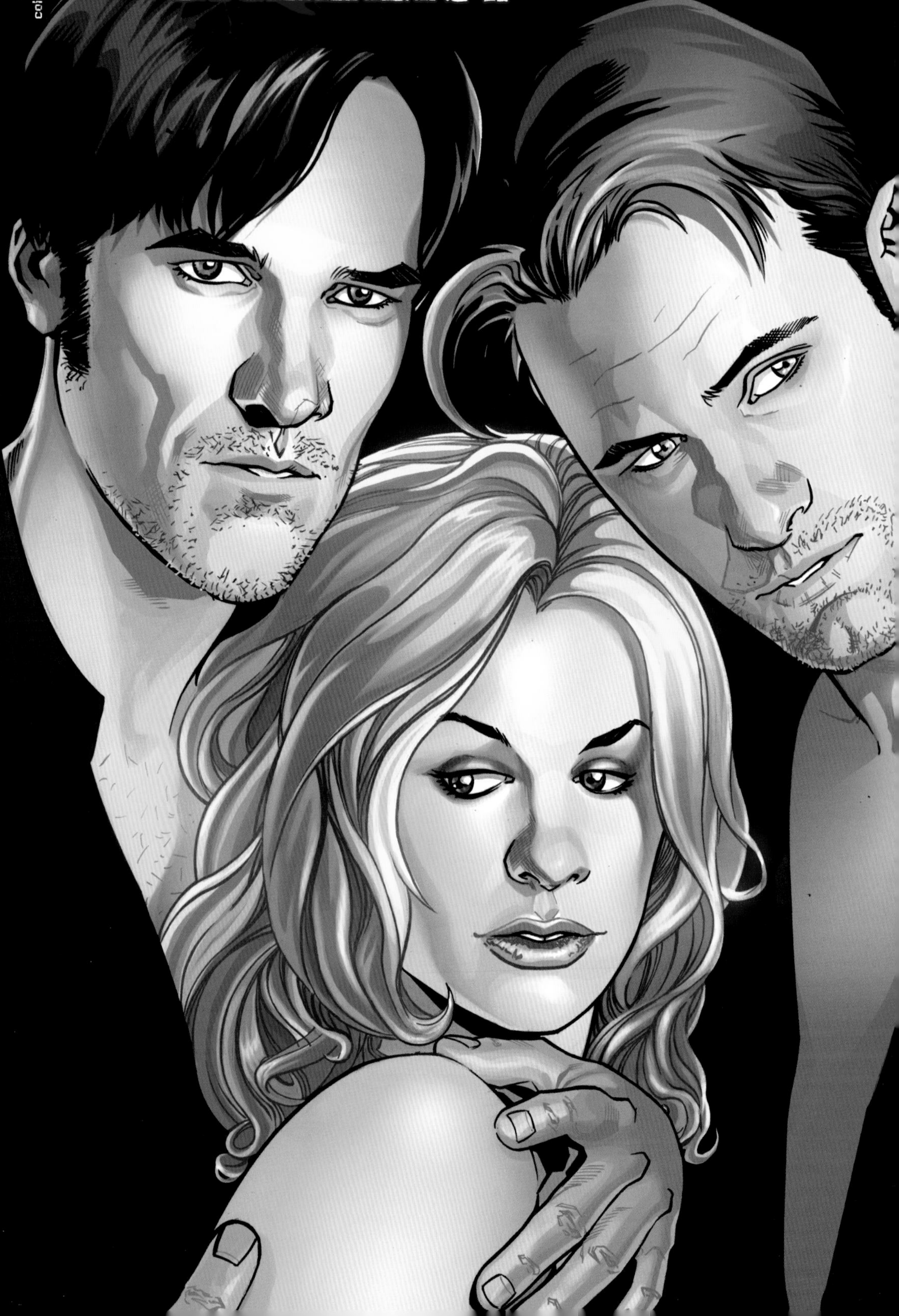

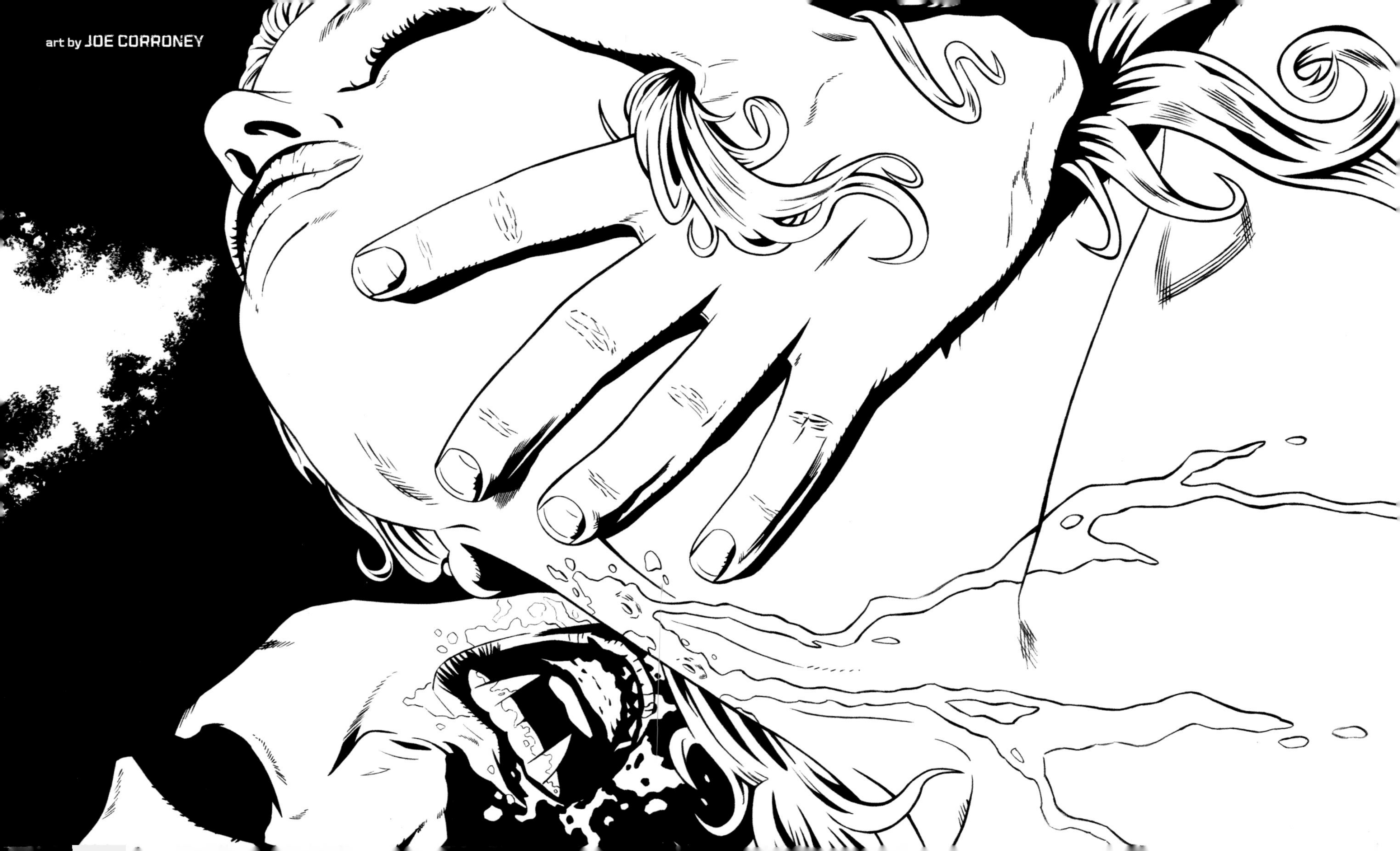
art by JOE CORRONEY

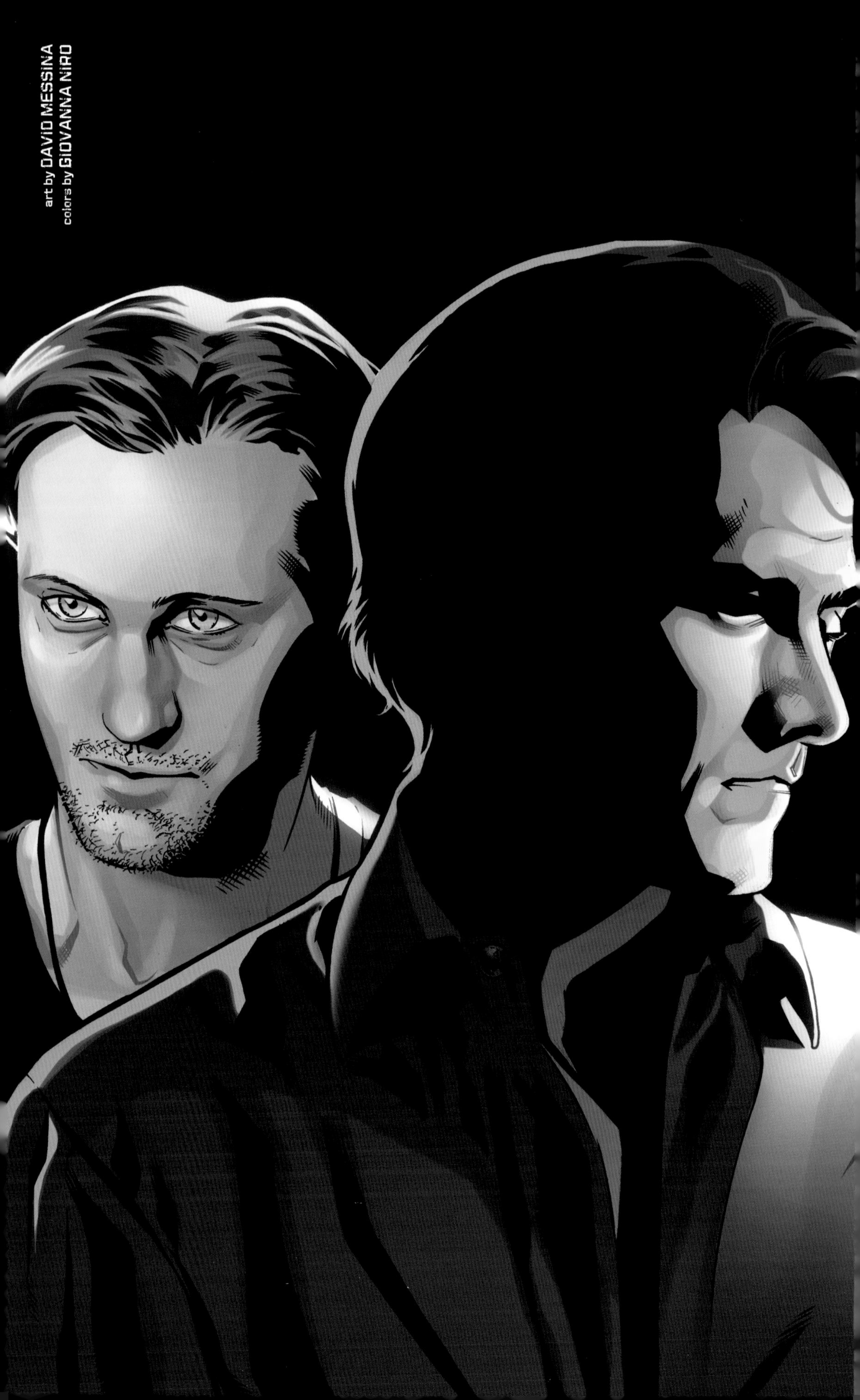

art by DAVID MESSINA
colors by GIOVANNA NIRO

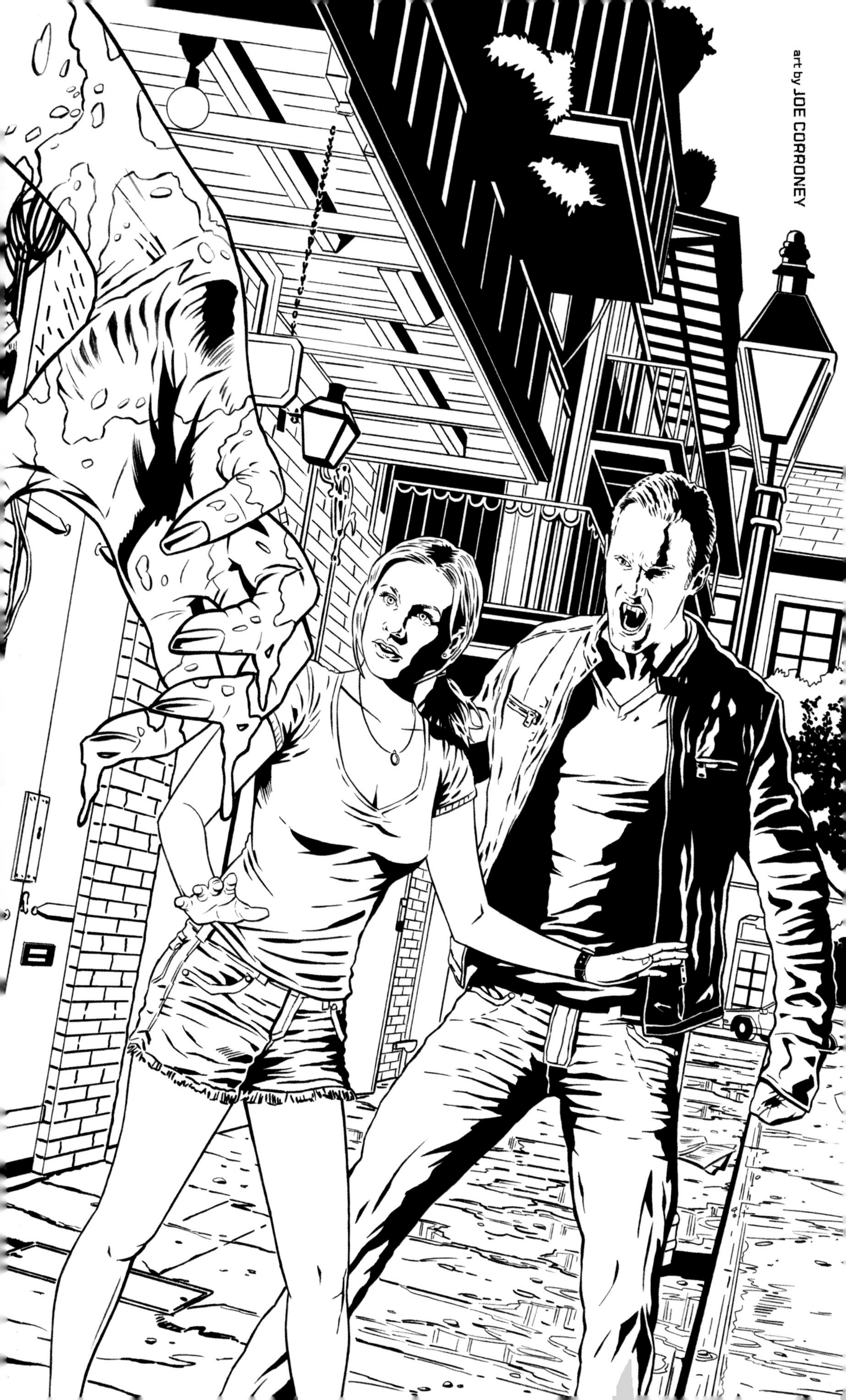
art by JOE CORRONEY

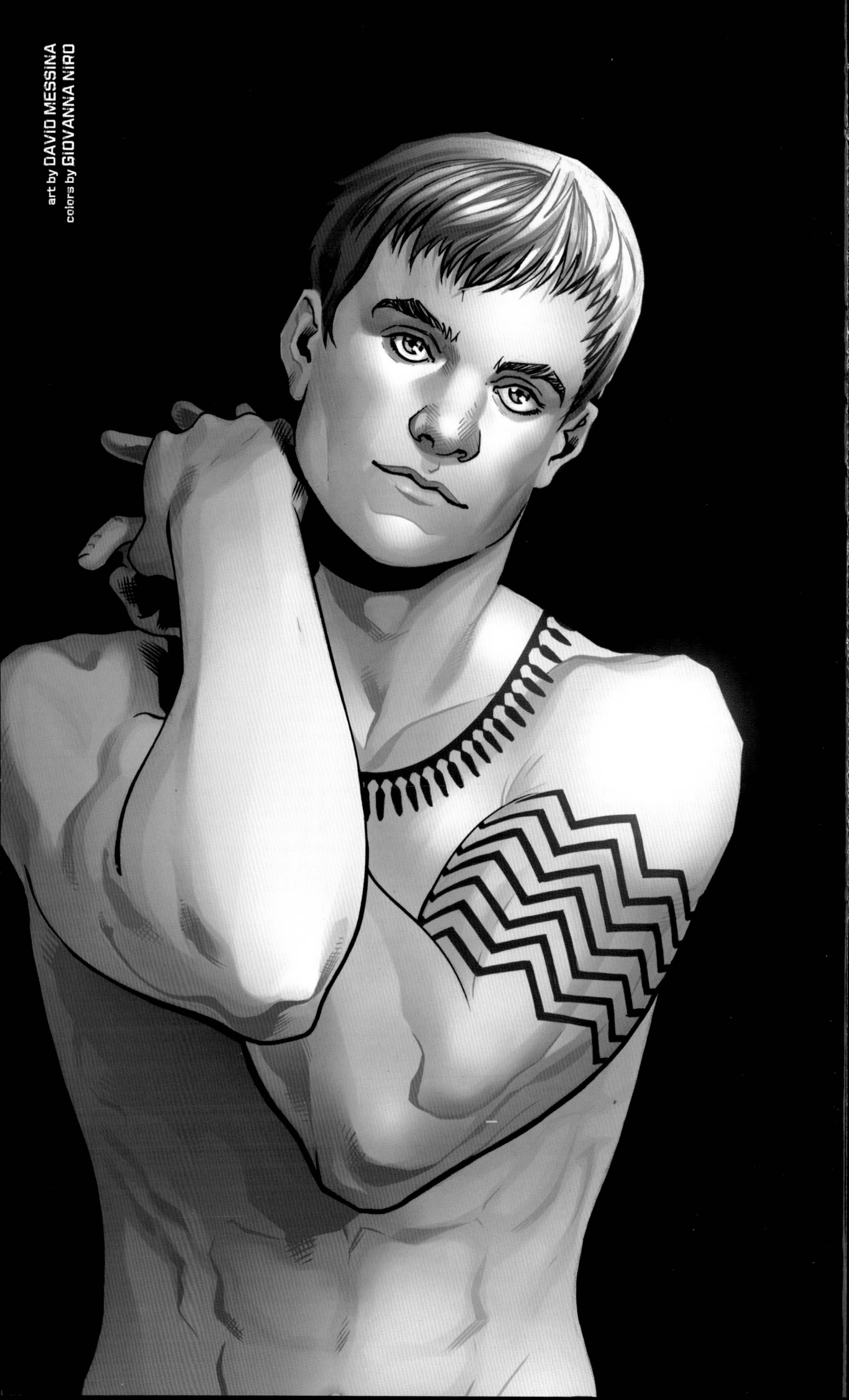
art by DAVID MESSINA
colors by GIOVANNA NIRO

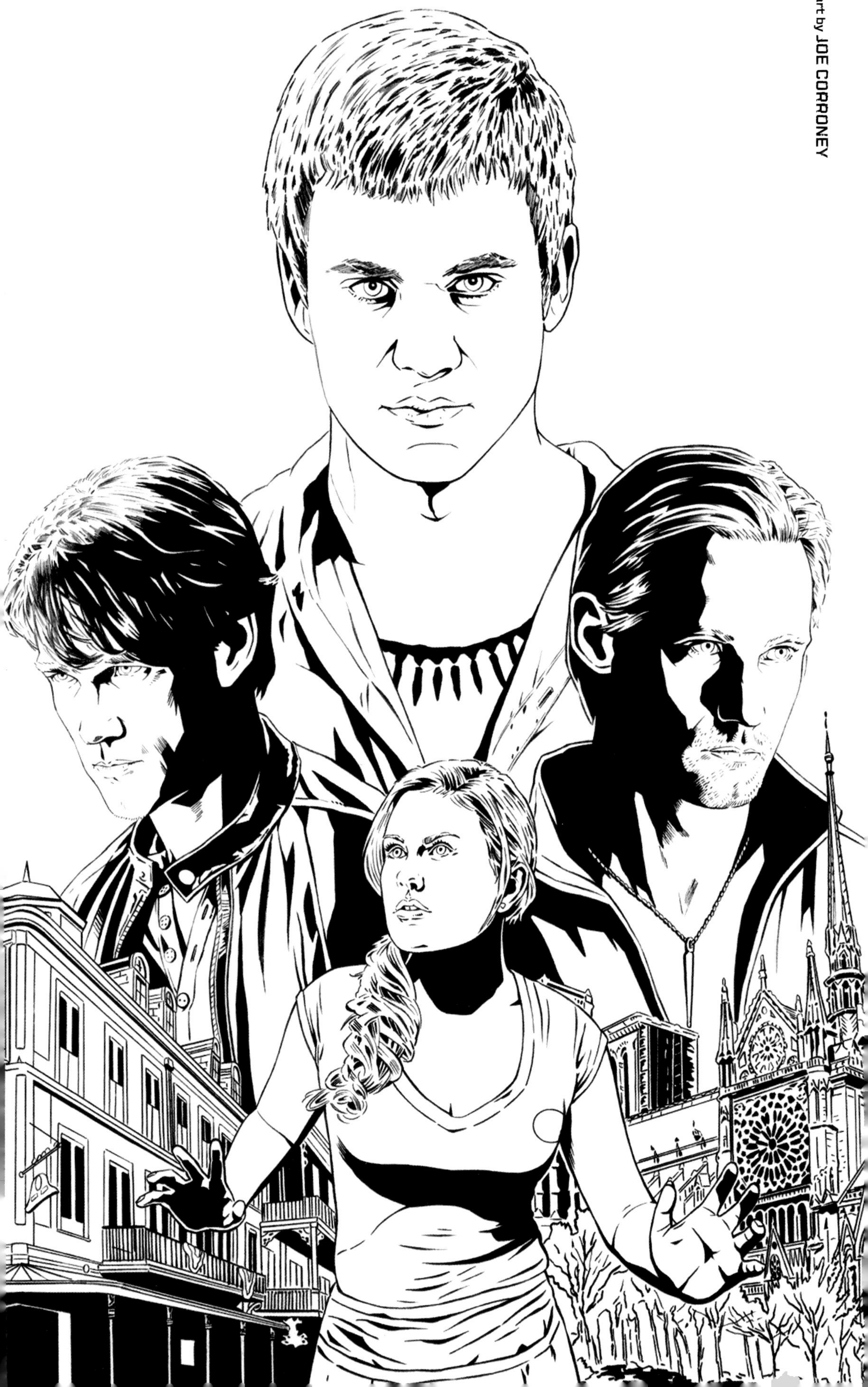

art by JOE CORRONEY

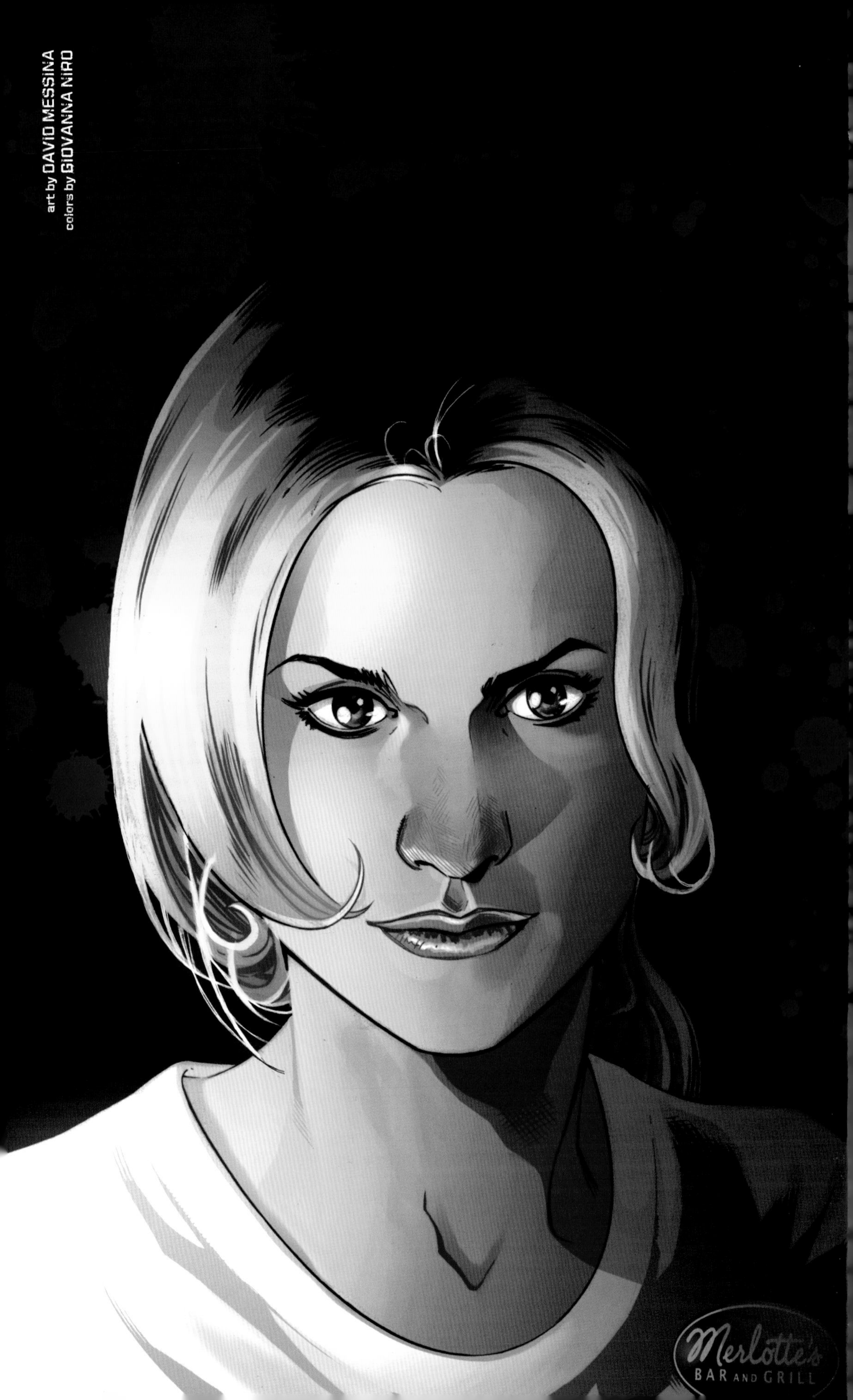
art by DAVID MESSINA
colors by GIOVANNA NIRO
Merlotte's
BAR AND GRILL

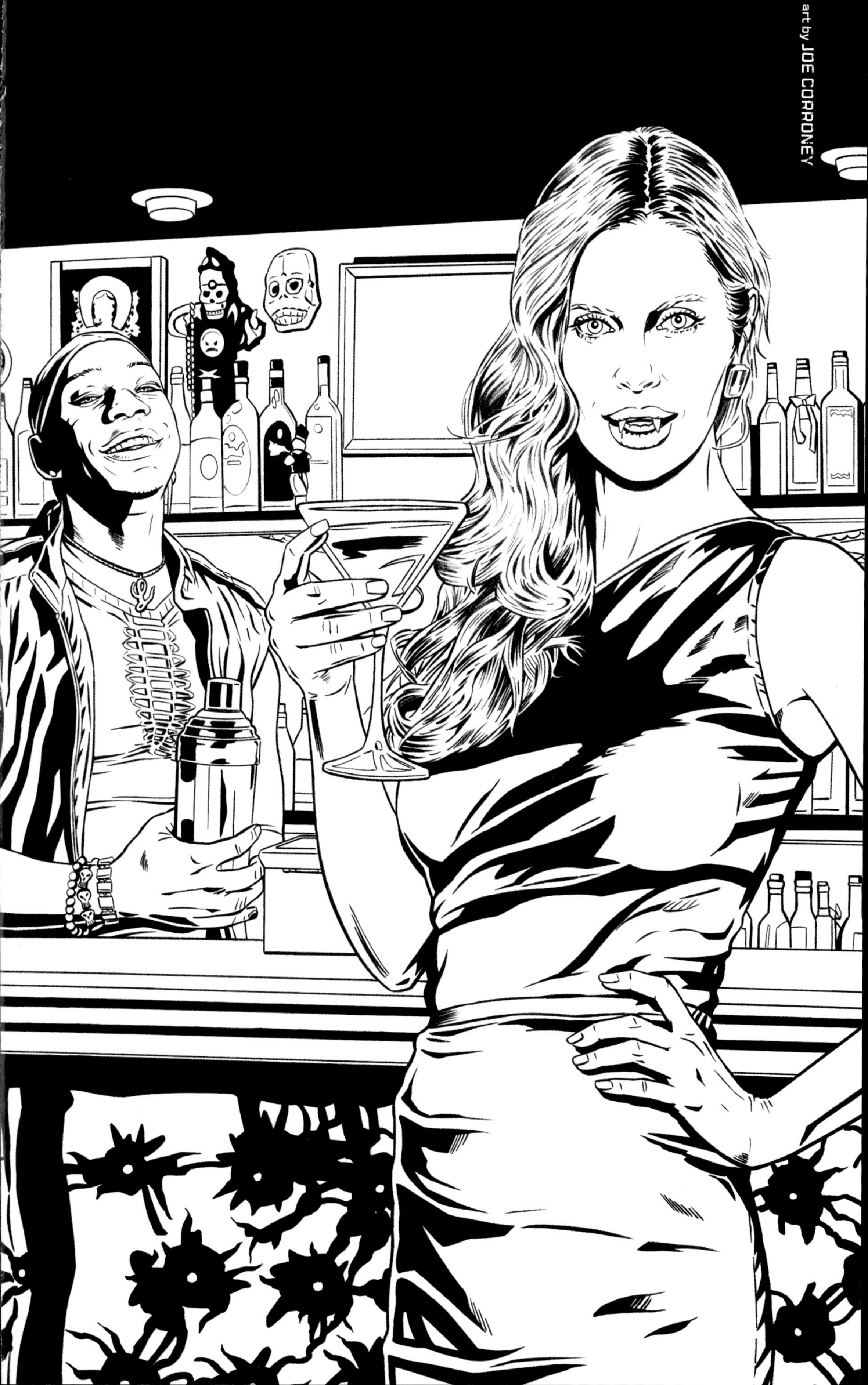

art by JOE CORRONEY

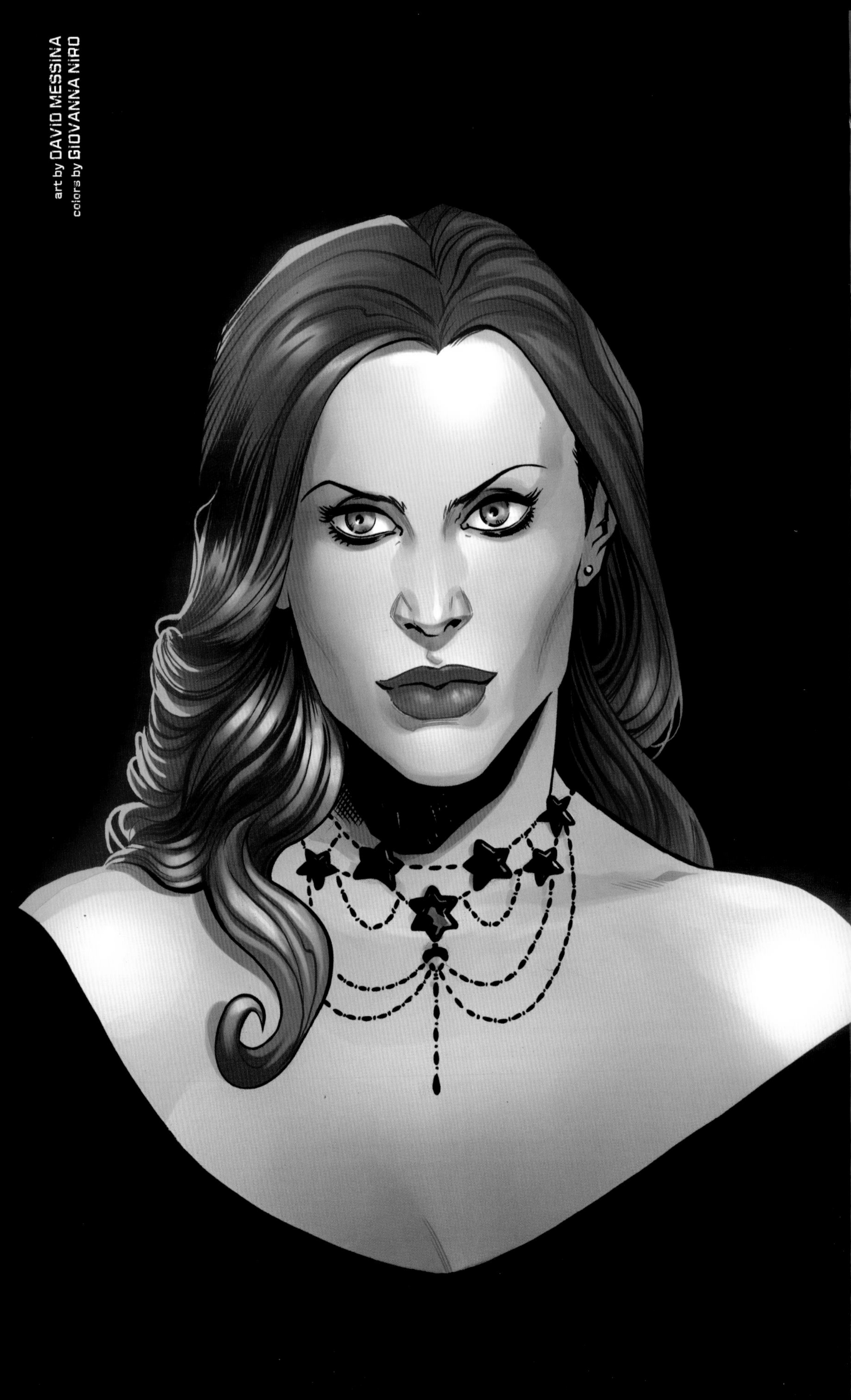
art by DAVID MESSINA
colors by GIOVANNA NIRO

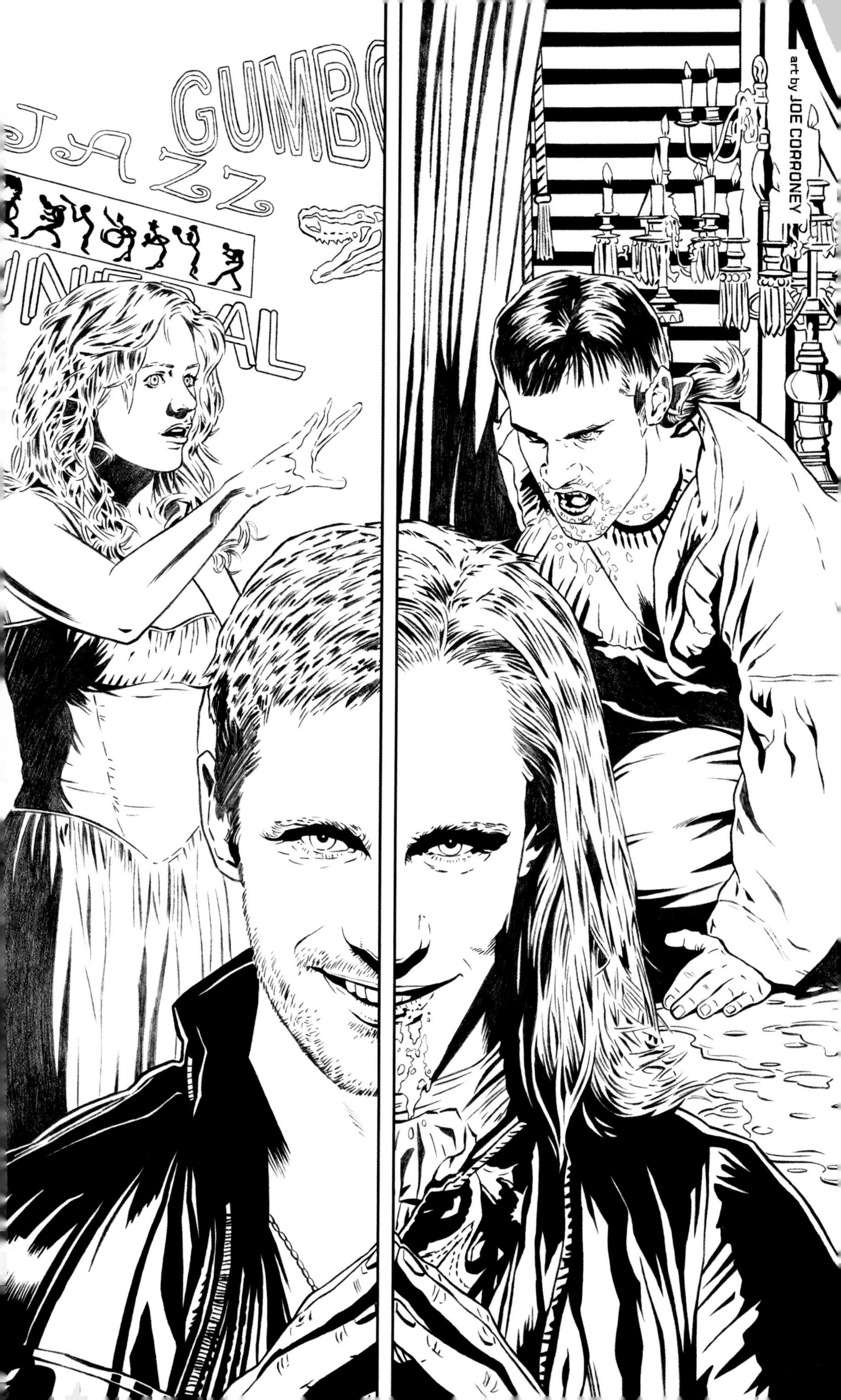
JAZZ

art by JOE CORRONEY

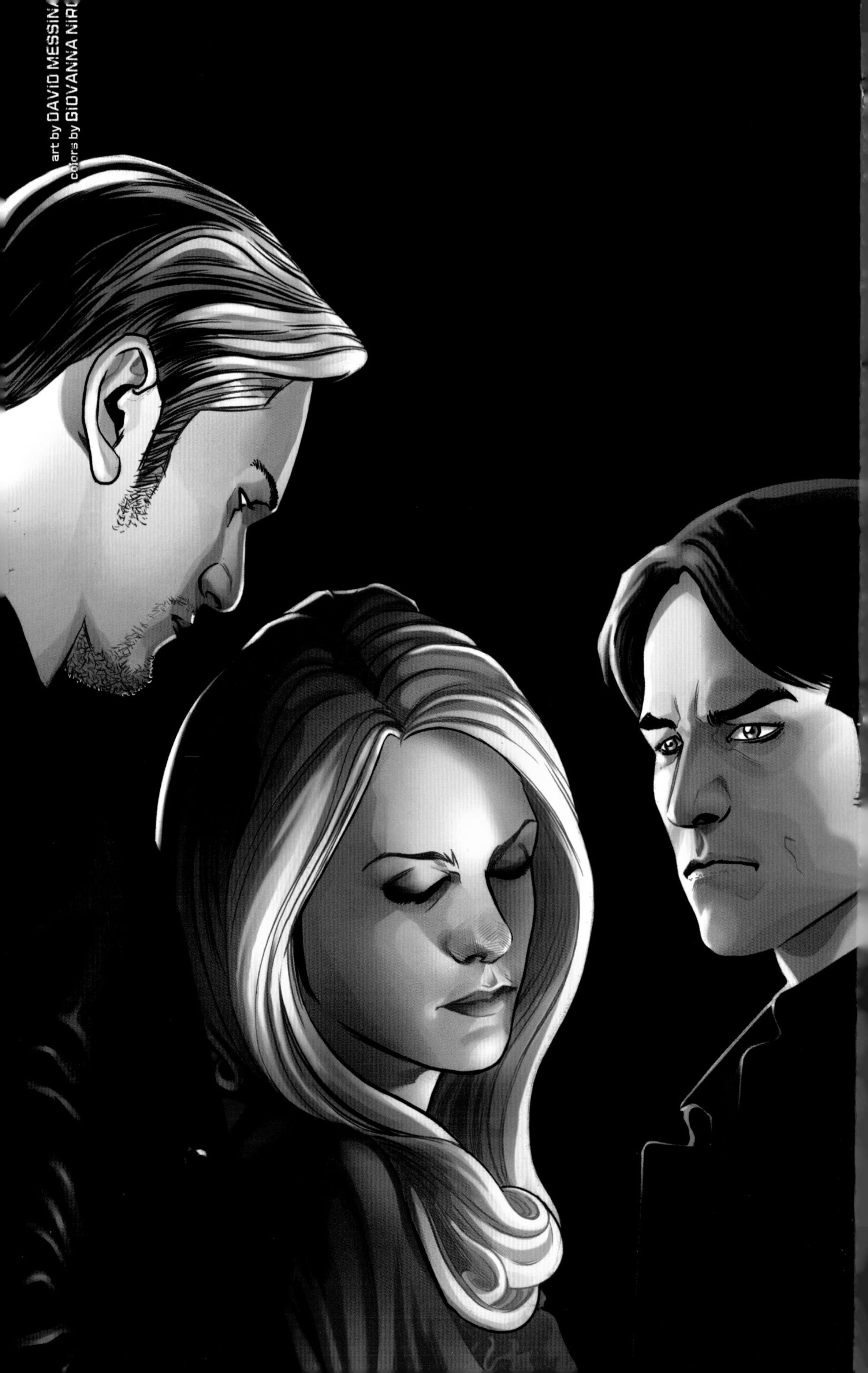
art by DAVID MESSINA
colors by GIOVANNA NIRO

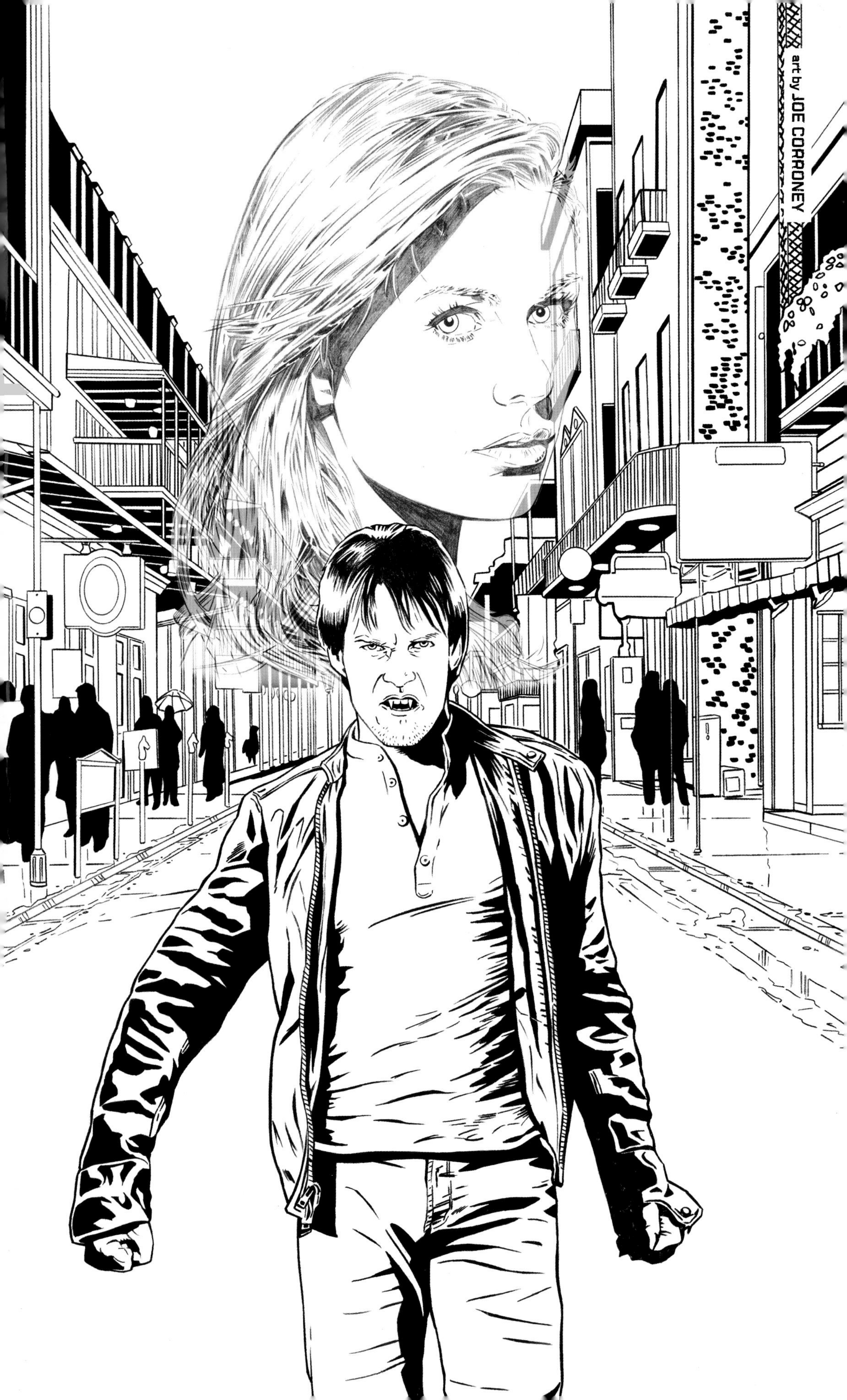
art by JOE CORRONEY

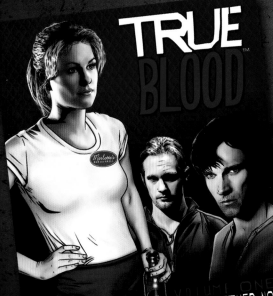